THE CHURCH AND CULTURE SINCE VATICAN II

The Church and Culture since Vatican II

The Experience of North and Latin America

Edited by Joseph Gremillion

UNIVERSITY OF NOTRE DAME PRESS
NOTRE DAME, INDIANA 46556

The editor and publisher gratefully acknowledge the following permissions to reprint:

Excerpts from the Pastoral Constitution on the Church in the Modern World (*Gaudium et Spes*) are from *The Documents of Vatican II,* Abbott and Gallagher, eds. Reprinted with permission of America Press, Inc., 106 West 56 Street, New York, N.Y. 10019. © 1966. All Rights Reserved.

Excerpts from "Evangelization in the Modern World" by Pope Paul VI are from the translation of Polyglot Press, Rome.

The address of Pope John Paul II to UNESCO as well as his addresses to the 1983, 1984, and 1985 sessions of the Pontifical Council for Culture are reprinted by permission of *Osservatore Romano,* English edition.

The translation of the 1984 Christmas Message of Pope John Paul II, "One Church, Many Cultures," is copyrighted by NC News Service and reprinted with their permission.

Excerpts from the Puebla Documents "Evangelization at Present and in the Future of Latin America," copyright © 1979 by the National Conference of Catholic Bishops, Washington, D.C., are used with permission.

Excerpts from "The Hispanic Presence: Challenge and Commitment," copyright © 1984 by the United States Catholic Conference, Washington, D.C., are used with permission.

The selection taken from *'What We Have Seen and Heard'–A Pastoral Letter on Evangelization From the Black Bishops of the United States,* copyright 1984, St. Anthony Messenger Press, 1615 Republic Street, Cincinnati, OH 45210. All rights reserved.

Library of Congress Cataloging-in-Publication Data

Main entry under title:

The Church and culture since Vatican II.

Includes index.
1. Christianity and culture—Congresses.
2. Catholic Church—America—Congresses. 3. Catholic Church—Doctrines—Congresses. I. Gremillion, Joseph.
BX1753.C427 1985 261 84-40364
ISBN 0-268-00753-5 (pbk.)

Contents

Presentation

John Paul II, in January 1983, created the Pontifical Council for Culture. To this new Council of the Apostolic See the Pope gave two main purposes and focuses: the evangelization of cultures, really a mutual understanding of culture and Christian values; and the promotion and humanization of cultures which contribute so mightily to the inner dignity of the human person.

By setting up this new body in the Church, John Paul opens fresh dimension and depth for the outreach of "The Church in the Modern World," the Pastoral Constitution *Gaudium et Spes* of Vatican II. Major portions of this seminal document are devoted to "culture." The whole of it, in fact, places the Church in the incarnational context of the modern world and its multiple cultures, deeply affecting thereby our theology of the Church and of ministry in all pastoral settings. Now the Pope has created an official channel to facilitate and carry forward communication, critique, and understanding among the Church and the many cultural creations of humankind, so that ecclesial self-consciousness might grow amidst the reality of today's world and through our ministry to all areas of society. This new papal focus on culture has promising potential for the Church of America.

In conversation following the inaugural session of the new Pontifical Council, Pope John Paul warmly encouraged my suggestion that a regional conference be held here at Notre Dame on the Church and cultural concerns of both Latin and North Americas. Archbishop Paul Poupard, Council President, and its Secretary, Father Hervé Carrier, S.J., offered close cooperation. With the help of Archbishop Marcos McGrath of Panama and Father Richard McBrien, Chairman of Notre Dame's Department of Theology, the Conference reported in this volume was organized and held here at Notre Dame in November 1983.

This University has in recent years deliberately reaffirmed its *Catholic* character – in the very sense signified by Vatican II's Pastoral Constitution on Church, world, and culture and by the new Pontifical Council for promoting evangelization and humanization of culture in the modern world. A Catholic university, especially since Vatican II, must provide a meeting place for the Church, her people, leaders, and pastors, with the surging creative élan of our society, manifest in multiplying currents and manifold cultural forms. These "new creations" of human mind, will, and initiative are repeatedly invited to encounter here on this campus the Good News of God's love for all humankind, as embodied more insistently in the Catholic Church since Vatican Council II.

We are especially honored when Notre Dame sponsors such a Conference in cooperation with a department of the Holy See, and particularly with the Pontifical Council for Culture so recently established by Pope John Paul, by his own special initiative. As he said to us at our first meeting: "Culture is important since it is what makes us human." It is therefore with particular pleasure that I present this book which reports our unique Conference on "The Church and Culture since Vatican II: Ecclesial Creativity to Meet Pastoral Needs in North and Latin America of the 1980s." I cannot do so without a special word of thanks to all who have been involved, especially Msgr. Joseph Gremillion, whose imaginative and dedicated efforts have brought this project to a happy conclusion, no easy task.

(Rev.) Theodore M. Hesburgh, C.S.C.

November 1984
University of Notre Dame

Rev. Theodore M. Hesburgh, C.S.C.
President
University of Notre Dame
Notre Dame, Indiana, USA

Dear Father Hesburgh,

The Seminar that the University of Notre Dame organized last November on "*Gaudium et Spes* and Culture" with the cooperation of the Pontifical Council for Culture has been a most interesting and fruitful event. I wish to thank you for your personal commitment, as a member of our Council, and for the generous support offered by the University of Notre Dame in preparing this meeting, which could set the pace for further encounters of the kind in other countries.

The fine papers presented by the speakers and the lively discussions that followed among the experts invited to the Seminar have underlined the continuing validity of *Gaudium et Spes*. In perspective, it appears as a central document of Vatican II that has deeply influenced the life of the Church and, particularly, as we have seen, in Latin America and in North America.

The book that the University of Notre Dame Press is publishing on the outcome of the Seminar will be very useful for Bishops, Catholic leaders, scholars, persons committed to research and action in the field of culture and for all those interested in an ongoing dialogue between the Catholic Church and the cultures of today.

Major documents from John Paul II and Paul VI, and also excerpts from *Gaudium et Spes,* included in this book, will offer a ready means for consultation and a useful reference for readers looking for a compendium of the Church's thinking regarding culture and the modern world.

With warmest thanks to you, dear Father Hesburgh, and with my best wishes for the well-deserving University of Notre Dame, I remain,

Yours devotedly in our Lord,

Msgr. Paul Poupard
Executive President
Pontificium Consilium Pro Cultura

(John Paul II named Poupard a cardinal in May 1985–Ed.)

The Pontifical Council for Culture, Vatican City

PRESIDENTIAL COMMITTEE

Cardinal Gabriel-Marie Garrone, President
Cardinal Eugenio de Araujo Sales
Archbishop Paul Poupard, Titular Archbishop of Usula

EXECUTIVE COMMITTEE

Archbishop Paul Poupard, Titular Archbishop of Usula, President
Archbishop Achille Silvestrini, Titular Archbishop of Novaliciana, Councillor
Archbishop Antonio M. Ortas Javierre, S.D.B., Titular Archbishop of Meta, Councillor
Rev. Hervé Carrier, S.J., Secretary

INTERNATIONAL COUNCIL

Rev. Georges Anawati, O.P. (Arab Republic of Egypt), Director of the Dominican Institute for Oriental Studies, Cairo.

Prof. Adriano Bausola (Italy), Rector of the Catholic University of the Sacred Heart, Milan.

Sister Mary Braganza, R.S.C.J. (India), former President of Sophia College, Bombay, and Secretary General of the All India Association for Christian Higher Education, Delhi.

Prof. Carlos Chagas (Brazil), President of the Pontifical Academy of Sciences; Director of the Biophysical Institute, University of Rio de Janeiro.

Rev. Theodore M. Hesburgh, C.S.C. (U.S.A.), former President of the International Federation of Catholic Universities and President of the University of Notre Dame.

Dr. Jean Larnaud (France), Secretary General of the International Catholic Centre of UNESCO, Paris.

Prof. Nikolaus Lobkowicz (Federal Republic of Germany), former Rector of the Ludwig-Maximilians Universität, Münich; Rector of the Katholische Universität Eichstätt.

Prof. Julian Marias (Spain), philosopher and writer, member of the Real Academia Espanola, Madrid.

Dr. Kinhide Mushakoji (Japan), Vice-Rector of the United Nations University, head office in Tokyo.

Mrs. Victoria V. I. Okoye (Nigeria), President of the Catholic Women of Nigeria.

Sir William Rees-Mogg (Great-Britain), former editor of the London *Times,* Vice-President of the Board of Administration of the B.B.C., and President of the Arts Council of Great Britain.

President Léopold Sédar Senghor (Senegal), former President of Senegal, poet and philosopher, member of the French Academy.

Prof. Alberto Wagner de Reyna (Peru), former Ambassador, philosopher, member of the Peruvian Academy of Language.

Prof. Jacek Wozniakowski (Poland), writer and Prof. of History of Arts, Catholic University of Lublin, Director of ZNAK publications, Cracow.

Preface

The body of this book is divided into two parts. The first part gives texts of the seven major papers presented during the Conference, together with reports of discussions these engendered among the sixty participants. Part II provides documents concerning Church and culture since Vatican II. These are offered as a handy collection of basic official sources on this subject, the first such vade mecum in the English language.

The Conference was introduced by Father Hesburgh as a member of the Pontifical Council's International Committee and Conference host. The President of the Council, Archbishop Paul Poupard, presided formally at the Notre Dame meeting. Father Hervé Carrier, Secretary of the Vatican's new office on Culture, besides making the keynote presentation on "Understanding Culture: Ultimate Challenge of the World-Church?" also prepared the concluding paper of the Conference, bringing the topic of Church and culture into the future.

Following this Preface, the six original papers of the Conference are summarized and the subject as a whole is placed in its wider setting by Denis Goulet, Fellow of the Kellogg Institute and O'Neill Professor for Justice Education at Notre Dame.

The titles of the three sections of Part I identify overarching themes and currents which flow from the papers and discussions, to enrich the central agenda of the Church of both Americas into the future:

1. The Church's Evolving Concept of and Global Role Concerning Culture
2. The Latin American Church's Option for the Poor and Their Cultural Creativity since Vatican II
3. North American Power Structures and the Church's Societal-Cultural Mission

From tapes which recorded all proceedings, I have prepared three Discussion Reports, one for each of the three sections listed above. These identify discussants, many of whom raise strong counterviews to those of the six presentors. The give-and-take is shared, with an editorial eye and ear for the more significant thrusts of often sharp exchanges, seeking however to follow and highlight major themes and convergences, trajectories for future focus on Church and culture.

From notes he kept throughout, Carrier made a concluding statement during the last hour of our meeting, to which participants added brief comment. He has since reworked this paper, and it is now made available here. We fervently hope that the discussion which this Conference has initiated will be further pursued by the regional and local Churches of the universal Church, in their respective societal and cultural settings.

Part I closes with "After-Thoughts of a Protestant Observer at Vatican II" by Professor Albert Outler of Southern Methodist University, Dallas. These are after-dinner remarks made off-the-cuff by this notable ecumenist at Hesburgh's urging during our closing repast. At my further urging Outler has prepared a written summary of these thoughts. His observations provide second-stage impetus to Church-and-culture trajectories launched by our Conference.

Ten Church documents compose Part II of this volume. Of these, the Pastoral Constitution on the Church in the Modern World, *Gaudium et Spes*, is foundational, above all because of its authority and range as coming from the Ecumenical Council Vatican II. Most of the others are papal statements; one from Paul VI, on "The Evangelization of Peoples," deserves added status because it draws largely from the 1974 Synod of Bishops on that subject.

The centrality of "culture" in the vision and ministry of John Paul II becomes increasingly clear from his numerous explicit addresses on the subject, of which five are given here. Perhaps more telling still, we note his penchant for inserting "culture" on other occasions, as gathered for this collection by Poupard and Carrier.

Long excerpts from the Puebla document are especially fitting in view of the Latin American dimension of our Conference and the direct focus on Puebla's attention to the region's cultures, especially the enduring *mestizaje* hybrid of Ibero-Christianity and the original culture of the Indians, plus African imports. Extracts are also chosen from Pastoral Letters issued in 1984 by the U.S. bishops on Hispanic Presence and Ministry, and on Evangelization and Black Culture by the ten black bishops of the country.

The United Nations Educational, Scientific and Cultural Organization is the primary worldwide body, formed by member-nations at the highest governmental level, which addresses culture widely conceived, including the areas of science and education. The papacy has sought close cooperation with UNESCO from its inception forty years ago, and maintains formal relations with that body through its Permanent Observer in Paris. The address of the Pope to the General Conference of UNESCO in 1980, included here, provides insight into John Paul's views on government and culture, and their relation to the *humanum*, as individual and as community.

I wish to express warm gratitude to Matthew Fitzsimons and Denis Goulet for their editorial assistance, and to my secretary, Margaret Boggs, for typing and retyping the several drafts of the authors. To James R. Langford, Director of our University Press, and to his staff, I express appreciation for wholehearted cooperation in the design and production of this volume.

(Msgr.) Joseph Gremillion
Director, Institute for Pastoral
and Social Ministry
University of Notre Dame

January 1985

Introduction to the Papers

Denis Goulet

In his UNESCO address of June 1980, Pope John Paul II declared that national sovereignty derives from each nation's "own culture." Every nation's culture must therefore be protected to preserve "this fundamental sovereignty" against becoming the prey of "political or economic interests" or "a victim of totalitarian and imperialistic systems or hegemonies."

By rooting national identity and freedom so deeply and directly in every nation's "own culture," the Pope reveals his motivation in creating the Pontifical Council *Pro Cultura*. The scope of influence John Paul assigns to culture extends from the freedom of each person's "own human existence" to "the future of the great human family."

Since the Second Vatican Council issues of peace, justice, and human rights have become constitutive dimensions of evangelization and Church ministry. John Paul II now calls us to recognize that culture has become the central arena in which struggles for peace, justice, and human rights are waged and in which the Good News is proclaimed. He summons the Church to meet and serve today's cultures in their rich diversity and in their agonizing confrontation with depersonalized technology and rapid social change, in their struggles against domination over national sovereignty and human creativity.

The essays from the Notre Dame Conference, which form the core of this volume, illustrate some of the ways in which the dialogue between religion and culture is conceptualized and practiced. The first two papers outline "The Church's Evolving Concept of and Global Role Concerning Culture." Papers three and four present "The Latin American Church's Option for the Poor and Their Cultural Creativity since Vatican II." The final two papers tell of two controversial pastoral statements, by the bishops of the United States and of Canada, on nuclear arms and on the economy: "North American Power Structures and the Church's Societal-Cultural Mission."

PAPER ONE: UNDERSTANDING CULTURES: ULTIMATE CHALLENGE OF THE WORLD-CHURCH?

Hervé Carrier, S.J., former Rector of Rome's Gregorian University and now Secretary of the Pontifical Council for Culture, Vatican City, traces the evolution in definitions of *culture* during the past hundred years. *Culture* long signified intellectual achievement in classical instruction, humanism, science, and the fine arts. Gradually a more anthropological definition gained sway and *culture* became an operational term to analyze social reality. We now speak of cultural policies, cultural liberation, and cultural development.

Nineteenth-century social scientists applied the term *culture* to "primitive" societies, which they distinguished from "civilized" societies. Now, however, thanks to the work of Margaret Mead and Ruth Benedict, culture designates the pattern of values, behaviors, and meanings found in all societies, including our own. Marx introduced a new dimension by stressing the role played by the ruling class in shaping the cultural values of all classes of the whole society. Twentieth-century liberation movements affirm their own cultural identity as a necessary arena of struggle, especially since World War II and the collapse of Western-held empires in Africa and Asia. Tanzania's Julius Nyerere, for example, makes of culture a basic category of development.

As society evolved its view of culture, so did the Church. Carrier traces changes in the Church's understanding of culture, from Leo XIII, who spoke in the neoclassical mode, to Pius XII, who viewed culture as a dynamic, not a static, social category. Vatican II marks a significant departure, particularly in the Pastoral Constitution *Gaudium et Spes*, by assigning a high positive value to contemporary cultures.

Carrier compares Church conceptions of culture with that advanced by the United Nations Educational, Scientific and Cultural Organization. Because UNESCO includes spiritual values in its understanding of culture, a high degree of congeniality between Catholic concepts and those of UNESCO is possible. When discussing post-Vatican II trends, however, Carrier becomes pessimistic: Culture is rapidly becoming an arena of dramatic confrontation and a domain where Gospel values are threatened. Because of close links between evangelizing, promoting justice, and defending human cultures, cultural dialogue becomes an urgent task for the Church. Carrier notes that religious leaders such as Mother Teresa, Mahatma Gandhi, and Helder Camara themselves create culture. He concludes that "for Christians the message should be clear. They are called to be builders of culture."

Cultural dialogue is the *ultimate* challenge, Carrier claims, because when societies do not dialogue, their opposing values breed conflict. He asks whether anyone more than the Christian, therefore, is called to foster the dialogue of cultures with the realistic hope of promoting human brotherhood?

Carrier poses anew the question of how God works in history. We are reminded of the ancient proverb which saw God's providential wisdom as his unique ability to "write straight with crooked lines." Today's Christians see the crooked lines well enough: the contradictions, dangers, and uncertainties of this world. But only recently has the Church begun to discern how God's providential incursions into human history here and now might render those lines straight. This is the cultural meaning, for instance, of the invitation of Vatican II to "read the signs of the times." By creating the Pontifical Council for Culture, John Paul II stamps the cultural arena as crucial for the survival of human values, and for the Church's evangelizing mission.

PAPER TWO: *GAUDIUM ET SPES* AND THE TRAVAIL OF TODAY'S ECCLESIAL CONCEPTION

Bernard Lambert, a Dominican theologian from Quebec, poses five questions to Catholics. Should we maintain the old Christian order or build a new one? How should we react to secularization in the world? What is the human person becoming amidst the turmoil of change? How can we build community peace? How should the Church evangelize today?

1. A Christian order, Lambert declares, is the social expression of the Gospel. Over the course of twenty centuries, however, societies have found varied forms to express the Gospel. Before Constantine, small communities lived spiritually and withheld their political and psychological allegiance from the social order. After Constantine the Church became identified with established political and economic powers. It took centuries to reach a new decisive turning point as Paul VI renounced the tiara and John Paul II opened Vatican finances to public scrutiny.

If Christians cannot maintain the old order, which new order should they strive to build? One that respects the diversity and autonomy of the secular or natural world, Lambert replies, adding that a new Christian order has already begun to emerge in the cultures of our times.

2. Secularization is the progressive shift toward this-world affairs and away from the authority of revelation or Church tradition. Although there are normative limits to the process, secularization is a natural outgrowth of creation. Yet the independence of earthly affairs does not do away with the existential ambivalence of human destiny, Lambert adds. It is good to be free, but free for what?

3. What will become of men and women caught in the vortex of rapidly changing times? The Church can help, for it understands both the nobility and the pettiness of human beings, their cruelty and compassion, their idealism and intractable *hubris.* That the deepest human aspirations have now become universal, powerful, and fully conscious constitutes a potent "sign of the times." Because human beings belong to the twin worlds of nature and of culture, the Church endorses a humanism of co-responsibility.

Discarding its former aristocratic definition of the term *culture,* the Church now discovers it in the midst of illiterates and outcasts, the "wretched of the earth." Christ, the Church teaches, is both the crowning exemplar of culture and the Savior of human beings, giving new shape to human reality and its works. Yet culture finds its perfection only in the Pascal mystery through which human beings are made free and nonviolent, ready to sacrifice personal interests to the common good.

4. The common good presupposes a community of nations and peace. Lambert asks whether the Church can help build the community of nations in peace. If so, on what foundations: those of justice, peace, power, reciprocity? Peace is not the mere absence of conflict, but the positive embodiment of values preached in the Beatitudes. Because Christ's judgment begins in the gospels with the cleansing of God's house, the Church must herself live what she preaches to the world. In the Beatitudes lies not only the secret of holiness, but of survival as well. If this be the new evangelization, how can it be carried out in the world today?

5. Evangelization should reject deductive or universal languages which leave Christians, and others to whom the Gospel is addressed, indifferent. Clearly the Good News speaks not only to the intellect of men and women, but to their hearts as well, to their passions and emotions. Because direct evangelization is often impossible, a pre-Gospel witness is necessary. Its best manifestation is solidarity with the dispossessed.

With a new language come new categories, the most central of which is life, for Christ came to make life more abundant. Therefore, the Church must extend his life-enhancing vocation. It must also demystify contemporary idols of the "ego" which always comes first, for there exist larger purposes than individual goals and the Church must display new parameters to incarnate these Gospel values in human experience.

PAPER THREE: IMPACT OF *GAUDIUM ET SPES*: MEDELLÍN, PUEBLA, AND PASTORAL CREATIVITY

Marcos McGrath, C.S.C., Archbishop of Panama, writes as a pastor describing the impact of *Gaudium et Spes* on Latin America. There the Church responded to Vatican II by validating the popular culture of the poor masses and by accepting responsibility for the concrete social conditions of the continent. Its distinctive contribution, says McGrath, lies in spelling out the values which Christians must build into the ideologies and politics for "the elaboration of historical models that conform to the necessities of each moment and of each culture."

The Latin American Church brought its own efforts at renewal to the Vatican Council. For over seventy years Latin America had been convulsed by social revolutions. The medical revolution tripled its population without a parallel industrial growth to support it. Two world wars generated sudden prosperity followed by prolonged recession. As city slums swelled, political conflict took on an explicit ideological content: Capitalism and Marxism drew their battle lines.

In the 1960s the Latin American Church began to reject the colonial structures of the past and to critically reexamine its relationship to privileged classes. It grudgingly acknowledged that class divisions within itself mirrored those found in the larger societies around it. McGrath dislikes English translations of the pastoral constitution as "The Church in the Modern World." A more accurate rendering, he argues, is "The Church in the World Today." The difference is important because the adjective "modern" applies to what has occurred in recent centuries, as when we speak of modern history or modern languages, whereas "today's world" means "here and now." This, precisely, is McGrath's point: The Latin American Church reads the signs of the times in concrete temporal settings of present-day social conflicts and human situations.

After the Council, a major breakthrough occurred in 1968 at the Latin American Bishops' meeting in Medellín, Colombia. Medellín's declarations publicly committed the Church to combatting the multiple injustices, personal and structural, operative in their societies. It took some bishops ten years, however, to catch up to the public positions taken at Medellín by their collective body. Indeed, strong rearguard actions were fought by conservative groups who tried to dominate the Third General Conference of Latin American Bishops held at Puebla, Mexico, in 1979.

Pope John Paul II himself urged bishops at Puebla to reflect upon the years since Medellín, to correct mistakes and wrong interpretations. The Puebla document ratified the Church's commitment to promote justice for the poor and to evangelize local cultures. A new and strong emphasis was placed on lay participation and the interplay of spirituality with political tasks.

At the very time when the Church was plunging more deeply into secular areas – a just economic order, struggles against repressive political systems, and a redefinition of the participatory roles of lay persons – it was also taking its distance from secular bodies. As it became more independent of these power structures, the Church gained more respect, a distance-taking McGrath considers to be a positive good. It places the Church in a stronger position to be a messenger of Gospel values in the midst of Latin America's turbulent cultures.

PAPER FOUR: EVANGELIZATION OF CULTURE, LIBERATION AND "POPULAR" CULTURE: THE NEW THEOLOGICAL-PASTORAL SYNTHESIS IN LATIN AMERICA

The Argentine theologian Juan Carlos Scannone, S.J., explores how the Latin American Church infuses ideological debates and social programs with a new incarnational reading of the Gospel. Since the Vatican Council, Scannone detects important shifts in pastoral practice and in how theologians define their mission. They now see that theory must be rooted in the living practice of communities and that the concept of culture needs to be broadened to cover the wider socio-political issues of society: problems of structural justice, the legitimacy of established authority, criteria for social change, prophetic liberation of oppressed masses from an alienating model of religious salvation (religion as opium of the people) and from subhuman conditions of life.

Gaudium et Spes, Scannone states, turned the Church's attention to contemporary problems in society by generating a new style of theological reflection grounded in Latin America's concrete situations. The Church now denounces as structurally unjust and exploitative those very societies which had traditionally called themselves Christian and whose leaders had historically harnessed Christianity's message to rationalize the status quo. Predictably, many Latin theologians criticize *Gaudium et Spes* for being conflict-free and for smoothing over the sharp edges found in their own societies.

Scannone identifies three theological and pastoral thrusts generated by *Gaudium et Spes.* The first distinguishes more clearly than before natural and supernatural domains, interior and exterior realms, what is public and what is private.

The second thrust urges social liberation if culture is to be evangelized. Latin America is an arena in which several cultures have disintegrated through the economic and political domination exercised by ruling groups. To affirm the value of popular or indigenous cultures, therefore, over against the dominant assimilationists, confers religious validation upon cultural resistance.

The third pastoral thrust analyzed by Scannone grants primacy to unity over conflict, without, however, dismissing class conflict. Because Latin America's poor and oppressed have resisted cultural aggressions better than others, their legitimate aspirations are today better oriented toward justice and the pursuit of the common good. They form the core of the liberation process and they are the historical agents of a new socio-cultural synthesis.

The preferential option for the poor made by the Church does not exclude pastoral concern for elites. For while denouncing structures of injustice, the Church must also promote the saving presence of the Lord in the efforts of all Latin American people to create a better society.

PAPER FIVE: THE PEACE PASTORAL AND GLOBAL MISSION: DEVELOPMENT BEYOND VATICAN II

Bryan Hehir of the U.S. Bishops Conference traces the recent pastoral letter of the American bishops on nuclear arms to the new dialogue with the contemporary world urged by *Gaudium et Spes* twenty years ago. Hehir explains that U.S. bishops could not have written their letter on war and peace, nor conducted the broad process of consultation leading to it, unless the groundwork had been laid earlier by Vatican II. The nuclear pastoral is therefore both a product of, and a response to, the Pastoral Constitution. As product, it stands on the theological foundations laid by the conciliar document; as response, it develops moral principles beyond the point reached by the Council.

The pastoral's teaching style is noteworthy: Bishops declare their willingness to learn from the world and to submit their moral views to the citizenry at large. The bishops' letter did generate widespread debate among the country's policy and media communities. In addition, throughout the country's parish halls and pulpits, in classrooms and retreat centers, through liturgies, fasts, and demonstrations, the pastoral animated soul-searching and debate on the implications of U.S. nuclear policy and plans.

No less significant than the pedagogical approach adopted by the letter is the substance of its teaching on nuclear war. The U.S. bishops move beyond the Council's doctrine by formulating concrete judgments about first strikes, deterrence, counterforce targeting, and other issues of concrete concern to policymakers and citizens. Ultimately, "The Challenge to Peace" invites the U.S. public to judge this nation's nuclear policy in the light of Gospel values and of Church tradition on the moral limits to violence and war, particularly as affecting civilian populations.

Specific challenges of conscience are addressed to political leaders, military commanders and troops, workers in war industries, researchers, university scholars, taxpayers, and citizens at large. In Hehir's concluding words, "The Council called us to be present in the world. The pastoral has given us a very visible presence. The quality of our presence is now going to be tested."

PAPER SIX: CULTURE, GOSPEL VALUES, AND THE CANADIAN ECONOMY: THE CHURCH ENTERS THE PUBLIC DIALOGUE

Remi DeRoo is Bishop of Victoria, Canada, and Secretary to the Social Affairs Commission of the Canadian Conference of Catholic Bishops. In this paper he summarizes the pastoral statement issued by that body in January of 1983 entitled "Ethical Reflections on the Economic Crisis" and tells of the vigorous dialogue which immediately ensued throughout Canada.

DeRoo reports that "Personally, the experience caused me to clarify my own role and personal mission as bishop. It led me to a clearer understanding of ecclesiology, namely the nature of the Church in its role of sacramentality, of mediation, and of communion." More significantly, his discussions with Canadians of all walks of life about issues of vital concern to them – jobs, economic security, safety at work, personal control over policies affecting their future, the economic role of Canada in the world at large – led DeRoo to discover in depth what it means for the Church to proclaim the Good News. "I have never been told by so many people," he writes, "many of them professed atheists, alienated Catholics, humanists, and members of other world faiths, that our pastoral statement revealed to them a different Church than the one they had known: a Church of compassion and hope."

Like its U.S. counterpart on nuclear arms, the Canadian economic document treats specific, conflict-laden issues, thereby illustrating the "new dialogue" the Church is to have with living communities of culture. Both texts invite all their country's citizens to undertake a joint learning experience as to what the Gospel has to say about "nitty-gritty" issues that truly matter in people's lives. There is no moral pontificating from abstract heights, no condemnation of personal sins, but rather a searching probe into the ethics of institutions, structures, policies, and social forces which shape the societies of Canada and the United States.

The Canadian statement is not a technical analysis of unemployment or the economic crisis in Canada but a series of moral reflections on structural disorders affecting Canadian society and on desirable future economic strategies to be adopted. Canada's bishops resoundingly affirm that human labor takes priority over capital.

They urge a reordering of values: Sound economics must serve human needs, not exploit people for corporate profit. They propose six short-term strategies which give priority to the fight against unemployment, to stemming the rate of inflation in equitable fashion, to developing an industrial strategy which creates permanent employment in local communities, to sustaining the Social Security safety net in a responsible manner, to giving labor unions a more decisive role in economic recovery, and to involving local communities in plans for coordinated economic action.

These resumes introduce the six papers which follow as well as a half-dozen key themes of Church and culture in both Americas. They offer introductory insights into the range of concerns which Pope John Paul II invites regional and local Churches to address, stimulated by pastoral needs and by his new Pontifical Council *Pro Cultura.*

PART I

The Papers and Discussions, Convergences and Perspectives

SECTION ONE

The Church's Evolving Concept of and Global Role Concerning Culture

The first set of papers, by Carrier and Lambert, explores secular understandings of culture and, principally, the Church's growing consciousness of culture's role in the call and ministry for humanizing and evangelizing all peoples. Carrier traces the Church's awakening to "modern culture" over the hundred years from Leo XIII, through Pius XII and the Second Vatican Council, to John Paul II.

Lambert focuses on the ecclesiology of culture brought forth by *Gaudium et Spes,* the Pastoral Constitution which breaks decisively from "the old Christian order" in response to the ecclesial challenge of today's secularization and human need. Cultural components are basic, the Council asserts, for the Church's evangelization and ministry in the world today "to reconsign matter to its divine origin and to integrate earthly hopes into the future promised by God."

Understanding Culture: The Ultimate Challenge of the World-Church?

Hervé Carrier

I. THE CULTURES OF POETS AND SOCIOLOGISTS

The metamorphosis of the word *culture* is perhaps one of the most revealing indicators of recent cultural changes. In the beginning of this century culture was a peaceful concept signifying intellectual enlightenment, classic education, and artistic refinement. The old standard dictionaries like the *Oxford Dictionary, Littré Larousse, Der Grosse Brockhaus,* limited themselves to the definition of culture in that classical sense. Culture, for the generation of the first part of this century, still meant: fine arts, humanism, science, instruction, and education.

Today culture has become a dynamic category for action. Slogans such as "cultural revolution," "cultural imperialism" are irritating but quite revealing. *Culture* now refers to a new frontier for social or political intervention. Analogously, Paul VI and John Paul II gave a dynamic meaning to *culture* in speaking of the "evangelization of cultures," and the "dialogue of the Church with cultures."

Strange destiny of a word: One is surprised, in consulting earlier editions of the great encyclopedias, to find that the term *culture* did not even deserve an entry in these scientific publications. The *Encyclopaedia Britannica,* the *Catholic Encyclopedia,* the *Dictionnaire de Theologie Catholique,* the *Enciclopedia Cattolica* did not even mention the word *culture* under the letter *c.*[1] Today, no serious encyclopaedia could fail to discuss the concept of culture, which has become indispensable in our way of apprehending social reality. It is not surprising, therefore, that the *Encyclopaedia Britannica,* in its latest edition (1977), devotes eight full columns to "culture" and indicates at least a hundred and fifty cross-references to cultural problems treated in various parts of the encyclopedia. The modern *Encyclopedia Universalis,* published in Paris, contains forty-one columns on "culture."

Culture has become an operational term with which to analyze social reality and to act upon it, to transform it. In this sense, today we speak of cultural policies, cultural programs, cultural liberation, and cultural development. For us, culture means not only achievements of the mind; it also indicates patterns of behavior typical of a group or a society. In other words, without rejecting the classical concept of culture, we have widened its meaning by giving it an anthropological and historical perspective.

II. TOWARD AN ANTHROPOLOGICAL APPROACH TO CULTURE

It may be rewarding to see how this concept of culture came to assume, beyond its intellectual meaning, an anthropological and historical dimension. Three causes or circumstances may be mentioned: 1) the borrowing of the word *culture* from the professional language of the ethnologists; 2) the influence of Marxist analysis; 3) the impact on modern thinking of cultural liberation movements.

1. The Influence of Ethnologists

During the nineteenth century, students of "primitive societies" had begun to use the word *culture* as an alternative to the term *civilization.* The concept of culture became a tool for analyzing the social habits of tribes or ethnic groups. The British anthropologist Edward Tylor was a forerunner. In 1871, he published *Primitive Culture,* in which we find one of the first systematic definitions of culture, understood in the anthropological sense: "Culture or civilization is that complex whole which includes knowledge, belief, art, morals, law, custom, and any other capabilities and habits acquired by man as a member of society."[2]

Tylor's definition has been refined, enriched and reworked many times since. In 1952, Kroeber and Kluckhohn offered a definition which has become a standard reference:

> Culture consists of patterns, explicit and implicit, of and for behavior acquired and transmitted by symbols, constituting the distinctive achievement of human groups, including their embodiments in artifacts; the essential core of culture consists of traditional (i.e., historically derived and selected) ideas and especially their attached values; culture systems may, on the one hand, be considered as products of action, on the other as conditioning elements of further action.[3]

The concept of culture which had remained the preserve of the professional anthropologists in Britain, France, Germany, and the United States, was progressively adopted by observers and students of Western societies, who were trying to analyze what was happening, especially after World War I, when the industrial societies experienced deep social changes and when modern communications intensified contacts and provoked a lively recognition of national differences and of cultural diversities, as we call them today.

The interesting point in this evolution is that the word *culture* gradually became a concept used to analyze our own societies. Books like Ruth Benedict's *Patterns of Culture* (1934) and Margaret Mead's publications contributed to extend the method of cultural anthropology to modern countries. In short, the growing interest and preoccupation of Western sociologists and of the public at large with what was happening in the institutions, patterns of life, and values in the emerging pluralistic societies facilitated the spread of cultural analysis applied to the industrialized collectivities.

2. The Marxist Analysis of Culture

Another factor in the popularization of the social notion of culture is the influence of Marxist analysis. For Karl Marx a dominant culture is the product of a dominating class. The owners of the means of production impose their values and their culture on the subordinate classes. For Marx there is a constant interplay between social classes manifested in the economic and cultural domination of the powerful over the poor.

In a famous passage of *The German Ideology,* Marx wrote:

> The ideas of the dominating class are, in all epochs, dominating ideas. That means that the class which is the material dominating power in society is, at the same time, its spiritual dominating power. The class which disposes of the means of material production disposes therefore, at the same time, of the means of intellectual production, in such a way that, generally speaking, the ideas of those who are deprived of the means of intellectual production are subjected to that dominating class.[4]

The Marxist approach to culture contains a dynamic and voluntaristic aspect: the proletarians, dominated by the culture of the bourgeoisie, will have to fight to change their culture. The proletariat itself has to supplant the dominating class, so that the proletarian culture will become the culture of tomorrow. Lenin commented: "The proletarian culture is not something that comes out of nowhere, it is not the invention of those who call themselves specialists. The proletarian culture must consist in the systematic development of all the knowledge that humankind has elaborated."[5]

In their approach to culture, the Marxists do not minimize, as the Western anti-intellectualists often do, the influence of formal education in promoting cultural change. Bakunin put it very clearly: "It stands to reason that the one who knows more will dominate the one who knows less."[6] The irony, Alvin Gouldner observed in commenting on Bakunin, is that the socialist intelligentsia "continues to exploit the rest of society as the old class had, but now uses education rather than money to exploit others."[7] Culture has become the new dominating power.

We should add that Marxist analysis is not only a method used by Communists. It is a mode of interpretation for the whole of social reality, and this method has pervaded the thinking habits of Western observers as well, even if they do not always consciously recognize it. The point has been made very well by Nicholas Lobkowicz, who urged that, while acknowledging some Marxist influence in our analysis of culture, we should be critical of the deterministic assumptions often linked with the method.[8] Moreover, we have come to realize that the relations between the so-called "popular" and "elite" cultures are not to be reduced to a one-way process of domination. The living culture of a people can even become a decisive factor in social change.

3. Impact of Liberation Movements

A third factor explaining the emergence of culture as a key social issue is represented by the liberation movements that have changed the map of the world after World War II. More than one hundred countries joined the community of nations in the last forty years. The process of decolonization was first seen as a political and economic movement toward independence. But it soon appeared that deeper aspirations were at work, namely *cultural liberation* and the affirmation of each people's *cultural identity.* Experts in international law and specialists in development programs were slow to understand the cultural factors in the struggle of the new nations for independence. The Tanzanian political leader Julius Nyerere put in strong terms a point that inspires the Nigerian novelist Chinua Achebe: "Of all crimes of colonialism there is none worse than the attempt to make us believe we had no indigenous culture of our own, or that what we did have was worthless–something of which we should be ashamed, instead of a source of pride."[9]

But to understand the cultural needs of the new nations seemed infinitely more complex than to satisfy their material necessities. In other words, in development and progress, culture has been revealed as the primordial reality to work with.

The Club of Rome, having discussed the economic and material implications of development for many years, came to appreciate the importance of the cultural factor. In 1979 it reported: "Cultural identity at both national and international levels remains one of the most basic non-material psychological needs which may well become an increasing source of conflict among and within societies."[10] There will be no development if we fail to see the decisive role played by the cultural factors:

> The immense issues that cultural identity raises are all the more complex because, unlike some material global problems, cultural issues are

not resolvable by a process of redistribution. Cultural autonomy is not granted (or withheld) at will through international agreements of redistribution of resources, indispensable as these may be in other cases.[11]

On the part of many governments and international bodies, like the United Nations, a profound revision of their approach to development is maturing. They now perceive development problems with all their cultural components. The Church itself has undergone an analogous evolution in its understanding of social reality.

III. THE CHURCH MODERNIZES ITS VIEW OF CULTURE

In fact, if we consider the use of the word *culture* within the Church, we notice an evolution comparable to the one we have observed above. The trend is clear from Leo XIII down to Paul VI and John Paul II, and a few indications of this evolution may be in order.

1. From Leo XIII to Pius XII

In his encyclical *Inscrutabili* (1878) Leo XIII came close to what we would today call the problem of culture. Against the revolutionaries of 1870, he sought to illustrate how the Church, by spreading the light of the Gospel, has dedicated itself to the advancement of humankind, by its fight against barbarism, superstition, backwardness and moral degradation as well as by promoting education, moral progress and intellectual refinement. Leo XIII had a classic view of culture. He wrote: "the very notion of civilization is a fiction of the brain if it rest not on the abiding principles of truth and the unchanging laws of virtue and justice." He vindicated the Holy See against all attacks: "In very truth it is the glory of the Supreme Pontiffs that they steadfastly set themselves up as a wall and a bulwark to save society from falling back into its former superstition and barbarism."[12] For Leo XIII, culture was the equivalent of civilization.

When we come to Pius XII and to the vast collection of writings and speeches he left, we see that whenever he treated the problems of culture or civilization, the accent was still on culture understood in the traditional sense. Pius XII provoked admiration and respect for the richness and breadth of his intellectual vision. Nothing pertaining to the knowledge acquired by his contemporaries seemed to be left out of his preoccupations. He appeared as an impressive "man of culture," in the humanistic sense. But there are also clear indications that he was inclined to understand in a wider anthropological perspective, especially when he had occasion to speak to groups interested in "the unity and universality of culture," or when he addressed ethnologists, or when he described modern mentalities confronting the problems of war and peace.

We also find in his writings a strong plea for the respect and understanding of the identity of each people—an element particularly important, he insists, in the training of future priests.

2. Vatican II: A Modern View of Culture

At the time of Vatican Council II, a decisive step was made in adopting officially the most modern view about culture. In the preparation of *Gaudium et Spes,* theologians and sociologists worked together and their cooperation was very helpful in coining a definition of culture which incorporates, in a perfectly balanced way, the classic as well as the anthropological dimension of culture. The main reason is that the Council boldly adopted a concrete and historical view in discussing the problems of the modern world. It is significant that the documents of Vatican II used the word *history* sixty-three times.

To recall the definition of culture elaborated by *Gaudium et Spes*:

> In the broad sense of the word, "culture" means everything which man uses to develop and refine the many capabilities of his body and his mind. Or, by his toil and his knowledge, bring nature and the universe to serve his ends. Or, through steps forward taken in customs and institutions, make his community life—both in his family and his group—a human life. Or express, communicate, and preserve, in the course of time, his great spiritual experiences and his higher aspirations, so that they can better the life of many people and even of all mankind. This is why human culture necessarily has an historical and social aspect, and why the word "culture" often is given a sociological and ethnological meaning. This meaning leads to the expression "plurality of cultures." For, different styles of living and different scales of values come from the particular ways which human groupings have of using things, of working, of expressing themselves, of participating in religion, of behaving, making rules and laws and setting up juridical institutions, of developing the arts and sciences, and of cultivating beauty. This is the way that, starting from inherited usages and customs, a patrimony is formed which is peculiar to every human community.[13]

In adopting a modern definition of culture, the Council wished to underline a few important points. First, it strongly affirmed, right from the beginning, that the human being cannot exist without culture: "man can come to an authentic and full humanity only through culture."[14] Second, between culture and the Gospel there are living links: "there are many links between the message of salvation and human culture. For God revealing Himself to His people, to the extent of a full manifestation of Himself in His Incarnate Son, has spoken according to culture proper to different ages."[15] Third point, cultural conditions can have a great influence on the religious life of believers. Christians are urged to understand cultures different from their own and try to promote cultural understanding. "May the faithful, therefore, live in very close union with the men of their time. Let them strive to understand perfectly their way of thinking and feeling, as expressed in their culture."[16]

We should note, also, the very positive approach to culture revealed by *Gaudium et Spes*. One is impressed by the optimistic and positive value attributed by Vatican II to culture as such. It speaks of cultural progress, of the benefits of culture, of culture as a right for all individuals: "For this reason, the Church recalls to all that culture must be subordinated to the integral development of the person, to the good of the community and the whole of society."[17]

3. Comparison with UNESCO's Conception

Having discussed the evolution of the notion of culture in the Church, it is interesting to compare the definition of *Gaudium et Spes* with the concept of culture used by international bodies like UNESCO. UNESCO has undergone a similar evolution in its view of culture. In its first years of existence, after 1946, it usually defined culture as including arts, science, education, literature. In a word, classical culture was the working concept used by UNESCO. In its usage nowadays culture has a clear anthropological dimension as well. Let us consider the definition that was given in Mexico, in 1982, at the International Conference of UNESCO on "Cultural Policies":

> In its widest sense, culture may now be said to be the whole complex of distinctive spiritual, material, intellectual and emotional features that characterize a society or social group. It includes not only the arts and letters, but also modes of life, the fundamental rights of the human being, value systems, traditions and beliefs. . . . It is culture that gives man the ability to reflect upon himself. It is culture that makes us specifically human, rational beings, endowed with critical judgement and a sense of moral commitment. It is through culture that we discern values and make choices. It is through culture that man expresses himself, becomes aware of himself, recognizes his incompleteness, questions his own achievements, seeks untiringly for new meanings and creates works through which he transcends his limitations.[18]

It is worth noting how this definition of culture includes spiritual as well as material values and how it stresses, as positive values, freedom, moral responsibility, fundamental rights and the search for transcendence. It would probably not be erroneous to think that some Christians have been at work in the drafting of this Declaration, as well as representatives from other great religions who believe in spiritual and transcendent values.

IV. NEW TRENDS SINCE VATICAN II

In the face of the rapid changes that have occurred in the twenty years since Vatican II, can we still say that the concept of culture elaborated by *Gaudium et Spes* remains valid? Speaking as a sociologist interested in cultural and religious problems, I would not hesitate to answer *yes*. But I would want to observe that, when we speak of culture now, new connotations are added to the optimistic and almost euphoric concept of culture contained in *Gaudium et Spes*. To make my point briefly, I would say that, when we deal with cultural problems today, we have: 1) a more dramatic view of cultural issues; 2) we give much greater importance to culture seen as a political goal; 3) we are rediscovering the unique role of creative individuals in culture.

1. A More Dramatic Perception of Cultures

First we say that our view of culture is more dramatic than that of twenty years ago. Paul VI expressed that aspect very eloquently in *Evangelii Nuntiandi* (1975): "The split between the Gospel and culture is without a doubt the drama of our time, just as it was of other times. Therefore every effort must be made to ensure a full evangelization of culture, or more correctly of cultures."[19]

In 1979, John Paul II, speaking to an extraordinary meeting of the cardinals, reaffirmed the same dramatic insight, describing culture as that "vital field, in which the destiny of the Church and of the world is at stake," in this final quarter of our century.[20]

The Church realizes more vividly today the close connection that exists between the complementary tasks of evangelizing, promoting justice and defending the culture of human beings.

In 1971, the synod of bishops, dedicated to the theme of justice, had stressed in a forceful way how acting for justice and preaching the Gospel were closely linked: "Acting for justice and participating in the transformation of the world appear to us clearly as a constitutive dimension of the preaching of the Gospel."[21] At the same time, the synod recognized how the pursuit of justice and development was related to the preservation of cultural identities.

> While we reaffirm the right of peoples to conserve their own identity, it appears ever more clearly how absolutely inefficient is the fight against modernization, considered as a threat to the proper characteristics of nations, if one appeal only to the sacred and historical traditions, or to venerated life styles. If modernization is interpreted in the sense that it serves the good of the nation, men will be able to create a culture that represents a true and proper heritage almost like a social memory which

> is an active element capable of modelling an authentic and creative personality in the concert of nations.[22]

So we see that the pursuit of justice is inseparable from the promotion of culture. Joseph P. Fitzpatrick explains this clearly in an article "Justice as a Problem of Culture":

> We generally think of justice in terms of economics: how much food does a person have; can one clothe oneself and one's family; does a person have a decent place to live? But the critical question about these practical issues is not the economic activity or the economic arrangement. The critical question is: what do they mean in terms of human interests, in terms of human destiny, in terms of what human life means? This aspect of 'meaning' is what constitutes culture; and that is where the heart of the problem lies.[23]

The natural connection which is seen today between the inseparable requirements of justice and of culture gives a sense of urgency to the commitment of Christians in favor of cultural progress, because the needs of culture are no less pressing than the basic biological necessities.

2. Political Approach to Culture

As we have noted above, culture nowadays is becoming an important field for social and political intervention. It is a trend that deserves close attention.

In a way, governments and central institutions in society have always had an influence on culture. What is new today is that governments are spelling out an explicit policy for culture. In August 1982, more than one hundred twenty governments came together at the Mondiacult Conference of UNESCO in Mexico to discuss the very subject of "cultural policies." At the Conference it was interesting to note the variety of objectives that the policies of different governments had. A cultural policy can range from a traditional interest in the arts, monuments, libraries, museums, sites, to a much more ambitious program embracing cultural development in its widest sense, that is, the promotion and defense of human values as such in all government policies. In this sense, it is the whole policy of the government that tends to be *cultural.* Today ministries of culture or their equivalent exist in more than one hundred countries. Substantial budgets are voted and programs and legislation enacted in order to pursue a cultural policy. Such a policy can stand for the noblest ideals, but it can also be destructive of freedom and human dignity.

An advance in the art of governing. On the one hand, we should recognize that the pursuit of a cultural policy can be an advance in the art of governing; for a cultural policy favors the education of all, the widest participation of all in the benefits of culture, with a particular attention to the poor, minorities, the isolated groups in a nation. Cultural policies in democratic countries tend to reaffirm the centrality of human aspirations in all sectors of government: health, education, communications, tourism, youth, scientific research and international relations. At UNESCO and at the Council of Europe, they speak today of "the cultural finalities of development," meaning that progress cannot be limited only to an economic point of view. All factors contributing to the quality of life are underlined explicitly, and non-materialistic values are pursued. Cultural democracy is the intended goal. The twenty-one countries forming the Council of Europe are carefully studying policies for the common pursuit of "cultural objectives." A recent report from Nordic Europe underlines the point: "In the beginning there was political democracy; then came social democracy; and now the movement is towards cultural democracy."[24] Cultural development, therefore, becomes a clear political objective. In November 1983, with the unanimous approval of 130 governments, UNESCO decided to launch a World Decade for Cultural Development.

Thus understood, a cultural policy fosters the free cooperation of all living sectors of a nation. It should be stressed that the role of the government is not to create or impose culture, but to favor the participation of each individual and group in the country. The state is no more a producer of culture than it is an educator, but it can play an indispensable role in trying to optimize the conditions that render educational and cultural progress available to all groups and individuals. True cultural advance can be achieved only with the participation of all live components in a society. Cultural policies that pursue such an objective of cultural democracy represent progress in the art of government, because the conditions of cultural participation tend to be equalized with greater equity, so that no group in the nation is excluded from the benefits of culture only because of adverse or unjust situations. Therefore, modern citizens become better equipped to resist the manipulation of ideological groups, or to oppose the economic imposition of certain cultural industries represented by producers of films, TV programs, magazines, books, video cassettes. It thus becomes possible to prevent cultural domination and to remedy the cultural discrimination or segregation imposed on minorities or marginal groups. In this sense we agree with *Gaudium et Spes* when it speaks of the function of the state in relation to cultural progress:

> It is not the function of public authority to determine what the proper forms of culture should be. It should rather foster the conditions and the means which are capable of promoting cultural life among all citizens and even within the minorities of a nation. Hence in this matter

> men must insist above all else that culture be not diverted from its own purpose and made to serve political or economic interests.[25]

The perversions of cultural policies. But, as experience teaches and *Gaudium et Spes* reminds us, any noble project may be perverted by ideological or economic interests. In the name of culture crimes against humanity have been committed and are still perpetrated. The Nazis pretended to pursue a cultural policy and Joseph Goebbels boasted: "We will become ourselves a Church."[26] It may be remembered that one hundred days after Hitler came to power on the night of May 9, 1933, Goebbels ordered the public burning of more than twenty thousand books in the major cities of Germany. That was also, unfortunately, a form of cultural intervention, the totalitarian imposition of an ideological view of culture.

In the name of culture, entire countries under Communist regimes have their true national identity threatened and are subject to constant pressure, re-education, and moral violence. This also is a cultural reality of today, which, of course, perverts the notion of culture that we have made our own.

Some socialist regimes, even in Western countries, have taken a radical view of their cultural programs. One socialist party in Western Europe proclaims that "socialism is a cultural project." I read in the socialist program of one of these parties that an absolute priority must be given to the ideological training of young children:

> Early childhood until the age of six is a decisive period of life for each individual. It is at that time that habits of speech, forms of thought, traits of mentality are acquired which become enduring structures for life. It is also at that age that the socialization of children is made easier. This is why early childhood considered in itself constitutes an absolute priority.[27]

Worse still, in order to restore cultural identity, some governments are regressing to primitive and inhuman methods of domination. Whipping is reintroduced for those who drink alcohol; cutting off the right hand for those who steal; death by stoning for those caught in adultery; decapitation for those who kill. These measures were announced in Khartoum, in September 1983, as "new Islamic legislation."

These perversions of cultural policies, inspired by extreme interpretations of the Koran, are matched by the attitudes of politicians who distort Buddhist or Hindu sentiments to impose cultural programs that are violently sectarian. Similar violence is committed by so-called Christians who use the ideology of national security to justify the worst abuses of military regimes.

In the end, religious and political dogmatisms of the extreme right or the left achieve the same results: culture becomes a means to dominate. This is one of the most violent contradictions of our time, which makes it all the more urgent to restore *culture* to its true meaning, as a genuine sign of human progress, dignity, freedom.

Confrontation of cultural policies. In the face of the conflicting ideologies that sustain opposed cultural objectives, it is not surprising to see that *culture* has become the *locus* of today's confrontations. Nations that feel dominated will fight for their cultural liberation. Some analysts even claim that culture is becoming one of the decisive grounds for international confrontation. Some even add that imperialism today does not mean only the conquest of lands, markets, or resources. Imperialism has become cultural: the minds themselves have to be conquered. The conquest of the minds, *La conquête des esprits,*[28] is precisely the title of a recent book on this theme, in which the author argues that, apart from its economic and military superiority, the United States aspires to spiritual domination of the earth by imposing its values, its way of life, and its culture.

A rejoinder to that thesis is, of course, the parallel view which sees the Soviet Union as the other imperialist power seeking the conquest of minds, since it is the explicit aim of communism to create a new man, through a new society formed by a new culture.

The practical consequence of these confrontations between East and West is that the peril of war comes not only from economic or political divergences, but from the radical opposition of cultures. That is why dialogue between cultures, which is a constant effort at mutual recognition, is an indispensable condition to peacemaking.

In spite of such cultural tensions, so artfully orchestrated today, I find great hope in the fact that we are rediscovering the decisive role of leading individuals in cultural change and are convincing ourselves that a new voice has to be given to wisdom and moral creativity.

This brings us to the third development to be observed since *Gaudium et Spes.* It confirms an intuition that was at the heart of Vatican II and that is too often forgotten.

3. Rediscovering the Role of the Individual in Culture

In our present view of culture, closer attention is given to the creative person, and it is recognized that, even in a society often marked by apparent fatalism, by massive conformity and easy compliance to dominant values, gifted individuals can play a very significant role in society. This is not something entirely new, but we tended to lose or overlook the tremendous potential of the individual in history. We now rediscover as something promising what our anonymous societies were strangely inclined to dismiss: creative persons can have a decisive impact on the culture of their epoch. Recent historical research is reinterpreting in that sense the social and cultural influence of such figures as Dante and Leonardo da Vinci. For instance Dante, whose genius had been interpreted as reflecting and sublimating the religious and intellectual treasures of the Middle Ages, is now recognized as one of the great creators of the culture of his times and a forerunner of the epoch to come. "He is not simply the representative or the mirror of his age; but, much more, he is one of its builders and not one of its least powerful creators."[29]

There are other examples still more surprising, especially for those who restrict themselves to an intellectualist view of culture. It often happens in history that individuals we would not have considered cultivated in the classical sense, have deeply changed the culture of their time. For example, Leonardo da Vinci, in his dialect called himself "omo sanza lettere," a man without letters, meaning that he did not know Latin or the classical authors. He never mastered the ability to compose a whole book, however his studio notes and drafts show how this self-made man came to re-create the world of forms, mathematics, mechanics, architecture, anatomy, and color. He gave a new dignity to the so-called servile or mechanical arts, which were still despised and considered less noble than the liberal arts. He developed mathematics, the experimental method, and the modern rules of mechanics. After him, we do not see arts, painting mechanics, anatomy, architecture, even engineering as before. He was a forerunner of our modern age. All this because of "the image of the world he had drawn in his own mind."[30]

A more familiar example is represented by Henry Ford, who has been called the father of modern automobile transportation. Ford certainly was not an intellectual. He once said: "I do not believe that I ever read a book until the end. Literature confuses the mind." But who can deny that his genius for producing and marketing popular automobiles has transformed the geography of our societies, our modes of communication, our notions of space and time. It would be difficult to assess the influence of Ford's activity on modern culture, which, according to sociologist James Flink, is typically a "car culture."[31]

The example of Gandhi belongs to the moral dimension. Mahatma Gandhi, as we now see him today, exerted the deepest influence on the culture of his country in spite of his poverty, austerity and moral independence. Gilbert Murray, who had known Gandhi at Oxford, later wrote an essay in which he underlined the extraordinary freedom and moral authority of Gandhi, precisely because he was attached to nothing on earth, apart from his desire to serve his brothers and sisters:

> Persons in power should be very careful how they deal with a man who cares nothing for sensual pleasure, nothing for riches, nothing for comfort or praise, or promotion, but is simply determined to do what he

> believes to be right. He is a dangerous and uncomfortable enemy because his body which you can always conquer gives you so little purchase upon his soul.[32]

In our society marked by mass-culture, the rediscovery of the unique influence of individual leaders, capable of intellectual and moral creativity, calls for a particular remark. It is refreshing to see that, beyond the trend toward fatalistic resignation, or beyond the pressures for passive conformity in our societies, there is always an important role reserved to inventors, heroes, and saints. Recognized examples today include the extraordinary influence of Mother Teresa of Calcutta, the lasting example of Martin Luther King, the impact of the many men and women in recent years who gave their lives in defending the poor and the oppressed in Latin America and in Africa. To them, I would add the increasing number of Church leaders and especially the recent Popes who stand firm for peace and human rights. All these are eloquent testimony to the cultural wisdom of the Christian tradition of prizing the social role of the moral leader and the saint. They are true creators of culture.

VI. DIALOGUE WITH CULTURES: A VITAL AREA FOR THE CHURCH

1. The Ultimate Challenge

It is in this context of the cultural evolution of humanity that the Church feels an urgent need to commit herself in favor of the cultural defense and progress of humankind. Culture has become the crux of the future and the real challenge of the world of tomorrow. For John Paul II this is a strong conviction he has repeated over and over again and in a very solemn way when he created the Pontifical Council for Culture in May 1982:

> Since the beginning of my pontificate, I have considered the Church's dialogue with the cultures of our time to be a vital area, one in which the destiny of the world at the end of this twentieth century is at stake. There in fact does exist a fundamental dimension capable of strengthening or shaking to their foundations the systems into which mankind as a whole is organized, and of liberating human existence, individually and collectively, from the threats which hang over it. This fundamental dimension is man, in his totality. Now man lives a fully human life thanks to culture. "Yes, the future of man depends on culture," as I said in my speech to UNESCO on 2 June 1980.[33]

As we have shown above, the Church has now acquired a dynamic, historic and operational view of culture. This has become evident in the innumerable pronouncements of recent popes in defense of human rights, freedom, peace, dignity for all men and women of today. The whole Church is becoming more aware of these deep aspirations which represent the ultimate defense of the human being.

A very significant example of this attitude of the post-conciliar Church is the cultural program which all the bishops of Latin America, meeting with Pope John Paul II in Mexico in 1979, have elaborated in the document called the "Declaration of Puebla." If we look at the major questions treated in this document, we find that "culture" occupies a central place among the subjects considered at this continental assembly: Latin America, the Church, evangelization, communion, youth, the poor and justice. The theme of "culture" is the one most frequently discussed in Puebla, immediately after those of the "Church," "evangelization" and "Latin America." In the index, more than one and a half pages of cross-references are given to various parts of the document on subjects pertaining to culture and evangelization.

Our analysis does not call for particular conclusions. The grave problems raised by the evolution and confrontation of cultures are all before us. But we take confidence in the fact that, since Vatican II, we have acquired a new approach to cultural realities. Catholics can now think modern about cultural problems, and we know that when a question is formulated correctly, a great step has been taken toward its solution.

What is required of our generation is essentially the ability to interpret cultural changes and the will to find the new cultural channels to announce the permanent truths of the Gospel. At this point, the testimony of an anthropologist and of a theologian might be in order.

2. The Anthropologist and the Theologian

The anthropologist is Clifford Geertz, who wrote that cultures are constantly created by human beings who have faith in their future and the worst mistake would be to think that the present cultural crisis is unique and insuperable. He cites the pertinent quotation:

> These times are times of chaos; opinions are a scramble; parties are a jumble; the language of new ideas has not been created; nothing is more difficult than to give a definition of oneself in religion, in philosophy, in politics. One feels, one knows, one fights, and at need, one dies for one's cause, but one cannot name it. It is the problem of this time to classify things and men. . . . The world has jumbled its catalogue.[34]

After reading this passage, it is somewhat consoling to check and find that the poet Alphonse de Lamartine wrote it around 1840 in the reign of Louis Philippe. Geertz's point is that culture is what we make it. "Without man no culture certainly; but equally, and more significantly, without culture, no man."[35] The words are very like those used by *Gaudium et Spes* in defining culture. For Christians the message should be clear: they are called to be builders of culture. No cultural crisis should be insuperable, because culture and hope can be closely associated.

The theologian is Bernard Lonergan, who reminded us that teaching and preaching remain sterile if they do not choose or seek to have the proper cultural channels. Speaking to his fellow Jesuits, Lonergan said:

> There is a crisis of the first magnitude today. For a principal duty of priests is to lead and teach the People of God. But all leadership and all teaching occurs within social structures and through cultural channels. In the measure that one insists on leading and teaching within structures that no longer function and through channels that no longer exist, in that very measure leadership and teaching cease to exist.[36]

It is with these considerations in mind that John Paul II decided to "found and institute a Council for Culture capable of giving to the whole Church a common impulse in the incessant encounter of the Gospel's message of salvation with the plurality of cultures."[37]

In practice, the Church is called to act on a twofold level: to give testimony to the Gospel's capacity to enrich and build human cultures; to pursue the defense of human beings and their cultural development for no other reason or pretext but only because they are human and deserve love as such. These two lines of action were clearly stated by John Paul II when he addressed the Pontifical Council for Culture in January 1983, insisting on:

> Two principal and complementary aspects which correspond to the two levels on which the Church carries on its activity: that of the *evangelization of cultures* and that of the *defense of man and of his cultural development*. Both tasks demand that new means for dialogue between the Church and the cultures of our time be developed.[38]

For our world, cultural dialogue has become a vital urgency and it might well represent the ultimate challenge. It is the pressing plea that the Church addresses to the human family:

> To the extent that the modern world stifles dialogue among cultures, it heads towards *conflicts* which run the risk of being fatal for the future of human civilization. Beyond prejudices and cultural barriers of racial, linguistic, religious, and ideological separation, human beings must recognize themselves as brothers and sisters, and accept each other in their diversity.[39]

Who, better than Christians, with their hope of effectively promoting human brotherhood, can foster the dialogue of cultures? For us, the ultimate challenge is the defense of the human being, created in the image of God and deserving our unconditional love.

NOTES AND REFERENCES

1. The respective volumes containing letter *c* were published in the following years: *The Encyclopaedia Britannica* (1922); *The Catholic Encyclopedia* (1908); the *Dictionnaire de Théologie Catholique* (1907); the *Enciclopedia Cattolica* (1950).
2. Edward B. Tylor, *Primitive Culture* (London: John Murray, 1871), I, p. 1.
3. Alfred L. Kroeber and Clyde Kluckhohn, "Culture: A Critical Review of Concepts and Definitions," in *Papers of the Peabody Museum of American Archaeology and Ethnology* 47, no. 1 (Cambridge, Mass.: Harvard University Press, 1952). See note 34 below.
4. Ernesto Mascitelli, ed., *Dizionario dei termini marxisti* (Milan: Vangelista Editore, 1977), pp. 78–82; see p. 80.
5. *On Youth and the School,* quoted in *Dizionario dei termini marxisti,* p. 82.
6. M. Bakouinine (Bakunin), *Oeuvres* (Paris, 1911), p. 106, quoted in Alvin Gouldner, *The Future of Intellectuals and the New Class* (New York: Seabury Press, 1979), p. 103.
7. Alvin Gouldner, p. 6.
8. Nicholas Lobkowicz, "Marxism as the Ideology of Our Age," *Center Journal,* Fall 1983, pp. 9–30.
9. Julius K. Nyerere, *Ujamaa* (London: Oxford University Press, 1974) p. 66.
10. J. W. Botkin, M. Elmadjra, M. Malitza, *No Limits to Learning: Bridging the Human Gap,* "A Report of the Club of Rome" (Oxford, N.Y.: Pergamon Press, 1979), p. 114.
11. Ibid., p. 116.
12. Leo XIII, Encyclical Letter, *Inscrutabili* (On the Evils Affecting Modern Society: Their Causes and Remedies), April 21, 1878, nos. 5, 7; in *The Church Speaks to the Modern World: The Social Teachings of Leo XIII,* ed. Etienne Gilson (Garden City, N.Y.: Image Books, 1954), pp. 278–290.
13. Pastoral Constitution *Gaudium et Spes,* December 7, 1965, no. 53; cf. W. M. Abbott and J. Gallagher, the *Documents of Vatican II* (New York: Association Press, 1966), p. 259.
14. *Gaudium et Spes,* no. 53.
15. Ibid., no. 58.
16. Ibid., no. 59.
17. Ibid.
18. *Mexico City Declaration: Final Report,* "World Conference on Cultural Policies," Mexico City, July 26 to August 6, 1982 (Paris: UNESCO, CLT/MD/1, 1982).
19. Paul VI, *Apostolic Exhortation Evangelii Nuntiandi,* December 8, 1975 (London: Catholic Truth Society, 1976), see no. 20.
20. *L'Osservatore Romano* (English), November 10, 1979.
21. Ibid., December 16, 1971.

22. Ibid.

23. Joseph P. Fitzpatrick, "Justice as a Problem of Culture," *Studies in the International Apostolate of the Jesuits*, December 1976, pp. 13–32.

24. See "Towards Cultural Democracy," in Barry Turner and Gunilla Nordquist, *The Other European Community: Integration and Cooperation in Nordic Europe* (London: Weidenfeld and Nicolson, 1982), pp. 252–297.

25. *Gaudium et Spes*, no. 59.

26. Quoted in *Documentation Catholique*, no. 1852 (May 15, 1983), p. 524.

27. *Projet de Plan socialiste pour l'EducationNationale* (Paris, September 16, 1976).

28. Yves Eudes, *La conquête des esprits* (Paris: Maspero, 1982); see also Corrado Medori, *L'Imperialismo Culturale*, International Conference of Algiers, 1977 (Milan: Franco Angelini, 1979), in particular; "English language as a vehicle of imperialism," pp. 64–73.

29. Giorgio Petrocchi, *Vita di Dante* (Rome: Laterza, 1983).

30. Augusto Marinoni, *La Matematica di Leonardo da Vinci* (Milan: Ente Raccolta Vinciana, 1983).

31. James J. Flink, *The Car Culture* (Cambridge, Mass.: MIT Press, 1975).

32. Quoted in B. R. Nanda, *Mahatma Gandhi: A Biography* (New York: Oxford University Press, 1958, reissued 1981), p. 89.

33. *L'Osservatore Romano* (English), June 28, 1982.

34. Clifford Geertz, *The Interpretation of Cultures* (New York: Basic Books, 1973), p. 221; see his concept of "culture" and his discussion of such formal definitions as those of E. B. Tylor and of Clyde Kluckhohn, pp. 3–30.

35. Ibid., p. 49.

36. Bernard Lonergan, "The Response of the Jesuit as Priest and Apostle in the Modern World," *Studies in the Spirituality of Jesuits* 2 (1970), pp. 89–110, quoted in *Social Action* 32 (January–March 1982), p. 68.

37. *L'Osservatore Romano* (English), June 28, 1982.

38. Ibid., February 28, 1983.

39. Ibid.

Gaudium et Spes and the Travail of Today's Ecclesial Conception

Bernard Lambert, O.P.

My task is to tell how *Gaudium et Spes* came to be, what it tried to do and what it has achieved; in sum *Gaudium et Spes,* yesterday and today.

Under the direction of Cardinal Garrone, and in collaboration with Monsignor Pierre Haubtmann, principal editor of the Pastoral Constitution on the Church in the Modern World, I was closely associated with the formulation of that conciliar document, especially in the decisive period of the last session in 1965. One more reading of the passages, once my joy and torment, raised many questions, when I sought to think of the document as a living force in our culture. To avoid being overwhelmed, I decided to try to select from the range of problems that assailed the authors of *Gaudium et Spes* a few issues of commanding eminence in their day that are still with us.

The questions are: Shall we maintain the old Christian order or shall we build a new one? How shall we react to the secularization of the world? What is to become of man amidst the turmoil of our changing world? How can we help man build the world community in peace? How shall we evangelize today? Each of these queries may be considered as the center of a constellation of questions that foreshadow some new order dimly taking shape in the minds of men.

I shall deal with the five central questions but not with the constellations. It will not be possible to treat or even enumerate proposed answers and solutions as well as their likely consequences. The subject matter is enormous and we are fully engaged with it. We conceived and created *Gaudium et Spes* yesterday; we continue to do so today.

I. CHRISTIAN ORDER

We begin with the first question: Shall we maintain the old Christian order, or shall we build a new one?

The very pertinence of the question may be doubted on the ground that on the eve of the Second Vatican Council little of the old Christendom seemed to be in evidence: the diminutive city-state of the pope, a distant reminder of a temporal power that had its origin some fifteen hundred years ago; and here and there throughout the world there were Christian churches. The Reformation had disrupted Christendom. After the cultural hostility to faith so marked since the beginning of the nineteenth century, and after the ravages that accompanied the Marxist invasions of the globe, where or what was Christendom?

The Church is accustomed to encounter the changes of centuries. She experiences them, then sorts them out, and only later makes lasting pronouncements. And it is not her style to bury alive whatever may still be breathing.

A general definition of a Christian order is that it is the social expression of the Gospel. In a cursory summary of Church history, one may say that first there was a broad period of Christian order which began in apostolic times. Beginning with the Emperor Constantine there was a second Christian order which had many avatars during fifteen centuries. This papacy-empire, church-state order was frontally attacked in the 1700s, especially by the French Revolution, and underwent a time of gradual erosion and total rejection until Vatican II. Now we are at the beginning of a new stage.

I must allow that this division may be seen as a terrible simplification, for it covers the forms of expression over so many centuries. Nevertheless, it is valuable. One may even argue that the five successive versions of *Gaudium et Spes* were so many stages in a growing recognition that certain matters were finished and that others should command the stage or, at any rate, win recognition on the world stage. When, on the first day of the Council, Cardinal Lienart of Lille proposed to discard the list of commissions that had been prepared before the Council, so that the Council could proceed as it wished, he in effect gave an alert, a signal of what the future was to bring.

During its first three centuries the Church thought of itself as Noah's ark, the ark of salvation. History was the deluge and the Church had to protect the elect. The Lord was soon to come and the ark, the Church, would finally cast anchor on the shores of eschatology. This frame of mind persisted until the days of the Emperor Constantine and the contemporary Pope, Sylvester I. Constantine decidedly had no intention of bringing history to a halt when with the cross that appeared in the heavens were the words: "In this sign you will conquer." For his part Pope Sylvester had come to think that the triumph of Christ necessarily implied neither an uninterrupted succession of persecutions and deaths nor the annihilation of Rome, the great Babylon. Did not Constantine in effect offer the conversion of Rome with his conversion?

When the Son of God came on earth, the world assuredly entered upon the last age, but that did not mean an imminent working out of eschatology. Nothing required that the bark of Peter, the ark of salvation, soon reach the shores of its final goal. Christ had, indeed, warned his disciples to be vigilant, but he had also prayed to his Father not to take them from the world. The voyage could be a long one. The Pope understood that the reign of Christ had to be universal and that with the protection of the Roman emperor the successors of Peter would be the principal agents of that reign. The Church could thus be in the world and be a part of it. It could also be in the world and spiritually be apart from it.

Before Sylvester I the Church depended solely and exclusively on spiritual authority. After him, though it took many forms, the spiritual authority of the Church always had a political and financial authority joined to it.

Vatican II marked a turning point. Paul VI gave up the use of the tiara, as did his successors. He spiritualized the diplomatic service of the Vatican. Pope John Paul decided to make information about Vatican finances accessible. All his activity affirms, so to speak, that the world must have a place where the Beatitudes should stand out as the standards of the Great King.

Was Pope Sylvester disavowed? But how can one speak in such terms about a man who established a formula which 232 successors were to maintain? Did we, in our future course, set by Vatican II, place ourselves apart from him? Not completely, for, even by human reckoning and in spite of apocalyptic threats that menace us, the Church still has areas of time to traverse before reaching the end of time and history.

The question remains: If we cannot sustain the old order, toward what kind of new order shall we direct ourselves?

This major question, surprisingly, issued from the labors prescribed by the third chapter of the first part of *Gaudium et Spes.* The phrasing of the text is detached and untroubled, without references likely to rouse passions or provoke infinite discussions. New things are presented almost as matter-of-fact. There is no looking for any modern Constantine. In it the Church says simply: Here then is man and it is with the humanum that we are going to forge an alliance. In this statement there is no looking on the temporal order as simply a support to the spiritual order; on the contrary, the Church fully acknowledges the autonomy of earthly affairs. Nor is there finally any question of saying: Creation has its value but let us bestir ourselves to absorb it into the realm of eternity. *Gaudium et Spes* declared: Creation and redemption are two categories of God's action which are to coexist to the very end and will achieve perfect coincidence only in eschatology.

There are other traits to be noted. The chapter on culture in the second part of the Pastoral Constitution states that the Gospel is open to a plurality of cultural models. May not, then, the new Christian order be compared to a network or galaxy? Pope Paul VI had declared in *Octogesima Adveniens* that in the future it would be difficult to make a single social pronouncement that was valid for the Universal Church and for all humankind. And John Paul II by his travels confirms the word that each regional Church has to say, that each culture has to express. To carry the point further: Christian institutions will always be necessary, but that does not imply the maximal and systematic confessionalization of the profane.

In his admirable book *Sources of Renewal: A Study of Implementation of Vatican Council II* (Cracow, 1972; French translation, Paris, 1981), Cardinal Wojtyla gives a central position to personal conscience. On what else, indeed, can Christianity count in a profane world, if not on the jealously maintained identity of its Church and on the mediation of consciences? It is conscience, having itself been transformed, that changes the world. Being part of the profane order, conscience respects that order's autonomy, but in its awareness of what man is existentially, conscience is located in the profane order and makes salvation the focal point in dealing with the culture.

Light will be given to us each day, our daily light, for the task of devising a new Christian order. It is already upon us and around us. Synods of bishops have taken up, apportioned, and forwarded the work of the Council. To mention only the synods, in 1971 there was the Synod of Justice in the World; in 1974, Evangelization Today; in 1977, on Catechesis; in 1980, on the Family; in 1983, on Reconciliation—all themes of *Gaudium et Spes.* Its very style, inductive, concrete, and pastoral, creative of the formulas and fashions of the future, has been incorporated in the style of the Church as a whole.

The proximity of events as we experience them may prevent us from seeing them as they really are, in their newness.

If other examples are required, it might be noted that institutions have been provided to implement the entire second part of *Gaudium et Spes,* in the Roman Curia first and then in a considerable part of the Church at large: The Pontifical Council for the Family derived from the first chapter on marriage and the family; the Pontifical Council on Culture had its lines of development sketched by the Council's extensive statements on culture; the section on social-economic life was extended by Paul VI's encyclical *Populorum Progressio* and by *Laborem Exercens* of John Paul II; the chapter on peace and the community of nations provided the basis for the Pontifical Commission on Justice and Peace; and the Council *Cor Unum* was founded to be, as it were, the soul of the charity of Christians in international mutual assistance.

From *Gaudium et Spes,* then, have issued movements on behalf of the poor, movements for nonviolence, movements of liberation and justice, and movements of brotherhood and peace. All these are in line with the renewed definition of the Church. The Church of the old order considered that she had reached her goal in this-world and could therefore rest statically, satisfied with repetition of formulas from the past. The Church of Vatican II renews herself in movement as a pilgrim, begins again to create the future in place of simply adjusting to it, and thus again becomes a presence which nourishes the world and is nourished by it.

The language of the Church has also begun to change; it becomes more clearly the language of the Gospel. Christ's language involved three elements;

he proclaimed the Beatitudes, he spoke in parables, he performed miracles. The Church again proclaims the Beatitudes. In a number of countries it has fashioned living parables and in those same places it has performed miracles. Today the Church performs miracles: when she tells the poor to raise their eyes, when she tells a paralyzed people to take up their beds and walk, when she urges upon those held in bondage that their deliverance is at hand, when she insists to a world supine in its sense of fatalism that there is hope. Thereupon miracles bloom, new parables are fashioned, the Beatitudes come alive.

The future of the Church is already under way, in spite of our lack of awareness. The Lord goes before us and we have only to follow him, to decipher his ways, to imitate him.

In the light of such facts, the conclusion is inescapable: A new Christian order has begun to grow within the culture of our age. There is, as well, the unmistakable sign that martyrs give their life for that new order.

II. SECULARIZATION

Granted that the Church can neither follow nor remake the Christian order of former times, it must then construct another one. The force of the evidence compels that conclusion. But what course should the Church take? In whatever direction the Church looks, the secularization of the image of the world presents itself. If one excepts Islam, where the Koran considers the sacred and the profane as one whole, the contemporary world embraces the image of a secularized world. Sacral forms of society have been torn down. The culture of Western origin, which has penetrated the land mass of the globe, desires to be autonomous, profane, laic.

What is secularization? It is the process by which a society strips itself of the religious ideas, beliefs, and institutions that once governed its life in order to make itself autonomous; that is, to find within itself and solely by reference to itself, the methods, structures, and laws of societal living.

I shall not attempt to deal with the distant antecedents of its long evolution. That would require going over the history of Western civilization since the Middle Ages, when the laic spirit appeared. It proceeded through many stages to the liberation of the profane order from religion. Its triumphant influence not only meant the affirmation of man's autonomy and his works but the enormous cultural developments of our day.

Is secularization so understood an evil in itself? In no way is this necessary, according to Vatican II:

> If by the autonomy of earthly affairs we mean that created things and societies themselves enjoy their own laws and values which must be gradually deciphered, put to use, and regulated by men, then it is entirely right

> to demand that autonomy. Such is not merely required by modern man, but harmonizes also with the will of the Creator. For by the very circumstances of their having been created, all things are endowed with their own stability, truth, goodness, proper laws, and order. (*Gaudium et Spes,* no. 36).

Secularization carries through the logical development of creation. God, however, has set up two orders, or structures: He is the originator of creation and redemption, and he upholds both until the end of time. As sole author of each and as supreme wisdom, God could not set up a contradiction of one order with the other. The conflicts come from us, not from him. The very logic of the two orders makes possible the fulfillment of each without chopping off the other. Man then lives in two orders, creation and redemption, which are ontologically distinct, the existentially each is involved with the other. Man is so much the more human as he lives in both, and by doing so he gives more glory to God. On the contrary, what we refuse to creation or to redemption, we take away from God.

Saint Thomas Aquinas clearly and simply formulated these views. In doing so he was well aware that he was expounding the bases of a revolution, for the spirit of Saint Augustine—may one say political Augustinianism?—governed the Christian order in which he lived. Although Aquinas was probably the greatest theologian of his time, his thought did not decisively shape the mind of the Church in the following centuries. Only in the nineteenth century did Leo XIII give Thomism such a position. That Pope's work made possible the influence, the prophetic force, of the teachings of Saint Thomas Aquinas on the Second Vatican Council. The third chapter of the first part of *Gaudium et Spes,* "The Activity of Man in the Universe," is based on ideas presented in the *Summa Theologica* and the *Summa Contra Gentiles.* During Vatican II, to explain and defend pertinent drafts, I compiled and distributed a series of Thomist texts to the members of the Theological Commission. Nourished by these, long labors went into formulating a chapter that would meet the demands both of the Council and the contemporary mind.

This meant that the Church had to change its course, not without regret and nostalgia, as though it were propelled by an irresistible wave. One could understand that the past was past. But to deal intelligently with the future was another matter, requiring courage and clarity to prepare new relations between the Christian faith and the new culture.

In that culture, secularization, above all, had been pushed to extreme limits by an atheistic secularism which became the object of policy, financially supported and presented as the whole of life by powerful states. State policies aimed at total control of human formation, to create a one-dimensional man.

The Pastoral Constitution confronted modern atheism, systematic and state-sponsored. In place of simple recourse to anathema the Church sought reconciliation with the healthy, even the revolutionary elements of our time. It entered upon that course in the hope of overcoming the contradictions between matter and spirit set up by the philosophical currents of the nineteenth century.

When matter, having excluded spirit, is abandoned to itself, it engenders madness. Men grasp it and are turned into its slaves. For that matter, medieval Augustinianism, or more precisely what some minds have made of Saint Augustine, did not have the seeds of an authentic liberation of matter but deprived matter of its proper realm, more by default than by a positive decision. Thereafter ensued a period of secularization, and then secularism: the triumphs of the material order, as it were an explosion of the material order and of earthly values, including materialistic atheism.

The task of the Council was to reconsign matter to its divine origin and integrate earthly hopes into the future promised by God. An urgent task followed: to distinguish the different senses of the term *world* in order to be able to involve the world in Christian hope.

Gaudium et Spes had to work on many fronts at the same time. It had to deal with man who set himself up as a rival of God. It had to make use of the abundant resources of the new and dynamic anthropology. It had to winnow the grain from the chaff in the new mythologies of our time. It had above all to make man of our time understand the dimensions of the autonomy of the secular. This independence or autonomy, in which the methods and laws of terrestrial things may be sought, leaves completely open the issue of man's use of earthly values, of the existential ambiguity of man and his works.

> A monumental struggle against the powers of darkness pervades the whole history of man. The battle was joined from the very origin of the world and will continue until the last day, as the Lord has attested. Caught in this conflict, man is obliged to wrestle constantly if he is to cling to what is good. Nor can he achieve his own integrity without valiant efforts and the help of God's grace. (*Gaudium et Spes,* no. 37)

The teaching of the Council draws on two fundamental points: The autonomy of the profane, of the order of culture – that is to say, all human development – and the ambivalence of all. The autonomy is in the very ground of being, and the ambivalence is not an invention of the Church but an existential fact. Every secular value, no matter how authentic ontologically, is always ambivalent when we confront it in man himself, as a divided being, an enigma to himself: He wishes to do good and does evil; he wishes to be master of himself and is burdened and twisted with alienations; as soon as man renounces God, he finds that he cannot live as though he were spiritually weightless, but falls rather under the ascendancy of false gods and idols.

A significant achievement of the Council appears in the third chapter of *Gaudium et Spes,* "Man's Activity throughout the World." An inspired feature of that work was to connect the fundamental structure of the history of each man, continuity-discontinuity-recommencement, which is the rhythm of everything in humanity and in nature, within the structure of the great Easter mystery of death and resurrection. No Council had ever attempted such an integration of creation and redemption. True enough, death and resurrection had been linked with the soul and with man, but all man's earthly activity and the values of culture had been seen as alien to such ultimate matters or as instruments of a higher goal. Thereafter, the Holy Week and Easter mystery were to be bound with man, body and soul, man on the earth and man bound for heaven, individual and social man, man suffering from the world and man refashioning the world. This was to be an alliance which in its full strength would pervade nature and culture. The teaching of the Council, then, pointed to the recomposition of culture and the image of man.

Similarly the Church reclaimed her responsibility to change the world and undertook to promote human welfare, that is, human development and liberation, and to participate in social action as an expression of following Christ. It, therefore, undertook the labor of making changes of unjust social structures which prevent men from fulfilling their vocation.

These ideas were amply taken up by the Synod of Bishops on Justice in the World (1971), in that on Evangelization (1974), in the conferences of Medellín (1968) and of Puebla (1979), and in many pastoral letters of episcopal conferences, of which the best have come, in my judgment, from Latin America.

Has the Church since *Gaudium et Spes* succeeded in convincing Marxists throughout the world that God is not the rival of man? Has it won the acceptance of the politician, the scholar, the entrepreneur, the great financier, the atheist, the academic, that its recognition of the autonomy of the profane is sincere? At the same time the Church insists on the ambivalence of culture and the Church's right and duty to intervene in matters of conscience.

There are serious questions and many great difficulties for all who would promote *Gaudium et Spes* as living experience, both for those people who are free and for those who live in totalitarian regimes. If we are not animated by a concern for personal advantage, then and only then shall we take the lead.

III. MAN IN THE CHANGES OF OUR TIME

What is man becoming?

The question, directing the attention and commanding the mission of the Church through the centuries, presses more insistently today. Man, persistingly a tangle of contradictions, who cannot live without myths and utopias, who unceasingly makes them, unmakes them, and reconstitutes them. Man happy as a child with his dreams, and upon their shattering unhappy unto death. Man, the deviser of marvels and in fear that he will be the victim of his own inventions. Man, without guile, unaffectedly good, who abruptly turns bloody, pitiless, and cruel. Man who to reassure himself parades through halls of fame and whistles in the darker galleries of history, then gets lost in labyrinths.

Man, tireless in his demand for new experiences, who then begs his fellow man to relieve him of a terrifying liberty. Man and his strange heart at war with itself, ardent and weak, impetuous, garrulous and given to abrupt silences. Man who goes to meet death without understanding it and who seeks survival, reincarnations, resurrections.

Man humble and submissive in the presence of the divine, while ready at the next moment to set himself against God as against a rival. He may adore his almighty Father and then put him to death so that he can reign in the Father's place. Just as man is capable of conversion and profound repentance, so he may be wracked by the anti-beatitudes, cultivating them, and making of them a counterparadise.

Man in his turbulence suddenly smashing all his toys in order to begin from scratch only to tell the tale of history again, a history which he pursues, distractedly and without end. Man, unexpressed, without words for the depth of his mystery, who greets the morning with enthusiasm and has failing nerve at night. Man possessed of the divine without knowing it, himself a storm center of grace, vanity, greatness and meanness. Man for whom Christ died.

Man as such "a piece of work" possessed the mind of the Church in Vatican II, especially in composing the Pastoral Constitution. Every chapter of *Gaudium et Spes* begins with the questions: What is man? What is he becoming? Is he still the master of his works? How do states and powers in their various regimes deal with him? What has he to say for himself in these changing times? In his search for perfection has he successfully redefined himself? In such redefinition has he truly come close to a synthesis? After taking into account the contributions of anthropology, has he inadvertently forgotten the key of the whole affair? Will the changes of our time make man greater or less?

Rarely, probably never, has the Church gone so far in questioning herself about man. In no earlier Church document has she tried anything quite like *Gaudium et Spes*: to reformulate for our age the article of the Credo: "For us men and for our salvation he came down from heaven."

The Pastoral Constitution was written above all to meet the deep aspirations of modern man: to harmonize the relations between spirit and matter; to achieve the wholeness and completion of the self; to create a new earth. Perhaps every age has had such aspirations; in our time they have become more conscious, powerful, and universal; they figure among the signs of our times.

Why indeed did stunning upheavals in human relationships and reversals of world power occur if not to create a new world quite different from that controlled by colonial regimes? What is the meaning of our vast scientific and technical enterprise if not a quest for wholeness and completion? Fascism and nazism envisaged a new type of man, as communism still does. And to cite the disillusion that the materialist view has left in its wake, is there not in it a search for a new relationship between matter and spirit?

What did the Pastoral Constitution propose in order to deal with man in his present changes? I shall mention points which persist in being relevant today.

First, it recognized that the world today desired a new humanism, a humanism of co-responsibility. The document warmly welcomed this.

We can decidedly say, *as Gaudium et Spes* puts it in the chapter on culture: "We are witnesses of the birth of a new humanism, one in which man is defined first of all by his responsibility toward his brothers and toward history" (no. 55). The issue here is assuredly an ethical humanism which grows in the universal conscience and on which men of every culture would eventually base themselves as they would find themselves in it. The Pastoral Constitution gladly greeted this sign of the times, because this humanism of co-responsibility for a future world, becoming interdependent, forcibly or willingly, was sustained by the secret power of love.

Thus, my neighbor approaches me with a cry for help. What does he expect from me? Primarily that I do not look on him as something to get rid of after use, but as a person. This neighbor also asks that I give up my will to power and domination over him. When he is in chains, he requests me to free him. When his rights are denied him, he looks to me to take up his defense, then to go beyond simple justice and even compassion to love and to give him the kiss of peace. Each of history's twenty-one major civilizations has provided different kinds of humanism. In all likelihood our world, more aware than ever of world needs, is moving toward a global humanism of interdependence and co-responsibility.

What more did *Gaudium et Spes* attempt in this effort to join man and keep him whole in the midst of changes? It proceeded to a new manner of defining man.

At first that may seem surprising, because man has for a long time believed that he knows himself. But as man does not call a halt to self-discovery, the definition of man will remain open-ended until the end of time. Only then will he have a satiety of those approximations of himself.

Marxism has defined man as an economic being. The consumer society sees him as a creature of needs, of avidity. Bourgeois culture envisions him as concerned with possessing, knowing, and power.

During recent generations the great cultural anthropologists have defined man as a cultural being. The vast scale of contemporary cultural development is testimony indeed that the new reality of man as a cultural being must be included in the definition of man. Man, the rational animal, an earlier definition, is not thereby contradicted; but one must go beyond it. Depth psychology and the history of religions and of cultures have disclosed dimensions which that definition did not take into account.

Has the former concept of culture been similarly surpassed? The answer is clearly affirmative in the chapter on culture in *Gaudium et Spes*. There the use of the word *culture* has two meanings: 1) the *topical* meaning or usage covers those matters which concern ministries of education and culture in modern states as well as centers, institutes and houses of culture; 2) a more *radical* meaning designates the entire set of values that man in a particular society discovers and works out to serve his living in the world and to fulfill his humanity. It denotes a many-faceted reality: all of man's dealings with nature, himself, other people, and the divine; all that shapes his life, emotionally, socially, historically, traditionally, institutionally.

Man is not an animal plus culture; at the very core of his being he is involved in culture. He makes culture, is made by and for culture. Culture is the individual's way of being human, of life in the world, of being mind and body. Subjectively, experiences, events, the processes of growing, learning and revelation, liberation, interpretation, and appropriations are elements of culture. Objectively, values, things, heritage, patrimony, and institutions are among the creations of culture. Subjectively, and objectively all kinds of forms, frames, and models are possible. Levels, shades, and nuances of every sort may be found in the history of man as culture.

This view of culture implies the rejection of an aristocratic manner of looking at culture. This went along with a habit of dividing people in two categories: those who are fully human and those who are not. Among the latter were to be found illiterates, pariahs, or untouchables; those banished, those called "colored," "non-Aryans," "domestics," etc. A man is always in danger of having another man regard him as a non-man or an under-man.

But the revolution which has gone around the world has brought into the open all those people who were denied definition and classification as men. They first called for the reclamation of their human status, their right to development and culture. They wished to be men and women like all other men and women. Manhood or womanhood is not a pretension but something so fundamental that no one has the right to deny it.

The chapter on culture, then, has proved to be of growing importance.

This is in contrast with opinion voiced during the Council that this chapter was weak, ranked among the Pastoral Constitution's minor achievements. There were, however, some acute judges who perceived the strategic importance of the chapter, because culture was an area where all other points merged. This judgment proved prophetic.

To pursue the matter a little further there are two realities in all creation: nature and culture. The cosmos does not cultivate itself, but it can be cultivated by man. An animal can be trained, but culture is not within its capacity. Only man is simultaneously nature and culture, not nature alone. For then he would not be man. And not culture alone, for then culture forgets its origin and becomes madness, as is evident in such matters as nuclear weapons, abortion on demand, and non-natural methods of birth control.

If we look at the second part of *Gaudium et Spes,* what do we see if not nature and culture? And does not the very title of the Pastoral Constitution mean the Church in creation that has reached the state of culture which today is ours? To go a step further: The chapter on the activity of man in the world, in the first part of the document, is the immediate basis of the chapter on culture in the second part. All human activity in the universe is decidedly cultural activity that corresponds to the concept of man as a being of culture. Man, of course, remains more important than all his cultural achievements, but culture, in its full sense, is the process by which a man and a woman become fully human. Culture has the central place. As the process of humanization, all aspects of a society and its institutions form part of culture as a way of life and should serve to make man human.

Consider the place that John Paul II has been giving to culture. Doubtless, his Polish origin accounts for much of this development: The centuries-long role of the Church of Poland as the safeguard of its culture is a matter of common knowledge. Only a few months before his election, he and his fellow bishops issued an important declaration on the matter. The Pope's abundant references to culture in his addresses at Rome and elsewhere should not cause surprise. He gave a new impetus to the convictions he brought to the papacy, extending to the universal level what he had learned in his local Church.

There are, as well, other reasons for the references to culture in Church documents and addresses of the last two decades. The main one is the position on culture adopted by the Council after a long evolution within the Church. The new orientation was strengthened by the Synods of Bishops on Evangelization (1974), and on Catechetics (1977). John Paul's speech on culture to UNESCO (1980), a forceful papal initiative, was no mere matter of formalities. In the following years he developed what now appears to be a deliberate policy of broadening the commitment of the Church to culture seen as the meeting place of the Church and the world. This way of thinking, presented by the Pope, has begun to influence the organs of the Roman Curia, its diplomatic service and episcopal conferences. It provides a favorite theme for the Church in Latin America, Africa, and China.

When man is conceived as a cultural being, the full and integral meaning of culture comes to the fore. This concept of culture goes hand in hand with the concept of man. To quote the first lines of the chapter on culture in *Gaudium et Spes*: "It is a fact bearing on the very person of man that he can come to an authentic and full humanity only through culture, that is, through the cultivation of natural goods and values" (no. 53). This shows how forcefully the Pastoral Constitution presented natural grounding for its vision of Christian anthropology.

Pope John Paul II likes to quote two passages which he has made the subject of his meditation: "The truth is that only in the mystery of the incarnate Word does the mystery of man take on light" (no. 22); and "A man is more precious for what he is than for what he has" (no. 35).

The Pastoral Constitution did not limit itself to declaring that Christ decodes the mystery of man. It firmly insisted that Christ has refashioned the image of man. Christ does indeed illuminate the world, but it is also he who restores creation, as the completion of his role as savior requires. Man-in-culture finds his completion and reaches a new earth and a new heaven in the paschal mystery.

Gaudium et Spes certainly sought to form a new man for our time. To suggest what is this new image of man: He is a man aware of the condition of the most deprived people and responsive to them; he is imbued with the spirit of nonviolence; a free man himself and the liberator of others, he has a lofty idea of the dignity of each person and of his rights; he is capable of compassion and therefore solicitous to provide opportunities for those in any way disadvantaged–individuals as well as nations; ready for dialogue and communion, ready also to sacrifice his interests to the higher interests of the community, he places "being" before "having," and Christ is his model; in Him all man's cultural values converge, because from there all value originates.

IV. THE COMMUNITY OF NATIONS AND PEACE

The fourth major question that the Church in Council had in mind while writing *Gaudium et Spes* was: How can we help contemporary man to build a community of nations in peace?

What is the stage we have reached in our history of the world? At the end of World War II there were only eighteen independent nations in Asia and Africa. Now there were more than eighty. Our epoch was, and still is, a time of world revolutions. Restrained with great difficulty, it always threatens a breakout that may have disastrous consequences.

It is also a time when people look for and prize the cultural sovereignty of their nations. Many older nations have intensified the self-awareness of their people; younger ones seek to express their cultural identity. Each knows that the liberation of the soul of peoples is not simply won at the end of a rifle or by economic or political agreements. Only when people create and express themselves do simple phrases like being myself, to be a man, to be a woman, to live freely, acquire their meaning. If a nation has had that experience, though dominated by another, only its body is in subjection; its soul remains free.

New means of social communication have made these cultures and consciences of the world present to one another, universally and simultaneously. The millennial cultures of Asia and Africa experience resurgence, often against the culture that Europe has imposed.

It is also the time of political giants. Superpower ambitions now seek to extend political sway based on a vast area, into a network of influence over the whole world or to dominate a major portion of the globe, in contest with others.

Equally we have witnessed the rising role of nations of the Third World in the forum of the United Nations. They thrust themselves forward to demand a new international economic order. It is necessary, therefore, to rethink the whole issue of development.

What picture of the world does this produce? If I should say that the world is in pieces, that would suggest that it had once been one. But when was that? What exists is a unity-in-becoming which at every moment is strained by disruptive forces.

What must be done so that the new world will come into being, the new state of human affairs, the new manner of man and being, of living and of living together?

The Church, having recognized the autonomy of the temporal order in *Gaudium et Spes,* had no intention of substituting herself for the efforts that the nations of the globe would have to undertake in order to become a community. But claiming an expertise in humanity and knowledge issuing from Revelation, the Church offers her services on behalf of the universal common good of all humans, of all nations. This offer included observations, questions, and suggestions from the chapters on political community and the international community. Only a few points will be cited.

First question: In the quest of an international community what values are to have primacy? Will it be wealth and possession, or knowledge, or power? If the first goal is wealth or "economism," man and the human will be subordinated to economic considerations and the result will be new divisions and conflicts.

The economy, of course, is an absolutely necessary matter, but it must be looked on as a means toward the integral human development of people. If knowledge has priority, there doubtless will be great progress but not necessarily with respect to the breadth of culture. Culture in its traditional sense may get lost in sheer intellectualism. Only culture in its existential sense does justice to the range and variety of people as they actually are. Alternatively, if power is made the criterion of the world organization, it will be in order to reread the history of civilization, where the failure that frustrated the builders of Babel has been repeated again and again.

Other values must provide direction: the dignity of man and of nations, the right of everyone to live and to act in the concert of nations, vigilance about the common good of humanity, striving toward a humanism of co-responsibility and interdependence.

A second point concerned justice and its role in promoting reconciliation and peace. This justice has its beginning in respect for the identity and development of individuals and people.

A nation is basically a community of men and women held together in many ways, but preeminently by a common culture. As a political entity, a nation is derived from its cultural reality, because in its culture the nation has its being, develops its personality, and acquires its sovereign right. That does not mean any absolute homogeneity. The culture of a people is apt to be the result of the mutual adjustments of several subcultures, each endowed with liberties and with recognized collective rights against infringement by the other subcultures. God has created a pluralist world. His wish is for a family of men. Modern pluralism, then, provides the opportunity for an apprenticeship devoted to the varied abundance of creation and to the promotion of fraternity. No individual as well as no nation has the right to make other individuals or peoples serve as a pedestal for its glorification.

Every nation has, therefore, a right to cultural sovereignty, to be what it is, to live its own experiences, and to work out its own ways of being human, of growth and expression. It has the right to preserve its patrimony. This radical right of the nation as a cultural reality involves the right to liberation—if that is necessary. The means and manner of liberation must be a matter for political judgment.

Another consequence is respect by the state for the soul of the nation. The state has become the most influential power in defining national culture. It takes on the role that the Church filled for centuries in much of the West. Nowadays national culture plays the role of a collective superego. It affords the resources which enable the state to ascertain and develop its new personality. No doubt the state has enriched the national culture and in turn has profited immensely from the national culture. On that cultural basis the national state desires to articulate its state language.

Today's nation-state disposes of an endless variety of means for intervention among its people. Through legislation, programs, regulations, decisions and publications, via promises, propaganda, and financial power, the state purveys, distributes, and establishes values. It shapes imagination and desire and creates a clientele for itself. When the state then gives free rein to the instinct of domination that in man goes with all power, it aspires to a shocking control of human life. Sometimes even total control. It may even restrict and curtail the dimensions of the national soul, for example, the traditional religion and the cultural values which have issued from it.

Such state efforts to reshape the national soul in ways hostile to its traditions are properly considered monstrous. A similar judgment may be passed on powerful states imposing their culture on other countries, entirely oblivious of that basic rule, a culture's right to sovereignty. *Gaudium et Spes* spoke explicitly of these concerns in the chapters on culture and on the construction of the community of nations.

The last point deals with a new world cultural order, a subject that emerges between the lines of the Pastoral Constitution. To arrive at a sense of the whole world requires a cultural change which includes giving to young people in their formative years an awareness of the world, a sense of the universal. To attain a sense of being a citizen of the world is no longer sheer romanticism but a practical necessity. And in some measure it has begun. Each culture must open itself to others, to the wider world.

This is a requirement of the new way of life, the humanism of coresponsibility. It calls for a general, though gradual, reappraisal of the ensemble of our values and their interrelations, beginning with the ideal of an integral or complete man. States must be questioned about their role as principal definers of national culture, for theirs is the power to intensify divisions among nations or to work to rise above them. The same applies to powers other than states, on the international scene; the United Nations and its several bodies, global press and information chains, powerful multinational corporations, international labor organizations, and relief and monetary agencies, professional associations of parliamentarians, scientists, lawyers, and others. The building of a human, world order depends on everybody.

These are among the works of peace and to the subject of peace *Gaudium et Spes* gave much attention. In re-examining the theory of the just war and the use of modern weapons the Council went beyond a casuistic approach, which could neither deal adequately with the problems posed by new armaments nor touch the consciences of men and women. Besides, the Council felt that the future life and survival of the community of nations should be rooted in evangelical peace through intense cultivation of the peace of the Gospel.

At the same time the Church could not forget that man is a pilgrim, that culture is history, that education is appropriation, that in the human order, if things are to be done, they must be done gradually. There is a basic law of gradualism drawn from the experience of nations and the Church. The declaration of the bishops of the United States on disarmament and peace has two major emphases: a refocusing on evangelical peace, and the application of the law of gradualism. These are, as well, the fundamentals of the approach of *Gaudium et Spes*.

One point, on education for peace, presented in the teaching of *Gaudium et Spes* deserves to be made more explicit. The way to peace may be sought directly or indirectly. The former means taking peace as the immediate subject of investigation and education and considering all aspects relating to it. There is, as well, an indirect approach, one that deals with time more spaciously and may not be an option in moments of urgency but yields sound results in the long run.

By way of explanation, the ordering of the Eight Beatitudes in Saint Matthew's Gospel has peace in seventh place, which means that each of the six preceding Beatitudes is a step leading to peace. Some exegetes have proposed that the Beatitudes are an eclectic grouping of values randomly put together. In opposition, Saint Augustine followed by Thomas Aquinas thought that the Beatitudes have a meaningful sequence going from first to last. Whatever may be the truth of the matter, it will be agreed that if there is no spirit of poverty (first Beatitude), if the Beatitude enjoining meekness and nonviolence is ignored (second), if there is no concern for liberty and liberation (third Beatitude), if there is no willing of justice (fourth Beatitude), if there is no pity and compassion (fifth Beatitude), if there is no will for communion and love (sixth Beatitude), peace is a cause vainly striven for. The only peace that will then appear is a semblance of peace, a peace of fear and armament races, a negative peace.

A society which has given itself to acquisition, or to major violence, a society which treats one of its classes or ethnic groups as hostages, which fails to seek justice, a hard, unloving, and pitiless society cannot establish peace. This applies to the international community as well within the nation.

The Eight Beatitudes are found in the Pastoral Constitution's imperatives to the Church: espousing poverty and renouncing privileges, choosing to be with the poor, and undertaking humble and disinterested service; working for the integral liberation of man, for justice, for another opportunity to those who have fallen, failed, or suffered reverses; and seeking to become the bond of communion among men. The Church so concerned is the preacher and herald of peace. It declares that Christ has taught us the way to peace and he is the prince of peace, the Word Incarnate who lived the Beatitudes. He is the cornerstone on which to build the community of nations in peace.

But as the judgment of God begins with the cleansing of his house, the Church has to be what she preaches: Her first option has to be for the poor, her second for nonviolence, her third for liberation, her fourth for justice, her fifth for compassion, her sixth for love, her seventh for peace, and her eighth for the persecuted.

The Word Incarnate knew the heart of man and in the Beatitudes he taught man the secret of holiness and, we may hope, the secret also of survival in our fragile planet.

V. A NEW EVANGELIZATION

This is the last question but has it not been the underlying question of all that precedes: How shall we evangelize man and the world today?

In fact, it was not the Pastoral Constitution that alone dealt with the question. The entire work of the Council, all its documents, contributed to answering the question of evangelization today. It opened new channels for relating with other churches, non-Christian religions, and nonbelievers. It fostered the formation of Christians in the modern world. It enlisted all Christians to rebuild the world with all men of goodwill. The last point is the very ground of *Gaudium et Spes.* It is necessary, therefore, to study it carefully to see how it envisages evangelization.

Before Vatican II it had become evident that there were pastoral methods and styles of evangelization which were no longer effective. Excessively deductive, objective, and uniform methods left some Christians and people of other spiritual convictions untouched or indifferent. The Church had many members and numbers could be made to argue that all was going well. The postconciliar crisis had a sobering effect. It made us see the fragility behind the apparent solidity of the Church before Vatican II. Our Catholics had been trained to stand up under attack. But they did not know how to change. Whether the Council were held or not, a crisis in the Church was inevitable due to the new age reached by the world's history. Thanks to the Council the Church did not lose self-control during those turbulent years.

Several lessons about the "new evangelization" are found in the Pastoral Constitution.

First of all, it has *changed the language* of evangelization. In reading it we see the Good News as Good News for man as a whole person, and for all men and women. The Good News announced is addressed to the intelligence, the reason and the mind, but is far from being exclusively so addressed. It is also for man's heart, sensibility, and passions, for daily living.

This evangelization carefully distinguishes between the sin and the sinner, between the person and error. It is cautious about readily made abstractions, because it recognizes that there is always more to man that his doctrines or his errors. It is well today to recall that at Vatican II there were those who wished to brandish anathemas, those who thought of dialogue between atheists and Christians as an exchange between two intellectual positions or two systems rather than between fellow human beings.

In *Gaudium et Spes,* "Joy and Hope," we find an evangelization with the kind of confidence in man that was first expressed in the opening pages of Genesis when God entrusted the world to man. This evangelization denies fatalism to history and measures man amidst the great fears which beset him from unending change and nuclear apocalypse. Evangelization need not always be direct. To revive human confidence, to foster insights that contribute to a sense of human responsibility, to strengthen courage in the face of threats, to work out new parameters are real expressions of the Good News.

What people feel and live is usually their basic language. It is superficial, at best, to think that language always has to be abstract or even the sound of words. A Church, experiencing the severity of those without mercy, the wants of the poor, the hatred of those who refuse human communion with others; a Church taking upon itself the lot of captives and those who suffer persecution, risking retaliation for their daily defense and the spiritual patrimony of a nation, this Church has found the way to be understood by many people who could not otherwise be reached. But such language may be meaningless to others, even some pastors and theologians, members of diocesan or national offices who may for decades talk about the new language without understanding a word of it. It is the language of the heart, of the humble and the "little ones," beloved of the Father.

Besides a new language, the *subjective in man* is rediscovered for evangelization by the Pastoral Constitution. Introducing the Faith always means teaching doctrinal truths. But evangelization now recovers the full sense of the Gospel from formulations that were too one-sidedly intellectual and abstract. *Gaudium et Spes* recognizes the value of friendly approaches, of the law of gradualism, of walking along with people, of companionship. It deals with man where he is, converses with him about his condition, clears a path for values.

Do we sufficiently realize the degree to which men, even many Christians, have become strangers to the Church, to Jesus Christ and, in fact, to being human? This basic Church mission of evangelization has then vast new ground for the good seed of the Gospel.

The new language of evangelization will address also *new categories* with fresh grasp of their faith content: life more abundant, man as problem and potentiality, culture as the "flesh" to be incarnated by the Spirit.

First, and most radical of these new categories is life above all. In *Gaudium et Spes* the Church shows herself as the partisan of life, life in abundance, in fullness. She strives now to set forth parables of life among men, as they will recognize that the Good News is again among them. What kind? Parables of solidarity and sharing, of nonviolence and meekness, of liberation and justice, of communion and peace, of help to the persecuted and oppressed, of confidence and hope.

The second series of new categories relates to man. *Man is the central problem,* and the question of "I" dominates all human situations the Church must address.

Man is restless with his very mystery. He is all too aware of his inclination, that real temptation, to make himself the center of the world and to consider others only so far as they advance his self-interest. That is the beginning of idolatry, which by degrees trains itself to reject the necessity of God's true image. The new false gods of our idolatry today appear superior to older ones in their brilliance, sophistication, and abundance. After all, even our false gods, today's idols, are recent developments of our changing culture. Later generations will laugh at them, as we find those of past ages a source of amusement and incomprehension.

Could the Church pass over in silence new idols and false gods? Could she let oblivion nullify the very first Commandment? True, the ambivalence of earthly affairs means that they may be under the rule of God or of idols. *Gaudium et Spes,* being emphatically clear about the powers competing to control man and culture, pointed to anthropology, theoretical and practical, as a strategic area for evangelization.

The third set of new categories concerns culture understood in the full sense of the *development of all the potentialities of man.*

The Gospel becomes present in the world of creation through the medium of culture. Jesus Christ was profoundly a man of his culture; the same may be said of the entire Bible. The history of Revelation is a perpetual going and coming between the souls of peoples and reaction to the Word received from God. Only the ensemble of cultures, viewed as complementary, makes possible a sense of the scope of that message. Jesus Christ has not ceased to listen to and to question humans.

Pope Paul VI in *Evangelii Nuntiandi* makes culture the focal point of evangelization. His teaching builds upon what *Gaudium et Spes* presented on the same subject. Each culture is called to pronounce the Gospel. But the Gospel cannot be incarnated if the Good News of God's love does not become culture.

Basic communities appear very promising today because they present a strategic point of focus in evangelization. The culture borne by the members interacts with their expression of the Gospel. Experiencing in their own persons the life and issues of their culture and the life and tension of faith, they incarnate both life and faith as a Christian community. Action which flows out of this advances the Kingdom. These local beginnings with everyday life can change the world.

For the new categories to be effective there must be concentration again on the fundamental values of the Kingdom, the Eight Beatitudes which animate the Pastoral Constitution. Even the atheist, agnostic, and nonpracticing Christian cannot remain indifferent to them. To some degree the Beatitudes are found as well among the great world religions. The City of Man also senses that it will survive only if it finds place for the Sermon on the Mount. What indeed can the earthly City do with its poor, its victims of violence, of enslavement, of injustice and harshness, of hate, of wars and division, if it receives no nourishment from the Beatitudes? Modern states incur enormous expenses with their police forces and prisons, rehabilitation and re-education services without achieving the effects brought by the Beatitudes in all their simplicity.

The essence of evangelization is expressed, therefore, by Jesus Christ, the Way of Life, way of renewed life for individuals and nations. The cult of Jesus is more than liturgical activity; it embraces all that man has created and acquired; all his culture.

IN CONCLUSION: INVENTING NEW PARAMETERS

What man has made, he can unmake, and what he has destroyed, he can rebuild.

The epic materialism of last century has been replaced by doctrinal and state materialism. This has left a spiritual void and already appears largely as a gigantic and terrible historical failure. It promised man possessions – that is, "having" – but it did not deliver adequately. The greater failing of materialism is the incapacity of elevating man's "being." For to do that, it would have had to be spiritual. The man of materialism was left one-dimensional.

Time and again, explicitly and implicitly, *Gaudium et Spes* returns to this point: The touchstone of human progress, of the authenticity of humanization, of the truth and integrity of culture lies in the difference between "to have" and "to be." The Pastoral Constitution was not mistaken or neglectful about "having." It listed basic physical rights of man: "to have" life, food, water, unpolluted air, housing, It then passed on to the higher rights which make man more and more fully human, because more centered on "being." The Pastoral Constitution sums up simply: "A man is more precious for what he is than for what he has" (no. 35).

Gaudium et Spes, indeed all of the Council, clearly called upon modern man to build a new world order to provide what every human needs *to have.* However, the constant compass of the Pastoral Constitution is oriented towards *being,* the quality of life, for "man does not live by bread alone, but by every word that comes from the mouth of God." (Matt. 4:4; Deut. 8:3)

From the issues and problems raised by *Gaudium et Spes* I chose five major questions which stand out as peaks commanding immense mountain ranges. Responses to them mark out the new parameters: a new Christian order, nonhomogenous, constructed as a network; a frank acceptance of secularity in its laws as well as in its tragic existential character; a view, renewed and holistic, of the new man desired by all humanity; as part of the new human order, a new world cultural order ruled in peace; and, finally, the issue that touches all the others, evangelization.

These important subjects must draw upon fervent hopes and will require mighty and sustained efforts. Nothing, Ernest Renan has said, nothing great has been achieved in the world without exaggerated hopes.

But should we conclude with the *bon mot* of a nonbeliever? Instead I repeat the words used by John Paul II upon his installation onto the Chair of Peter: "Be not afraid!" Because Christ our pastor goes on ahead of us. He goes ahead of us as the cloud column preceded the Hebrews in their journey to the Promised Land. What at night they sought rest it remained over the meeting tent and during the day's march it went before them as a pathfinder in the desert.

Discussion Report One*

A dozen themes flowed swiftly through the discussion. Most converged with nearby currents; a couple diverged sharply to preserve inherited cultural concepts against the threats of post-conciliar modernization. Resulting discord, however polite, showed that doubts still run strong among some Catholic intellectuals over Vatican II's open embrace of the modern world – as "world," and especially as "modern."

Early on Doherty decried applause for "this friendly and open Church of yours, which would become only one more modern institution among many others." Out of her rich religio-cultural heritage, "of which Rome, Jerusalem, Athens, and Oxford are symbols, the Church must act as a critic of men and the secular world." Until now, the Church has offered "man a self-transcending and transcultural vision." Her role as critic of the secular world is still much needed, but the Church can no longer act as a critic because she now becomes so "modern . . . emasculated."

Grappling for the meaning or meanings of culture or cultures became a major exercise for most participants. This showed how novel the subject still is in Catholic academia, posed by *Gaudium et Spes* and now proposed by John Paul II as major agenda among Church intellectuals. Many puzzled over that "metamorphosis of the word *culture*," introduced by Carrier from the opening line of his paper, from "classical education and artistic refinement" among Enlightenment elites to the anthropologists' primitive and folk cultures of 1900, to our current dynamic categories: cultural revolution, cultural imperialism, evangelization of cultures.

Cuen offered his own multiplex definition of culture as the product, intellectual and historical, of the struggle to attain man's self-fulfillment and

*Editor's footnote: This and other discussion accounts are taken from tape recordings of the proceedings. Discussants are identified by last name only, usually without titles. I have ordered each account according to themes, so speakers are not always reported in chronological succession. Comment and response from the principals, Carrier and Lambert here, are interposed also at logical points. In brief, these are not recorded minutes. Rather, this is my report of *my understanding* of the more significant thrusts of the exchanges. The accounts are interlarded with editorial comment and opinion, which is clear from the context and for which I alone am responsible. Finally, it must be remembered that direct quotes have not been reviewed by the speakers; by no means are their remarks to be taken as definitive views. They are, again, merely what I heard them say in this particular discussion. – Gremillion plentitude; the struggle is constant, to discover the realities and mysteries of man, society, nature, and God, from which comes civilization as product: buildings, institutions, etc. Crosson observed that sometimes culture, in the singular, is normative, but it can also be merely descriptive, usually in the plural as cultures; Aristotle describes man as a social and political animal. Above all, Crosson wanted Lambert to clarify his phrase that man is "a being of culture," *un être de culture*. (This relates to Cuen's concept: Does *homo* become human as the product of cultural struggle? Does culture then produce *homo*?)

Ever the promotor of social justice, Ryan (who founded the Center of Concern in Washington and contributed heavily to the Jesuits' 1974 document on "Faith at the Service of Justice") showed suspicion over the new papal focus on culture. Since Vatican II, Ryan noted, promotion of justice has received great emphasis throughout the Church as a "constitutive dimension" of evangelization. This new focus has occasioned pastoral and theological controversy within the Church of most regions and has been a deep concern of the papacy. Now of a sudden, the pope himself singles out culture, a much less controversial issue, for major attention. Does this indicate a pastoral tactic aimed at reducing concern for justice to quiet the controversy? If not, what are the deep ecclesial and pastoral motives for this recent focus on culture exemplified by the new Pontifical Council for Culture and by this conference?

Lambert countered that John Paul II continues to champion the cause of justice, especially in his pastoral visits to the regional Churches of all continents where controversy, even struggle, is rife. The present pope now highlights the significance of culture as a central element of *Gaudium et Spes,* an element barely recognized thus far. He urges the new Pontifical Council to focus on culture from the double angles of humanization and evangelization. Man becomes human through culture, Lambert observed, and becoming fully human is not possible without justice.

This close linkage of humanization and evangelization, of justice and culture, recurs in the Latin American papers and discussion below. Participants begin to grasp that culture, in the meaning of *Gaudium et Spes* and the Pontifical Council, appears to encompass all human and societal categories other than nature.

(The term *nature,* as distinct from *culture,* would seem to apply then to those physical and psychic traits which are transmitted "naturally" through the genetic code, without creative mediating acts of human reason and will. Justice, Lambert seems to imply, with Carrier concurring, is a requirement within the whole cultural process of "becoming fully human." Justice, therefore, is more than a moral imperative and much more than "natural" law.)

Lobkowicz brought up a wider debate about Church problems. Some allege that *Gaudium et Spes* has caused many of the troubles that the Church has experienced since Vatican II. If the Pastoral Constitution is really to blame, would Lambert indicate the reasons?

Lambert responded by contrasting Church positions and self-awareness before and since the Council, amid the welter of cultural changes and societal conflicts which began penetrating ecclesial consciousness. *Lumen Gentium* took fresh options of ecclesiology, that opened the way for the new pastoral and cultural options of *Gaudium et Spes* and other documents, such as those on ecumenism and religious freedom. Lambert compares the Church before and after the Council by stark contrasts:

- from defensive tradition since Trent, to openness of mission to "Go fishing!"
- from juridic institution, to gathered community who answer the call "Come, follow me!"
- from a static "perfect" society, to the ongoing event of encountering God, directly and in his People.
- from the means to individual salvation, to awareness of social sin.
- from monolithic hierarchy, to a network of servants.

These developments of ecclesiology were stimulated by the signs of the times, manifested through vast cultural changes, and discerned in the Spirit by the Council's twenty-three hundred bishop-pastors. They warmed each other's zeal in St. Peter's Basilica, their hearts sensitive to the human needs of their people–and God's–in a hundred new nations, among the awakening religio-cultural regions of Africa, Asia, Europe, and the Americas.

Underlying this global shift of Church theology and ecclesial consciousness, Lambert explained, was new doctrinal awareness that *creation and redemption* are both from God, "inter-rooted" in the same Trinity: therefore, *Church and world* are inter-rooted also. From these roots *Gaudium et Spes* sprouted forth into our "new cultural age, which explores everything," which enters space, the atom, and the human psyche. Homo, Lambert concluded, now "sees himself as formed by culture–*un être de culture.*"

And what now happens, Doherty asked, to the tradition we Catholics have so long treasured. Lambert replied that most of us were formed in and by that tradition and we are grateful. It was a fitting cultural expression of a specific historical consciousness "and must be honored today as integral to our community memory–for there is no culture without community memory." However, since Vatican II, "we have left the defensive security of tradition's Tridentine walls. Now our Church is again in the desert of a new Exodus, as a people whose identity is the New Alliance of Christ, on pilgrimage toward the goal of evangelizing today's world."

Returning to Carrier's paper and the discussion's mainstream of "Understanding Cultures," Outler affirmed Vatican II's opening to the "cultural enterprise." As an official Observer for the Methodist Church, the veteran ecumenist watched and lived the developments in St. Peter's Basilica which Lambert and Carrier ably describe, as the Roman Catholic Church abandoned its fortress stance to address the "full humanum of the collective human community." He applauded then, and still does twenty years later.

However, on this occasion by which the new Pontifical Council for Culture is introduced to the North American region and Church, Outler feels some unease about the degree of confidence most express for this new "cultural enterprise." These positive views should be balanced by the critical fact that "all culture shows as well its *shadow side*. Tragic flaws appear in all human endeavors. All human cultures thus far have shown serious miscarriages of cultural expectations." Outler only asks his Catholic friends to recognize this: "People who live by culture also mess it up. How account for this? Original sin? Freud? Sociologists? Who knows – but just recognize this tragic dimension of all human cultural endeavor."

Thanking Outler for his timely warning, Carrier assured that "*Gaudium et Spes* is not pelagian. It defines the humanum in the context of original sin. It promotes man who is a sinner," and directs the social ministry of the Church "against social sins. Christ himself began his ministry among the poor and ill, prisoners and the oppressed, victims of sin and human failure."

Sister Braganza, who directs India's association of two hundred Christian colleges – Protestant, Orthodox, and Catholic – brought up three problems which center on education and the transmission of culture:

– Formal education in her distinctive national setting causes conflict between the "classical culture" of Western style schools and local traditional culture.

– Since newly introduced Western culture does not build up Indian traditions, the erosion of all particular cultures results and danger arises of homogenizing all culture.

– The family has filled for millennia a dominant role in transmitting culture, but now in India the role of family fades and the main transmitter of our culture is being lost.

Schmitz led from Braganza's observations to the more global field of cultural policy and planning by national governments, individually or together through UNESCO, and by private foundations and study groups, such as the Club of Rome. Traditional culture, Schmitz observed, was the millennial product of human activity in community handed down through generations. As a whole it evolved spontaneously without prior planning; the community was not conscious that they were creating and transmitting their culture. It was lived, not reflected on. More recently, however, cultures have become the object of study by anthropologists, and now in most countries culture is the object of national policy, governmental planning, and political projects.

The overall human experience of inherited culture is changing radically and rapidly.

Carrier agreed with this view that we enter now a new cultural age, in which culture takes on a more self-conscious role. The entry of other cultures spurs this process, because the cultural interloper leads to questions of identity: Who are we? Who am I within our cultural we? Who is this stranger-culture as compared with the cultural-us? This process of cultural self-consciousness intensifies when national traditions are threatened. Carrier cited the current cases of Poland, and his home province of Quebec. They ask, "What is the soul of our people?" and revive in response their cultural roots. In both these cases the Church played a major role in the creation of the threatened cultures and now in their continuation.

Goulet raised questions central to worldwide evangelization and culture. In its missionary endeavor the Church has acted as "the bearer of a particular culture." Upon encountering other cultures the Church was "reductionist, and only tolerated a plurality of cultures" when advantageous to itself. Raimundo Pannikar and others now insist that "cultural plurality is now constitutive of global reality." Goulet suggests that "the Church must change its view as to what universality demands today."

Carrier responded by quickly surveying several levels of Catholic cultural identity:

–In the respective Catholic countries, cultural adaptations are found which identify Irish and Polish, Italian and Mexican, African and Indian Catholicism as distinctive, one from the other.

–We have also spoken of our "Catholic culture" which embraces traits found in most nations.

–Definitely, Carrier readily admitted, "the Catholic Church has been long identified with *Western* culture. It now realizes that true inculturation of the Gospel requires a difficult adaptation to different structures, to other values and styles of life." Study and stimulus toward such adaptation is "the role of the Pontifical Council for Culture," for as Vatican II and Pope John Paul have said, "The Church of Christ is not a Western church."

–"*Catholic* culture," in Carrier's view, is now being created in diverse cultural settings "from the special concepts of man, family and education, of justice and peace, for which we stand." These values and views, and resulting ways of life, should become our distinguishing cultural marks; not our clothing, as is said in the Letter to Diognetus.

Finally, Carrier stresses that "culture is a relative reality." As Paul VI states, culture itself is neither evangelization nor religion. However, to the mind of John Paul II, faith that does not "become culture" does not become a living faith.

Carrier's substantive survey, in followup to Braganza's perceived danger "of homogenizing all culture" and Goulet's view on "cultural plurality" as constitutive of today's global reality, prompted Gremillion to introduce Karl Rahner's ideas about inculturation by the Church in the several regions of the world. He suggests that "a basic theological interpretation" of Vatican II is the Church's approach "to the discovery and realization of itself as *world-Church*" (*Weltkirche*), with plural ecclesial incarnations in the several religio-cultural regions of the globe. (Rahner, *Concern for the Church* [Crossroad, 1981], pp. 77–186)

Carrier expresses thanks that Rahner's "seminal work" has entered the discussion. He is familiar with these stimulating views, with Rahner's "whole project" that Vatican II has opened toward the realization of the Church becoming universal in a new way.

The Church, Carrier summarizes, is now "working as a living organism to become the best servant of this world of ours, which is itself still in construction." Evangelizing culture includes therefore promotion of world structures which render true service to the humanum and to all humankind.

SECTION TWO

The Latin American Church's Option for the Poor and Their Cultural Creativity since Vatican II

The second pair of papers focuses on the "evangelization of culture" by the Church of Latin America, as it awakens to *Gaudium et Spes* and to the fresh voice of its three hundred million Catholics – two-thirds of whom are poor and powerless by North American norms.

Archbishop McGrath, theologian-pastor of Panama's poor, and Father Scannone, a pastoral theologian of their "popular" culture, present overviews of two complementary ecclesial events: 1) the evangelical response of God's Latin people to the call of his Spirit through Vatican II; and 2) the pattern of creative community aroused by this new-found *vox populi Dei.*

McGrath traces major phases in the evolution of and follow-up to *Gaudium et Spes,* Medellín, and Puebla. In each of these historic events he played key roles for seventeen years, 1962–79, as a member of their central and drafting committees. McGrath is among the few remaining notable actors in all three of these ecclesial dramas involving a cast of millions, on stages global and continental, directed by the Spirit of Father and Son – with denouement unto the eschaton.

The archbishop writes and speaks here primarily as a pastor: that these churchly documents and flowing phrases might become Good News flesh among peasants and slum dwellers, who for generations have endured their situation with patience, prayer, and persistence. In this process of cultural evangelization launched out of *Gaudium et Spes,* Medellín, and Puebla, McGrath derives great hope and joy from the promise of basic Church communities: *comunidades ecclesiales de base* (CEBs).

Scannone, a Jesuit theologian of Church-and-culture, profiles the five centuries of Latin America's history, secular and ecclesial, shaped by three interweaving cultural currents:

1) The Iberian culture of imperial Christendom crossbred since 1500 with indigenous Amerind civilizations plus African roots, to form Latin Amer-

ica's foundational matrix, the hybrid of *mestizaje*, despite efforts of Church and empire to suppress the native heritage during the first period of evangelization.

2) The European Enlightenment culture of the 1800s, mainly French and English, which accompanied the first wave of neocolonialism, intellectual and bourgeois, after national emancipation from the empires of Spain and Portugal; though it deeply affected educational and political ideologies and systems, the press, professionals, and cosmopolitan elites, it bore little impact upon the *cultura popular* of the *mestizo* poor.

3) Industrial and commercialized culture of our century, with pervasive economic neocolonization by multinational business corporations and from political centers of world power, especially from the United States since World War II; in our century cultural elements of Marxism have penetrated as well, notably philosophic materialism, to affect worker and peasant consciousness, class struggle, ideologic and political movements.

To this ensemble of cultures so marked by intrusive power structures, dominant classes, and leader-elites, Scannone contrasts the humble ethos of *mestizo* culture assimilated through the centuries from religio-natural and evangelical sources, and expressed as the *popular* (people's) *religiosity* of Latin Catholicism. For Scannone, this cultural ethos of divine presence and human meaning–amid the rhythms of life and season, the folk wisdom and values of family, community and work, the *convivencia* of festal joy and sorrow and hoping anew–needs, of course, renewed "evangelization," even "aggiornamento." Howsoever, it does provide promising ground and fertile soil for planting the future of the Latin people of God. Scannone rejoices that Puebla clearly recognizes this faith-filled field of cultural Christians, ready anew for Gospel sowing:

> So our culture is impregnated with the Faith, even though it frequently has lacked the support of a suitable catechesis. This is evident in the distinctive religious attitudes of our people, which are imbued with a deep sense of transcendence and the nearness of God.
>
> It finds expression in a wisdom of the common people that has contemplative features and that gives a distinctive direction to the way our people live out their relationship with nature and their fellow human beings. It is embodied in their sense of work and festiveness, of solidarity, friendship and kinship; and in their feel for their own dignity, which they do not see diminished by their own lives as simple, poor people. (Puebla Document, no. 413)

The Impact of *Gaudium et Spes*: Medellín, Puebla, and Pastoral Creativity

Archbishop Marcos McGrath, C.S.C.

My contribution will carry our theme of *Gaudium et Spes* and culture into a concrete area of the Church: into Latin America, the "continent of hope," as Pope Paul VI called it when he went there in 1968. It is a vast expanse of nations, large and small, where almost half the Catholics of the world now live. As the only predominantly Christian part of the Third World, it is a bridge, a meeting point between the culture and civilization of the West and the poverties and resentments Latin America shares with the nations on the southern half of the great world divide.

After almost twenty years, how has Vatican Council II and, specifically, how has *Gaudium et Spes* influenced the relationship of Church and culture in this important area? The area is the subject of two Conference papers here that allow for different approaches which should complement and help to explain each other.

As a bishop-pastor from Latin America who had the good fortune to work on the drafting committee of *Gaudium et Spes* and later on the drafting committees of Medellín and then of Puebla and has labored with his local Church in their application these many years, I will describe for you some of our pastoral efforts to apply *Gaudium et Spes* in general and in relation to culture. Father Juan Scannone has developed a theological reflection on the evangelizing of culture in Latin America, a reflection which I am sure will be very rich in pastoral and social significance.

I. HISTORICAL AND CULTURAL SETTING

Walter Buhlman, in *The Coming of the Third Church,* has dramatized the emerging importance of Christianity, and specifically of the Catholic Church, in the southern half of our planet, in Latin America and Africa.

Europe dominated the theological and pastoral formulations of Vatican Council II. The very Church movements which bore fruition in the Council – biblical, liturgical, lay apostolate, ecumenical, social – were largely born in Europe. Their most articulate spokesmen in the Council were bishops and theologians of middle Europe: Austria, Germany, France, and Belgium.

Nonetheless, the makeup of the Council was the most worldwide in history, in numbers of bishops and experts who were natives of all the continents. Their physical presence gave voice to regional preoccupations. It became a familiar sound for us to hear on the Council floor a bishop speaking for several hundred bishops of Latin America, or for "all the bishops of Africa as well as Madagascar." What these interventions expressed were generally preoccupations, desires, or problems not yet spelled out into theological reflection nor into precise formulas for the Council documents. But they told on the consciousness of all present. The entire Council paid attention. *Lumen Gentium* reflected its attention in a renewed theology of the local Church, and *Gaudium et Spes* in the care it took to reflect the diverse situations of these local Churches around the world.

For these and similar reasons, Karl Rahner, in *Concern for the Church* (New York, 1981), said of Vatican II: "There really was a world-council, with a world episcopate such as had not hitherto existed and with its own autonomous function" (p. 80). He adds: "In *Gaudium et Spes,* in an act of the whole Church as such, the Church as a whole became expressly aware of its responsibility for the future history of mankind" (p. 81). He concludes: "This, then, is the situation: either the Church sees and recognizes these essential differences of the other cultures, into which it has to enter as a World-Church, and accepts with Pauline boldness the necessary consequences of this recognition, or it remains a Western Church and thus in the last resort betrays the meaning of Vatican II" (p. 86).

The Church of Latin America was providentially prepared to bring to the Council its efforts at renewal, *aggiornamento.* Since the first Latin American Synod, held in Rome in 1899, there had taken place a slow but steady renaissance of the Latin American Church, urged and guided by the Holy See, and much influenced by the Churches of Europe, especially that of France.

It is helpful to the understanding of what the Council has meant to our continent to trace the movement of our Churches in the generations between 1899 and 1962. Latin America was convulsed by social revolutions that hit it from abroad. The medical revolution tripled its population without an industrial growth sufficient for its support. Two world wars meant sudden prosperity, followed by prolonged recession. Agricultural production suffered. City slums began to swell. Political conflict took on a stronger social content. Capitalism and Marxism began to draw their lines of battle.

The Church as an institution, linked intimately to the colonial structures of the past, began to be separated from the structures of power: first from official union with the state, and then progressively from an implicit alliance with the interests of the upper classes and their conservative parties. This process was irregular. Sometimes, as in Chile, it was by choice; in other cases, as in Mexico, it was by force of revolution.

Of all the movements of renovation which led to the Council, perhaps the most important for our Churches were those of Catholic Action and social action. They stood for responsibility and participation in the Church and in the world. These gave new vigor and new participation to the Church in many of our nations.

The growth of the Latin American Church and its needs caught the attention of the Holy See and of the West after World War II. The Churches of Europe and North America began an intense campaign of aid in personnel and funds which continues to our time. It has been very effective, especially since it has become less and less paternalistic as the Church in Latin America has become more able to direct its own course.

To this end the institution of the Council of Latin American Bishops (CELAM) was very important. Created after the International Eucharistic Conference of 1955 in Rio de Janeiro, it came into its own through the services and the coordination it provided the bishops of Latin America through the four sessions of the Vatican Council, 1962–1965. The developments of the Council, to which we have referred above, conferred upon CELAM its raison d'être and its mission.

II. THE PLACE OF THE PASTORAL CONSTITUTION IN THE COUNCIL

Cardinal Gabriel Garrone, a key figure in the Council and especially in the formulation of *Gaudium et Spes,* has a thesis on the Council which I would largely share (see G. M. Garrone, *50 Ans de Vie d'Eglise,* Paris: Desclee, 1983). He reminds us that the fundamental concern of the Council is the presentation of the Church, and it is contained in the Dogmatic Constitution *Lumen Gentium,* of which the Constitutions on Revelation and on Liturgy can be considered as appendices.

The remaining documents of the Council were meant to be decrees, in the proper sense of concrete directives. They were meant to apply *Lumen Gentium's* vision of Church to the diverse areas in question. The mistake was, in Garrone's opinion, that each document tended to become a little constitution in itself, establishing once more the background and the principles for the decree, repeating or even redoing *Lumen Gentium* without really getting around adequately to the concrete determinations proper to decrees. For this reason, in part, *Gaudium et Spes* took on such importance. It offered a method and a pathway for the application of *Lumen Gentium* to the key problems of the Church in the world today, a task which the decrees had not adequately carried out.

I repeat this opinion of Cardinal Garrone because I think it has much merit. I would disagree that the Council could have developed *Gaudium et*

Spes in less time than the three years it took to do so. The various stages and successive texts illustrate a process of maturation that could not have been hastened more than it was. But it is true that some of the other texts—for example, on education and on communication media—came out too soon to share in the maturing process and that these and other decrees and declarations lack the sharp edge of application Cardinal Garrone describes as their proper function. All of which does bear out in practice what Cardinal Garrone himself stated in a 1965 press conference in the closing days of the Council: *Lumen Gentium* is the foundation of the Council; *Gaudium et Spes* is its application.

Another vital fact is that the title of our pastoral constitution is not "The Church in the Modern World," as it is sometimes badly translated, but rather *Ecclesia in Mundo Hujus Temporis,* "The Church in the World Today." The adjective *modern* can apply to what has occurred in recent centuries: as when we speak of modern history, or modern languages. *Hujus temporis* means very specifically the *here and now,* today. This title was not easily acquired. In a long and intense session of the drafting commission, late in November of 1963, the idea that an ecumenical council could or should take up contingent situations of the *here and now* was forcibly opposed, not only by exponents of the Oriental Church and its theological tradition but also by some of the most outstanding European theologians. They reminded us that theology, as a rational reflection on revelation and as an exposition of sacred doctrine, deals with the transcendent, the permanent; not inductively, but rather deductively, from the principles or articles of our faith to their due conclusions.

This is, of course, the Thomist (basically Aristotelian) vision of theology as science, the sacred and supreme science. While fully accepting this view of theology, several bishops on the mixed commission argued that we had to develop a complementary manner of addressing present mentalities and present problems of Christians and of the Church today, taking our model from Pope John XXIII, who addressed himself, especially in *Pacem in Terris,* to all men of goodwill, and did so beginning with the consideration of the "signs of the times." These Pope John took up, not in a biblical eschatological sense, but as indications of the key preoccupations and currents affecting men today, and of what the Lord wants of the Church in this world, and for the future.

This was clearly the desire and intention of John XXIII for the Council, a desire to be fulfilled specifically in *Gaudium et Spes,* once given the vision of Church assured in *Lumen Gentium.* It was clearly the vision and the desire as well of Pope Paul VI, who made *Gaudium et Spes* his own and insisted that even though it speaks of the contingent it be called a Constitution of the Council. This gradually became the vision of the mixed commission and of the entire Council. It had enormous influence upon the manner in which *Lumen Gentium* would be lived and applied in the post-conciliar Church.

We discover in *Gaudium et Spes,* then, an intention, a method, and a content:

An *intention* of dialogue: on the Church, in the Church; and on the world, from the Church; and in the Church, in the world.

A *method* for this dialogue is the simple inquiry of specialized Catholic Action: see, judge, and act, which had developed in the Church in recent decades. This had become a pastoral habit for many persons and sectors of the Church: an application, in effect, of pastoral discernment, choosing action after due consideration of situations, seen in the light of faith; nothing more nor less than Christian prudence, the virtue and the act. Many have written on the "inquiry" method. There is, for example, the little book by Archbishop Garrone, *L'Action Catholique* (Paris: Desclee, 1958, pp. 72–74). I shall discuss this method further when I consider its application in the Puebla document of 1979.

Thirdly, the *content,* consciously reflecting the historical, salvific, sacramental, communion sense of Church in *Lumen Gentium,* sign and instrument of the coming together of human persons, in all their dignity, among themselves, and in God. This content is more richly expressed in the first part of *Gaudium et Spes,* which was composed later, in a more mature stage of the Council, than in the second part, which was largely composed early on, although meant to be an application of the first part. This helps explain why the method of *Gaudium et Spes* is unevenly applied in various parts of the text, and why also perhaps some would later twist the method somewhat in their applications, to the detriment of the content of Church faith and life.

III. MEDELLÍN: VATICAN II IMPACTS LATIN AMERICA

There has always been a prevailing sense of some overall unity in Latin America. The dream of Simón Bolívar was that of a continental nation federated out of all the previous dependent colonies, with the center and capital in Panama. It was in 1826, during Bolívar's lifetime and at his invitation, that the first Pan-American congress took place in Panama in search of that dream: the dream of the *Patria grande,* the "Great Homeland," which so haunts Latin American leaders, even today when we are so divided among ourselves and our nations.

The Church has always felt herself to be at the core of Latin America: the strongest element of its spiritual, cultural, and social unity. Pope Paul VI stressed this awareness in his message to the extraordinary meeting of CELAM in Marl del Plata, Argentina, in 1976, on the theme: "The Church in the Development and Integration of Latin America." The Pope's exhortation was pointed. The Church, he said, which was present at the birth and throughout the history of these nations, had to be present in these crucial moments of their history.

But it took the Council to give impetus to the Church's presence in the new circumstance of this century. Not now as a dependent ally of the Spanish or Portuguese crown, nor as a center of vested interests in the liberal-conservative, clerical-anticlerical struggles of the nineteenth century, but as a renovation Church called to the evangelizing mission spelled out by Vatican II.

The Episcopal Council of Latin America, CELAM, had been established in 1955, during the International Eucharistic Congress at Rio de Janeiro. This continent-wide Council is made up of twenty-three national Episcopal Conferences, whose delegates elect a presidency from among themselves. Early during Vatican II, CELAM began to point toward post-conciliar applications. It set up a series of departments, roughly corresponding to the key areas of pastoral action of the Council and of our Churches. It began also to promote meetings on a continental level of bishops and experts in each of these areas. The first of these was held in Porto Alegre, Brazil, in May 1964, the mid-point of Vatican II. Leading priests from all our countries were invited, after careful contacts with their bishops, to hear about the Council firsthand from three Council theologians, Italian, French, and Brazilian. The meeting which lasted fifteen days was very enthusiastically received by the sixty participants. CELAM's departments were encouraged to promote and carry out additional meetings on the effect of Vatican II throughout the Latin American Church in specific fields: liturgy, catechetics, social action, pastoral action, secular and Catholic universities, seminaries, etc. These meetings opened new horizons. Their effect was far-reaching. For the first time there began to develop Latin American reflection and consciousness on each of these pastoral areas. To do so CELAM leaders brought together some of the most competent specialists in each area, which was very rewarding and motivating for all participants. They encouraged initiative in the local Churches of their homelands, and to relate these with the whole Church of Latin America. This was done in the spirit of Vatican II and, in each of the areas, following the method of inquiry developed in *Gaudium et Spes.*

Medellín, the 1968 General Conference of the Latin American Bishops, grew out of these meetings. I remember when the idea came up. In 1966, on the death of Bishop Manuel Larrain, the much loved Chilean president of CELAM who had given the first post-conciliar push, I was elected second vice-president. The presidency, assessing our continent-wide situation, decided to propose to Pope Paul VI the idea of a special meeting of the hierarchy to discuss in a more integrated fashion the application of the Council in our region, which the various departments of CELAM had been studying piecemeal. In an audience with the presidency early in 1967, Pope Paul VI immediately approved the idea and suggested it take the form not of a synod but rather of a General Conference, similar to the first in Rio, in 1955, which had created CELAM. He also suggested the date and place: Colombia, August 1968, when he would be present for the International Eucharistic Congress in Bogotá. He would convoke the CELAM Conference, and himself inaugurate it. So it happened: the inauguration was in Bogotá, and, thereafter, it met in Medellín for two weeks.

The formal announcement of the Conference took place in 1967. The specific preparation was not extensive. A working document was prepared in January 1968 and sent to the Episcopal Conferences. These elected their representatives to Medellín in the manner of Vatican synods, according to the number of dioceses and bishops in each Episcopal Conference. The Conferences' commentaries on the initial document were combined into a second edition of the document which was sent to the elected participants before the General Conference. But it was not the main basis of discussion at the Medellín Conference. The principal preparation, as to content, proved to be the half-dozen specialized pastoral meetings organized between 1967 and 1968 by CELAM, on the continental level, and the documents they had generated and approved. The spirit of Medellín really flowed directly from the Council itself, so fresh in the memory of all the participants. It was heightened by several opening talks and forums on the "signs of the times" in Latin America and their interpretation for the theological and pastoral mission of our Churches.

There was a strong sense of divine action making history at Medellín. Paul VI, in his opening words, said that with this first visit of a pope to Latin America, "through a convergence of prophetic circumstances, a new period of ecclesial life begins today." There was a feeling of Pentecost. Many commented on it. The bishops refer to it in the introduction to the final documents; in the style of *Gaudium et Spes* they speak of entering upon a new era of history (no. 4).

Here was the spirit of the Council overflowing upon Medellín. The title of the subject CELAM gave the Conference made this clear: "The Presence of the Church in the Actual Transformation of Latin America, in the Light of the Council." The use of sources did also. Of 340 references which Medellín makes, 219 are from the Council (47 from *Gaudium et Spes* and 28 from *Lumen Gentium*) and 76 from Paul VI (almost half of these from *Populorum Progressio*).

Medellín was a quick, bright shining forth of the Council's light upon the reality of Latin America and its Church. Therein lay its strength, and also a certain weakness, or perhaps immaturity.

There was and still is great strength in the sixteen documents of Medellín; in the conciliar doctrine and message they broadcast to all the continent; in the method followed, after the model of *Gaudium et Spes,* of casting each document into the inquiry frame: first the facts and reality; then the light of doctrine; leading in turn to pastoral recommendations.

This was a great breakthrough–so quickly and at a continental level. The Bishops of Latin America had heeded the Council fathers and carried the method and the contents of the Pastoral Constitution *to its own people, adapted to their own mentality* (no. 91). The Church of Latin America, traditionally the passive recipient of Church movements and inputs from abroad, had truly entered a new era in which it would take much more initiative in its tasks.

There was a significant breakthrough, also, in the fact of addressing itself so strongly and decidedly to the situation of the Latin people: "Their basic cultural richness" runs throughout the message of Medellín. The cultural values and Christian virtues latent in the religiosity of the people pervades the section on *Popular Pastoral Action.* Above all, the document on *Peace* makes sharp denunciation of suffering, as the result of injustice, both personal and structural.

The two documents on *Justice* and on *Peace* are very strong in their call for necessary changes, but through peaceful nonviolent means. They call for action, for liberation.

There was a weakness in the follow-up and use of the texts. The sixteen documents were not edited into one whole. This made it more difficult for the reader to get an integrated sense of Medellín. Most readers would look only at those documents that interested them most. Many would only read the first two, *Justice* and *Peace,* forgetting to relate them to the other texts on *Evangelization* and *Church Structure.*

A second problem was that much of the content was far ahead of the thinking and attitudes of some bishops, priests, and lay leaders at home. It took time for Medellín to be fully accepted by them, even after the Holy See gave its approval to the documents. One major Conference of Bishops did not really accept them until Puebla, a decade later.

Medellín was the first rapid projection of the Council, its spirit and demands, throughout the Church of Latin America.

IV. PUEBLA: COMMUNION AND PARTICIPATION, IN CHURCH AND WORLD

In his opening address to the Third General Conference of Latin American Bishops, at Puebla in January 1979, Pope John Paul II called upon us to consider the decade since Medellín, including the mistakes and wrong interpretations. He reminded us that without the Council there would have been no Medellín. He placed special emphasis upon Pope Paul VI's great exhortation in follow-up to the 1974 Synod, *Evangelii Nuntiandi*. Having reviewed the excruciating situations of poverty and injustice imposed so often upon our people, John Paul II offered the three basic truths around which we could develop the content of our evangelizing response to our people: the truth about Jesus Christ, about the Church, and about man.

Following the Pope, Cardinal Aloysio Lorscheider spoke as President of CELAM, outlining the topics we would treat. These were based upon the consultations held during the previous two years in all our countries. A committee of five was elected to coordinate the single final document. Its first task was to receive the criticisms of the Conference members on the outline proposed by Lorscheider and reform it accordingly. This done and approved, the Conference dug into its work: in the numerous commissions assigned to the different parts of the document, in the plenary sessions, and in the task of coordination. We aimed at producing a single document, overcoming the piecemeal effect of Medellín's sixteen documents, and to maintain throughout the underlying and unifying theme: "A Liberating Evangelization for Communion and Participation, in the Church and in the World."

There had been much fuss and publicity about discords within the hierarchy before going into Puebla. There was fear, in progressive circles, that the liberation themes, suggested in Medellín and developed since, would be excluded. In fact, most of the more controversial theologians having this view were excluded from the Conference, though they set up their own nearby forum in the city of Puebla.

The marvel is—a marvel of grace—that so much work, and such profound accord, in genuine consonance with the Council and with Medellín, was attained in those two short weeks.

I do not intend to go deeply into the Conference of Puebla, its document, and its applications in our Churches. These are already well known. Rather I would suggest that the process of Puebla, a direct result of the Council and especially of *Gaudium et Spes*, is in a very real sense part of a profound process of acquiring self-identity in the Church of Latin America, and in each of our local Churches in communion with Rome and the universal Church, and at the same time in communion with our own people. It is my very clear impression that in our part of the world these two decades since the Council have gone mostly into that effort: building up our Churches, in effective inner dialogue, communion, and participation within our cultures, so as to be able, from this double identification of Church and culture, to address more effectively the problems—cultural and others—which so deeply trouble our peoples. It is not that the dialogue with our world has not begun, but it has not gone very far in most areas. Now I think it will.

The most striking feature about Puebla is dialogue within the Church, with all the people of God, under the direction of its pastors.

The first round of consultations on the Conference begun two years before, in 1977, was done mostly at the level of the bishops. It produced a working document that was interesting, full of topical issues, and somewhat fearful of prevalent errors. A second round of consultations was held throughout 1978 on the document produced the year before. But this time thousands of groups–priests, religious, and especially parishes and Church Base Communities–participated. Their contributions, which were voluminous, were sent in, carefully integrated, by the Episcopal Conferences. These made Puebla. They manifested a deep and widespread process of evangelization through our Churches, with ever broader lay participation and responsibility–deep sacramental participation, solid spirituality, and a general rejection of the ideological or political interferences which would try to manipulate Church groups to their ends. The increase of Church vocations–lay, religious, and priestly–was a sign of inner life. Even more so was the clear sense of the Church's mission to its own people.

The descriptions of poverty, suffering, and injustice were graphic. The call for liberation was strong. Puebla reflects this in the opening section of its document, which, in the style of *Gaudium et Spes,* is a pastoral description of the social and religious situation of our peoples.

Indeed, Puebla has carried further and perfected the method of *Gaudium et Spes,* to which it is faithful throughout its work and document. It gives us a remarkable example of theology, especially pastoral theology, developed out of consideration of our realities.

In this theological process we are very careful to look at that reality pastorally, with the eyes of faith, excluding any ideological interpretation that would prejudice this view or bend the Gospel to its end. Secondly, the doctrinal or evangelical reflection, within the second part of Puebla's document, should address itself specifically to the problems raised in the pastoral vision of our reality. Thirdly, the pastoral recommendations should result from this double process. In fact, most of our Churches had been busily applying these methods in the decade since Medellín. These pastoral-reality methods of theological reflection had become habitual since 1968, so their application in preparation for Puebla and during the Assembly itself came to us naturally.[1]

To conclude, I wish to go very briefly into Puebla's projection of this dialogue outwards–to culture and all that it portends. But before doing so I must say a few things about dialogue and participation within the Church, or within our Churches. I must generalize. You will understand that we are many nations, with many individual differences.

Two major points, both concerning the laity: one a decided gain; the other still a challenge.

The participation of our laity–as delegates of the word, or catechists, or responsible community coordinators, or whatever the title, including the diaconate—manifests a growing reality that brings the Church in its communities, small and large, more closely together as Community: in communion and participation. This is a remarkable fact in Churches long marked by strong clericalism and the distance created by authority between clergy and lay.

Another fact is that the formation of base communities, and of active parishes, is more common among the workers, the city poor, and the *campesinos* on the land. Our upper classes practice their faith and attend Mass, but more as individuals. Their lay movements are less integrated with the general community and are more given to spiritual formation of the individual. The result is that our Churches, in many dioceses and countries, are literally becoming more and more the Church of the Poor: made up of the poor, who are becoming its leaders, not only in their local communities but on diocesan and national levels.

This lends much force to the call of Puebla, not only that we have a preferential option for the poor in economic and political terms, but that we apply this option first of all to the evangelization of the poor, so that with them and from their point of view we can carry out the evangelization of the entire community. This is absorbing the Church fully in the culture of our poor, in the great virtues hidden in their popular piety, purifying this and bringing it to the conversion of us all: to life-styles of participation and communication of our goods that are the heart and soul of our social message to all of society.

The second major point is a deficiency, a challenge to be met. If we have learned to dialogue and share responsibility with our laity in Church action, we have not learned yet to do so in the projection of Church into guidance for the temporal order. The very nature of the inquiry, in the "observe" step especially, should lead us to rely upon and consult mostly with lay persons in order to inform ourselves adequately of the social, economic, political, and other realities which require the light and guidance of the Gospel. This kind of consultation is yet infrequent in our countries. There are exceptions. There are some dioceses which have permanent consultations, commissions of dialogue, etc., in key cultural and social areas. But most do not.

It is as though the local Churches have to feel their own consistency, in inner dialogue within our cultures, in order then to be able to face the "outside," as it were, with greater confidence. In this regard, we experience in some countries the strength that comes from confident dialogue and consultation among the bishops and pastors, and with the theologians, in the local Churches. Where these two levels of teaching work together in due collaboration and communion, with respect for theology and with respect for the magisterium, local and universal, the effects of union and communion in our Churches are edifying. Where they do not, as in some Central American nations, the divisive effects upon our people are lamentable and the Church's possibilities of furthering her dialogue with the culture of the nation are much diminished.

V. EVANGELIZATION OF CULTURES IN PASTORAL MINISTRY

The theme of dialogue with culture, and with the cultures, came into Puebla at a late hour as an explicit theme. There had been much discussion on the topic, particularly among outstanding Argentinian theologians, including Father Scannone, the other Latin American contributor to this volume. But the topic was not in the working document of 1977 nor prominent in the document which wound up the consultations of 1978.

At that point the coordinating team in the preparation of Puebla and the committee of coordination within Puebla (to each of which I belonged) felt it wise to indicate some gaps in the presentation of themes for our document. Among them was the lack of real reference to specialized environments. Puebla's document reflected the pastoral reality of our Churches, based predominantly upon community groups (base and parish), vertically organized but not actively organized in the universities, the labor unions, the professions, etc. This void in the document was filled by adding the third chapter in the fourth part, with the heavy title: "The Church's Action with the Constructors of the Pluralist Society in Latin America." But the gap in our organized pastoral presence in all these areas still exists, and it is a cultural gap.[2]

Another lacuna in the considerations advanced by the local Churches for Puebla was the whole international order. There were references to international economic structures bearing unjustly upon our nations, but little else. The fourth chapter of the fourth part was added, with another heavy-sounding title: "The Church's Work for the Human Person, in the National and in the International Society."

The question of culture came in much more directly. *Evangelii Nuntiandi* of Paul VI inspired the Church of Latin America greatly from the time of its publication in 1975. Latin America had made significant contributions to the Synod of 1974, of which that document was a projection. Also Latin America needed this strong centering of its Church action upon evangelization, taken in the integral sense from the announcing of the word to the building up of the civilization of love, which the Synod and the subsequent document stressed.

The remarkable points about what Puebla has to say concerning culture are: 1) the length of the section and the many cross-references throughout the text to the same, a sign of a growing awareness; 2) the acceptance of the humanist or human-person-centered definition of *Gaudium et Spes* on culture, but then specifying the religious dimension as the nucleus, the heart of culture; 3) the subchapter on the evangelization of culture, which comes immediately after the description of evangelization itself and before the other areas are treated.

It is obvious that culture is taken as the global whole in which the other subjects are to be understood and carried out. The evangelization of "popular religiosity," for example, is largely the discovery and developing of the germs of the Gospel already present and developing there. Evangelization for liberation and human promotion is in large measure developing the sense of Christian values in an articulated social doctrine which must be present in all of our religious and educational labors toward social consciousness and social action. In evangelization of both ideology and politics, it is the Christian values which responsible Christians in the world must build into their ideologies, and into their politics, for "the elaboration of historical models that conform to the necessities of each moment and of each culture."

CONCLUSION

This has not been a scientific, but rather a pastoral presentation of our theme. It might be summed up by the statement (for me an experienced conviction) that our Church, or our Churches, in Latin America have taken the Council and *Gaudium et Spes* seriously. They have developed more as local churches, in stronger self-identity, communion, and participation, as a result. They are more independent of the secular powers than in the past, and on the whole much more respected, and perhaps feared.

Our Churches, I think, are now on the threshold, and in better condition, for a more serious and conscious effort to bear this cultural identity which is theirs into contact and dialogue with the surrounding cultures on our continent. We are ready also to relate evangelically with the world cultures which affect us so deeply as to constitute often a genuine aggression against our very being.

NOTES

1. See Marcos McGrath, *El Método Teológico–Pastoral de Puebla,* vol. 33 (1982) of the *Annales de la Faculdad de Teología,* Universidad Católica de Chile.

2. See "La participación de los laicos en la vida y misión de la Iglesia en América Latina; pistas de evaluación" in *Los Laicos en la vida y la misión de la Iglesia* (Rome: Consejo Pontificio para los Laicos), pp. 17–61, esp. p. 39.

Evangelization of Culture, Liberation, and "Popular" Culture: The New Theological-Pastoral Synthesis in Latin America

Juan Carlos Scannone, S.J.

Two of the central issues of Latin American Church life and theology after the Council are *liberation* and *evangelization of culture*: It suffices to recall, on the one hand, Medellín and Puebla, or, on the other, the theology of liberation and the current Latin American theological and pastoral concern with popular religiosity, culture, and wisdom. From the Latin American point of view these issues are intimately related.

The influence, direct and indirect, of the Constitution *Gaudium et Spes* on both issues was decisive, for the new contributions as well as for the problems it brought and for the reinterpretations and other effects that issue from it as put into practice in the Latin American context.

In this exposition I shall try to state briefly some of these influences. After a general consideration I shall distinguish three theological and pastoral trends that have extended the influence of *Gaudium et Spes* upon the issue of the evangelization of culture in Latin America, with special attention to its relation to the question of liberation. Thereafter I shall indicate what, in my opinion, is now the main challenge to the evangelization of culture, and finally shall suggest how in the light of *Gaudium et Spes* and its effect on Latin America this challenge may be met.

I. *GAUDIUM ET SPES* AND THE EVANGELIZATION OF CULTURE IN LATIN AMERICA

This matter has already been discussed by Archbishop McGrath in the light of Medellín and Puebla and, therefore, I will limit myself to points necessary for my further exposition.

The main contribution of *Gaudium et Spes* to the issues was the new pastoral attitude of the Latin American Church: its resolute turn toward Latin American man, society, and cultures. That change went along with a new mode of theological reflection that, in the light of faith, took its starting point from the historical situation. Both elements were central in Medellín and

Puebla and contributed greatly to the rise of liberation pastoral practice and theology.

A second important contribution of *Gaudium et Spes* was its revaluation of the historical activity and responsibility of man in the world as well as the autonomy of the temporal sphere and culture, perceived historically—that is to say, in the framework of the integral vocation of man, in which salvation in Jesus Christ and human development are intimately united. This brought on a crisis in the mood of Christendom which still prevails in many Latin American Catholic circles. It called for an extensive theological elaboration of the "intimate relations" between the Church and culture and of the mission of the Church with respect to both society and culture.

I should note as well the influence exerted by the Pastoral Constitution's conception of culture. That conception, neither objectivist nor "culturalist," is anthropocentric, historical, and integral and has deeply inspired Latin American reflection and pastoral practice. Indeed, the Constitution notably influenced the growth of a Latin American formulation on the pastoral practice of culture which the Synod of 1974 expressed in *Evangelii Nuntiandi.* In my opinion, however, the main influence of *Gaudium et Spes* was not its mere "application" to Latin America but the dynamic *process* involved in applying it, experiencing the subsequent reactions and effects, and then comprehending the situation anew: the ongoing sense of continuity and critical fulfillment that the application provoked. The Latin American Church thereby gained a greater awareness of its own special identity and of the history of the evangelization of culture on the continent.

The theological and pastoral shift in the direction of the socio-cultural realities of Latin America, already in turbulent passage—a reality marked by injustice and violence—served to correct the rather naive optimism with which some Latin American groups had received *Gaudium et Spes* and its openness to the modern world. Within the possibilities of Christian hope this openness is not to be questioned. Nevertheless, confronting the existing situation in Latin America and such explanations of it as may be afforded by social science brought about an awareness of great social maladjustments. The reconciliation of the Church and modern values made it possible to address these issues. There was structural injustice and widespread and humiliating dependence in a continent self-styled as Christian. Those conditions gave rise to sharp conflicts and a recognition of the Church as having a mission to promote human liberation. This recognition proved to be ever more influential in the issue of the evangelization of culture in Latin America.

Such an increased awareness moved some Latin American theologians, who acknowledge their indebtedness to *Gaudium et Spes,* to criticize what they call its "irenism."[1] According to these critics, the Constitution had blunted the sharp edges and avoided the more conflicting aspects of the meetings between classes and nations, because it had spoken about development mostly from the perspective of the developed countries, rather than from that of the poor ones, as subsequently Medellín, dealing exclusively with Latin America, would do three years later, in 1968.

The method of pastoral-theological thinking in *Gaudium et Spes* and Latin American circumstances inspired a "new way of doing theology," the starting point of which is appeal to the poor and the oppressed and the agape-oriented (*agapica*) praxis of liberation that the appeal requires. This theology makes use of the human sciences of society and of history. From the perspective they afford, it works toward a new understanding of the relationship between eschatological salvation and historical liberation. Critically inspired by *Gaudium et Spes,* this enterprise proposes courses designed to reveal concrete forms of this relationship. In so doing it affirms the unity between salvific history and salvation in Jesus Christ on the one hand and, on the other hand, the secular history of human oppressions and liberations, although it must also distinguish among those dimensions which are not mutually reductive.[2] The importance of this, not only for the theoretical understanding of the evangelization of culture but also for its praxis, is obvious.

A third consequence of the influence of *Gaudium et Spes* in Latin America was the pastoral revaluation of Latin American popular religiosity and, as a consequence, of popular culture, topics which *Gaudium et Spes* had not dealt with. The shift toward Latin American society, history, and culture allowed the Church to discover, reflexively and globally, not only her evils and conflicts, but also the human and Christian richness, however ambiguous, of popular religiosity and the wisdom in it. This religiosity and wisdom are, to no small degree, the fruit of evangelization. Such a re-evaluation, however, was also a reaction against the secularizing and at times iconoclastic interpretations which some post-conciliar groups in Latin America gave to the autonomy of secularity.[3] All of these brought about, at a later period, the formulation of a proper and well-placed understanding of the process of modernization and secularization and of the relationship between religion and secularity of culture and between evangelization, liberation, and popular culture.

The slogan was no longer "Christianity" or "New Christianity," not even "autonomy of the temporal order" or "liberation," but rather "evangelization of culture," understood as a pastoral option, fundamental and all-encompassing. This provided a theoretical formula for understanding the relationship between the Church (evangelization) and world (culture) along the lines of *Gaudium et Spes.* Furthermore, this perspective contributed to Latin America's renewed comprehension of the challenges of modern society and culture to evangelization and theology, seen in the light of the wisdom of the poor.

II. DIFFERING THEOLOGICAL AND PASTORAL APPROACHES

The so-called Latin American "post-conciliar Catholics" began to divide into different groups around the time of Medellín, 1968. I shall not attempt here to describe in a nuanced fashion particular positions, but rather to indicate three main force-lines issuing from *Gaudium et Spes* and point out their principal characteristics. In doing so, I shall risk some oversimplification. The differences among them lie, above all, in their emphases, and they are frequently due to the mediating factors (philosophical, scientific-social, historico-hermeneutical) used for their respective comprehensions of reality and faith. Initially, I shall sketch each of these three main lines and then explain how, in my opinion, the perspective of the third position allows the contributions of the other two to be subsumed within it.[4]

1. Distinction of Levels

There is, in the first place, the pastoral and theological approach which takes up the position that Gustavo Gutierrez, in 1971, called "the distinction of levels"—that is, the distinction between the level of salvific realities and that of temporal ones, within the unity of God's plan.[5]

The center of his attention is the clear affirmation of the autonomy of the temporal order and respect for its consistency, on the one hand, and, on the other, the affirmation of and respect for the pre-eminently religious character of the mission of the Church. To do this, he resorts to a spatial schema of levels. This can easily lead to a somewhat dualistic interpretation of the relation between faith and culture, the supernatural and the natural, the interior and the exterior, the individual and the social, what is private and what is public.

This line, therefore, can become an extreme spiritualist and interiorist view of the mission of the Church in society and culture. It tends to reduce to mere spirituality the institutional action of the Church, which in Latin America can have great moral and social weight. This spiritualist-interiorism serves to deter the Church from making institutional pronouncements on temporal and controverted questions, favoring instead action through the rightly formed conscience of the Christian laity. This approach insists on the distinction between the religious and the technical levels, or between the level of principles and values and that of concrete realizations. It also stresses the pluralism of the temporal options of Christians. Even though this spiritualist approach emphatically opposes the manipulation of the Church by national-security regimes, on occasion its division of levels has favored silence in the face of harshly dehumanizing economic or social policies, and merely abstract denunciations of flagrant violations of human rights.

For this line of thought, cultural-pastoral praxis is primarily in the education and formation of individual consciences, above all, of social and cultural agents, without adequate consideration of the collective conscience of the people and of the structures and systems of living together. Sometimes its understanding of the concept of culture tends to be individualistic or idealistic, with overtones of Renaissance or Enlightenment humanism.

In some cases this understanding of respect for the autonomy of the secular order—especially for science and scholarship, technology and politics—according to the schema of "levels," hinders the influence of faith on culture from its very beginning. There arises here the danger that the all-encompassing horizon of meaning as disclosed by faith does not intrinsically affect the all-encompassing horizon of meaning in which the cultural praxis is factually carried out—be that cultural praxis ethical, political, economic, scientific, technological, or other. In many cases faith serves only as a sort of added corrective to a cultural praxis whose horizon of human meaning was adopted without any reference to the meaning of man and life which is presupposed by faith.

That all-encompassing horizon of meaning always in fact affects the basic orientating perspective of lively self-knowledge and of the concrete praxis of each one of the dimensions of culture, even economics, politics, science, and technology, insofar as they are human actions. Then, the horizon itself continues to be distorted by the position of sin, without having been "cured" of its distortion of perspective. It will have a distorting effect as well on the regional perspectives that observe the human activities mentioned above and on the concrete elaboration of objective cultural dimensions that are the historic result of the same. Such a view, such an all-encompassing horizon of meaning, may actually permeate the understanding and the practical activity of economics, science, technology, and politics, and be wholly untouched by faith.[6]

In looking at the situation in Latin America this interiorist view judges it to be unjust and violence-ridden, and tries to mitigate the ordeal of its transformation. In the main it holds that this transformation will be achieved through the modernizing process of capitalism, already under way, provided that the personal morality of its agents improves. In general it believes that the modernization process is an inevitable and positive development, although it has problems with which it must deal. The proponents of this view, therefore, concern themselves with the evangelization of modern culture in Latin America, inasmuch as they think that traditional cultures must adapt to modernity or perish. To effect the transformation, they look to elite groups, and they emphasize the urgency of Christian formation of leading elites.

2. Socio-historical Liberation and Evangelization of Culture

There is second a force-line represented by important groups of liberation theology and the pastoral practice inspired by it. Their formulation regarding the evangelization of culture and their corresponding reinterpretation of *Gaudium et Spes* draw from their view of the *system of labor as the basis of culture.* At times they develop an integral understanding of culture; on other occasions they confine it to the level of conscience and suprastructure;[7] but they always focus their attention on the decisive conditioning of cultural values, meanings, and cultural expressions effected by the labor system and by the power systems which issue from it. When – as is the case in Latin America – the economic base and the political system are marked by oppressive domination, this is expressed in the suprastructure in the form of a confrontation between a dominant culture and a dominated one. In this line of thought the analysis of social class – taken, more or less critically, from the Marxist tradition – is a necessary preliminary for effective evangelization of culture.

This very understanding of culture presupposes a clear affirmation of its secularity and autonomy with regard to religion and faith. As a consequence, some representatives of this line – as well as some of the preceding one – maintain that in contemporary society the Church should not assume leadership in cultural processes, nor should religion attempt to monopolize the cultural realm or to be the exclusive shaper of the collective conscience on the national or the continental level.[8]

Proponents of this line of thinking look on the evangelization of culture as an inescapable task which primarily means putting the Gospel into practice, not so much at the level of ideas, intentions, or meanings, but on the level of social relations, institutions, behavior, and structures. Because, after all, salvific reality is present in a praxis informed, sometimes anonymously, by love. Essentially this praxis is ethico-historical, to be found not only, or necessarily, on the level of an explicit knowledge of faith or of religious symbols. If, then, the culture is to be evangelized, there must first be the liberation of oppressed cultures, which in turn will be conditioned by the liberating transformation of the labor system and of social power. This transformation is conceived along socialist lines.

This particular line of thinkers denies that there is *one* homogeneous Latin American culture. After all there have been three violent colonizations of the continent, which by introducing new economic and political domination disintegrated existing cultures. In every case there was a new confrontation of the oppressed races or classes and their dominated culture and the hegemonic races or classes and their dominant culture, which, in turn, was alienated by its dependence on the cultural colonization existing at the time.[9]

These three cultural invasions were: a) Iberian Catholic culture, during the period of the Spanish and Portuguese conquests and settlements; b) European Enlightenment culture (mainly French or English) which accompanied the neo-colonialism of the nineteenth century after national emancipation from the empires of Spain and Portugal; c) contemporary culture in our century (with the marked dominance of United States culture), a kind of cultural colonization which increased in the last two decades as neo-colonialism – that is, dependence on multinational corporations and the centers of world power.

The advocates of this second line very often acknowledge the efforts to bring about a "cultural *mestizaje*" (cross-breeding). During the first colonization and after the "great immigration" of the late 1800s, these efforts at cultural mixture were made. Some of those advocates, however, judge that these attempts as well as the traditional *mestizo* culture, which has been mainly a culture of peasants, have already failed, and they think that the indigenous or Afro-American cultures are nothing but "canned cultures." Other representatives of this line, on the other hand, see in popular culture – whether it be *mestiza, criolla,* or indigenous – an effective force of cultural resistance. They claim to see as well a capacity for integral human liberation, manifested above all in many central aspects of popular religiosity.[10]

These last-mentioned proponents of the second line, who are gaining more and more influence within it, although they assign priority to the analysis of class struggle, recognize a cultural resiliency, grounded and expressed in religion, as the result, but not the exclusive result, of several centuries of evangelization. This challenges the more or less orthodox use of Marxist analysis in the evaluation of culture. And this brings them closer to the third force-line.

The approach to the evangelization of culture and its relation to sociohistorical liberation will vary according to the different understandings of popular culture and religiosity. Some will insist, as proposed in the first line of thinking, on the need to evangelize modern culture, dismissing the importance of specific Latin American cultures. On the other hand those who value popular religiosity maintain that the liberation and the evangelization of modern culture should be carried out in the context of popular culture, that of the poor and the oppressed, a culture which is, in fact, religious. Here, popular culture is not looked upon as intrinsically alienated or threatened by extinction. Rather, in spite of its ambiguities and some areas of alienations, popular culture is likely to be an important and decisive factor in evangelization and liberation.

Examples of this are the basic church communities and other free popular organizations. For those who think along these lines, these communities are not only a new way of conceiving the Church, but also an essential factor in the task of evangelizing Latin American culture and incorporating, within popular culture, the valid dimension of the modernization process. The hoped-for synthesis may liberate this very process through the liberation of the poor.

3. Evangelization and Latin American Cultural Ethos

A third force-line sprang up—at any rate, in Argentina—thanks to the direct influence of *Gaudium et Spes.* When its text was read by Latin American eyes, readers in their interpretations gave great significance to the meaning of culture which in *Gaudium et Spes* is designated as "ethnological," an emphasis also evident in the document of Puebla.[12]

Gustavo Gutierrez has characterized some of the representative thinkers of this line of thought as proponents "of a current bearing its own unique features within the scope of liberation theology."[13] In addition, some authors share important elements of this current of thought even though they are not, properly speaking, within the camp of liberation theology. Representatives of this third force-line may not ignore the role of conflict, but they accord primacy to unity and, though they do not ignore class analysis, to historico-cultural analysis. This has a major bearing upon their concepts as well as upon their interpretation of history, of the present situation, and of the contemporary Latin American historical challenge.

The advocates of this line believe there is a Latin American culture; although this culture is neither uniform nor homogeneous nor without sharp contradictions, it has sufficient historical unity and similar nuclei to allow us to conceive it in terms of a pluralistic or analogical unity.

The culture is the result of a common history. Its foundation event was the cultural intermingling of the Iberian and the indigenous cultures, which formed a new culture. The new culture was the product of conquest and violence, but also of a vital encounter and synthesis. The culture that issued from such mingling has its own distinct quality, different as a child from its progenitors. Furthermore, the same subsistent indigenous cultures and the Afro-American ones mixed with one another in a process of cultural *mestizaje,* in which the aboriginal cultures sought to respect and retrieve their own aboriginal values.

Evangelization was decisively influential in the birth of the mestizo culture and in some of the most important aspects of its history. It thereby influenced intrinsically the formation of the "cultural ethos" of Latin America and the traditions of wisdom and ethics which find expression in various forms of popular Catholicism. The Puebla Document declares:

> So our culture is impregnated with the faith, even though it frequently has lacked the support of a suitable catechesis. This is evident in the distinctive religious attitudes of our people, which are imbued with a deep sense of transcendence and the nearness of God. It finds expression in a wisdom of the common people that has contemplative features and that gives a distinctive direction to the way our people live out their

relationship with nature and their fellow human beings. It is embodied in their sense of work and festiveness, of solidarity, friendship, and kinship; and in their feel for their own dignity, which they do not see diminished by their own lives as simple, poor people. (no. 413)

External and internal oppression – economic, political, and social – prevented this nucleus from achieving sufficient expression in the form of structures of community life and in institutions which could articulate it socially. Nevertheless, it gave Latin American people sufficient strength to resist cultural alienation and it offers them the drive and guiding inspiration of a socio-historical liberation intrinsically influenced by the Gospel.

The words *people* and *popular* – popular culture, popular religiosity, popular wisdom – as they are used in this current of thought are not fundamentally based on the concept of class conflict but rather in the unity of a common historical experience, life-style, and historical project.[15] Those, however, who deny their own people and oppress them, exclude themselves from the project. The line of demarcation between "people" and "anti-people," then, crosses through the hearts of persons and groups, according to whether or not they practice justice, a justice measured not only by abstract ethical criteria but also historical ones.

In Latin America, the poor and the oppressed resisted cultural aggression better than other groups and have preserved Latin American popular culture in a more vital form. Their legitimate aspirations are more oriented toward justice and the common good than those of other groups. That is why they form the core of the cultural and social liberation process.

Without denying the anthropocentric concept of culture found in *Gaudium et Spes* and its affirmation of cultural autonomy, this third line of thought, perhaps because of its Latin American viewpoint, upholds a more religious understanding of culture, as Puebla also does. For, in this particular perspective, the fundamental ground of a given culture is constituted by the ultimate meaning of life and death, even within the secular and socio-structural dimensions of the culture, if one may assume the absence of an interposed dominating culture. In this particular line of thought the basic religious or anti-religious attitude of a culture is a key dimension of it.

This line, therefore, suggests that the evangelization of culture, starting from the religious dimension, through the mediation of ethics, ought to affect all the other dimensions of human life and dialogue. To achieve this, however, it does not look to a church-state partnership, an ecclesiocratic regime, but rather to the influence of the faith of the People of God upon the collective conscience of the people, a conscience which, in Latin America, has already been evangelized. This approach respects the secular autonomy of the peoples and their cultures, but does not limit itself to evangelizing only the individual persons who are the bearers of the respective cultures. To be sure, it respects the importance of structures, but considers as more important the cultural *ethos* of the people, that is, the totality of lived principles and really existing values which animate it and which should find expression in institutions and structures.[16]

Indeed, popular piety in Latin America often bears within it a profound Christian wisdom that reveals in its fundamental values the influence of the evangelical spirit of the Beatitudes. The Puebla Document declared concerning this wisdom:

> As its core the religiosity of the people is a storehouse of values that offers the answers of Christian wisdom to the great questions of life. The Catholic wisdom of the common people is capable of fashioning a vital synthesis. . . . This wisdom is a Christian humanism that radically affirms the dignity of every person as a child of God, establishes a basic fraternity, teaches people how to encounter nature and understand work, and provides reasons for joy and humor even in the midst of a very hard life. (no. 448).

According to the advocates of this persuasion, the culture which emerged from the first cultural *mestizaje* (European indigenous) was threatened in its very foundations, first of all, by the rationalist Enlightenment in the nineteenth century. Today it is threatened by the secularism of the liberal-capitalist and Marxist ideologies, both of which are practically or theoretically atheistic, and which are accompanied by structural neo-dependency and cultural intrusions.

According to this third line, the present challenge to Latin-American nations is to achieve liberation by finding a new vital synthesis between their human and Christian cultural heritage and what is valid in modern progress, society, and culture. This synthesis must be creative; it cannot duplicate external models which do not respond to the cultural distinctiveness and to the Christian view of life that animates it.

For most of the representative proponents of this line, it is not the task of the Church, but rather of the Latin American peoples, to undertake this creative and liberating cultural project. But a suitable pastoral program of culture, to bring the light and strength of the Gospel to this process of responding to the challenge of socio-cultural changes, should be a part of the effort. Furthermore, the evangelization of culture should take as a starting point the implantation of the Gospel within popular culture.

4. The Third Line Enriched by the Other Two

Each one of these lines that in Latin America issue from *Gaudium et Spes* can make valuable contributions to the evangelization of our culture. But, in my opinion, the general orientation of the third line is the more acceptable one, both for its theoretical understanding of culture and its relationship with evangelization, and also for its grasp of historical-pastoral possibilities in Latin America. It must, nevertheless, incorporate the contributions of the other two lines.

In my exposition I have pointed out how this third line assimilates meaningful truths from the first one, such as respect for the autonomy of culture and legitimate pluralism. For, from the perspective of this third line, we cannot bring cultural systems out of a religious system, but we should rather influence them indirectly from the perspective of the ethical-wisdom nucleus of the different peoples and their view of the ultimate meaning of a human person and of life. This in turn allows a plurality of options—religious, ideological, political, etc.,—within the *ethos* of a given people.

Such indirect influence yields to the conversion of the heart to Christ and the healing effect of grace in those persons of a society who have a hand in molding together, at the point where they meet, authentically human value attitudes and their corresponding cultural forms and social structures. This is applicable not only to values and value positions that are wholly of the "natural" order, but also to those that originate from the influence of the theological virtues in life and, indirectly, in culture. Nevertheless these last values, because they are deeply human, can be acknowledged and shared also by non-Christians.

At this point I should note that the proponents of the third line may profit by adopting some of the contributions made by the second line's proponents who provide an alert to dangers in the third position. These are notably: 1) The risk of a certain kind of "populism" or "romanticism" which might conceal conflicts and contradictions by means of an idealized, or organismic, concept of "people"; and 2) the danger of "idealism" or "culturalism," concerned with the idea-form of the contents of consciousness and its symbolic expressions, overlooking the socio-material reality which is their living base.[17]

To avoid the first danger, it is important that the pastoral program of culture in Latin America recognize and take sufficiently into account the structural domination and dependency, internal and external, which are the products of the three previously mentioned colonizations. In every case, therefore, it will be necessary to analyze the concrete cultural situation by means of a historico-cultural methodology of analysis and hermeneutics. This methodology, in turn, will have been shaped by a critical examination and adaptation of the socio-cultural analysis of interests and class struggles.[18] But this is not enough: It is necessary that such hermeneutics be taken up and critically assessed by human comprehension of the historical, global situation in terms of the Christian faith. This is how theologico-pastoral thinking in the service of the evangelization of culture must go through the medium of social analyses and historical hermeneutics. Its ultimate criteria for discernment, nevertheless, should always be theological. These theological criteria must not ignore the dimensions of history.

Among the concrete tasks of evangelization of culture in Latin America which the preceding line of thinking should illuminate I may mention: 1) to provide special attention to indigenous and Afro-American oppressed cultures, very often insufficiently evangelized by the first evangelization; 2) to guard popular culture and religiosity from possible alienation, to recognize their basic capacity to resist against foreign intrusion, and that, in the last analysis, they usually represent a true popular Catholicism; 3) to criticize, from a Gospel perspective, the idols of the dominating culture—that is, consumerism, the absolutizing of the quest for money, sex, power, national security, etc., as well as the ideologies which protect and nourish them; 4) to help the people pastorally in the actualization of the ethico-historical potentialities implied in resistance to cultural domination[19] and the potentialities of self-affirmation of the individual's dignity and culture, as well as potentialities of an effective and organized struggle for justice and against structural injustice and oppression; 5) to continue to promote popular pastoral practice and the ecclesial base communities.

These tasks are to be carried out especially among people who are in transition from a rural or slum culture to an urban and modern culture so that they will not discard their own human and Christian values and symbols in the process.[20] To assist the people in this process is an inescapable pastoral and educational task, as is also study of the models which issue out of it, in order to incorporate them in pastoral, educational, and politico-cultural strategy.

Because the third line of thought accepts that in the cultural unity of Latin America the poor are the axis of its history. Therefore, since the evangelization of culture must be approached from the vantage point of the preferential option for the poor, it cannot overlook the factor of conflict in Latin American history and in its present situation. It allows for this element of conflict without, however, making it the ultimate key in interpreting history or in its liberating pastoral strategy. For the proponents of this third line the socio-historical liberation and the evangelization of modern culture should be carried out in Latin America, by and through assimilation of the poor into popular culture, which in turn should be continuously evangelized.

In that popular culture there will be perceived, promoted from the Gospel, the transforming and vivifying influence of the spirit of the Beatitudes. Indeed, this is frequently encountered in the Christian wisdom of the poor of Latin America, in matters of the heart and of feeling.

The second danger to which we have alluded is that of an eventual cultural "idealism." But the preferential option for the poor obviates the danger, at least partially, because it readily draws attention to the material dimension and material dynamics of history and culture in order to discern how material aspects (which do not determine history or culture) condition collective and personal conscience. This third line stresses the influence and role of ethics and history in fostering the attitudes, value-dispositions, and collective actions of peoples, including, of course, those of the individual persons who constitute them. Consequently, it focuses its understanding of culture and its evangelization on ethics and freedom. Its understanding of the latter is neither abstract nor individualistic, but rather social and historical. Therefore it does not neglect either the conditioning of ethics and freedom by socio-material structures, or the effort to make ethics and freedom effective through structures and their socio-economic dynamics and energies. Liberation so conceived and so promoted will be a human, integral liberation, and the evangelization of culture—while respecting secular autonomy—will influence intrinsically the very same socio-historical liberation.

III. CONCLUSION

It seems clear, in my opinion, that the main actual challenge to the evangelization of culture in Latin America lies in the scandal already denounced by Puebla: Peoples whose cultural nucleus has already been evangelized live in conditions of acute, structural injustice and violence.[21] By criticizing precisely those "structures of sin" from the standpoint of the Gospel and the Christian sense of man and life that goes with that cultural nucleus and by promoting cultural forms and social structure in accord with the conscience and culture, that scandal can be removed.

I have argued that the response to this historico-cultural challenge should not be sought by adopting alien models of development and liberation, which, in the past, have not been authentically humanizing and did not respect Latin American culture's character.

The likely response is to be sought in an attempt to bring about a new socio-cultural synthesis, the historical agent of which would be the Latin American people, whose core are the poor and the humble. This historical synthesis should continue to develop through the cultural *mestizaje* between the Latin American cultural heritage, confirmed by Christianity, and the legitimate contributions of modern systems of thought, technology, participation, and dialogue. To accomplish this it will be necessary for the scientific, technical, political, educational, artistic elites to turn to the people, to their popular culture and wisdom, and their fight for justice, and to become an organic part of their activity.

In this way, this Latin American, human and Christian wisdom will inspire, albeit indirectly, social theories or technical models which will be more suitable to the historico-cultural reality and the ethical goals of justice. This is possible by means of an analogical projection of human attitudes, and its corresponding analogical projection of the all-encompassing perspectives of the specific action of the elites in their respective fields, and within the community of people.[22] Perhaps, in this fashion, modern culture will receive the ethical presence and orientation which it does not yet have, transforming it from within the context of popular culture, while at the same time modern culture transforms the popular one toward a new liberating cultural synthesis.

It is not the mission of the Church as such to actualize such a cultural project, but rather to walk, from within the Gospel, with the Latin American peoples in the pursuit of this attempt, at a decisive moment of socio-cultural transformation.[23] Such an evangelizing task must start from the inculturation of the Gospel already achieved in Latin America, and it must take its orientation from a preferential option for the poor.

One of its objectives must be the conciliatory mediation of the elites (religious, scientific, political, technical, artistic, etc.) with the poor and simple people, and the promotion of that from within the people itself. And it should be characterized by an attentive historico-salvific discernment, which should not only recognize and denounce historical sin but recognize and promote in the concrete history of Latin America, the salvific presence of the Lord of History.

NOTES

1. See G. Gutiérrez, *Teología de la liberación: Perspectivas* (Salamanca, 1972), pp. 64–66.

2. See my article "La teología de la liberación: Caracterización, corrientes, etapas," *Stromata* 38 (1982), 16ff., and in *Teología de la liberación y praxis popular* (Salamanca, 1976), pp. 55ff. In English: "The Theology of Liberation–Evangelical or Ideological?" *Concilium* 10 (March 1974), 150. Those works, as well as the present article, are in the same vein with the author's other works done with the accepted method and terminology of philosophy but against an explicit horizon of faith which transforms them "as water into wine" in order to put them at the service of theological theorizing and evangelization.

3. Cf. A. Methol Ferré, "Marco histórico de la religiosidad popular," in *Iglesia y religiosidad popular en América Latina* (Bogotá, 1977), p. 47.

4. On the different post-conciliar trends in Latin America, see my treatment, "Theology, Popular Culture and Discernment," in *Frontiers of Theology in Latin America* (New York, 1979), pp. 213ff. On the different currents within liberation theology, consult the first article cited in note 2 of this work, pp. 18ff.

5. See Gutiérrez, pp. 88ff. Gutiérrez wrote on pp. 91–92: "It is the theology that, with different nuances, is mostly represented in the texts of Vatican II. There are however, points of view and intuitions that point out further, for example, in *Gaudium et Spes.*"

6. I develop these ideas in my article: "Hacia una pastoral de la cultura," *Stromata,* 31 (1975), 237–259; in French, *Convergence,* 1975, pp. 44–53.

7. Compare, for example, the concept of "culture" of J. Comblin, taken from *Gaudium et Spes,* in "Evangelización de la cultura en América Latina," *Puebla,* no. 2 (1978), 91–109, and that of Cl. Boff in "Evangelizacâo e Cultura," *Revista Eclesiástica Brasileira* 39 (1979), 421–434.

8. See Boff, p. 424. See also, by the same author: "A Ilusâo de uma Nova Cristaodade," *Revista Eclesiástica Brasileira* 38 (1978), 5–17. About the topic of "New Christendom" in the Working Papers for Puebla, see also: N. Zevallos, "El documento de Puebla y la filosofía de la cultura," *Puebla,* no. 2 (1978), 109–115.

9. Cf. J. Comblin, article cited above in note 7, pp. 107ff.

10. Cf. J. L. González, "Teología de la liberación y religiosidad popular," *Páginas* 7 (1982), 4–13.

11. That was one of the principal sources of group ideas gathered by F. Boasso in *Qué es la pastoral popular*? (Buenos Aires, 1974). One of the main members of that group was Lucio Gera.

12. In the Puebla Document there is added to the citation of *Gaudium et Spes,* no. 53-b, the specification, "in a people" (see Documento de Puebla no. 386). On our topic at Puebla see G. Remolina, "Evangelización y cultura. Qué hay de nuevo en Puebla?" in *Análisis de Puebla* (Bogotá, 1979), pp. 125–143; and "La Cultura en el Documento de Puebla," in *Religión y Cultura: Perspectivas de la evangelización de la cultura desde Puebla* (Bogotá, 1981), pp. 11–35; in the same work see the summary of the discussions of the Study Group of CELAM, composed by J. C. Terán, "En torno a la tarea de evangelizar nuestra cultura," pp. 327–367.

13. Gutiérrez, *La fuerza histórica de los pobres* (Lima, 1980), p. 377; see also his article, "Evangelizar la cultura: Evasion de un compromiso?" *Servir,* 14 (1978), 408, n. 8.

14. L. Gera, "Fe y cultura en el Documento de Puebla," *Criterio* 52 (1979), 749–754; and "Iglesia, cultura y realidad temporal en América Latina," *Sedoc-Documentación,* no. 34 (1978), pp. 3–23. See also: C. Giaquinta, "Cultura latinoamericana y evangelización: Apuntes, reflexiones y digresiones en torno a Puebla," *Criterio* 53 (1980), 239–252.

15. On people, religion, and culture, see L. Gera, "Pueblo, religión del pueblo e Iglesia," in *Iglesia y religiosidad popular en América Latina,* already cited in note 3 above.

16. John Paul II spoke of the "set of principles and values which constitute the *ethos* of a people," in relation with "live culture" and "popular culture," respectively, in the Letter to Cardinal Casaroli on the creation of the Pontifical Council for Culture (see *Osservatore Romano*, Spanish ed., no. 701, June 6, 1982, p. 391) and in his address to the Bishops of Lombardy (see *Osservatore Romano,* Spanish ed., no. 685, February 14, 1982, pp. 110–112). On the notion of "*cultural ethos,*" see "Cultura y Evangelio," in G. Farrell, J. Gentico, L. Gera, and others, *Comentario a la Exhortación Apostólica Evangelii Nuntiandi de S.S. Pablo VI* (Buenos Aires, 1978), pp. 259–276.

17. Also in some texts dealing with the Puebla Document it has been called "idealism and populism": see P. Trigo, "Evangelización de la cultura," *Puebla,* no. 5 (1979), c. 298 and 299.

18. I treat the interrelation among the socio-analytical, historical-hermeneutical and ethical-historical criteria to determine—at the level of philosophical discourse—the authentic notion of "popular" in my work "Volksreligiosität, Volksweisheit und Philosophie in Lateinamerika" that will appear in *Theologische Quartalschrift* of 1984. I think that it is also relevant for pastoral-theological thinking.

19. I intend to work out philosophically a dialectic of liberation different from the Marxist one, starting off from the experience of cultural resistance, in my work "La mediación histórica de los valores. Aporte desde la perspectiva y la experiencia latinoamericana," *Stromata* 39 (1983) 117–139.

20. Cf. P. Trigo, "Espiritualidade e Cultura. Diante do Impacto da Modernizacâo," *Revista Eclesiástica Brasileira* 39 (1979), pp. 632–643. We think that in the labor milieu of the Greater Buenos Aires area one can sense already the beginnings of that new synthesis that must be taken into consideration by popular pastoral practice.

21. On that challenge as it appears in the Puebla Document see my article "Interpretations of the Puebla Document," *Lumen Vitae* (Eng. ed.) 35 (1980), 368.

22. The points briefly made in this paragraph are developed in my article, "La racionalidad científico-tecnológica y la racionalidad sapiencial de la cultura latinoamericana," *Stromata* 37 (1981), especially pp. 158–164.

23. According to J. Ladrière, *Les enjeux de la rationalité. Le défi de la science et de la technologie aux cultures* (UNESCO, 1977), the danger of cultural disarray and the loss of goals in contemporary culture are caused by science and technology through an indirect process of transference. On the consequent threat to the ethical-mythical nuclei of cultures, see P. Ricoeur, "Civilisation universelle et cultures nationales," in *Histoire et Vérité,* 3rd ed. (Paris, 1955), pp. 286–300.

Discussion Report Two

In his paper McGrath gives us a profile of the process through which *Lumen Gentium* and *Gaudium et Spes,* Medellín and Puebla came to be produced by the awakening ecclesial consciousness of Vatican II and the Latin American Church, 1962–79. It is fitting that this book on culture – as creative communal memory – should record this prominent leader's account of historic events which engraft fresh life onto the millennial roots of the Catholic Christian Church, the oldest communal memory and creative cultural body of Europe and both Americas.

The learned discussants, however, largely ignored historical glories to focus on very recent pastoral experiment and creative theology, *promocion popular* and people's participation, introduced in tandem by Scannone and McGrath. Many conferees showed awareness that perhaps we now become observers and/or participants privileged to attend history in the making and the Church being reborn, through fresh incarnations of nature and culture and grace in triune symbiosis.

"Evangelization of culture" becomes a clear pastoral priority of Puebla, of Latin pastors and theologians, of Pope John Paul and his new Pontifical Council for Culture. The priority role of the Latin poor as participants and leaders is *the new* good news, according to McGrath and Scannone.

The poor are not only objects of "the preferential option for the poor." They are also subjects, main actors and initiators. Not only as *delegados* of the Word, and as *animadores* of basic communities: After five or six years in these local ministries, despite their elementary level of formal schooling, they have become so knowledgeable about the Bible and Vatican II, Medellín and Puebla, that some have chosen the priesthood. Special seminaries are created for them. Latin America's "Church of the Poor," McGrath explained, is becoming the Church *led by* the poor – as laity and as clergy.

Scannone repeated several times in discussion the most telling theme of his paper: "Evangelization of culture" in Latin America must aim above all at further and deeper evangelizing of the *cultura popular* of the peasant and slum-dweller, who have assimilated Gospel values and spiritual wisdom, a communal ethos and worthy ethics through five centuries of popular religiosity, nourished often by Amerind and African religious traditions. This *mestizaje* crossbred culture, too long despised by Europeanized elites, still bears many Gospel values and must be further evangelized today.

This is a main function of the *comunidades eclesiales de base* – full of promise though still so young—together with other Vatican II pastoral and theological methods, liturgical and educative practices, adapted to local reality.

These themes dominated three hours of discussion, stimulated by questions and comment which probed the ecclesial scene and cultural stage of both continents. The Latin Church and culture of the *poor* is difficult to perceive by Catholics imbued with North America's culture of *power*—economic, political, technological, military, and media power.

Cardinal Dearden addressed the first question. He cited McGrath's assertion that leadership within the Latin Church now arises from the poor and moves up to challenge and influence the middle and upper classes. The opposite is the usual case. Leadership normally comes from the higher and educated levels, then moves downward through the rest of society. How explain this remarkable reversal? Above all the former Archbishop of Detroit, who helped draft *Lumen Gentium,* wanted to know: "How do wealthy Catholics react toward clergy and Church in view of Puebla's preferential option for the poor?"

McGrath readily admitted this pastoral dilemma between poor and rich: "Moving around Latin America, upperclass Catholics do complain to us that we give our attention and priority only—or mainly—to the poor." Some of the wealthy do show resentment; they reproach the Church for forgetting that "we also have souls and need to be saved." The charge is justified in some areas, where the poor have become the exclusive option; in McGrath's view, "We have indeed lacked adequate concern for evangelization of professionals, technicians, and others."

A main reason for this lack, however, is "the urgent need for justice ministry." To heighten consciousness of the plight of the poor and encourage their active participation as believers, the *comunidad eclesial de base,* CEB, has evolved since Vatican II and Medellín in most of Latin America's 650 dioceses. McGrath explained the evangelizing motives and pastoral steps that have led to the formation of tens of thousands of these basic Church communities. He also cited current results and trends which could affect not only the "evangelization of culture," but the "acculturation of the Church" by the ecclesial experience and ministry of the poor themselves. The points that follow were elicited from McGrath by questions and comment from a dozen conferees.

1. In the past clergy lived in the larger towns and waited for the faithful to come to services in the large central churches, usually built by the wealthy or the state. The priest traveled a few times each year to outlying villages, perhaps a dozen or more, for special feastdays. In our generation the population of Latin America has doubled; over a hundred million peasants have moved to new slum areas (barriados, favelas, callampas) around the cities. In recent years, as McGrath put it, "the Church has moved out among them and their misery."

2. A priest or sister goes into the new slum, visits around, and gathers forty or fifty families for prayer and the sacraments. They talk over their situation. After a few visits leaders come forth, one of whom becomes responsible in the locality. They meet first in a family's shack, under a tree, on a vacant lot; within a few months they have built a shed–as combination church and neighborhood hall–of bamboo and reeds, scrap, tin cans, cardboard. Leaders from twenty to thirty little communities gather for monthly training sessions with a sister or priest or lay minister at the parish church, a mile or two distant. They come from the country, five to fifteen miles away, often afoot. Together the lay delegates prepare Sunday liturgy of the Word for the coming weeks. They return with the Eucharist from the parish church for communion and worship as a neighborhood group in their own ecclesial shed.

3. CEBs do not "spring up," McGrath insisted. An evangelizer must go out to sow the seed. The new leaders require–and desire–formation and instruction. As these mature they are commissioned by the priest or bishop as *delegados* of the Word, as *animadores* of the basic community. McGrath recounted the development of a rural vicariate of his archdiocese during the past fifteen years. Six parishes from the area, each with about fifty base communities. From these CEBs about 600 lay ministers gather every three months in a diocesan training center for four days of instruction, formation, and experience-sharing. These are workers and farmers with four or five years of schooling on the average. However, McGrath reported, "They can stand up and talk. They become familiar with the main teachings of Vatican II, with the documents of Medellín and Puebla–and with the New Testament."

4. Prior to the Puebla Conference in 1979, these 600 lay delegates of the Word, these community leaders of rural Panama, held special sessions to ponder and discuss the preparatory documents and to counsel their archbishop from their own faith experience as lay ministers and citizens, spouses and parents. Many dioceses all over Latin America followed the same process, McGrath recounted, so Puebla was deeply influenced by these voices of the poor. To an increasing degree "these are elected heads of Catholic organizations in the dioceses. The Church now becomes *led* by the poor, in lay ministry and, of late, in the priesthood as well."

5. Before Vatican II, McGrath explained, very few from worker or peasant families became priests. The prior requirement of a classical education over a dozen or more years was the privilege of the upper class only. Now, however, after a few years of training and service in lay ministry, some of the *delegados* desire to become priests. In McGrath's diocese, forty of these CEB alumni are now candidates for priestly ordination in a special seminary set up two years ago, modeled on an experiment of longer duration in Colombia. The archbishop predicted that the "entry of peasants and workers as priests in sufficient numbers will give a new hue to the Church and its leadership."

McGrath foresaw the possibility of comparable leader training programs in social and economic ministry.

6. To put these developments in the perspective of the past twenty years, the concept and phrase "Church of the poor" was introduced to the Universal Church by Latin bishops in St. Peter's Basilica during the first session of Vatican II, October 1962. McGrath recalled that six years later at Medellín, *communidades ecclesiales de base* were mentioned: "They had begun, but most bishops had not yet experienced CEBs. Medellín was a prophetic announcement. It impacted the Latin Church and its poor with a great glare of light, which stirred dramatically initial awareness of injustices and oppressive situations."

7. By 1979, eleven years later, some three hundred dioceses had begun basic Church communities through which the poor find their voice. "Puebla," McGrath emphasized, "received much more preparation than had Medellín, from the people themselves in their faith communities. The bishops brought a great amount of documentation and a much more assimilated ecclesial presence to Puebla from the people themselves—from the hills and valleys and countryside, all over Latin America. Puebla was *made by the people,* from the life of the Local Church."

Scannone's paper and follow-up commentary uncovered for us the root culture of the Latin poor which generates and nourishes their young pastoral progeny, the basic ecclesial communities, as set forth by McGrath. Dozens of questions and much critical commentary during joint discussion of both papers showed the surprise of most participants, and the chagrin of some, at the key role assigned to cultural *mestizaje,* first conceived in the 1500s and still alive today.

This *mestizo* culture, as the Spanish term indicates, is a mixture, a crossbreed, whose "foundation event," Scannone repeatedly explained, "was the cultural intermingling of the Iberian and the indigenous cultures," Amerind and African. "This new culture was the product of conquest and violence, but also the product of vital encounter and synthesis, with its own distinct quality, different as a child from its progenitors."

During this "process of cultural *mestizaje,*" Scannone insisted, "the aboriginal cultures sought to respect and retrieve their own aboriginal values." At the same time, "evangelization was decisively influential in the birth of the *mestizo* culture," leading to "the formation of the 'cultural ethos' of Latin America and the traditions of wisdom and ethics which find expression today in various forms of popular Catholicism." Scannone and McGrath kept returning to the fresh significance given at Puebla to this popular religiosity and to the recent movement for positive evaluation of *mestizo* culture, among scholars and theologians as well as in pastoral method and community settings.

European and North American discussants raised a score of questions.

Issues about mixed-bred *mestizaje* and basic Church communities, both closely identified with the poor and the preferential option they now receive from Latin pastors, might be summarized in this overarching query: How is the *mestizo* culture, five centuries old with roots in millennial Amerind civilizations and Afro-tribal myths, related (or opposed) to the "modern world" culture with which the Catholic Church now seeks to catch up via aggiornamento, as urged by *Gaudium et Spes*?

Cuen noted twin global thrusts of the Church since Vatican II: 1) promotion of economic and human development among all peoples, and 2) evangelization by open dialogue with international movements and cooperation with transnational organizations. In his view, these positive steps for evangelizing the cultures and structures which affect Third World development require profound knowledge of underdevelopment and its causes. Bishops have approached these issues "in pastoral style," but most are not aware of the economic, historical, and geographic causes. The cultures of many "less-developed countries are permeated with societal irresponsibility – in the family, the economy, and work, concerning the common good." Cuen cautioned that raising vain hopes "among those we want to liberate can lead to resentment; this is dangerous, anarchical, explosive."

Bartell warned about the "heavy policy implications" if the Church overidentifies with the localized culture of the poor. "This could be a trap," because the Church must deal with culture today as a universal phenomenon. To an increasing degree, Bartel continued, as economic and political systems take on global dimensions, the Church's apostolate also becomes more international. Worldwide systems controlled by the rich and the local cultures of the poor must both find place on "the Church's total global agenda." The Gospel calls us to reconcile the two sectors, not to "seem anti-rich and anti-international."

Pike evoked the Spanish experience of popular culture eight centuries ago as a possible historical analogy to the role of Latin *mestizaje* today. He explained that "twelfth-century Spain was converted to *cultura popular* by the masses," mainly by their exaltation of the Virgin. While this analogy offers much hope today, Pike recalled "its seamy side of interaction between the masses and elites." In Spain this popular religiosity stimulated "intolerance of the masses toward nonbelievers, which led to the Inquisition." A comparable "danger of manipulation" arises if "the poor of Latin America become intolerant of the rich, especially if supported by ideology."

Lobkowicz affirmed that in Germany and France also the Church succeeded by the fourteenth century in evangelizing the culture of the peasants. This provided an anchor of faith which enabled the Church to survive the Enlightenment. He asked for other historical examples of cultural and leadership roles by the poor.[1]

Gremillion, drawing from boyhood and pastoral experience in Louisiana, cited the stirring history of the black churches, mostly Baptist, begun in the plantation South of the U.S.A. after the Civil War: "The blacks were serfs, sharecroppers, without economic or political power, with little schooling, deprived of social status by whites, rich and poor alike. In the 1870s they began organizing small rural churches of twenty to a hundred members, very similar to the Latin basic communities of today, with one of their number as part-time preacher. This provided for blacks the only gathering and leadership opportunity in most localities, a place for communal discussion and decision, where cultural expression was stimulated. The spirituals were born and oratory flourished, jazz and the blues resulted; sense of community and group initiative were cultivated. After World War II, these Baptist churches, rural and city, provided the network and leadership for the struggle toward social equality, political participation, and economic justice–exemplified by the work of Rev. Martin Luther King, Rev. Andrew Young, and Rev. Jesse Jackson, their congregations and colleagues."

Besides the *mestizaje* culture of the poor and the basic communities which it animates–and their relation to "the powerful rich" and global modern culture–two other discussion subjects must be highlighted: Liberation theology and Marxist analysis. Neither of these two elements of today's Latin ecclesial "problematique" received systematic attention during the Conference. As touched on in the give-and-take, only snatches can be reported.

Lambert asked whether "theology of liberation is an impulse or an obstacle to the development and identity of CEBs." McGrath emphasized that for him, and for pastors as a whole, the basic community is above all an *ecclesial* creation, a community of the Word and of the Eucharist, and that in most the members and the leaders are the poor, with very modest education. "Among these, liberation theology is not usually posed and discussed theoretically. Starting from their own social and cultural situation, they become aware of their struggle, including the sense of striving to form their own community. From Church documents, especially from Puebla and local pastorals, they perceive overall support for the liberation they seek."

Normally, McGrath continued, although CEB members do "theologize" about God and Gospel, concerning themselves and their situation, "they do not work out any particular theology of liberation." Their own sense of and thinking over liberation provides an impulse, rather than a hindrance, for CEBs. McGrath stated that, "As a pastor, I avoid the term *liberation theology.* Puebla does also. Because significant differences have arisen among the many authors during its evolution." This required identifying each theology by name and by its historical stages for accuracy. In discussing this process, we must constantly ask: "What and whose liberation theology are you speaking about?"

Scannone expressed the view that "theologies of liberation" as a plural group "are helpful to basic Church communities." They do have differences, as McGrath said, because they are "really historical creations formed through the light of faith applied to particular pastoral situations." These pastoral situations vary enormously in different historical periods and today in the diverse regions of the world. "If the Gospel is truly God's Good News for all humans," Scannone went on, "then evangelization takes place via varying cultural mediations." In the past these took on and transmitted diverse cultural forms – Greek, Roman, Byzantine, baroque, etc. Similarly, in Latin America today, "there are elements of Marxist analysis which are valuable for evangelization."

Such elements of "Marxist analysis" listed by Scannone include: 1) clearer acknowledgement of the *material* element of culture, not as determining but as conditioning human society; 2) more energetic grasp of the *symbols* of culture, as set forth by Ricoeur, from Marxist and Freudian insights; 3) *conflict* as historical reality, of which the Cross is the primary Christian symbol. Scannone warned that cultural mediation can expose theology and evangelization to ideologies which, "if Marxist, can lead to politicization."

McGrath affirmed that if a particular theology of liberation "becomes connected with a particular political movement, serious problems can arise." Some leftists would like "to take over the CEBs and orient them toward Marxist revolution." For that reason, the bishops at Puebla insisted on the *ecclesial* nature of the base communities and so identified them by name. In some cases, the archbishop of Panama reported, leftists enter a community and fail to politicize it, then abandon the pastoral milieu to join more radical groups, even guerillas. On the other hand, some "more mature CEBs now acquire a social presence and punch. Such is the case in Brazil; there the role of the basic Church communities for the social mission of evangelization becomes substantive."

In Argentina, the Society of Jesus now attempts to "evangelize the culture of the poor" within the formation program of its own members. Scannone explained the experiment: Heretofore almost all Argentine Jesuits were recruited from the upper class. Even the occasional candidate from the lower class was "de-culturized" and "re-formed" along the ideals of classical education and lifestyle. Currently, however, "men from the barrio are sought out. These sons of workers are not stripped of their *cultura popular.* They join an intercultural, interdisciplinary group of candidates." Mixing with other candidates educated in Paris and Munich, Fribourg and Rome, they are challenged to develop a philosophy and theology "rooted in the popular wisdom of their origins, to develop a leadership nourished both by this culture of the poor and by the best of modern scholarship."

These are some of the ways in which the Church of Latin America attempts the evangelization of that region's culture, to humanize the society and lives of its 400 million people. In closing this discussion which he chaired, Goulet stressed that we here, and the post-conciliar Church of the Americas, only now begin to discern the function of culture in evangelization and the role of Gospel values in the humanizing process innate to true evangelization. This dynamic relation of culture and Gospel values, of humanizing and evangelizing, will become ever more central to the mission of the Latin and the North American Churches in the next two decades after *Gaudium et Spes,* into the third millennium.

NOTE

1. Gustavo Gutiérrez has written recently on this very subject in *The Power of the Poor in History* (Maryknoll, N.Y.: Orbis, 1983).—Ed.

SECTION THREE

North American Power Structures and the Church's Societal-Cultural Mission

The third set of papers offer pastoral responses of the North American Church in face of the dilemmas raised by new levels of technological-industrial *power,* that vitally affect and mortally endanger all humankind. These two pastoral documents are: "Ethical Reflections on the Economic Crisis," by the Social Affairs Commission of the Canadian Conference of Catholic Bishops (CCCB), January 1983; and "The Challenge of Peace," the pastoral letter of the U.S. bishops on nuclear weapons and war, May 1983.

Both papers offer the "insider's view" of the aims, procedure, and problems of each document: by Bishop DeRoo, a member of the Canadian Commission and co-author of their statement; and by Father Hehir as chief of staff for international affairs in the U.S. Catholic Conference (USCC), and principal aide to their ad hoc committee, chaired by Cardinal Bernardin, during the three-year process of hearing, draft, hearing, and draft anew. Both papers put forth fresh approaches to the societal mission of the Catholic Church in North America, which shows a marked rate of maturation only twenty years after *Gaudium et Spes.* And both papers probe new ecclesial relations with and critique of the plural cultures of the socio-economic, geo-political region comprised of Canada and the United States, including its "superpower" dimension and grave responsibility among all nations of the globe.

The central challenges faced by the sister Churches of Latin and North America, among their regional cultures, stand forth now in startling contrast: One contends with human poverty, struggle, and hope amid societal injustice and weakness. The other confronts the technological might and political-ideological hubris of the superpowers. Both Churches respond to the pastoral Good News of God's love for all his human family.

The Peace Pastoral and Global Mission: Development beyond Vatican II

J. Bryan Hehir

This paper examines the pastoral letter of the American bishops, "The Challenge of Peace," as a theological document. Since the pastoral is an exercise of the teaching ministry of the bishops of the United States, it should be understood in light of the broader framework of Catholic social teaching.

The key to locating the pastoral letter in the wider tradition is found in the Introduction where the bishops explicitly state their dependence upon the Second Vatican Council's "Pastoral Constitution on the Church in the Modern World."[1] This chapter will examine "The Challenge of Peace" as both a product of and a response to the Pastoral Constitution. Specifically, the case argued here is that the American pastoral letter stands *theologically* on the ecclesiological foundation of the conciliar text, while *morally* it develops the arguments of the Pastoral Constitution beyond the point reached at Vatican II.

I. THE CHALLENGE OF PEACE: A PRODUCT OF THE PASTORAL CONSTITUTION

There are two ways in which the Pastoral Constitution establishes a framework for understanding the letter of the American bishops. First, the ecclesiology of the Pastoral Constitution, its description of "the presence and function of the Church in the world of today,"[2] laid the theological and pastoral foundation on which the bishops of the United States stood in writing their letter. Second, the moral argument of the Pastoral Constitution on modern warfare defined the starting point from which the bishops proceeded to address concrete aspects of the nuclear age. Both of these contributions of the Pastoral Constitution need to be explicated.

1. The Church in the World: The Conciliar Vision

In the secular media the specific positions which the pastoral letter took on contemporary questions of strategy and politics dominated all commentaries. In the Church, it is necessary also to see the place of the pastoral letter in the wider ministry of the Church.

The Pastoral Constitution of Vatican II has proven to be one of the most influential of the conciliar documents.[3] It is difficult to imagine the bishops of the United States issuing their pastoral letter in 1983 if they had not been schooled in the ecclesiology of the Pastoral Constitution for the last eighteen years. There are three aspects of the theology of the Pastoral Constitution which prepared for the pastoral letter: 1) its definition of the *place* of the Church in the world; 2) its description of the Church's *presence* in the world; and 3) its *perspective* on the Church's teaching style.

The Pastoral Constitution provides the most comprehensive statement in modern times of the Church's *place* in the world. The conciliar document is not content either with homiletic statements that the Church should be active in the affairs of the world, or even with a repetition of previous moral teaching on specific social questions.

Rather, the distinctive contribution of the conciliar text is that it provides a theological rationale for the entire social ministry of the Church. The significance of this contribution can be grasped by showing what the Pastoral Constitution adds to the social teaching of the last hundred years. Embodied in a succession of papal encyclicals from Leo XIII through John Paul II, the "social teaching" has been principally devoted to an articulation of the dignity of the person and the defense of the spectrum of human rights and duties which flow from and protect that dignity. These twin themes of human dignity and human rights have been incorporated in a developing moral vision which has assessed the conditions of the industrial revolution, the postwar interdependence of the globe and today's post-industrial society.

Noticeably absent, even in the best of the social encyclicals, has been an explicit discussion of how the social vision is related to a theological understanding of the Church's nature and mission. The gap has been an ecclesiological one, a failure to join the activity of the Church in the world to the inner nature of the Church. The lack of such a statement has the effect of leaving the valuable social tradition at the edge of the Church's life; it resides there as an aspect of the Church's ministry but not a central focus of its life.

The Pastoral Constitution establishes an explicit theological relationship between the moral vision of Catholic social teaching and its ecclesiological significance. The linkage is made in two steps.

First, the Pastoral Constitution takes the key concept from the social teaching and describes the Church's role in society in light of it. The Church, says the conciliar text, "is at once the sign and the safeguard of the transcendental dimension of the human person."[4] In this passage the tasks of protecting human dignity and promoting human rights take on ecclesial significance. They are not purely "secular" functions toward which the Church is benignly but distantly disposed. Rather, the Pastoral Constitution calls the Church to place itself in support of these tasks in every political system. The engagement of the Catholic Church, as an institution and a community, in defense of human rights in political cultures as diverse as Poland, Brazil, South Africa, and South Korea testify to the impact of this linkage of moral teaching on human rights and the ecclesial teaching on the ministry of the Church.

Second, the authors of the conciliar text recognized that it was insufficient to leave the theological argument at the point of linking the moral and the ecclesial themes. For as soon as the Church takes this linkage seriously and engages in a consistent pursuit of human rights, the question which inevitably arises is whether such activity is beyond the scope of its competence or involves a politicization of religion. The deeper issue which needed to be addressed, therefore, was how the Church influences the socio-political order without itself becoming politicized.

The response of the Pastoral Constitution, found in paragraphs 40 to 42, is clear and basic. The place of the Church in the socio-political order is shaped by the following principles: a) the ministry of the Church is religious in nature, it has no specifically political charism; b) the religious ministry has as its primary object the achievement of the Kingdom of God – the Church is in a unique way the "instrument" of the Kingdom in history; c) the power of the Kingdom is designed to permeate every dimension of life; d) as the Church pursues its properly religious ministry, it contributes to four areas of life which have direct social and political consequences; e) these four religiously rooted but politically significant goals are: 1) the defense of human dignity; 2) the promotion of human rights; 3) the cultivation of the unity of the human family; and 4) the provision of meaning to every aspect of human activity.[5]

In the theology of the Pastoral Constitution the *place* of the church in the world is set by two principles: transcendence and compenetration. On the one hand the Church, because of its religious ministry, transcends every political system, it cannot be identified with or contained within any one political system. On the other hand, the Church, precisely in pursuit of its religious ministry – adequately defined – should be engaged in the daily life of every socio-political entity. The engagement is "indirect" – that is, through the pursuit of the four goals outlined above; this form of witnessing to the life of the Kingdom in history is what the late John Courtney Murray called the principle of "compenetration."[6]

Examination of the place of the Church in the world led the Pastoral Constitution to discuss the mode of the Church's *presence* in the world. The Church must contribute to each and every political system in a manner which preserves its identity and still makes an effective contribution to a just and peaceful society. The style of presence outlined in the Pastoral Constitution is the method of dialogue: "And so the Council, as witness and guide to the faith of the whole people of God, gathered together by Christ, can find no more eloquent expression of its solidarity and respectful affection for the whole human family to which it belongs, than to enter into dialogue with it about all these different problems."[7]

The Pastoral Constitution describes the attitude which the Church brings to this dialogue with the world: the Church has something to learn and something to teach. In a spirit strikingly different from that of the eighteenth and nineteenth centuries, the Church acknowledges its need for and its desire to draw upon the various disciplines and areas of expertise which contribute to the building of contemporary society. In a major teaching document of the Council, the bishops committed themselves to a teaching style which seeks a precise understanding of contemporary problems in all their complexity prior to making moral judgments or providing religious guidance about these questions.

The willingness to learn from the world is partly motivated by the desire of the Church to contribute to a deeper sense of the human and religious significance of contemporary life. While the Pastoral Constitution exhibits an attractive modesty in the face of secular complexity, the Council was not paralyzed by the data of the empirical sciences. The pastoral desire to dialogue moves beyond listening to that of interpreting: "The Church likewise believes that the key, the center and the purpose of the whole of man's history is to be found in its Lord and Master. . . . And that is why the Council, relying on the inspiration of Christ . . . proposes to speak to all men in order to unfold the mystery that is man and cooperate in tackling the main problems facing the world today."[8] At the heart of the dense technical complexity of the age lie problems of meaning, purpose, and moral direction.

The method of dialogue was a central theme in the preparation of "The Challenge of Peace." The Bernardin committee, charged with the drafting of the letter, followed the style of the Pastoral Constitution: it first listened, then it spoke. The first year of the committee's work was largely given over to a series of "hearings" in which a number of people were invited before the committee to share their expertise and experiences.

The "witnesses" included a panel of biblical scholars, a dozen moralists of differing persuasions, a spectrum of arms control experts, two former Secretaries of Defense, a physician, two retired military officers, a panel of peace activists, and specialists in nonviolent defense and conflict resolution. The hearing process closed with a full day of discussion with representatives of the Reagan administration: the Secretary of Defense, the Under Secretary of State for Political Affairs, and the Director of the Arms Control and Disarmament Agency. Through these hearings the bishops were immersed in the problems of nuclear strategy, arms control, and the likely consequences of a nuclear war.

The process of dialogue extended to the whole Bishops' Conference when the various drafts of the pastoral letter were published for analysis and debate.

The scope of the dialogue and the degree of detail the committee addressed went beyond that used in the Pastoral Constitution, but the method of dialogue was drawn from the conciliar experience.

The dialogue was carried on within the *perspective* of the Pastoral Constitution. That perspective is expressed in the following passage from the document: "At all times the Church carries the responsibility of reading the signs of the times and of interpreting them in the light of the Gospel. . . ." The biblical phrase "signs of the times" points toward a methodological principle of the Pastoral Constitution. It means beginning the process of theological analysis with a concrete examination of the nature of the questions to be addressed, then moving to a theological reflection on the major characteristics of the problem.

The American pastoral letter began with an assessment of the "New Moment" in the nuclear age. The bishops sought first to understand the content and dynamics of this "New Moment" prior to making their contribution to it. They went on in the letter to assess the *nature* of deterrence as a predominant sign of the times before they tried to make a *moral* judgment on the policy of deterrence.

On all three of these ecclesiological themes, the place of the Church in the world, its style of presence, and its perspective, the contributions of the Pastoral Constitution directly shaped how the American bishops pursued their task.

2. The Morality of Modern Warfare: The Conciliar View

The Pastoral Constitution was approved at Vatican II twenty years after the atomic bombing at Hiroshima and Nagasaki. The letter of the bishops of the United States was published almost twenty years after the Council, but its point of departure was the assessment of modern war found in the Pastoral Constitution.

The American pastoral letter said: "The Catholic tradition on war and peace is a long and complex one, reaching from the Sermon on the Mount to the statements of John Paul II."[9] The Pastoral Constitution is one chapter in this long narrative, but it was a crucial chapter. It has determined the state of the question of Catholic teaching on warfare for the post-conciliar Church. The contribution of the Pastoral Constitution lay in its synthesis of major elements of the classical Catholic tradition and in its statement of a contemporary theology of peace for the nuclear age.

The classical character of the Pastoral Constitution is evident in the way it proposes a positive vision of peace (an idea rooted in the Scriptures and Augustine) and joins it with an ethic of limits on war (a concept found in Augustine, Aquinas, Vitoria, and recent papal teaching). Positively, the Pastoral Constitution defines peace as "more than the absence of war"; peace is "the fruit of that right ordering of things with which the divine founder has invested human society and which must be actualized by man thirsting after an ever more perfect reign of justice."[10] The building of peace at every level of society, shaping it through the values of justice, truth, freedom, and love, is the primary way to prevent war.

The Pastoral Constitution reaffirms this ancient idea, but it does so in conjunction with an equally venerable part of the classical Catholic tradition: "Insofar as men are sinners, the threat of war hangs over them and will so continue until the coming of Christ. . . . As long as the danger of war persists and there is no international authority with the necessary competence and power governments cannot be denied the right of lawful self-defense once all peace efforts have failed."[11]

These two dimensions of the classical case, mediated by the Pastoral Constitution, flow directly into the American bishops' letter. Other elements of the classical tradition are highly visible: the categories of noncombatant immunity and proportionality as key ideas of an ethic of force; a sober realism about the difficulty of building peace in a world of sovereign states, and healthy skepticism about claims that force can be both used and precisely limited.

The Pastoral Constitution mediated more than a restatement of the classical concepts for the pastoral letter. The conciliar text was acutely conscious of the different circumstances posed for any moral doctrine by the nuclear age. Its assessment of the signs of the times gave the Vatican II document a distinctively contemporary tone. The Pastoral Constitution shaped the state of the question for the American letter in three ways: its description of facts, its development of the tradition, and its definition of the moral problem of deterrence.

The contemporary tenor of the Pastoral Constitution is found in its description of the qualitatively new danger of the nuclear age and in the theological response evoked by such a new danger. The opening sentence of the conciliar text asserts that "the whole human race faces a moment of supreme crisis in its advance toward maturity."[12] The moment of supreme crisis is formed by the destructive capabilities of "the kind of weapons now stocked in the arsenals of the great powers"[13] and in the complexity of international relations today. In the face of this moment of supreme crisis the Council states a theological imperative which leads directly toward the American bishops' letter twenty years later: "All these factors force us to undertake a completely fresh reappraisal of war. Men of this generation should realize that they will have to render an account of their warlike behaviour; the destiny of generations to come depends largely on the decisions they make today."[14]

The Pastoral Constitution not only called for a "fresh reappraisal," it began the task itself. Key developments in the moral analysis of warfare are present in the conciliar text; the American letter is shaped by these concepts. An example of this is the stress on individual conscience found in the Pastoral Constitution. Precisely because the destiny of future generations depends upon present choices, the Council sharpens the responsibility of conscience which each person bears regarding decisions of war and peace. The classical formulation, which held that on questions of this magnitude the "presumption of the laws" meant that the burden of proof rested upon the citizen who dissented on moral grounds, is not found in this document. Instead there is a reaffirmation of binding principles of natural law and an instruction that "Any action which deliberately violates these principles, and any order which commands such actions is criminal and blind obedience cannot excuse those who carry them out."[15]

This stress on conscience is then extended to include praise for those who "forgo the use of violence to vindicate their rights . . . provided it can be done without harm to the rights and duties of others and of the community."[16] This position in turn is complemented by a statement to governments that "it seems just that laws should make humane provision for the case of conscientious objectors who refuse to carry arms, provided they accept some form of community service."[17]

All this development on the doctrine of conscience and warfare is articulated within the context of a reaffirmation of the "just-war" ethic of the classical tradition. But the new weight given to the protection of the rights of conscience illustrates the stress placed on the classical vision by the conditions of modern warfare. The classical case holds, but with modifications. Both the lines of continuity and of change will be evident in American pastoral.

Finally, the contemporary character of the Pastoral Constitution is manifested by its willingness to grapple, however tentatively, with the dominant ethical question of the nuclear age, the policy of deterrence. The direct linkage between the Pastoral Constitution and "The Challenge of Peace" is more visible here than on any other topic. The Council opened the question of deterrence but did not move very far in the direction of providing guidance about it. The conciliar text admirably grasped the political and moral paradox of the problem in the following sentence: "Since the defensive strength of any nation is thought to depend on its capacity for immediate retaliation, the stockpiling of arms which grows from year to year serves, in a way hitherto unthought of, as a deterrent to potential attackers. Many people look upon this as the most effective way known at the present time for maintaining some sort of peace among nations."[18] This lucid statement of the problem was not followed by an equally clear assessment. In the next two decades leading to the American pastoral, many would struggle with the question whether deterrence is the "most effective way" or even a morally acceptable way to maintain the peace. By the time the bishops came to write their letter, the specifics of the issue could not be avoided.

In a sense the deterrence issue symbolized the challenge faced by the American bishops. Forty years into the nuclear age, twenty years after the Council, and faced with increasing political tension, galloping technology and dim prospects for effective arms control, what should a "fresh reappraisal of war" look like? The Pastoral Constitution had provided the framework of a response, but there was need for a specific address to the "moment of supreme crisis."

II. THE CHALLENGE OF PEACE: A RESPONSE TO THE PASTORAL CONSTITUTION

The purpose of this section is not to provide a detailed commentary on "The Challenge of Peace," but to select three themes which illustrate both continuity with and development beyond the Pastoral Constitution. Each topic is rooted in the conciliar document, but each is given its own distinctive character in the letter of the American bishops.

1. Dimensions of the Dialogue with the World

In the opening section of the pastoral letter the bishops establish their objectives as teachers: "Catholic teaching on peace and war has had two purposes: to help Catholics form their consciences and to contribute to the public policy debate about the morality of war. . . . As bishops we believe that the nature of Catholic moral teaching, the principles of Catholic ecclesiology and the demands of our pastoral ministry require that this letter speak both to Catholics in a specific way and to the wider political community regarding public policy."[19]

An explicit choice of which audiences they would address was one of the early decisions the bishops had to make. Both the Pastoral Constitution and Pope John's encyclical *Peace on Earth* had explicitly stated that they were written for consumption beyond the community of the Church. Both had been examples of the Church speaking to the world, but they had used different means for the dialogue.

The encyclical *Peace on Earth* exemplified the natural law ethic which has been such a major part of Catholic social teaching.[20] Its mode of discourse is philosophical, not theological; it makes extensive use of secular categories and minimal use of biblical imagery; it engages complex public issues in a detailed and sophisticated fashion. The conciliar document, written only two years after the encyclical, is distinctively different in style. The role of natural law is minimal; the categories of analysis are explicitly biblical, theological, ecclesial, and christological. The document, while addressed to all people in terms of the topics analyzed, uses an analysis which presumes some identification with the Christian faith.

The two documents, both products of Catholic teaching in the 1960s, exemplify two quite distinct ways for the Church to engage in dialogue with the world.

The differences between them are not confined to questions of language (philosophy *versus* theology); in deciding *how* the church is to conduct its dialogue with the world, we move from issues of language to ecclesiology and theology. One purpose of the natural law ethic, exemplified in the concepts and terminology of the just-war ethic, has been to allow a community of faith to address its concerns to the wider civil community. The natural law ethic is designed to provide a mediating instrument which allows an ethic rooted in a faith perspective to be explained and expressed in a way which others can grasp and support.

The issue of *language* is related, therefore, to which *audiences* the Church seeks to address in a given document. The choice of audience in turn depends upon how the Church conceives its pastoral responsibility.

The choices made by the Bernardin committee and then affirmed by the bishops in the final document took a "traditionally" Catholic position. They decided to speak to both the Church *and* the wider society. This decision shaped not only the language of the pastoral, but the logic of its moral reasoning. If appeal was to be made to the society as a whole, then mediating language, in this case "just-war" ethics, would be needed. If the Church sought to shape not only Christian witness but public policy, then engagement in highly technical issues (the nature of the deterrent, targeting doctrine, negotiating positions) would be necessary. The letter uses both mediating language and detailed analysis of intricate policy issues.

At the same time the style of the Pastoral Constitution is evident. The sharp distinction between an ethic of reason *versus* an evangelical ethic is not clearly drawn. The appeal to the witness of the Scriptures and specifically to the way of life of Jesus is a major focus in the pastoral. The extreme choices posed for Christians by the nuclear age run through the pastoral.

The trade-offs made in shaping this letter are similar to those which have been debated for centuries in the Christian Church. To choose to speak to *both* the Church and world is to lose some of the "prophetic edge" of the Scriptures. To attempt to shape public policy leads inevitably to consensus positions which are not a clear witness against the evil threatened by nuclear war.

The pastoral letter at times speaks directly and clearly to the community of the Church, particularly in Parts I and IV. For many these sections constitute the real message of the letter. Others, particularly in the media and the policy community, focus on Part II and Part III. Here the consensus choices – which should not imply that consensus is possible on every choice – are hammered out. For some in policy circles the choices made by the bishops are beyond what can be followed. For some in the Church the choices give away too much to the prevailing presumptions of policy.

There is a tension in the way the bishops chose to shape their dialogue with the world, but they found the method of speaking to both the ecclesial and civil communities closest to their sense of pastoral responsibility.

2. From Principles to Cases: The Issue of Specificity

The effective role played by the Pastoral Constitution in setting the state of the question on issues of war and peace is demonstrated by the dependence of the pastoral letter on it. At the same time, it is clear from reading the two documents that the eighteen-year interval was a time of significant development in Catholic theological thought on the ethics of war in the nuclear age. The best way to illustrate both themes – dependence by the pastoral on the Council, and development beyond the conciliar analysis – is to examine the principles of the Pastoral Constitution and the conclusions of "The Challenge of Peace."

To examine both principles and conclusions is to highlight a fundamental decision made by the bishops in the preparation of their pastoral. It involved the willingness to draw specific conclusions in a teaching document. The Pastoral Constitution is strong on the articulation of basic principles, but not very expansive about the consequences of applying these principles to policy choices and personal decisions. Such caution is very understandable both in terms of the *kind* of document the Council produced (a document for the whole Church) and the *time* when it was written (twenty – not forty – years into the nuclear age).

When the U.S. bishops chose to address issues similar to those faced by Vatican II, they did so as pastors in one of two major nuclear nations. This meant that the pastoral responsibilities they exercised were more specifically defined than those of a general council of the Church. The specific choices they had to address were more concretely articulated by the widespread public debate going on in the United States about nuclear policy, and the need to indicate the role of moral principles in policy choices was more urgent. The risk of maintaining the same level of generality as the conciliar text was that the meaning of the moral principles would be blunted, the opportunity to place the voice of the Church decisively in the midst of the public debate would be lost, and the developments which had occurred theologically since the Council would not be well utilized by the episcopal magisterium of the local Church.

At the same time the willingness to be specific needed to be balanced by principles of interpretation which made clear that increasing specificity on the part of the bishops meant declining moral authority. This is a general principle of moral analysis; as one moves from statements of clear principle to the application of such principles to complex and concrete situations, the mixture of principle and fact means that a number of contingent judgments must be made which are open to debate by others.[21] The acknowledgment of this general principle was particularly necessary in the pastoral letter, not only because of the intricacy of the nuclear issues, but also because other episcopal conferences in other parts of the world were also addressing many of these same issues and could quite legitimately differ from judgments made in the American pastoral letter. The decision, therefore, to be specific in judgment and flexible in interpretation was an attempt to reconcile several legitimate concerns of the bishops as teachers in the Catholic Church. They desired to use the wisdom of the universal Church, to fulfill their responsibilities as pastors of a local Church, to open a process of serious examination of these issues in their congregations, and to be fair to their brother bishops in other parts of the world.

The issues of the *use* of nuclear weapons and the strategy of *deterrence*, both found in Part II of "The Challenge of Peace," illustrate how the American bishops sought both to use the classical moral teaching and to extend its contemporary application.

Three cases of use were considered. The Pastoral Constitution had performed a significant service by restating with great clarity the just-war principle of noncombatant immunity.[22] The American bishops not only reaffirmed the binding force of this principle but applied it to one of the key questions in the strategic debate when they ruled out retaliatory strikes against civilian centers, even if our cities had been hit first. Such a judgment stands as a moral barrier against a tactic which has been proposed more than once in the nuclear age.[23]

The clarity of the principle of noncombatant immunity and its very special role in Catholic ethics made the step between principle and application very short. This was not the case when the bishops addressed two other cases of use: "first use" and limited nuclear war. On both questions the pastoral letter entered an arena of intense controversy. On both questions one finds the debate among strategists yielding very different views.

The bishops examined both issues from the perspective of moral principles, but they were aware that in neither case could they escape the task of reading the signs of the times, of understanding why the technical authors divide over the empirical data. Both *Peace on Earth* and the Pastoral Constitution had questioned whether the criterion of proportionality could be observed in a nuclear exchange. The American letter, using proportionality as its principal but not exclusive criterion, made a specific judgment against the moral acceptability of first use of nuclear weapons and expressed radical skepticism about the possibility of containing a "limited" nuclear exchange.[24]

In both instances the bishops of the United States took specific positions not previously found in either the papal literature nor, to my knowledge, in any statement of another episcopal conference. On both questions the bishops staked out a position for themselves in the public debate, and they openly acknowledged that the very strength and specificity of their moral judgments invited debate about them within the Church and in the society.

The complexity of first use and limited war pales when the topic of deterrence arises. This has been the key political and moral issue of the nuclear age. It does not yield easily to the resources of reason or faith. We have already seen how the Pastoral Constitution opened the topic for consideration in 1965. In the period from 1965 to 1980 the debate in the Church about deterrence intensified in theological writing and in the community of peace activists. In the United States, Cardinal Krol's congressional testimony in 1979 served as a catalyst in the discussion. The Cardinal had rendered a judgment of "toleration" of the deterrent on the condition it be used to move the superpowers toward effective arms control and disarmament.[25]

A qualitatively new impetus was given to the debate when Pope John Paul II addressed the deterrence question in a message sent to the U.N. Special Session on Disarmament (1982): "In current conditions 'deterrence' based on balance, certainly not as an end in itself but as a step on the way toward a progressive disarmament may still be judged morally acceptable."[26]

The bishops were already deeply into the deterrence debate when John Paul II spoke to it. They continued to struggle with the question for the next year. The final version of the pastoral letter illustrates the dynamic of development which had occurred since Vatican II. The essential judgment of the American bishops on deterrence is that of "strictly conditioned moral acceptance."[27] Each word is necessary to put the judgment in perspective.

Shorn of all modifiers the verdict is "acceptance" rather than "condemnation." Clearly the Holy Father's statement plus the bishops' own struggle with the various elements of deterrence were the moving forces in this final judgment. But it is not their intent to give a blank check to every form of deterrence or to every proposal made in the name of deterrence.

Hence the meaning of "strictly conditioned" must be precisely understood. The phrase is designed to place two kinds of limits on deterrence. The first is temporal: the argument of the pastoral is that the marginal justification accorded deterrence means it is acceptable *only* if it is used as a step toward a different kind of basis for national and international security. We are not to be complacent, politically or morally, about deterrence.

The second limit is analytical: deterrence is such a faulty and dangerous way to keep the peace, that it must be contained to its most limited function.

The bishops enumerate a series of nine conditions designed to limit the role and function of deterrence. Here again they must be specific to be effective. They oppose: 1) hard target kill weapons; 2) blurring the distinction between nuclear and conventional forces; 3) the quest for superiority in the arms race; and 4) the extension of deterrence into war fighting strategies.[28]

All of these specific judgments on use and deterrence go beyond the analysis of previous Catholic teaching. But each judgment is rooted in the principles and perspective of the prior teaching. In this way the pastoral letter seeks to preserve what has been received and to use it creatively and constructively.

3. From "Presence in the World" to Issues of Identity

The Pastoral Constitution called the Church to be present in the midst of the drama of history, to be visible and vocal at all the key places where decisions are made which shape the fabric of human life. The pastoral letter is an attempt by one local hierarchy to respond to the conciliar call, to be present in the midst of the nuclear debate.

But "presence" is not a static category. To be present in the style of the Pastoral Constitution is to face questions about our identity as a Church and our vocations as Christians. These are the questions which the Church in the United States struggles with in virtue of its response to the Pastoral Constitution.

The questions of identity arise from the dialogue to which the Church is called by Vatican II. As the pastoral letter was being prepared and the successive drafts were published for public scrutiny, four different forms of dialogue became evident.

The first, perhaps the most dramatic, was a classical church-state dialogue. The ethic of war and peace touches upon issues of "national security." No state can be indifferent when a major institution in society questions the legitimacy or morality of the means proposed to guarantee the security of the nation. But the pastoral letter raises precisely these questions. One commentator wrote of the pastoral: "The Catholic bishops' logic and passion have taken them to the very foundation of American security policy."[29] In brief, neither Church nor state can be neutral when a serious examination of "national security" occurs. The issues of politics and morality are so closely linked that each will feel its identity is at stake. But to enter this argument the Church needs a clear sense of its role in society, of its teaching obligation, of the limits and the scope of its pastoral responsibility. All of these themes surround the concrete questions of war and peace.

A second dialogue which has been a byproduct of the pastoral involves religion and science. This topic has not been a happy one since the Enlightenment, and it has touched upon the identity of religious faith and its meaning in a scientific age. Many times the Church appears on the defensive. The experience of the pastoral has been one of positive engagement of religion and science, an opportunity to illustrate that at the heart of scientific power, as embodied in the nuclear age, there stand moral questions which must be addressed and do not yield simply to more technical data. But the dialogue also is an opportunity for the church to use the resources of science to probe the very problem it seeks to assess in moral terms.

A third dialogue involves the Church and the university. The terms of the nuclear debate have been set in the academic world. The very complexity and dynamism of the nuclear age forces the government to rely upon research to define the questions it must decide. Shaping the intellectual debate means helping to shape political decisionmaking. The pastoral has become a much discussed resource in university communities. This too provides an opportunity for the Church to define its identity as a major contributor to one of the intractable intellectual and political problems of the day.

Finally the dialogue between Church and state and the Church and other major institutions in society moves back inside the community of the Church itself. The bishops have conducted the dialogue which led to the pastoral letter. Now they put their finished product into the hands of the people of the Church. The attention which the other levels of dialogue with the world have attracted means that our dialogue in the Church will be watched carefully. As we discuss war and peace, the Catholic moral tradition and the American political tradition, we will be forging an image of the Church in our culture. The discussion will cut across the proper role of the Church on public issues, the questions of personal and professional choice in the nuclear age and the cooperation of the Church with other institutions. How we decide these issues will project an identity for the Catholic church in American society.

The Council called us to be present in the world. The pastoral has given us a very visible presence. The quality of our presence is now going to be tested.

NOTES

1. "The Challenge of Peace: God's Promise and Our Response," A Pastoral Letter of the National Conference of Catholic Bishops (Washington, D.C.: U.S. Catholic Conference, 1983) no. 8. Cited hereafter as "The Challenge of Peace" with paragraph number.

2. Vatican II, The Pastoral Constitution on the Church in the Modern World, no. 2 in A. Flannery, O.P., ed., *Vatican Council II: The Conciliar and Post-Conciliar Documents* (Collegeville: Liturgical Press, 1975), cited hereafter as The Pastoral Constitution with paragraph number.

3. For commentary see: J. C. Murray, "The Issue of Church and State at Vatican II," *Theological Studies* 27 (1966) 580–606.

4. The Pastoral Constitution, no. 76.

5. Ibid., no. 40.
6. Murray, p. 600.
7. The Pastoral Constitution, no. 3.
8. Ibid., no. 10.
9. "The Challenge of Peace," no. 7.
10. The Pastoral Constitution, no. 78; the same theme is found in John XXIII, *Peace on Earth* in J. Gremillion, *The Gospel of Peace and Justice* (New York: Orbis Books, 1979).
11. The Pastoral Constitution, no. 78.
12. Ibid., no. 77.
13. Ibid., no. 80.
14. Ibid.
15. Ibid., no. 79.
16. Ibid., no. 78.
17. Ibid., no. 79.
18. Ibid., no. 81.
19. "The Challenge of Peace," no. 16
20. *Peace on Earth,* in Gremillion, cited.
21. For comments on this theme see: John Courtney Murray, *We Hold These Truths* (New York: Sheed and Ward, 1960), p. 272; R.B. Potter, *War and Moral Discourse* (Richmond, Va.: John Knox Press, 1969); J. Gustafson, "Context Versus Principles: A Misplaced Debate in Christian Ethics," *Harvard Theological Review* 58 (1965), 171–202.
22. The Pastoral Constitution, no. 80.
23. "Under no circumstances may nuclear weapons or other instruments of mass slaughter be used for the purpose of destroying population centers or other predominantly civilian targets. . . . Retaliatory action whether nuclear or conventional which would indiscriminately take many wholly innocent lives must also be condemned." "The Challenge of Peace," nos. 147–148.
24. "The Challenge of Peace," nos. 50–161.
25. Cardinal John Krol, Testimony on SALT II, *Origins,* 1979, p. 197.
26. John Paul II, Message to the Second Special Session of the United Nations General Assembly Devoted to Disarmament, June 1982.
27. "These considerations of concrete elements of nuclear deterrence policy, made in light of John Paul II's evaluation, but applying it through our own prudential judgments, lead us to a strictly conditioned moral acceptance of nuclear deterrence. We cannot consider it adequate as a long term basis for peace." "The Challenge of Peace," no. 186.
28. Ibid., nos. 188–191.
29. Stephen S. Rosenfeld, "The Bishops and the Bomb," *Washington Post,* October 29, 1982, Op-Ed page.

Culture, Gospel Values, and the Canadian Economy: The Church Enters the Public Dialogue

Bishop Remi J. DeRoo

In his discourse to the Pontifical Council for Culture, January 18, 1983, Pope John Paul stated our task with uncommon clarity: "It is in the name of the Christian faith that the Second Vatican Council committed the whole Church to listen to modern man in order to understand him and to invent a new kind of dialogue which would permit the originality of the Gospel message to be carried to the heart of contemporary mentalities. We must then discover the apostolic creativity and the prophetic power of the first disciples in order to face new cultures" (no. 3).

Gaudium et Spes has in fact set in motion a new dynamic in the dialogue between the Church and contemporary humanity. That Vatican II constitution is also the reflection of an already developing awareness within the Church that contemporary humanity must be addressed where it is, in time and place, in culture and language.

The Canadian experience of this reality, as reflected through the Conference of Bishops, can be traced back more than thirty-five years, although it was only with their statement of January 1983, "Ethical Reflections on the Economic Crisis," that the nature of the dialogue became more clearly focused. This sudden taking hold of a bishops' statement by the general community was perhaps due to the topic itself, or to the kind of language used, or to the readiness of the listeners to hear, but more probably it was due to the urgency of the situation.

The Social Affairs Commission (SAC) of the Canadian Conference of Catholic Bishops (CCCB) issued the document in its own name rather than in that of the whole Conference. Of course, the President's authorization to publish assumed the tacit agreement of the other bishops whose previous teachings were herein developed. The statement broke on the Canadian scene with such energy that it set in motion a dialogue within the whole community that lasted throughout the year.

As a member of SAC and a coauthor of the statement, I experienced a most intense pastoral year in 1983. I was tested, as in a crucible, by pressures and counterpressures within both the Church community and the general community. Indeed, all the members of the SAC and a number of CCCB members had the same experience.

Personally, the experience caused me to clarify my own role and personal mission as bishop. It led me to a clearer understanding of ecclesiology, namely the nature of the Church in its role of sacramentality, of mediation, and of communion.

I now have a deeper perception of the episcopal office, understood as shepherding, overseeing, and unifying. A bishop is related to the pilgrim people of God not only as sacramentalized by Baptism, but also as called to a deeper experiential faith by discipleship and mission. The bishop, as well, relates to all those people who accept the transcendent dimensions of humanity, but do not identify their search for meaning with the Roman Catholic institutional or intellectual categories.

More specifically, I have never been told by so many people, many of them professed atheists, alienated Catholics, humanists, and members of other world faiths, that our pastoral statement revealed to them a different Church than the one they had known: a Church of compassion and hope; a Church that proclaims the "good news."

While not consciously following a master plan or detailed blueprint, the CCCB in general and the SAC in particular have followed experiential and inductive processes similar to those stated in *Gaudium et Spes* and found in the experiences of Latin America and the United States of America.

What I present here now is a concrete example of this new dialogue with contemporary humanity. In this case, it is a dialogue with the economy. We call it "Ethical Reflections on the Economic Crisis."

THE STATEMENT

New Year's Event

The interaction between Gospel values, cultural priorities, and economic institutions has so far received only limited study. As a modest attempt to further this vital investigation, I submit the following observations. They are based on a recent, much publicized experience which has proved to be a historic episode in the Canadian annals of Catholic Social Action.

When the Canadian Bishops Social Affairs Commission issued its statement "Ethical Reflections on the Economic Crisis" at the beginning of 1983, few people anticipated the storm of publicity that greeted its appearance. No Church document in Canadian history ever created an equivalent reaction. It held center stage in the mass media for several weeks. Subsequent events continued to draw attention to it as the months went by. Network television did a half-hour special on the statement and its effects for the first anniversary.

The Social Affairs Commission's "Ethical Reflections" was released on New Year's Eve. The media generally disregarded any distinction between the eight-member Social Affairs Commission and the total Bishops' Conference comprised of one hundred and thirty members. Therefore, the message became known as the "Canadian Bishops' New Year's Statement." That perception has remained in the public mind. Many people, puzzled by the furor surrounding the Commission's statement, did not realize that such declarations were not unusual on the part of the Canadian bishops, who have been issuing messages on topics of social concern for some thirty-five years.

Crisis in the Canadian Economy

The impact of "Ethical Reflections" in Canada stemmed in part no doubt from the climate of despondency and confusion reigning throughout North America in the winter of 1982–83.

The social malaise had been the object of much analysis and comment. *Time* (January 17, 1983) indicated after a lengthy study that while leadership was required as never before from economists, their language through North America resembled "the economic Tower of Babel."

The bishops' statement made an appraisal of this continental situation. It noted that the structural crisis in the economy was endemic and international, not only limited to Canada. It described the malaise as a continuing systemic crisis, not merely a downturn phase in the economy. The future did indeed look bleak for the majority of working people who saw their opportunities for employment increasingly eroded. The specter of massive structural unemployment hovered over the horizon, threatening to become permanent.

The solutions proposed by governments and business, mainly of a monetarist nature, were seen as inadequate. "Social Darwinism" was reflected in suggestions that people should "tighten their belts" during the economic struggle, in appraisals that the survival of only the fittest elements was inevitable, and in statements by Prime Minister P. E. Trudeau during his October 1982 "fireside chats" that Canada had no choice but to compete fiercely in the international struggle. Such draconian proposals only compounded the problem and malaise.

Canadians were faced with alarming problems: an ever deepening urban crisis, poverty and illiteracy in a context of plenty, a technology seemingly beyond control, a welfare state leading to deepening alienation, increased electoral passivity, *anomie* on the part of many. All these were signs something was seriously wrong in the very structures of society. The Social Affairs Commission assessed this as a major moral crisis. It challenged people to move beyond current popular liberal political theory to a renewed biblical vision of a transformed society.

The Content of "Ethical Reflections"

"Ethical Reflections on the Economic Crisis" expressed the Social Affairs Commission's pastoral concern about the scourge of massive structural unemployment affecting millions of Canadians. The statement, while using a language familiar to the marketplace, was not a technical treatise on economics, since that is not the role of Church leaders. Rather, it offered some moral reflections about the structural disorder affecting Canadian society. It then proceeded to a series of observations concerning the social and ethical issues at stake in developing future economic strategies for Canada.

The bishops based their judgments, not on specific partisan political options, but on two fundamental Gospel principles: 1) the preferential, though not exclusive, option for the poor; and, 2) the special value and dignity of human work in God's plan for creation. They used as their central socio-economic principle, the priority of human labour over capital.

The statement identified a moral disorder in Canadian society. This disorder was brought about by certain structures in society which reversed the God-given priority of human labor over capital. The result is endless suffering of weaker people.

The Commission called for a reordering of values. The basic purpose of sound economics is to serve human needs, not to exploit people for corporate profit. Massive unemployment constitutes a social evil as well as an economic problem. Alternative solutions are urgently required.

The bishops placed their analysis in the context of the larger structural crisis of international capitalism, where changes in the structure of capital and technology impact negatively on working people. With the weakening role of the nation-state vis-à-vis multinational corporations, the poor have no global protector. The result is that on a world scale the survival of capital has taken priority over the rights of workers.

"Ethical Reflections" proposed that all Canadians henceforth work together as an authentic community in order to develop strategies for economic recovery which would realize three goals: 1) to have the needs of the poor take priority over the wants of the rich; 2) to have workers' rights come ahead of maximization of profits; and 3) to have participation of marginalized groups take precedence over the preservation of a system which excludes them.

The statement went on to suggest six short-term strategies as alternative approaches more in keeping with Gospel values.

1. Give priority to the fight against unemployment, while not ignoring inflation.
2. Stem the rate of inflation equitably, not by putting the burden on low-income people.

3. Develop an industrial strategy to create real permanent employment in local communities.
4. Sustain the social security net in a responsible manner.
5. Give labor unions a more decisive and responsible role in economic recovery strategies.
6. Involve local communities in plans of coordinated action.

The bishops also proposed some long-term alternative policies or structural orientations based on their central principle, the priority of human labor over capital.

Without halting technological progress, but re-emphasizing human values, the economy could serve basic needs and redistribute wealth and power more equitably among people and regions. Renewed emphasis would be placed on alternative models for the economy: socially useful forms of production, labor-intensive industries, appropriate forms of technology, more self-reliant economic development, community ownership and control of industries, new forms of worker management and ownership, and greater use of renewable energy.

These were suggestions, not prescriptions. They were offered as a challenge for community and political leaders to involve all the people affected by the economy in developing new alternatives. They were accompanied by a commitment on the part of the bishops to stimulate public dialogue and action to overcome what was perceived as a grave moral disorder. The bottom line was a call to conversion–societal and personal.

REACTIONS, SECULAR, AND ECCLESIAL

The reaction to the document was predictable, but the intensity of the reaction had not been anticipated. Praise and condemnation echoed back and forth in the media. The avalanche of comments and debate more than fulfilled the expectations of the Social Affairs Commission which had been to stir up many Canadians to further reflection, dialogue, and action.

Through the year 1983, countless lectures, conferences, and workshops occurred in cities and towns across Canada. The members of the Commission, along with the Commission staff, and joined by numerous supporters delivered many lectures and talks to all kinds of community groups, from parish gatherings to business meetings, from union assemblies to college seminars.

An awareness of a new model of Church came out of this experience. While the bishops were the high-profile people, the lay staff and supporters also took initiatives, and an encouraging network developed with various social activists of all persuasions and with many competent people in the social sciences.

Also, the statement served as a catalyst for a number of citizens' coalitions. It afforded these groups an opportunity to focus their concerns more precisely. The very nature of the economic dialogue and debate changed. The movement was from the technical sphere of esoteric economics to a discussion of values, priorities, and culture in Canadian society.

"Ethical Reflections" turned out to be a unifying statement causing people to work together beyond ethnic, religious, and political barriers. Positive response came from more than the Christian Churches. Humanists, atheists, members of major world faiths, and alienated Roman Catholics, all seemed to discover in this statement a kind of "new Church" of the good news.

In the months elapsed since the statement first appeared, there are signs of the beginnings of various citizens' coalitions which may engender a broad popular movement in Canada.

Naturally, a number of people have disagreed with parts of the statement or questioned some of its proposals. Among the criticism leveled at the document were its limited consultation process, its failure to recognize more clearly the benefits of modern scientific discoveries and to acknowledge beneficial Canadian achievements, its reticence about the job-creating potential of small businesses and business people. Critics claimed that while the document referred to the global context and wider implications of Canadian economic disorders, it did not adequately develop the links with the Third World. The claim was made that proposals for Canadian national self-reliance or sufficiency might impinge on the poor in the Third World and eventually prove counterproductive.

These and other objections have some validity but they overlook the fact that the statement was not intended to be an exhaustive treatise. It focused mostly on domestic aspects of the unemployment crisis. Rightly or wrongly, it assumed a certain familiarity with the many other statements that the Canadian bishops had made over the years. It had a limited and specific aim. Its function was to act as a catalyst rather than to provide a fully developed and refined treatise. The title itself indicated its limited purpose, offering some ethical reflections about an acute, contemporary malaise within Canada, even though closely linked to the global economic crisis.

THE BACKGROUND

Tackling Social Issues

The Canadian Conference of Catholic Bishops can look back over a growing tradition of social teaching and action. It began with the French-speaking "Semaines Sociales" in the 1920s and expanded into the English "Social Life Conferences" of the early 1950s. The bishops established the first Social Action Commission in 1947. From 1956 until 1976 it issued a major document each year, around Labor Day, on various aspects of social or economic issues.

A brief review of the topics of these Labor Day Messages reveals a great variety of concerns: Review of Some Socio-Economic Questions (1956); Appeal to Spiritual Values (1957); Economic Warfare (1958); Christian Attitudes Towards Social Problems (1958); Toward a Greater Collaboration between Management and Labor (1959); Labor and Immigration (1960); Social Teachings of the Church (1961); Socialization (1962); Indispensable Collaboration between Public Authorities and Intermediate Organizations (1963); Automation (1964); International Solidarity in the Distribution of the World's Goods (1965); Poverty in Canada (1966); The Economic Conditions under which the Canadian Family Lives (1967); The Church's Solidarity with Workers and Victims of Social Injustices (1968); New Powers (1969); Liberation in a Christian Perspective (1970); A Christian Stance in the Face of Violence (1971); Simplicity and Sharing (1972); Inequality Divides: Justice Reconciles (1973); Sharing Daily Bread (1974); Northern Development: At What Cost? (1975); From Words to Action (1976).

In 1977 the Social Affairs Commission set aside the practice of yearly Labor Day Messages with a fixed publication date. They chose instead to issue topical messages as current events would require.

The Bishops' Plenary Assembly of 1977 issued their most radical critique of Canadian social patterns. It was entitled: "A Society to be Transformed." It dealt with ideological problems concerning capitalism, Marxism, and possible new alternatives to these. It declared that Christians acting in the light of Gospel principles should feel free to engage in reflection and action leading to new social orientations and structures.

The Commission's bishops in 1979 next prepared a set of working documents entitled: "Witness to Justice." In these, following on their own guidelines of 1976, they invited people to move beyond theoretical considerations to more action-oriented policies. Their aim was to assist community leaders by providing a follow-up, a five-year plan of action.

Further messages followed: in 1980: "Unemployment: The Human Cost" and "Elderly Members of the Church," and in 1981 "The Neutron Bomb—Enough Is Enough."

Influencing Social Change

With the Second Vatican Council and *Gaudium et Spes* came a shift of emphasis. The bishops moved beyond the Social Life Conference format with its emphasis on explaining doctrine or adjusting to changes in society. The new orientation carried the commission in the direction of influencing social change itself.

Through a process of increasingly maturing social analysis, the bishops began to illustrate how doctrine is effectively applied to life. They moved beyond assessing the impact of public policies to deeper insights concerning their historic causes and their cultural foundation. By pointing to the structural disorders underlying social institutions, they guided people to see how the Gospel can challenge the very roots of social policies. Revelation then becomes more effectively an experiential Gospel. Its power and dynamism come alive through the personal and communal resurrections brought about by the Gospel's impact on life. Religion becomes a sign of hope.

As people are led from a superficial grasp of how social change affects them into initiating a pattern of actions that can influence the change itself, they become more conscious that they are free and responsible agents or subjects of their own history.

It is instructive to look back and identify some of the landmarks or highlights marking the evolution in the Canadian bishops' approach to social action since Vatican II.

Ecumenical Outreach

The first interchurch consultations on social issues began in 1964 between the Canadian Conference of Catholic Bishops and the Canadian Council of Churches. These dialogues involved the staff and resource people of both structures, not just the executive figures. The result was a flurry of creative activity coming out of this newly discovered interchurch mix.

In 1965 the Conference of Bishops was involved in what is now remembered as the "Medicare Coalition." It grouped people from all walks of life, involving many churches, popular groups, labor, business people, politicians, and other leaders anxious to guarantee for Canadians the reliable medical and hospital care which was their right as citizens. The united witness no doubt contributed to the growing public support for publicly administered health care insurance in Canada.

In 1968 the bishops participated with other church leaders and concerned groups in a conference on "Christian Conscience and Poverty" held in Montreal. It was described as a "watershed in concern and commitment on the part of Christians and the Christian churches in Canada." The governments of Canada and of six provinces participated, together with twelve sponsoring churches. Over twenty businesses and civic groups contributed resources in staff, money, and other facilities. Details of this major undertaking are recorded in a document entitled: "Pussy Cat Puurrrr or Tiger Roar." This conference came as a follow-up to the international ecumenical gatherings of Geneva (1966) and Beirut (1968).

An interchurch strategy committee report to the Canadian Council of Churches, to the Canadian Conference of Catholic Bishops and to all concerned Canadians was issued in 1969 entitled "Toward a Coalition for Development." Its recommendations for a unified strategy to combat poverty involved the following guidelines described as a fourfold ministry: 1) a review of resources and a revision of priorities – the Ministry of Penance; 2) committing more resources to development – the Ministry of Sharing; 3) animating people to action – the Ministry of Hope; 4) initiating political action – the Ministry of Justice.

It is interesting to recall that among the key issues proposed for attention were: world development, native rights, citizens' groups, and tax reform.

A joint interchurch brief to the Special Senate Committee on Poverty was also presented, on June 11, 1970. It referred to the coalition experiment which had been its launching pad. The brief asked the Canadian government to establish as its first priority social policies that would guarantee the basic rights of citizens, particularly the poorest. It suggested that the correction of unjust structures, with their negative social consequences for the marginalized and poorer elements of society, was not only a question of economic capacity or political consensus. It was primarily a question of willpower.

Ecumenical Coalitions

A further ecumenical development was emerging at the national level. It too was the result of the Second Vatican Council. Previously, Christian church relations in Canada had often been less than friendly. As late as 1945, the Protestant churches had formed a Committee to counteract what they perceived as Roman Catholic encroachments on Protestant rights. With the Council the quality of ecumenical dialogue changed dramatically.

By 1964 the Protestant churches actively sought an improvement in Roman Catholic relations. A 1965 working conference on the implications of a Canadian Health Charter led to the "Medicare Coalition" mentioned above. Common ecumenical efforts in Geneva (1966), Beirut (1968), and the Montreal Poverty Conference (1968) with its follow-up program helped the churches appreciate the need to set aside contentious differences and to concentrate on their common call to spread the Gospel and to manifest their compassion for the downtrodden members of society.

In 1969, the idea was born of a joint partnership on an *ad hoc* basis to address social issues together. The ensuing fruitful experience of practical social ecumenism encouraged the mainline Christian churches in Canada gradually to establish enabling coalitions of small-scale interchurch groups whereby the national parent bodies could more effectively deploy their limited resources to tackle major national issues of social policy.

This particular form of Canadian ecumenism is believed to have been unique in the world. It eventually (1980) became the object of a study by Sodepax under the authorship of Father John Lucal, S.J. This study, entitled "Coalitions for Social Ecumenism: The Canadian Story," was never published.

The following lists some major coalitions with the year of their foundation: ICCDR–Interchurch Consultative Committee on Development and Relief (1970); GATT-FLY (1972)–it monitors government performance at international events and on major issues like energy policy and the GATT agreement; ICPOP–Interchurch Project on Population (1973), occasioned by the World Conference in Bucharest, relates to population and immigration policies –now inactive; Ten Days for World Development (1973)–popular education on global justice issues; PLURA (1974)–an acronym representing the Presbyterian, Lutheran, United, Roman Catholic, and Anglican churches–it researches social justice issues and funds self-help group initiatives; TCCR (1975)–Task Force on Churches and Corporate Responsibility; Project North (1975)–Stewardship of Resources and Native Peoples' Rights; ICCHRLA (1976)–Inter Church Committee on Human Rights in Latin America–began with Chile; Project Ploughshares (1976)–Disarmament and Defense Policies.

These coalitions further illustrate the shift in emphasis taking place in the Canadian bishops' approach to social issues. This growth came from an early acceptance that the Canadian Bishops' Conference or some of its commissions would join in coalitions, task forces, and the like, not only to reflect on social issues, but to initiate concrete action regarding social or economic policies. In this regard, "Ethical Reflections on the Economic Crisis" represents a breakthrough.

Inter-American Involvement

The increasingly ecumenical undertakings of the Canadian bishops in matters affecting social policy also had their counterpart internationally at the level of joint Bishops' Conferences. Thus, an Inter-American Bishops' Meeting took place in Mexico in May 1971, bringing together bishops representing South America, Mexico, the United States, and Canada.

A document was produced and circulated under the joint authorship of the Inter-American Bishops' Meeting and the Canadian Commission for Justice and Peace. Its title was "The Liberation of Men and Nations: Role of the Church in the Americas." The report stated that "unjust social orders embody man's social sinfulness." It called for complete liberation from domination by both the forces of nature and the will of human beings imposing themselves on other people.

THE PASTORAL APPROACH

Contemporary Pastoral Method

The key issue is how does the Church evangelize in the world today? To evangelize in this period of cultural transition is to respond to the basic religious question of today, which is one of meaning.

To focus the question more precisely, how does the Church evangelize in a culture characterized and dominated by the market economy? Gospel values must be inserted into the culture in order to counteract "economic-ism" which reduces economics to the market economy model and thus stultifies the culture it dominates.

Some of the elements to be inserted into the culture are: the understanding of human beings as being in the image of God; an appreciation of human beings as co-creators with God of this world; a conscience for justice; a respect for human rights; the priority of labor; the opting for the poor; responsible participation of citizens in making society.

The Gospel will serve as a catalyst when inserted into the economic discourse of our culture. This is a new way of preaching. It will show that the Gospel values are in fact good news, because they point the way out of the closed circle of current economics, which produces hopelessness and despair. The hope offered is simply to point out that the people themselves, the very victims of the system, have the potential to create new futures and build up a new world.

In order to enable people to forge a new cultural vision, the long-term pastoral strategy is to return to the parables in action, following the example of Jesus.

This means firstly, to listen to the people who are the victims in order to understand the contemporary phenomenon of economic marginalization; as well, it means to develop a new type of dialogue which will permit the Gospel values to penetrate today's cultures and mentalities.

Secondly, it means exercising an apostolic creativity in modern form, by proposing a variety of alternatives; this makes manifest the prophetic power of the Gospel values.

Thirdly, similar to the parabolic actions of Jesus, which illustrated different models of action and thus brought new light and hope, so the alternative suggestions for action based on Gospel values become sources of hope and light. They hold the promise of change, of a new life, of fraternity, of participation in shaping the future, and of a respect for human dignity.

This pastoral approach presents us with a new vision of Church: not a Church content to accept the status quo as inevitable and unchangeable as in the case of an economy no longer at the service of the people; but rather a Church which calls people to create their own future instead of fatalistically resigning themselves to their marginalized condition. A Church which invents new parables and thus provides the Beatitudes or Gospel values with their new incarnation for today's world.

Thus people will understand that the Gospel is not just theory and principles, but a sign and an agent of hope in everyday life.

Gaudium et Spes marks the emerging of a new order in today's culture.

Pastoral Method for Ethical Reflections

This experiential pastoral approach can be traced back to the Vatican Council, and particularly to Canadian participation in the 1971 Synod of Justice. It is a consistent growth experience which parallels the approach of recent papal teachings, namely *Evangelii Nuntiandi, Populorum Progressio, Octogesima Adveniens,* and *Laborem Exercens.*

Part of this argument is to show how this inductive pastoral approach, based on an analysis of the signs of the times in the light of faith, has been effectively applied by the Canadian Conference of Catholic Bishops, especially through the Social Affairs Commission. The development of this approach can be seen in the bishops' "Words to Action" of 1976, through their "Witness to Justice" of 1979 and "Unemployment the Human Cost" of 1980; to the most recent "Ethical Reflections on the Economic Crisis."

The following outline demonstrates this pastoral approach as carried out by the Social Affairs Commission for "Ethical Reflections."

1. Pastoral reflection on the signs of the time:
   - immediate problems
   - deeper issues
2. Reference to Gospel principles:
   - perspective of the victims
   - option for the poor
   - priority of labor principle
3. Suggested new orientations:
   - short-term strategies to current problems
   - six points strategy for action based on new orientations
4. Long-term issues:
   - basic moral crisis indicated by structural disorders
   - suggested alternative approaches based on reordering of values
   - new priorities to combat the identified social evil
5. Challenge to the people of Canada:
   - to envision alternatives
   - to develop strategies through public debate
6. Invitation to follow a specific process involving:
   - commitment to the marginalized
   - experiential analysis directed at real problems
   - reflection on ethical principles in church teachings
   - elaboration of new visions
   - choosing new strategies aimed at solving specific problems
7. Conclusion:
   - identification of the aspirations of the poor with the voice of Christ, the Lord of History.

SOCIAL AFFAIRS COMMISSION STRATEGY

The Social Affairs Commission is committed to the empowering of the marginalized members of society, as the Canadian bishops previously indicated in 1969 in their statement on "New Powers" and their 1970 declaration of "Liberation."

The Commission will exercise a teaching role by continuing to propose to governments at various levels, and to community leaders in different spheres, social policies and social priorities which seek to guarantee the basic rights of people. It will affirm people so that they can enjoy fuller participation in shaping the future of society. Such proposals are not new, they were already voiced by the Joint Council of Churches and Bishops' Conference brief to the Joint Senate Committee on Poverty in June 1970.

The Commission will also exercise an animating role by promoting an outward process impacting on public awareness, through the mass media of communications, public forums, conferences, the staging of interdisciplinary debates, etc.

As well, this process will attempt to come to grips with the challenge of those ideological responses which distort the true nature of the Commission's message. These need to be countered by ever-increasing clarification, both of the Gospel premises from which we speak and the precise area of their application to secular issues. While the danger of ideological manipulation is ever present, it must be lucidly and courageously faced rather than evaded.

Interdisciplinary teamwork will be increasingly vital for the progress of our initiatives and the survival of the new institutions which we hope will eventually be launched through the dynamic action of the popular coalitions.

It will also be necessary to have recourse to the other disciplines, technical, sociological, behavioral, psychological, so important for a realistic teamwork approach to the complex issues of contemporary society. As we proceed, it is to be hoped that we will experience solidarity as an authentic religious act.

This will present a new image of the Church in the world. The Church will be seen as the defence of basic human rights, while accepting human beings precisely in their humanness. The Church will take the position of proclaiming the universal destiny of all created resources. In a preferential way, the Church will opt to stand with the poor and with the marginalized in society. The Church will announce a new awareness of humanity's common history and destiny. The Church will be the proclaimer of hope. The Church will stand in solidarity with all humanity beyond confessional borders. We will see a Church with a new understanding of political action, so that a political theology will develop to help handle political power and its implications for a developing culture.

TENTATIVE CONCLUSIONS

From all that has been said and from the experience of several decades of social action in Canada, one sees patterns beginning to emerge.

Pastoral Guidelines were proposed by the Canadian bishops for the construction of a new society. The did not proceed from a ready-made master plan, nor were they constantly conscious of the new values and priorities affecting society. But by proposing certain principles, Gospel insights, and authentic Christian humanism, the bishops gradually elaborated an alternative vision of a new culture that could help transform our economy.

They did not act alone, but in collaboration with others, as responsible leaders of their Christian communities. These communities expect leadership from them in focusing our collective "social memory" on our rich heritage and history, and suggesting new orientations for acceptable social alternatives. This will be done together with popular or basic communities. It will comprise the organized support not only of the Catholic faithful, but also of other churches and people of goodwill. It will include a crosscultural dialogue involving native peoples as well as the French and English communities and not forgetting the multicultural mix of the country. Thus the variety of gifts and ministries, the co-responsibility and stewardship will be made manifest as declared by the Second Vatican Council in *Lumen Gentium.* The Christian voice will be heard as the voice not only of a distant elite, but of all the people of God.

Social analysis will be appreciated not only as a scientific discipline but as an exercise in spiritual discernment as well. Thus will be encouraged forms of lay spirituality using discernment and social analysis in applying to everyday life the biblical themes of Exodus, Liberation, Salvation, and Resurrection.

Popular coalition building and solidarity networking will in turn be linked to a deeper understanding and more meaningful celebration of the Eucharist. For it is in the Eucharist that the Kingdom erupts into our lives and radiates its creative and salvific power into human relationships, social structures, and the total environment or culture. The historic struggle for justice becomes a source of hope.

Christian education too will be inspired by these insights. Popular groups and in a special way the families which are the basic units of society will be encouraged to reflect upon and adopt these insights. They will then become the source of new values and priorities in a faith-inspired culture which will promote economic renewal through a sense of sharing, respect for persons, renewed appreciation of the creative value of work, stewardship of the ecology and of natural resources. By reclaiming the Gospel as good news which authenticates their own history, people will be empowered to renew their own faith and promote its dynamic impact on a renewed culture.

This alternative culture will contribute to the promotion of an alternative economy:

- –where human beings are respected as "creators" made in the divine image;
- –where the dignity of human life is respected at all its stages;
- –where economic and industrial strategies are developed to guarantee creative full employment;
- –where a direct selective attack is made on the most urgent problems of the economy, rather than reliance on continued subsidies for the powerful sectors;
- –where a "basic needs" economy is fashioned to meet primarily the necessities of the majority, not the wants of the affluent;
- –where the arms race is set aside as economically unproductive as well as morally unacceptable;
- –where economic and industrial strategies to guarantee creative full employment are recognized as the productive human base for economic stability and social harmony.

The dialogue of faith with culture and of culture with the economy will come to a new level of consciousness as we deepen our awareness of the implications of Gospel values for the shaping of our society.

Thus we will respond more effectively to the call of Christ to imitate him by our efforts to transform society, so that people may have life and have it in abundance.

Though not explicitly elaborated in these terms, I believe some of these insights were operative in the minds of the Social Affairs Commission members when they published their "Ethical Reflection on the Economic Crisis." Hopefully these insights will continue to develop as the current crisis deepens. The Church in communion with the popular coalitions will continue its mission of promoting a more just and participatory society based on truth, justice, and love.

Discussion Report Three

Both papers begin by establishing at length the right and responsibility of the Church to address societal issues, such as the Canadian economy and the arms policy of the United States. During the entire first half of his essay, Hehir shows that *Gaudium et Spes* substantially deepened and enlarged the Church's self-understanding of her mission in society, for the achievement of the Kingdom of God in history and as "the sign and safeguard of the transcendental dimension of the human person."

Besides appeals for the same purpose to encyclicals and Vatican II, DeRoo lists by title the year-by-year messages of Canada's bishops, from 1956 until their "Plenary Assembly of 1977 issued their most radical critique of Canadian social patterns. It was entitled: "A Society to Be Transformed." It dealt with ideological problems concerning capitalism, Marxism, and possible new alternatives to these."

Discussion ranged from the new dimensions of *Gaudium et Spes* ecclesiology to the practicalities of Gospel witness and pastoral ministry within our continent's unique democratic, secularized culture. During the three-hour exchange, amid difference and debate, there grew a group consciousness of the "never-before" role to which we now awaken as North American Catholics—academics and pastors, laity and clerics alike—as a regional People of God, possessed of (and by) the industrial technological culture of a superpower, which imparts global duties and dangers of scale and substance never imagined by Augustine, Aquinas, or Assisi, by Calvin, Luther, or Loyola, by Newman or Leo XIII.

Criticism of content and doubt about the bishops' competence (and pastoral prudence) were expressed, in stronger terms than used during the previous discussions. Haas opened with very practical remarks about current political issues. The U.S. bishops, he charged, present a "partisan image of the Church, which will cause political fallout." To his mind some "Reagan supporters will feel that the Church has chosen sides. This diminishes the pastoral role of the bishops in the long run."

Dougherty criticized the U.S. bishops for descending from the level of moral teaching and general principles to the concrete cases of prudential judgments. While admitting the episcopacy's "right to influence public policy in areas of their competence, such as private schools and abortion," they have no particular expertise about armaments; rather they "draw heavily from other experts." Dougherty strongly objected to the self-assurance and pride of the writers, the "triumphalism with which the bishops have promulgated their document, almost enshrining it in a way no other has been." He compared them with "military leaders who have comparable moral concerns," but are "sometimes much more humble" than the bishops, who have much less expertise.

Hehir took these charges in stride: "All these are legitimate questions. None are outside the ambit of what we are trying to promote in our country. A person can rest comfortably in the Church with every position you have taken. Pull and tussle among us is part of what this is all about."

(As rapporteur and editor, I must raise here a signal flag: Hehir, head spokesperson for the U.S. Bishops' Conference on this issue, makes clear that promoting debate is a definite purpose of the pastoral letter. Criticism of the bishops was anticipated. Hehir clearly points to a significant development within the ecclesial consciousness of U.S. Catholics since Vatican II which this pastoral dramatizes: Disagreement, debate, and lively exchange now become quite acceptable within the maturing Church of North America, as it outgrows the immigrant's monolithic mindset of earlier years. Some long-range questions come to mind: Is America's "democratic" culture affecting this evolution? Is it invited and abetted by the openness of *Gaudium et Spes*? To what degree does this acceptance, even welcome, of difference and tension now mark ecclesial awareness in North America, as compared with other regions, such as Black Africa, Asia, Latin America, and Europe, East and West? How will this effect the evangelization of cultures and acculturation of the Gospel worldwide? And what will be the role for the Holy See?)

Returning to Hehir's response to attacks on the secular competence, political fairness, and pastoral prudence of the U.S. bishops' position on nuclear arms, he stressed that their letter criticizes the position of Democratic and Republican administrations alike since 1945. Hehir then outlined a "science of policy analysis" the bishops have followed, to arrive 1) at prudential choices, 2) from moral principles, 3) applied to empirical data, 4) in light of faith-insight. Hehir strongly reaffirmed the degree of specificity taken among the prudential choices made by the bishops, concerning "first use," for example. To show that such concreteness is characteristic of Catholic social teaching and teachers, he cited John Paul II, who praised the Camp David and SALT II agreements, who defended the right to expropriate farms in Mexico, who on landing in the Philippines told Marcos to his face that government could not impede human rights in the name of national security; add also the Pope's role in Poland, all the way back to John A. Ryan specifying a living wage sixty years ago.

Hehir noted that Catholic social teaching still joins moral principles with empirical data in the attempt to reach specific implications. The basic moral principle of the nuclear arms pastoral is identical with that of Catholic teaching on abortion: Innocents must not be killed.

Wilber asked why many Catholics accept this principle when applied to abortion, but not if applied to nuclear war. Hehir answered that such people *define* the issues differently: to them abortion is a moral question, war is political. The bishops insist that both acts are both moral and political; both involve killing innocents. In the United States, according to Hehir, the Catholic Church is the only nationwide body publicly taking the same position against both acts of killing innocents, abortion and war.

The arms pastoral purposely addressed several major groups: 1) the Catholic Church as a whole, at all levels; 2) the public policy community, including academia, media, and government, aiming especially at congressional committees, foreign and defense policy; 3) other religious communities, Protestant and Jewish. Hehir noted that, to the surprise of the U.S. bishops, the still broader community of Western Europe also showed interest, especially the German and French episcopal conferences and the Apostolic See. This raised another new issue for the North American Church: its relation to the Christian communities (and episcopal conferences) in other religio-cultural geopolitical regions of the globe, in view of the "superpower" effect of North America upon them in the economic, political, military, media, and cultural fields.

Archbishop McGrath asked Hehir to comment further on the relations of national conferences of bishops. In addressing peace and justice issues of mutual or reciprocal interest, different conferences sometimes arrive at different positions. Only since Vatican II have these episcopal bodies been constituted in about a hundred nations, and only since *Gaudium et Spes* have these justice and peace issues become major ecclesial concerns, both among nations of a given region and worldwide. The Holy See's role is also much expanded. What is the policy and procedure followed by the United States Catholic Conference in this new field?

Hehir explained the guidelines and process developed, and problems encountered, by the USCC during the dozen years of this new experience among bishops' conferences:

1. "The bishops' conferences and the Holy See seek to promote a *universal moral and ecclesial framework* to which all might appeal in arriving at their positions on particular issues." While sharing these principles within the same moral framework, however, episcopal conferences might arrive at differing positions, as McGrath indicated. Hehir cited the example of "first use of nuclear weapons, concerning which the French and German Conferences differ from the U.S. bishops. They appeal to the same moral principles; however, they do not come out with the same specific contingent conclusions. This happens with other conferences on other issues, such as human rights and economic justice." Still, Hehir insisted, sharing the same moral framework and principles counts enormously in building up the network of cooperation among national conferences on world issues.

2. *Problems of consultation* among bishops conferences, according to Hehir, fall in two main categories, *tactical and ecclesial*:

1) Tactical problems include "*safe access* to learn what is a conference's position. Often we cannot use the telephone, nor the mails. It is not easy to travel to Korea to see Cardinal Kim in person. And going to visit in some East European countries, about U.S. policy there, is out of the question. We keep working at this and acquiring experience. With you, Archbishop McGrath, it was easy; we met halfway in Miami, then you came to talk to the U.S. Conference about the Panama Canal."
2) Ecclesial problems exist, first of all, "if the national episcopal conference is *divided* on a serious issue. But even if we know what the bishops think, we are sometimes not sure that this represents a sufficient *consensus* of the whole Church of that country." Hehir cited Nicaragua, where serious divergencies exist. On the whole, however, the U.S. Bishops' Conference treats with other episcopal conferences almost exclusively and leaves *other groups* within the U.S. Church to communicate with nonepiscopal bodies of the sister Church.

3. The *formal object* of the U.S. Conference, Hehir stressed, "must be kept clear: It is within the competence of the U.S. bishops to comment on the impact of American foreign policy on the situation in the other country or region. It is not our business to tell other episcopates or countries what they should do." In this procedure Hehir's office follows three main norms:

1) Solid documentation and evidence concerning the alleged problem.
2) American foreign policy or involvement clearly and directly affects the issue and/or impacts the situation, for example, through U.S. military or economic assistance, or via American business enterprise.
3) Consultation is made with the bishops' conference of the country concerned.

(As editor of this report, I intrude on the discussion to underline this new role of the U.S. Church:

1) In the above paragraphs Hehir has briefed us on the guidelines, process, and problems involved in relations between the U.S. Bishops' Conference and those of other nations, concerning the impact of American power and presence among peoples and regions outside U.S. boundaries. To my knowledge this is the clearest and most concise outline of USCC policy and procedure given to date by an authoritative spokesperson of our episcopal conference.

2) This very significant development of the Catholic Church's role concerning American foreign policy, this deliberate entry of the U.S. Church onto

the global scene of "today's world," began only fifteen years ago and continues to expand. It marks a significant shift of North American ecclesial consciousness and conscience onto the whole new terrain of all humankind–alongside promotion of "justice and peace" by the papacy and synod, all in fitting follow-up to Vatican II.

3) Hehir states that the U.S. Bishops' Conference treats with other episcopal conferences almost exclusively, and leaves other groups within the U.S. Church to communicate with nonepiscopal bodies of the sister Church. He also expresses concern whether an episcopal position "represents a sufficient consensus of the whole Church of that country." This shows an expectation that other appropriate groups within the U.S. Church should continue to address their faith concern on *Gaudium et Spes* issues of the world-Church as a whole, and that the U.S. bishops by no means regard this as their exclusive terrain.

4) The Church in and of the United States begins to catch up with the "evangelization of culture" role called for by the fact that our nation has acquired superpower status since World War II. The economic and political and cultural systems of North America as they affect all 160 nations, their systems and peoples, now become the faith concern of Canadian and U.S. Church members.)

The discussion with Bishop DeRoo, like that with Hehir, gave close attention to the purpose of Canada's bishops in writing their statement, and to the audience it primarily addresses. Wilber opened with the observation that the Canadian pastors seem to stress that "the economic system should serve all people, particularly to help the disadvantaged." Further, the head of Notre Dame's economics department saw that while the U.S. Bishops address above all the nation's policyworkers, the Canadians speak to "a much broader range of the public as a whole."

(Wilber's interest in purpose and audience is more than academic: He is the principal economist on the team of experts assisting the U.S. bishops in drafting their new document on the American economy. A Notre Dame Conference on that subject, held December 1983 at the bishops' request, is reported in the book *Catholic Social Teaching and the U.S. Economy: Working Papers for a Bishops' Pastoral,* John W. Houck and Oliver F. Williams, C.S.C., editors, 450 pages, University Press of America, 1984; authors include David Hollenbach, Michael Novak, Peter Peterson, Marina Whitman, Dennis McCann, Daniel Finn.)

DeRoo confirmed Wilber's views on both points, and stressed the second: "Definitely! We do not address only policymakers. We insist on involving everybody, particularly the grass roots. We continue encouraging coalitions of popular groups and networking across political lines and religious bodies.

We cannot truly change the economic system unless we go back to the roots." DeRoo assailed the conceptual framework of power which has dominated among policymakers of industrialization; they look upon the economic system as a *machine*: "With their machine image, derived from the Enlightenment, they believe that tinkering will help the system to run more smoothly, but they will not change the machine. It now becomes uncontrollable. So we are coming with a new set of ideas and values – human and Gospel values – new creative imagination to rethink the whole system. This can arise only from the people, not from the possessors of all this power."

Schmitz, who is from Toronto, told the group that the *Globe and Mail* of that city, "comparable in English Canada to the *New York Times* and *Washington Post*," responded with much sympathy in their first editorial after the bishops' statement. They showed appreciation for the offer of a moral framework and stimulus, and gratification that "at last religious leaders are doing the sort of thing they should be doing." This mood however did not last, Schmitz reported. In follow-up articles the Toronto daily "became quite critical of a number of specifics."

Schmitz questioned the "operating conception" of the document, whether the bishops had thought out with sufficient depth the implications of "alternative strategies and models, alternative cultures and visions for an alternative economy." He asked about the process toward these alternatives, wanting detail about "labor-intensive industries, the competition of new technologies," and the whole set of problems these entail. Schmitz concluded by underlining the difference between the U.S. Peace Pastoral which has "immediate input for present policy and decision," as compared with the Canadian document which addresses the country's basic economic system, its long-range reform and evolution.

"Our statement," DeRoo replied, "is our way of speaking about the 'preferential option for the poor' from the basis of our Canadian experience. To bring about a new vision of society we must go to the people most affected by the economy as now structured, based on the needs of all, as experienced and expressed by them – not as artificially laid out by the media, or as determined by those who control the present system. This is the 'operating conception' of our Canadian document. The media in general treated it well by stirring up debate."

In answer to the desire of Schmitz for more detail about "alternatives," DeRoo explained that above all they offer an "alternative cultural vision. We needed as bishops to assure that our empirical assessment of the present economic structure and situation made sense and that alternatives we are proposing lie within the parameters of economic discipline and acceptable discourse. Schumacher and others have done most of the creative thinking which we present." This approach, DeRoo stressed, conforms with that put forth "so ably by Hehir in our previous discussion on the U.S. Peace Pastoral: Gospel values and moral judgments are applied to empirical reality in making societal policy."

Concerning "labor-intensive industries, competition of new technologies," and related issues raised by Schmitz, as well as the dire effect of the North's "high-tech power centers on the Third World," DeRoo carefully spelled out the episcopal role: "We only open up these questions. As bishops we do not pretend that we have solutions to offer. We want to help the Spirit to work among the people, especially at the grass roots–to empower these people. They will come up with economic and political projects not now anticipated, but no less valid than present ones. They will bring us to the original concept of economics: to meet basic needs of all people, not just the wants of a few."

Burrell commended DeRoo and his Canadian brothers for having "joined the issue. We use your document here at Notre Dame and find it very helpful. It flies in the face of so much conventional analysis and of so many existing institutions that implementation is the big question." How, for instance, might investors be challenged to risk funds on the type of economic models you suggest? Also, little is said about the global obstacle of institutionalized dependency on the high-tech North. "A Latin American document would probably have underscored dependency throughout."

Readily acknowledging these deficiencies, DeRoo explained that these issues were "too much to tackle. They would have taken us into the whole worldwide reality and ideology of *power.* I think we will be drawn in that direction; this is inescapable in due time. We first wanted a brief statement on *current* Canadian reality, to launch deeper and longer re-examination in which the people themselves participate. They will in due time discover this power-dependency relation which you cite."

Specifically cultural dimensions were raised by Houck and Goulet. Houck pointed out that Adam Smith focused on "division of labor" when he began modern economic discourse over two hundred years ago. "Today he would probably focus on *division of knowledge.* This and all universities are involved in this division of knowledge. Business corporations use great bureaucracies of technocrats. That's where the power is. We like to think of greedy capitalists and elitist policymakers, but the power is in the division of knowledge within the technocratic bureaucracies. Your document, however, doesn't address this power reality. You say you will listen to the 'little people,' and not to the technocrats. You speak of liberation and exodus, of getting away from where and in whom power resides and is exercised. You would do better to speak of *covenant* and *creation*–forming a social order which uses this division of knowledge, of developing new processes which enhance human life." Technocrats above all, Houck concluded, "need spiritual nourishment and vision, and I don't see you speaking to them. If they lack such a vision your goal of an alternative economy and society remains very doubtful."

DeRoo stated that although "talking covenant to technocrats is like talking covenant to Pharoah, the call to conversion must be addressed to everyone – the poor, the marginalized and powerless, as well as the rich and powerful, the technocrats." He recalled Paulo Friere's warning that the greater challenge is not making revolution, but rather how to keep the newly empowered (formerly marginalized) from becoming the dominant class after successful revolution. DeRoo cited the difficulty today's technocrats (many of whom are descendents of poor, immigrant families) have in relating their personal dreams and private lives with the society-wide vision of the Gospel.

The Canadian pastor told of visits in the homes of Catholic business executives: "They trot out their diplomas from Catholic schools and accuse me of considering them public sinners because they're making a profit. They have so totally bought the ideology, the philosophy, the policy of their company, that my criticism of that company's policy is taken as an individual moral put-down, as if they were bad people. I now realize how profound is the whole individualist morality of the West, rather than a society-wide morality, concerned for all the people. You have opened a wide area for the ongoing and future dialogue, including the technocrats."

Goulet brought the discussion back to "the two major themes we have been trying to analyze and deepen in the Conference as a whole: 1) the evangelization of culture and 2) cultural pluralism." Goulet alerted the discussants to "the confessional and reductionist sense we have been giving to 'evangelization of culture' in our exchanges. We 'cultured Christians' sound as though we proceed from a secure sense of possessing *the* truth, *the* real culture *a priori*, without approaching other cultures as richness to be discovered, in humility and reciprocity. We look at the culture of others primarily as something to be judged, something above all to be saved and redeemed. Maybe we should reverse the terms to 'acculturation of the Evangel,' to beget new cultural incarnations, multiples of the Good News."

Focusing directly on DeRoo's homeland, Goulet repeated the bishops' stated desire to "preach the Good News as authenticating the history and vision of the people of Canada and their own four cultures, as Anglos and French, as 'new Canadians' (immigrants post-World War II), and as 'native people.'" The statement of Canada's bishops seems to applaud that very vision and culture which is notable among the native people, with their views of nature and harmony: "They are clearly opposed to a Promethean stance toward resources and life rhythms, opposed to the machine as dominant cultural model, opposed to the people as instruments of production. The Good News certainly does authenticate such a vision." However, Goulet asked, "have you as Canadian pastors learned any of this from the native people and *their* culture?"

DeRoo related a personal pastoral experience: "I have lived in the Mackenzie Valley of the Canadian Rockies with the Innuit people. With them I perceived the cultural qualities which you describe, their respect for nature and the whole ecology. The extended family provides their economic framework and decision making. They explained to me: 'Our riches are in the forest, not in the bank; the ocean is our deepfreeze.' Certainly, I am not against progress," DeRoo continued, "but as Christian leaders we must promote participation and partnership, not competition and boom or bust."

Scannone noted convergences of these Canadian concerns with those he had outlined in the previous discussion about the indigenous people and cultures of Latin America. "Evangelization of modern culture," he insisted, "must start from the wisdom of the people, which has already been christianized in Latin popular religiosity." This wisdom must be exercized today through a triune process "involving: 1) creative imagination and symbol, 2) joint analysis of the social and scientific elements of the modern world, and 3) discernment of spirits. We need to develop strategies for mediating these themes."

DeRoo voiced his "indebtedness to so-called illiterate people, particularly Latin American peasants. I have sat at table with them after evening meals, listening to comments on the economic and political systems. They showed more wisdom than some of my highly schooled people in Canada. Latin bishops tell me they are now doing *less preaching* and *more listening* to their own base communities. In Sao Paulo I heard shared-homilies of favela people who taught me more than I could have."

Moved by such experiences, Bishop DeRoo has "started a 'Prayer Companion' program in his own Diocese of Victoria. This encourages lay persons to become spiritual directors, a ministry too long regarded as exclusive to the priest. I have discovered otherwise. We use the discernment procedure of the Jesuits, with emphasis on freedom via detachment, willing to live with less in a more sharing way. We draw from the ideas of Schumacher's *Small Is Beautiful,* and from *Small Is Possible* written by his successor, McCrory. We aim at rediscovering the Bible as a book of prayer; like the people of God in the Bible we worship by prayerful response to multiple human situations. Just as the biblical people found answers in human situations, we encourage this wisdom among our people today, and we are amazed at what they discover. I control the arrogant urge to tell them what direction to take; the Spirit, I now know, will move them."

Bartell applauded "the preferential option for the poor" and the human values exalted by the Canadian bishops. He strongly decried, however, "their failure to treat the international order within which Canada's economy operates." Further, this global economic system is embraced by the universal scope of the Gospel and by Catholic social teaching since Vatican II. Bartell repeated earlier criticism that DeRoo and his colleagues ignored the worldwide system of the South's dependency on the high-tech North: "The only concern for dependency I found is that of Canada on the United States and the desire for more Canadian self-sufficiency."

Elevation of *Small Is Beautiful* to the level of national policy, Bartell warned, would gravely harm the labor-intensive industries of Asia, in textiles for example. The industrialized North has the high technology for other products and should not try to recapture markets of labor-intensive industries whose demise would wipe out the jobs of millions who are much worse off than we North Americans. Any Canadian national strategy, therefore, especially that advanced by Catholic bishops as option for the poor, should relate especially to the needs of poor nations within the world economic system, with its global "division of labor" and "division of knowledge."

Archbishop Vauchon quickly reviewed cultural issues profiled throughout our Conference. He urged greater attention to "the new technics of the near future which will bring frenetic changes for all human life and the whole sweep of human culture." The Catholic Pastor of ancient Quebec quoted the warning of scientists and philosophers of culture whom he consulted as preparation for our Conference: "You bishops will be dealing in the future with a *new type of humanity every three years*. You will not escape this." The Archbishop urged that in follow-up to our conference each of us, in our respective roles and institutions, and the Pontifical Council for Culture in particular: "must seek to identify the *essentials of a truly human life* which we must try to save among these changing types of future humanity."

Gleason forewarned that the criticism he intended to make of the Canadian bishops' statement, and of DeRoo's explanations, would be distinctly negative:

1. "Your left liberal analysis," Gleason charged, "is merely warmed-over socialist analysis of the capitalist or free-enterprise system. This critique of capitalism, derived culturally speaking from Marxist analysis, has greater respectability in the intellectual world than any other at present. So it enjoys hegemonic status."

2. "By adopting this cultural analysis which enjoys priority in the intellectual world, the Church has in effect become co-opted by a cultural position. To put this in unpleasant language: The Church is baptizing this essentially Marxist-derived critique; the Church has aligned itself with a cultural position. In doing this the Church is always in danger of being absorbed by that culture and of finding its own truth redefined in terms of that culture. The Church is weakened thereby."

3. "Therefore," Gleason concluded, "how is sufficient vigilance to be exercized within the Church about this danger, if the option you [DeRoo and Canadian bishops] propose is followed? Alternative societies which are socialist or Marxist-inspired are not pure figments of imagination. You should

therefore give some attention to those societies which claim these socialist or Marxist bases."

DeRoo responded briefly that "North Americans are usually traumatized by the very mention of socialism and Marxism." There exist around the world "many kinds of socialist systems. There is a socialism more akin to Scripture insights than is capitalism in its raw form. This has been recognized by a number of popes, including John Paul II in *Laborem Exercens.* We must reassess our use of language."

To Bartell's criticism, DeRoo readily admitted that "our 1983 statement does lack global perspective. You should refer to our 1979 document which did cover world economy issues. We chose not to repeat these in our present pressing pastoral concern about basic needs within our own country." DeRoo warned that the high-technology, which Bartell urged for Canada, now spreads worldwide and will in turn wipe out many jobs in poorer nations, "leaving the Third World in deep trouble."

The Canadian bishop concluded by urging that the U.S. bishops address "the distortions which the nuclear arms race have caused within the total global economy. In much of the industrialized North economies are geared *for war.* Some say that if the manufacture of weapons would stop, our own North American economy would collapse. Let us strive then for an economy *for peace,* using all present 'for war' resources. I ask the U.S. bishops to speak out further on an economy 'for peace,' before it becomes impossible to challenge the whole 'for war' system."

The Church Meeting Cultures: Convergences and Perspectives

Hervé Carrier, S.J.

Concluding a conference, we all know, is an impossible task, but it is an expected ritual among debating colleagues who do not wish to part abruptly without pondering a little longer all they have said in days of intense work.

In the spirit of a continued exchange, let me try, first, to reflect on the results that seem to have been reached in our deliberations these last days. Then I will attempt to underline two major problems that have emerged as central during the whole conference: the question of cultural pluralism and the meaning of "the evangelization of cultures."

I. CONVERGENCES

1. Achieved Goal

Have we, first of all, achieved our major goal in this conference? I think we can answer: yes, the goal has been reached. Twenty years after Vatican II, we have seriously reconsidered *Gaudium et Spes*; we have discussed with specialists having participated in the elaboration of the document; we have heard sociologists who have analyzed for us the document in today's context, and, finally, we have listened to several representatives of local Churches deeply involved in the implementation of *Gaudium et Spes* in Latin America, in the United States, and in Canada. We have, indeed, achieved our goal. But, in all fairness, we have to admit that our goals were limited. According to the rules we had set for ourselves, we wanted our analysis to center on the local Churches of the American continent. Theoretically, we could have invited other bishops, from Europe, Africa, and Asia, and we would certainly have heard other points of view, quite different. Other important problems could have been considered, like inculturation, for instance, which is a very central question in many countries and local Churches, not only in Africa and Asia, but also in many countries of the Western world, including America, where deep cultural changes call for an urgent study of inculturation of the Gospel. This being said, let us acknowledge that we have achieved our limited goal and we should thank the Lord for that.

We have also reached a substantial convergence on several points.

2. A Valid Concept of Culture

We have agreed that we now have, in the Church, a valid concept of culture, which we have discussed at length, starting from the formulation given in *Gaudium et Spes*, no. 53. We have compared that definition of culture with other accepted concepts used by sociologists, anthropologists, philosophers, and international organizations such as UNESCO. Our notion of culture, which incorporates the traditional or classical view as well as the anthropological and historical perspective, is a modern and operational tool used to analyze the characteristic traits of human groups and societies.

We have tried to understand how *Gaudium et Spes*, in its assessment of modern cultures and societies, has opened some major avenues in the post-conciliar Church.

3. Alliance with Man Himself

Gaudium et Spes is a remarkable document, especially for having redefined the role of the Church in the modern world. The old Christian order, valid for other epochs, has not been repudiated, but a new approach has been formulated by Vatican II. The alliance of the Church will now be with the human beings as such in their historical condition, not with states, or kingdoms. The Church will try to pursue its mission in any kind of civil regime that respects religious freedom. The Gospel is accessible to a plurality of cultures. It is through the mediation of consciences that the Church will penetrate and transform humankind, by defending and promoting the *humanum*, that is, the fundamental value and dignity of human beings. In other words, serving the *humanum* means pursuing justice, peace, freedom, dignity for all, in view of the full development of all men and women in their physical, cultural, and spiritual potentialities. This new approach is manifested today in so many initiatives undertaken by Christians in all countries and, in a particular way, in new services created by the Holy See, which deal with the modern problems of the family, of justice and peace, of organized charity, of culture, of the laity, of the relations with other Christians, with other religions, and in a new dialogue with nonbelievers.

4. A Secularized World

This world is now recognized as secularized, not that it is seen as cut off from God, Creator and Redemptor, but civil societies are accepted in their legitimate autonomy, with their own consistency, their own structures, their proper responsibilities. Secularization can be seen as a positive development of culture, but it can also degenerate into secularism. In that case, the contradictions of modern cultures produce destructive effects on the *humanum*, especially through new forms of atheism. These cultural trends are submitted to moral judgment, but the Church, in a spirit of open dialogue, still continues patiently to remind all men and women that God is not a rival. Liberation, freedom, and an openness to transcendence are prerequisites toward an integral development of the *humanum*.

5. Man as Creator of the New Order to Come

A dynamic image of the human being emerges from Vatican II. It is through culture only that a person comes into being. Persons are greater than their works, their inventions, their belongings. Being, believing, and hoping are more important than having things. This applies to all human beings, not only to those who are said to be "cultivated" in the classical sense. The most humble individuals live also from a culture that deserves esteem. The human being is always in danger of becoming subhuman and, today especially, is threatened by political regimes, economic systems, oppressive ideologies, systematic manipulations, and, most of all, by deadly weapons. Men and women are in need of liberation and salvation in order to develop all their virtualities, their spiritual capacity, their compassion for others. All are called together to a new task, the construction of the human order to come. A new sense of community among nations is needed.

6. A New Community of Nations

Gaudium et Spes calls all human beings to be the builders of a new community of nations, that will recognize the cultural sovereignty of all peoples, as well as their growing interdependence. The inspiring dynamism of such a community cannot be based only on economic, technological factors, or on the blind rules of historical determinism. It is from a cultural inspiration—that means from a respect for the *humanum*—that states will endeavor to favor justice and development, with a particular concern for the weakest and the poorest. Moreover, states, between themselves, have to build peace as the universal culture of tomorrow. More than ever in history, nations come to realize that peace is not given passively; it has to be built up every day, out of good will and respect for all members of the human family.

States have become the great *definers of culture* and, in many instances, they have supplanted the Church in that function. The influence of the Church and of the state, in cultural matters, is often matched if not overcome by the power of the mass media, whose overwhelming impact deserves a new type of cultural discernment. These new sources of influence over mass culture–and the immense responsibility they have acquired–should be constantly submitted to an alert opinion and to the discernment of all living sectors of society.

Education for freedom, peace, and justice acquires therefore a major role in a pluralistic world if the *humanum* is to be insured and if a new human order is to take shape. It is in that context that a new approach to evangelization has been considered and proposed by *Gaudium et Spes.* This last point has been constantly present in all our discussions and we will return to it later, in a more explicit form.

7. Twenty Years after the Council

We have noticed that *Gaudium et Spes* had proposed a rather serene conception of cultural realities, culture being understood as an ideal and a heritage. Today, cultural problems have become considerably more radicalized and politicized, with more than a hundred new nations striving for their cultural liberation and with the ominous clashes between cultural blocks intensifying and generating a universal anguish for the survival of humankind. For John Paul II, culture is a very pressing issue, for it has become, in his words: "this vital field in which the destiny of the Church and the world is at stake in this final close of our century" (*L'Osservatore Romano,* 19 November 1979). Paul VI had already expressed the dramatic challenge that this raises for the Church, "the split between the Gospel and cultures is without doubt the drama of our time" (*Evangelii Nuntiandi,* 1975, no. 20).

Over the years, culture has become inseparable from social, political, and also pastoral action. In the Church, we are perceiving more realistically the close link that exists between *evangelization,* acting for *justice,* and promoting *culture.* Those three operations are not absolutely distinct; to evangelize is inseparable from the fight for justice, which comprises cultural promotion and the development of all human beings. We have agreed on these points and we have come to realize better how culture and justice are intimately related; in other words, justice is a problem of culture, just as culture is a problem of justice.

8. Culture and Politics

Another evolution to be observed after *Gaudium et Spes* is the extraordinary development that "cultural policies" have known in almost all countries. There are now more than one hundred twenty nations having a Ministry of Culture or its equivalent. A cultural policy can be an advance in the art of governing if it means reaffirming the priority of human aspirations in all sectors of public affairs and the pursuit of the "cultural finalities of development," according to the usual expression of UNESCO and the Council of Europe.

But cultural policies can be distorted, as happens too often today. Culture then becomes a means to dominate populations in the name of totalitarian ideologies or uncontrolled interests.

It has become urgent for today's citizens, especially for the believers, to support governments in their efforts to optimize the conditions for the widest participation of all in the benefits of culture; but public opinion worldwide should also be vigilant and condemn distortions of cultural policies that are pursued with a spirit of intolerance and discrimination in the name of religious, ideological, or economic dogmatisms.

II. THE IMAGE OF A COMMITTED CHURCH

Through numerous testimonies, these days, we have become more aware of the beneficial effects of *Gaudium et Spes* on the Church. Yes, the postconciliar Church has been changed by the message of *Gaudium et Spes.* This has come out quite clearly as we have analyzed what has happened in the Church these last twenty years, both at the local and at the universal levels.

1. The Universal Church after *Gaudium et Spes*

The Catholic Church, as a whole, appears ever more as a universal and pluricultural body, deeply committed to justice, peace, human rights, freedom, compassion for the poor and the oppressed, respect for life, international solidarity, universal brotherhood. The Church has become a central protagonist in the enterprise of promoting a new world order. Speaking in general, the Church projects the image of a major actor in fostering an order of justice and peace and in defending the highest values of the *humanum.* Our Church has given itself the mental tools (meaning by that renewed theological and phenomenological insights) to understand the historical events we are living and to pursue a credible dialogue with men and women of our time.

We proclaim a message of hope that reaches the highest expectations of our contemporaries. People see us as an institution that stands for the ultimate defense of the *humanum,* that is, for the true culture of humankind. Using the suggestive expression of our Latin American friends (coined by Simón Bolivar) we stand for "la Patria Grande," meaning that we defend with love the great *patria,* the fatherland or the motherland of the human family. "More than any others we have the cult of men," said Paul VI at the conclusion of Vatican II. With modesty, but with a sense of confidence and responsibility, let us acknowledge this social, cultural, and spiritual progress of the postconciliar Church.

2. The Church in the Americas

A similar testimony is given by the local Churches, as we have heard, in particular in the recent experiences of the Churches in Latin America, in the United States, and in Canada.

The maturing of the Medellín and Puebla documents, in *Latin America*, bears witness to an extraordinary renewal of the Church in that continent and, here again, we have been able to perceive how these achievements of the Church were directly inspired by the message of *Gaudium et Spes.* The Puebla Document stands as one of the most successful results of collective reflection and spiritual research concerning the modern problems of evangelization, and the promotion of justice, culture, and development. For several years, in all countries of Latin America, bishops, study groups, specialists as well as people involved in social and pastoral action have cooperated in the preparation of a continental program for the Church, which was finally approved in Puebla in the presence of John Paul II in 1979.

We have also reviewed the experience of the Church in the *United States*: its commitment for social justice and, more recently, its exceptional effort in defining the redoubtable moral problems raised by atomic weapons. It has been pointed out explicitly that the research, in all that reflection, was guided by the line of thought of *Gaudium et Spes.* The sum of consultations, studies and deliberations that has preceded the publication of this courageous document gives witness to the earnestness with which Catholics, after *Gaudium et Spes,* are invited to confront the most pressing problems of the human family. The U.S. bishops' document has had a worldwide echo and has stimulated a very lively exchange among other Episcopacies, especially in Western Europe, and also among many other religious leaders in the United States and elsewhere. In the U.S. the position of the Catholic Church has started an open debate among the most representative elements of the population, and one of the merits of the ongoing discussion has been to sharpen and deepen the extremely complex, but unavoidable, moral problem that atomic war raises in the conscience of humankind.

The impetus given by *Gaudium et Spes* has also brought the Church in *Canada* to commmit itself ever more courageously and competently in issues of major concern for the country. In recent years, authoritative statements have made a notable impact on public opinion, government, industry and labor unions. Specialists were called to work with theologians in the elaboration of high quality statements. The January 1983 declaration by the Canadian bishops on the "Economic crisis" is a clear example that the Church intends to involve itself in complex issues such as the economic and structural factors leading to a dramatic situation of unemployment. The intention of the Church, of course, is not a technical one; it is of a moral and cultural nature. The Church defends, as a preferential value and as a priority, the concrete opportunity for all citizens to work and to serve the common good. It is a question of dignity and security. The defense of the *humanum* should have precedence over the blind mechanism of profit making. The economic system should be encouraged for its creativity and its service to the community; which means that the *spirit of service* should never be forgotten. In other words, economic means should remain finalized toward cultural goals. The economic system is for man, and not vice versa: this is the right order of cultural values proposed by *Gaudium et Spes*.

III. TWO EMERGING PROBLEMS

Throughout our discussions, two major problems have emerged and retained our attention: 1) cultural pluralism; 2) evangelization of cultures. They deserve a special consideration and call for further study. Here are the main points that have come out of our exchanges.

1. Cultural Pluralism

True and false pluralism. How have we understood modern pluralism? First, we have rejected a false pluralism that simply flattens all values and spiritual diversities. Herbert Marcuse has written strong pages on the subject showing how this parody of pluralism simply kills the moral fibre of a society. A new totalitarian system, he contends, takes the form of a "harmonious pluralism," in which the most contradictory truths and values coexist in the most tranquil indifference.[1] This is a false pluralism, that is simply destructive of culture.

Moreover, pluralism is contradicted by violence, terrorism, totalitarianism, or by any forced unity in the name of an abstract society.

Pluralism as a situation and as an attitude. On the other hand, we have recognized that we are now faced with a plurality of cultures and that this situation is here to stay. It is a phenomenon inherent in modern societies, especially in those which are democratic, mobile, free, educated, interdependent. Even in totalitarian states, pluralities cannot simply be suppressed, although the diversity of cultures can be gravely threatened. In urbanized and industrialized societies, people pursue a plurality of life projects and a plurality of subjective absolutes. People are ready to give their lives for all sorts of absolutes, causes or values.

If this is a modern reality, if this observation of ours is correct, then a *new attitude* is needed on our part which we would call an attitude of *cultural pluralism.* It means that we accept the desirability of a human order respecting the complexity of ideologies, the diversity of life projects. We acknowledge the fact that there are realities simply not reducible to unity by force. There is a multiplicity of languages, beliefs, traditions, ways of perceiving and defining life, individually and socially. We have to pursue a new type of social unity that respects cultural disparities.

We practice tolerance, not only in a passive way. Positively, we favor the building up of a *communitas communitatum*, of a community of communities. We say: all cultures that promote the *humanum* deserve to be respected; but, in the name of pluralism, we maintain that all cultures must be open to mutual enrichment, appreciation and criticism.[2]

Homogenization of cultures. In the perspective of cultural pluralism, we have also encountered the problem of homogenization, or unification of cultures. Frontiers between cultures tend to disappear. For instance, the young behave the same way in all countries, they sing the same songs, dress alike, and react in a similar way toward traditional values. Standard ways of traveling, doing business, educating, communicating, recreating, tend to spread everywhere. Homogenization of cultures is an ambivalent phenomenon. It can mean progress for the human family, in the sense that it spreads positive values such as the aspiration toward greater participation in the benefits of science, technology, education, medicine, information, and art. In a word, it can bring a better service to all human beings and a better knowledge of the universe.

But homogenization of cultures can also provoke the destruction of a sane pluralism, the disappearance of cultural identities, and the domination of the weaker, or the minorities, by the strongest and the wealthiest. This problem of homogenization deserves greater consideration. It is not easy to study, objectively, because the partners in the discussion do not always consider themselves truly equals. For instance, representatives of the Western world often have some reluctance in questioning the superiority and universal value of their culture and they hardly accept that other traditions, some even older than their own, could widen the horizon of today's world culture.

In the Church. Even in the Church, the practice of pluralism deserves careful attention. Without entering into the complex question of *inculturation*, which, as I have said earlier, has not been on our agenda during this conference, we have recognized that special attention is needed in our way of dealing with various groups in the society and in the Church. For instance, there is a way to deal with the young that can alienate adults and vice versa. Another example: some of us dedicate our energies to higher education and to the dialogue with intellectuals in the hope of influencing in a Christian way the leaders of tomorrow; but such a preoccupation should never imply depreciating social commitment in favor of the least privileged groups, whose collective action might also be necessary for social change. On the other hand, a justified preference for the poor, as proposed courageously at Puebla, should not induce us to forget the importance of revealing the Gospel to leaders, technicians, entrepreneurs, scientists, media specialists, university representatives, whose contribution is also indispensable for development.

In a pluralistic society we feel free to hold a spiritual and normative view of culture, but we do not impose on others or on all groups a uniform cultural model for society. As Christians, we have, indeed, our own anthropological and historical notion of culture and we want others to respect our cultural characteristics. For us, culture contains a normative aspect that affirms a sense of transcendence. It is a kind of culture we want to transmit freely to the younger generations and we expect others to respect us for this. But we do not want to impose that culture on all, or as the unique model. We want to dialogue with others, we want indeed to defend our values, but in a concert of cultures. Pluralism, among Catholics, supposes that they do acknowledge this plurality in regard to socio-cultural models.

An ecumenical perspective. We are all learners when it comes to defining the rules for building a new kind of unity, respectful of all legitimate cultural and religious perspectives. We have insisted, thanks especially to the presence of some highly qualified representatives of other Christian denominations and of the Jewish community, that pluralism cannot be separated from an attitude of open ecumenism. It is rewarding to discover how close we are, when we attempt to define together the major ingredients of what we call the *humanum.* This is quite promising for future common reflection and action. We have also to extend our sympathy and our dialogue to other religious groups, like the Muslims, and the great religious traditions of the East, in particular. Even among those who profess no religion, we often recognize a sincere and stimulating commitment for the promotion of cultural progress. Culture is a common denominator that should interest all those who hope in a better future for the human family.

The management of conflicts. Pluralism, as we have noticed, raises at times the hard question of *divisions and conflicts.* How then do we manage conflicts? For such a question, we need a yes and no answer. *Yes,* we want to fight for justice, we want to free the oppressed, we want to use strength and organized action, in order to defend the cultural dignity of the oppressed; but we say *no* to violence, which is an attack on persons, which is destructive of our opponents. We reject the dialectic of hate and, at the same time, we want to be effective, and there is a tension we have to live with. There is no set of preestablished rules to deal with conflictual situations; we have recognized, at least, that a sincere attitude of cultural pluralism can lead to open dialogue, mutual respect, and, we can hope, to morally acceptable solutions.

Further dimensions of Vatican II. Before concluding this section on pluralism, I would like to add that in Vatican II there are two other documents that it would have been important to consider in this matter: the first is on religious freedom (*Dignitatis humanae,* 1965) and the second is the declaration on non-Christian religions (*Nostra Aetate,* 1965). The problem of diversity of religious faiths has been present in all our discussions, when we considered cultural pluralism. Freedom of religion is a major issue, especially in countries which pursue atheistic policies, even when affirming the liberty of religious belief.

In creating the Pontifical Council for Culture, the Holy Father has invited us to work not only with Catholics but with all men and women of good faith, whatever their religious convictions, even with those who profess no religion. Culture is the business of all sincere men and women. In our work, we also have to pay close attention to the recommendations of Vatican II on non-Christian religions. As we are reminded, Christians have to be firm in their own faith, but they are invited to fraternize with non-Christian believers and they are encouraged to "acknowledge, preserve and promote the spiritual and moral good found among these men as well as the values in their society and culture" (*Nostra Aetate,* no. 3)

2. Evangelization of Cultures

The second major problem that has dominated our exchanges is the *evangelization of cultures.* The expression has been used frequently by Paul VI and by John Paul II, especially in reference to the work of the Pontifical Council for Culture. Here, I think, are the main points that have come out of our considerations.

Evangelization directed to persons. First, we have tried to remind ourselves more explicitly of what we mean by *evangelization,* as such. For us, it means announcing the Good News. The Father has sent His Son who gave His life and has risen for our salvation, and His Spirit has been given to us for our sanctification. We are called to live together and render glory to God in the Ecclesia, founded by Christ. The Ecclesia helps us to convert ourselves daily and serve our brothers and sisters through charity. Together, in Ecclesia, we give testimony to the unity of men with God and to the unity of all men between themselves (*Lumen Gentium,* no. 1). This is the meaning of evangelization and Saint Paul says: "Woe to me if I do not preach the Gospel!" It is therefore an obligation for us to announce the Good News. The Gospel is directed to all *persons* willing to hear the message of Christ.

Is the Gospel valid for all? In regard to evangelization, it was asked if the Gospel or the Scriptures are valid *for all.* We answer yes, they are valid for all men and women who are willing to hear them and who want to adhere freely to the Word of God. In this strict sense, we talk of the evangelization of *persons* disposed to convert themselves and willing to join the *Communitas Fidei,* the Community of Faith. Indeed, faith is a very personalized and free act which we can elicit with the grace of God.

This being said, there is another way to test the universal validity of the Gospel and the Scriptures. From a cultural point of view, there are, in Scripture, elements which are valid for all. They are values of a universal nature which are conducive to human brotherhood, this being the most revolutionary idea that the Church has spread throughout the centuries. Along with the conviction of universal brotherhood, the Scriptures have spread the dynamic ideal of love, justice, compassion for the poor, the weak, the needy, the oppressed; and those moral values have, undoubtedly transformed cultures through history.

Cultures "evangelized": in what sense? Now we have to press the question further and see in what sense we can truly speak of the evangelization of *cultures.* It should help us greatly, at this point, to recognize that the term evangelization applies to cultures in an *analogous way.* Cultures, as such, do not pose an act of faith; cultures cannot repent or convert, cannot adore the Lord; only persons, individually or in communities, can do this. But, as in all analogy, there is an element of similitude to be noted here.

Cultures also need corrections, purification, "conversion" if you wish. History shows us constantly how cultures have been purified from superstition, barbarism, moral and intellectual backwardness. Speaking as modern observers, we say that if a culture is a typical way of thinking, judging, working, behaving, then the message of the Gospel can influence a collectivity in its manner of thinking, judging, educating, living and dying. Historically, that is the way many cultures have been evangelized, not simply by imposing values but by proposing a Christian life project. A point has been underlined in our discussion: it is through the conscience of the behaving persons that Christian values are transmitted; ethics and moral norms serve as the mediating factor.

Evangelization, therefore, is the contrary of pure accommodation to cultural trends. Evangelization supposes a critical attitude of discernment. Christians will criticize, for instance, unjust laws, immoral practices, racist, sexist, ideological, and tribal discrimination, or economic structures of domination. Christians will try to discern in cultures what contradicts the *humanum,* and they will act against whatever they consider to be countervalues or obstacles to the real cultural progress of men. In so doing, they will be evangelizing, because they are defending universal values which they think are inspired by their faith.

Contribution of Christians to Cultures. Let us go further. We advocate the legitimacy of common action on the part of Christians, who believe that they can contribute to better society by their corporate action. We even feel justified in creating, where possible, institutions of our own, schools, hospitals, associations that can render a special kind of service to the common good in a pluralistic society. Then one needs prudential judgment in order to decide whether Christians, as such, should organize political parties, labor unions, cooperatives, social projects, for pursuing their own goals and defending, with others, a concrete sociopolitical order. We claim that freedom of action is part of a pluralistic society and that the plurality of social commitments can contribute to the enrichment of culture. This also is a means of inserting the ferment of the Gospel in the cultural dynamism of a society.

Beyond these lines of action, we do not pursue the confessionalization of societies. There are still, today, countries where a particular religion is ingrained in a living culture, or is officially recognized as a state religion. These are historical situations which have grown out of a rich cultural experience. In today's pluralistic societies, evangelization of cultures will not follow the blueprint of a state religion. John Courtney Murray has very well analyzed the American experience and has shown how a pragmatic separation of church and state has finally been quite beneficial to the cause of religion as well as to that of culture, in the United States, by leaving channels open for an unending dialogue.

There is no one model for the dialogue of the Gospel with cultures. The plurality of cultures, therefore, will define the conditions and methods of evangelization. We have to assess cultures, to learn from them, to be enriched by their creativity, to participate in their progress. We also have to give witness to an order of values that defends and promotes the *humanum,* even if the *divinum* cannot always be affirmed openly. To evangelize cultures signifies that you understand them, live from them, always trying to discern their values from their countervalues in regard to the *humanum,* and give witness to the Christian ideal that you hold.

Acting through dialogue, discernment, testimony. Bringing Christian values to cultures supposes, essentially, an attitude of dialogue and free cooperation. John Paul II has given some clear orientations, in that sense, to the Pontifical Council for Culture in January 1983. It is not from a position of authority that you impose your values to cultures; you rather proceed through discernment, dialogue, understanding, presence, testimony. The Gospel acts as a ferment in the world and it is through their personal and social commitments that Christians will manifest "the fundamental link there is between the Gospel and man in his humanity itself," as John Paul II said in his address to UNESCO, on June 2, 1980 (no. 10). When the Pope says: "A faith that does not become culture is not a faith fully received, thoroughly thought through, not fully lived out" (January 16, 1982), he speaks directly to Catholics who have to bring their own cultural outlook in conformity with their living faith, in their personal, family, professional, social life. By so doing, they become the ferment we have been talking about.

This dialogue is practiced in a spirit of cooperation with all men and women of goodwill, as John Paul II has made clear, speaking to the Pontifical Council for Culture: "since the Church does not stand outside culture but inside it, as a leaven, on account of the organic and constitutive link which joins them closely together. The Council will pursue its ends in an ecumenical and brotherly spirit, promoting also dialogue with non-Christian religions, and with individuals or groups who do not profess any religion, in a joint search for cultural communication with all men of goodwill" (*L'Osservatore Romano,* 28 June 1982).

An enterprise of common research. What has come out of our discussions, finally, is the growing importance of discernment and research if we wish to work, with all men and women of goodwill, toward the solution of extremely complex problems that a new human order raises. How do you meet the challenges to modern cultures posed by international economic crises, by tensions that threaten the future of humankind, by the cry of those who cannot wait forever before they are liberated, fed, educated and really accepted in a true community of nations, each one respected in its dignity and cultural heritage? All this supposes a mobilization of the best minds in the world, as John Paul II has pointed out: "It is a moral imperative, a sacred duty, which the intellectual and spiritual genius of man can set about by way of a new mobilization of each person's talents and energies and by exploiting man's cultural and technical resources" (*L'Osservatore Romano,* 26 February 1981).

This is the historical challenge that Christians have to meet if they want to bring their proper contribution to the emerging culture of the human family.

NOTES

1. See Herbert Marcuse, *One-Dimensional Man* (Boston: Beacon Press, 1964) and *The Critique of Pure Tolerance* (Boston: Beacon Press, 1965).

2. See *The Catholic University as a Means of Cultural Pluralism to the Service of Church and Society* (Paris: International Federation of Catholic Universities [78A, rue de Sèvres], 1978); and Hervé Carrier, *Higher Education Facing New Cultures* (Rome: Gregorian University Press, 1982), chapters 5 and 6 (on cultural pluralism).

After-Thoughts of a Protestant Observer of Vatican II

Albert C. Outler

This conference stands in a great tradition here in this University–of pioneering explorations, of opening frontiers. It is my seventh such experience in two decades, reaching back to a remarkable colloquy in 1966: "Vatican II: An Interfaith Appraisal" (then puckishly labeled "Vatican Two and a Half"). This present gathering resembles that one in many ways, for you are taking up, at a still further stage of its development, the unfinished business of one of the pioneering ventures in Vatican II and formulated in its unique "*pastoral* constitution," *Gaudium et Spes.*

What was aimed at then, even more than in the Council generally, was the reorientation of the Roman Catholic Church, away from her open defiance of what passed for "culture" and "modernity" in mid-nineteenth-century Europe, toward aggiornamented understandings of, and more open attitudes toward, the new "world" that had emerged and its kaleidoscope of human cultures. The distance from *Syllabus Errorum* (1864) to *Gaudium et Spes* is a striking indication and measure of the development of "the Catholic mind and ethos" over the course of a single century. It may be just as well to ignore, for now, the question as to how much that "development" involved substantive change in that mind.

As well as I have been able to understand this particular variation in an endless discussion of a perennial issue, what marks your new initiative here off from its antecedents is the special linkage in its papal mandate: "the evangelization of cultures" *and* "the defense of man and his cultural advancement" as "*parallel*" and "*complementary*" –neither the one without the other, both in vital balance. Thus, it has been intensely interesting to follow your analyses of these paired concerns and to note the signs of your awareness of their unavoidable tensions–in a world unforeseen in 1965, and unforeseeable.

The most significant consensus that has seemed to appear in the papers and discussions thus far, is a decisive move away from "classical" notions of culture (with their "Western" overtones of aesthetic and elitist values and with their imperialist undertones) toward conceptions more pluralistic and ethnic, more concerned with universal humane values within the varieties of cultures in today's world, in which distinctive cultural values are respected and cherished. One senses an important synthesis in formation here: between the ecclesiocentric traditions of "evangelization" of any and all cultures and the sociocentric perspectives on "culture" and cultural diversity that run from Vico through Herder to Tylor and on into contemporary sociology and anthropology. What is clear is that both notions–"culture" as what the *humanum* adds to "nature" and "evangelization" as what the *humanum* needs from God–are under review, with no stabilization in sight as yet.

Nor is this surprising, in view of the inherent tensions in your enterprise. There never has been a simple or easy harmonization between "the humanization of culture," in all its contrarieties, and "the evangelization of culture" in any depth worth mentioning. For there is a shadow-side of the *humanum* and the cultures it generates. This, in turn, has always meant that the evangelization of any given culture has entailed alterations in ethos, in one aspect or other.

This is quite clear in the New Testament, where *cosmos* and *aion* have counterpoised connotations (with John 3:16–17 being more of an exception than the rule) and where Christians are enjoined not to be "conformed to the patterns of this world." This is an old story in church history with its succession of cultural crises with marked consequences in each case–and always with the lurking specter of *Ersatz-Christentums.* And now there is a veritable cluster of culture crises in the contemporary world, with the Catholic Church involved in every one of them. It has been encouraging to see how steadfastly, in your grapplings with this baffling situation, you have resisted the temptations to settle for simplistic or singularist "either-ors."

Even so, to a Protestant observer, it has seemed at least mildly remarkable that, thus far, you seem to have managed to ignore the extensive experiences of the interactions of "church and culture" in the various Protestant traditions–and most of all, the impact on "liberal Protestantism" of the radical changes that have come with "secularism" and "secularization." The general principle of the separation of church and state has seemed to be taken for granted, and yet its remarkable history not weighed–along with its import as a counterpoise to the rising tide of theocratic thought seen in so many parts of the world. It is almost as if the ideas in *Dignitatis Humanae* were now commonplace–as they certainly were not in 1964–65! Max Weber's demonstration of the formative influences of "culture" on religion has seemed to be assumed, but its problematics not much attended to. There are implied value judgments on "culture Protestantism" in Ritschl and Troeltsch that are not irrelevant to your inquiry, but these seem to have gone unnoticed, as if they did not apply to you and your problems.

Most of all, one might think, there is Richard Niebuhr's *Christ and Culture* and his typological analysis of five different modes of interrelationships between church and culture: 1) Christians' rejections of culture; 2) their accommodations to culture; 3) their attempted escapes from culture; 4) their experiences of paradoxical tensions in culture; and 5) their visions of cultural transformations. Beyond this, there are many lessons about accommodation and martyrdom to be pondered from Eastern Orthodoxy, from the churches in China, Africa, Indonesia, and so on. This is not just an old teacher adding bibliographical annotations; it is a veteran ecumenical observer wondering if there is an unconscious tendency here to restrict the total framework (ecumenical and interreligious) within which your inquiry might be well cast.

All of which is to say that this new Pontifical Council has its work cut out for it, with ample precedents but no set models for replication. And it is also to say that the cause of high religion – Christianity, Judaism, and others – is likewise at stake in what you are attempting and, therefore, that the wider its perspective, the better. In principle your twin mandates – "evangelization" and "humanization" – have identical premises and ends. But in history and practice they have easily drifted into unedifying polarizations. In resisting all such tendencies, you will be serving us all.

Gaudium et Spes made news in 1965 and has gone on altering church history ever since. This new Council, *Pro Cultura,* is clearly a further venture into the possibilities of guiding Christians into truly current applications of the Diognetian formula for being *in* the world without being *of* it. As your work develops, you can count on a host of interested observers, with lively concerns and high hopes. For we have come to a time when your achievements will also be our benefits – and the world's as well. In such an enterprise, our prayers and proffered help are with you – as you and other men and women of faith attempt to persuade humanity, in all its baffling diversity and yet also its shared perils, that (in Niebuhr's words) "the world of culture – man's achievement – exists *within* the world of grace."

PART II

Documents of the Church on Culture

Introducing the Teaching Magisterium

Joseph Gremillion

The papers and discussions of our Conference, reported in Part I, draw repeatedly from recent Church teaching about culture, evangelization and humanization. Significant texts on these subjects are provided here to facilitate direct reference, the first vademecum in the English language of basic official documents on Church and culture.

Three of these carry exceptional magisterial authority: *Gaudium et Spes* of Vatican II; "The Evangelization of Peoples in the Modern World" by Pope Paul VI in follow-up to the 1974 Synod; and the final document of CELAM's Puebla Conference, "Evangelization in Latin America's Present and Future." All three are issued from collegial bodies of pastoral bishops, convoked by the Chair of Peter, and published with full approval of its current occupant.

Further, the three episcopal bodies addressed their themes during week-long sessions, after months, even years of preparation, with participation and consultation of hundreds of members of the worldwide College of Bishops, many of whom consulted in turn their own Christian communities. In Vatican II all 2200 Catholic bishops participated, from all religio-cultural, geopolitical regions of the world. The 1974 Synod included representatives of the more than one hundred national and regional conferences of bishops. And CELAM's Puebla Conference was constituted by delegates from all Latin America's local Churches, plus observer-consultants from several other regional Churches, and was inaugurated in person by John Paul II. These elements of magisterial authority are cited to stress that "culture" has now become a major concern of the highest teaching and pastoral bodies of the Catholic Church as a whole.

This historic opening was launched officially only twenty years ago by the Pastoral Constitution on the Church in the Modern World. Its chapter on "The Proper Development of Culture" is reproduced here *in toto,* for it contains the seminal concepts and pastoral context for the more focussed teaching on culture of the past two decades. The ten introductory paragraphs of *Gaudium et Spes* are also given. They immediately relate "the hopes, the griefs and the anxieties of the men of this age, especially those who are poor," with mankind's "wonder at its own discoveries and its power." The issues of *poverty* and *power,* as products of cultural values and systems, have become central to the Latin and North American Churches, as well as the World Church, since Vatican II.

The 1974 Synod of Bishops elaborated the Council's opening insight into "evangelization of cultures," as reported faithfully and applied pastorally by Paul VI to the Universal Church. Five years later, CELAM's Puebla Conference developed this thrust of the apostolate in the concrete historical, political and economic, ethnic-anthropological and religious reality among the 300 million Catholics of the Latin continent. Extracts from these two collegial documents show how the essentials of Vatican II's opening, toward a more incarnational ministry, are applied increasingly by local Churches to their own cultural settings.

Two North American documents, both direct descendants from *Gaudium et Spes*: the Canadian Bishops on their nation's economy and the U.S. Bishops on peace and the nuclear threat, received major attention during the Notre Dame Conference. Issued in 1983, both show the influence of Puebla in their concern for the poor and the weak, nationally and globally. It is, however, North America's twin cultural constituents of technological power and democratic process which mark both pastorals. The series of hearings held by the U.S. episcopal committee introduces to the magisterium a model of people's participation adapted directly from American civil culture, from town council to state legislature and national Congress. Neither North American document is reproduced here because they are so readily available.

Long extracts are given, rather, from two U.S. pastorals on the Hispanic and black communities, with focus on their distinctive cultures. Issued in 1984, both recognize, at last, the constant adaptation needed in the fields of liturgy and catechesis, community life and structure, pastoral and social ministry among these some forty million members of Christian Churches, among whom Catholics number about one million blacks and twelve million Hispanics, over 25 percent of all U.S. Catholics. Of high significance for the Church of North America, these self-aware black and Hispanic Communities help to "conscientize" Catholics of European origin to the "evangelization of cultures" well underway in the regional Churches of Africa and Latin America within our Universal Church, and under a Chief Pastor constantly traveling to visit his global flock, well aware of and welcoming their cultural plurality among the religions and races of all six continents.

John Paul II is now devoting major attention to the importance of culture for the Church's whole apostolate. He gives his reasons in the five documents reprinted here: his three annual addresses to the new Pontifical Council for Culture, founded by him in 1983; his annual policy statement to the College of Cardinals, Christmas 1984, bearing the significant title, "One Church, Many Cultures," in which Puebla's "preferential option for the poor" receives particular attention; and an address to UNESCO, "Man's Entire Humanity

Is Expressed in Culture," delivered in 1980 in Paris. In the last-named the Pope offers key insights on the "humanization" role of the Church in the very process of the "evangelization of culture." This document also shows the Papacy's long-term support for UNESCO as the only assembly and agency for humankind's cultural concerns that is open to all nations.

Evidence of constant stress on culture in his teaching day by day is provided by sixty-nine citations from John Paul's talks and messages, 1978–82, summarized for this collection by Archbishop Poupard; also from scores of similar references covering 1983–84, gathered by Father Carrier.

The multifold subject of culture already figured prominently in the writings of Karol Wojtyla, professor and pastor and bishop, in the decades before he was called from Poland's national setting to become Teacher-Pastor-Bishop confirming his brothers and sisters amidst all human cultures. This collection of documents witness to the continuity of this Pope's unique vision of the Church's mission, and of his own holistic calling and ministry worldwide.

Pastoral Constitution on the Church in the Modern World

Excerpts from *Gaudium et Spes*, Second Vatican Council, December 7, 1965

PREFACE

The Intimate Bond between the Church and Mankind

1. The joys and the hopes, the griefs and the anxieties of the men of this age, especially those who are poor or in any way afflicted, these too are the joys and hopes, the griefs and anxieties of the followers of Christ. Indeed, nothing genuinely human fails to raise an echo in their hearts. For theirs is a community composed of men. United in Christ, they are led by the Holy Spirit in their journey to the Kingdom of their Father and they have welcomed the news of salvation which is meant for every man. That is why this community realizes that it is truly and intimately linked with mankind and its history.

For Whom This Message Is Intended

2. Hence this Second Vatican Council, having probed more profoundly into the mystery of the Church, now addresses itself without hesitation, not only to the sons of the Church and to all who invoke the name of Christ, but to the whole of humanity. For the Council yearns to explain to everyone how it conceives of the presence and activity of the Church in the world of today.

Therefore, the Council focuses its attention on the world of men, the whole human family along with the sum of those realities in the midst of which that family lives. It gazes upon that world which is the theater of man's history, and carries the marks of his energies, his tragedies, and his triumphs; that world which the Christian sees as created and sustained by its Maker's love, fallen indeed into the bondage of sin, yet emancipated now by Christ.

He was crucified and rose again to break the stranglehold of personified Evil, so that this world might be fashioned anew according to God's design and reach its fulfillment.

The Service to Be Offered to Humanity

3. Though mankind today is struck with wonder at its own discoveries and its power, it often raises anxious questions about the current trend of the world, about the place and role of man in the universe, about the meaning of his individual and collective strivings, and about the ultimate destiny of reality and of humanity. Hence, giving witness and voice to the faith of the whole People of God gathered together by Christ, this Council can provide no more eloquent proof of its solidarity with the entire human family with which it is bound up, as well as its respect and love for that family, than by engaging with it in conversation about these various problems.

The Council brings to mankind light kindled from the gospel, and puts at its disposal those saving resources which the Church herself, under the guidance of the Holy Spirit, receives from her Founder. For the human person deserves to be preserved; human society deserves to be renewed. Hence the pivotal point of our total presentation will be man himself, whole and entire, body and soul, heart and conscience, mind and will.

Therefore, this sacred Synod proclaims the highest destiny of man and champions the godlike seed which has been sown in him. It offers to mankind the honest assistance of the Church in fostering that brotherhood of all men which corresponds to this destiny of theirs. Inspired by no earthly ambition, the Church seeks but a solitary goal: to carry forward the work of Christ Himself under the lead of the befriending Spirit. And Christ entered this world to give witness to the truth, to rescue and not to sit in judgment, to serve and not to be served.

INTRODUCTORY STATEMENT

THE SITUATION OF MEN IN THE MODERN WORLD

Hope and Anguish

4. To carry out such a task, the Church has always had the duty of scrutinizing the signs of the times and of interpreting them in the light of the gospel. Thus, in language intelligible to each generation, she can respond to the perennial questions which men ask about this present life and the life to come, and about the relationship of the one to the other. We must therefore recognize

and understand the world in which we live, its expectations, its longings, and its often dramatic characteristics. Some of the main features of the modern world can be sketched as follows:

Today, the human race is passing through a new stage of its history. Profound and rapid changes are spreading by degrees around the whole world. Triggered by the intelligence and creative energies of man, these changes recoil upon him, upon his decisions and desires, both individual and collective, and upon his manner of thinking and acting with respect to things and to people. Hence we can already speak of a true social and cultural transformation, one which has repercussions on man's religious life as well.

As happens in any crisis of growth, this transformation has brought serious difficulties in its wake. Thus while man extends his power in every direction, he does not always succeed in subjecting it to his own welfare. Striving to penetrate farther into the deeper recesses of his own mind, he frequently appears more unsure of himself. Gradually and more precisely he lays bare the laws of society, only to be paralyzed by uncertainty about the direction to give it.

Never has the human race enjoyed such an abundance of wealth, resources, and economic power. Yet a huge proportion of the world's citizens is still tormented by hunger and poverty, while countless numbers suffer from total illiteracy. Never before today has man been so keenly aware of freedom, yet at the same time, new forms of social and psychological slavery make their appearance.

Although the world of today has a very vivid sense of its unity and of how one man depends on another in needful solidarity, it is most grievously torn into opposing camps by conflicting forces. For political, social, economic, racial, and ideological disputes still continue bitterly, and with them the peril of a war which would reduce everything to ashes. True, there is a growing exchange of ideas, but the very words by which key concepts are expressed take on quite different meanings in diverse ideological systems. Finally, man painstakingly searches for a better world, without working with equal zeal for the betterment of his own spirit.

Caught up in such numerous complications, very many of our contemporaries are kept from accurately identifying permanent values and adjusting them properly to fresh discoveries. As a result, buffeted between hope and anxiety and pressing one another with questions about the present course of events, they are burdened down with uneasiness. This same course of events leads men to look for answers. Indeed, it forces them to do so.

* * * * *

Excerpt from Part II: Some Problems of Special Urgency

CHAPTER II

THE PROPER DEVELOPMENT OF CULTURE

Introduction

53. It is a fact bearing on the very person of man that he can come to an authentic and full humanity only through culture, that is, through the cultivation of natural goods and values. Wherever human life is involved, therefore, nature and culture are quite intimately connected.

The word "culture" in its general sense indicates all those factors by which man refines and unfolds his manifold spiritual and bodily qualities. It means his effort to bring the world itself under his control by his knowledge and his labor. It includes the fact that by improving customs and institutions he renders social life more human both within the family and in the civic community. Finally, it is a feature of culture that throughout the course of time man expresses, communicates, and conserves in his works great spiritual experiences and desires, so that these may be of advantage to the progress of many, even of the whole human family.

Hence it follows that human culture necessarily has a historical and social aspect and that the word "culture" often takes on a sociological and ethnological sense.* It is in this sense that we speak of a plurality of cultures.

Various conditions of community living, as well as various patterns for organizing the goods of life, arise from diverse ways of using things, of laboring, of expressing oneself, of practicing religion, of forming customs, of establishing laws and juridical institutions, of advancing the arts and sciences, and of promoting beauty. Thus the customs handed down to it form for each human community its proper patrimony. Thus, too, is fashioned the specific historical environment which enfolds the men of every nation and age and from which they draw the values which permit them to promote human civic culture.

SECTION 1: THE CIRCUMSTANCES OF CULTURE IN THE WORLD TODAY

New Forms of Living

54. The living conditions of modern man have been so profoundly changed in their social and cultural dimensions, that we can speak of a new age in hu-

*The concept of "culture" as it is understood by sociologists and anthropologists is a relatively new one. It is not surprising, then, that Vatican II should find it necessary to spell out several definitions of the term. (Editor's note in Abbott edition)

man history. Fresh avenues are open, therefore, for the refinement and the wider diffusion of culture. These avenues have been paved by the enormous growth of natural, human, and social sciences, by progress in technology, and by advances in the development and organization of the means by which men communicate with one another.

Hence the culture of today possesses particular characteristics. For example, the so-called exact sciences sharpen critical judgment to a very fine edge. Recent psychological research explains human activity more profoundly. Historical studies make a signal contribution to bringing men to see things in their changeable and evolutionary aspects. Customs and usages are becoming increasingly uniform. Industrialization, urbanization, and other causes of community living create new forms of culture (mass-culture), from which arise new ways of thinking, acting, and making use of leisure. The growth of communication between the various nations and social groups opens more widely to all the treasures of different cultures.

Thus, little by little, a more universal form of human culture is developing, one which will promote and express the unity of the human race to the degree that it preserves the particular features of the different cultures.

Man the Author of Culture

55. In every group or nation, there is an ever-increasing number of men and women who are conscious that they themselves are the artisans and the authors of the culture of their community. Throughout the world there is a similar growth in the combined sense of independence and responsibility. Such a development is of paramount importance for the spiritual and moral maturity of the human race. This truth grows clearer if we consider how the world is becoming unified and how we have the duty to build a better world based upon truth and justice. Thus we are witnesses of the birth of a new humanism, one in which man is defined first of all by his responsibility toward his brothers and toward history.

Problems and Duties

56. In these conditions, it is no wonder that, feeling his responsibility for the progress of culture, man nourishes higher hopes but also looks anxiously upon many contradictions which he will have to resolve:

What must be done to prevent the increased exchanges between cultures, which ought to lead to a true and fruitful dialogue between groups and nations, from disturbing the life of communities, destroying ancestral wisdom, or jeopardizing the uniqueness of each people?

How can the vitality and growth of a new culture be fostered without the loss of living fidelity to the heritage of tradition? This question is especially urgent when a culture resulting from the enormous scientific and technological progress must be harmonized with an education nourished by classical studies as adapted to various traditions.

As special branches of knowledge continue to shoot out so rapidly, how can the necessary synthesis of them be worked out, and how can men preserve the ability to contemplate and to wonder, from which wisdom comes?

What can be done to make all men on earth share in cultural values, when the culture of the more sophisticated grows ever more refined and complex?

Finally, how is the independence which culture claims for itself to be recognized as legitimate without the promotion of a humanism which is merely earth-bound, and even contrary to religion itself?

In the thick of these tensions, human culture must evolve today in such a way that it can develop the whole human person harmoniously and at the same time assist men in those duties which all men, especially Christians, are called to fulfill in the fraternal unity of the one human family.

SECTION 2: SOME PRINCIPLES OF PROPER CULTURAL DEVELOPMENT

Faith and Culture

57. Christians, on pilgrimage toward the heavenly city, should seek and savor the things which are above. This duty in no way decreases, but rather increases, the weight of their obligation to work with all men in constructing a more human world. In fact, the mystery of the Christian faith furnishes them with excellent incentives and helps toward discharging this duty more energetically and especially toward uncovering the full meaning of this activity, a meaning which gives human culture its eminent place in the integral vocation of man.

For when, by the work of his hands or with the aid of technology, man develops the earth so that it can bear fruit and become a dwelling worthy of the whole human family, and when he consciously takes part in the life of social groups, he carries out the design of God. Manifested at the beginning of time, the divine plan is that man should subdue the earth, bring creating to perfection, and develop himself. When a man so acts he simultaneously obeys the great Christian commandment that he place himself at the service of his brother men.

Furthermore, when a man applies himself to the various disciplines of philosophy, of history, and of mathematical and natural science, and when he cultivates the arts, he can do very much to elevate the human family to a more sublime understanding of truth, goodness, and beauty, and to the formation of judgments which embody universal values. Thus mankind can be more clearly enlightened by the marvelous Wisdom which was with God from all eternity, arranging all things with Him, playing upon the earth, delighting in the sons of men.

In this way, the human spirit grows increasingly free of its bondage to creatures and can be more easily drawn to the worship and contemplation of the Creator. Moreover, under the impulse of grace, man is disposed to acknowledge the Word of God. Before He became flesh in order to save all things and to sum them up in Himself, "He was in the world" already as "the true light that enlightens every man" (Jn. 1:9–10).

No doubt today's progress in science and technology can foster a certain exclusive emphasis on observable data, and an agnosticism about everything else. For the methods of investigation which these sciences use can be wrongly considered as the supreme rule for discovering the whole truth. By virtue of their methods, however, these sciences cannot penetrate to the intimate meaning of things. Yet the danger exists that man, confiding too much in modern discoveries, may even think that he is sufficient unto himself and no longer seek any higher realities.

These unfortunate results, however, do not necessarily follow from the culture of today, nor should they lead us into the temptation of not acknowledging its positive values. For among its values are these: scientific study and strict fidelity toward truth in scientific research, the necessity of working together with others in technical groups, a sense of international solidarity, an ever clearer awareness of the responsibility of experts to aid men and even to protect them, the desire to make the conditions of life more favorable for all, especially for those who are deprived of the opportunity to exercise responsibility or who are culturally poor.

All of these values can provide some preparation for the acceptance of the message of the gospel—a preparation which can be animated with divine love by Him who came to save the world.

The Many Links between the Gospel and Culture

58. There are many links between the message of salvation and human culture. For God, revealing Himself to His people to the extent of a full manifestation of Himself in His Incarnate Son, has spoken according to the culture proper to different ages.

Living in various circumstances during the course of time, the Church, too, has used in her preaching the discoveries of different cultures to spread and explain the message of Christ to all nations, to probe it and more deeply understand it, and to give it better expression in liturgical celebrations in the life of the diversified community of the faithful.

But at the same time, the Church, sent to all peoples of every time and place, is not bound exclusively and indissolubly to any race or nation, nor to any particular way of life or any customary pattern of living, ancient or recent. Faithful to her own tradition and at the same time conscious of her universal mission, she can enter into communion with various cultural modes, to her enrichment and theirs too.

The good news of Christ constantly renews the life and culture of fallen man. It combats and removes the errors and evils resulting from sinful allurements which are a perpetual threat. It never ceases to purify and elevate the morality of peoples. By riches coming from above, it makes fruitful, as it were from within, the spiritual qualities and gifts of every people and of every age. It strengthens, perfects, and restores them in Christ. Thus by the very fulfillment of her own mission the Church stimulates and advances human and civic culture. By her action, even in its liturgical form, she leads men toward interior liberty.

Harmony between the Forms of Culture

59. For the aforementioned reasons, the Church recalls to the mind of all that culture must be made to bear on the integral perfection of the human person, and on the good of the community and the whole of society. Therefore the human spirit must be cultivated in such a way that there results a growth in its ability to wonder, to understand, to contemplate, to make personal judgments, and to develop a religious, moral, and social sense.

Because it flows immediately from man's spiritual and social nature, culture has constant need of a just freedom if it is to develop. It also needs the legitimate possibility of exercising its independence according to its own principles. Rightly, therefore, it demands respect and enjoys a certain inviolability, at least as long as the rights of the individual and of the community, whether particular or universal, are preserved within the context of the common good.

This sacred Synod, therefore, recalling the teaching of the first Vatican Council, declares that there are "two orders of knowledge" which are distinct, namely, faith and reason. It declares that the Church does not indeed forbid that "when the human arts and sciences are practiced they use their own principles and their proper method, each in its own domain." Hence, "acknowledging this just liberty," this sacred Synod affirms the legitimate autonomy of human culture and especially of the sciences.

All these considerations demand too, that, within the limits of morality and the general welfare, a man be free to search for the truth, voice his mind, and publicize it; that he be free to practice any art he chooses; and finally that he have appropriate access to information about public affairs.

It is not the function of public authority to determine what the proper nature of forms of human culture should be. It should rather foster the conditions and the means which are capable of promoting cultural life among all citizens and even within the minorities of a nation. Hence in this matter men must insist above all else that culture be not diverted from its own purpose and made to serve political or economic interests.

SECTION 3: SOME ESPECIALLY URGENT DUTIES OF CHRISTIANS WITH REGARD TO CULTURE

Recognizing and Implementing the Right to Culture

60. The possibility now exists of liberating most men from the misery of ignorance. Hence it is a duty most befitting our times that men, especially Christians, should work strenuously on behalf of certain decisions which must be made in the economic and political fields, both nationally and internationally. By these decisions universal recognition and implementation should be given to the right of all men to a human and civic culture favorable to personal dignity and free from any discrimination on the grounds of race, sex, nationality, religion, or social conditions.

Therefore it is necessary to provide every man with a sufficient abundance of cultural benefits, especially those which constitute so-called basic culture. Otherwise, because of illiteracy and a lack of responsible activity, very many will be prevented from collaborating in a truly human manner for the sake of the common good.

Efforts must be made to see that men who are capable of higher studies can pursue them. In this way, as far as possible, they can be prepared to undertake in society those duties, offices, and services which are in harmony with their natural aptitude and with the competence they will have acquired. Thus all the individuals and the social groups comprising a given people will be able to attain the full development of their culture, a development in accord with their qualities and traditions.

Energetic efforts must also be expended to make everyone conscious of his right to culture and of the duty he has to develop himself culturally and to assist others. For existing conditions of life and of work sometimes thwart the cultural strivings of men and destroy in them the desire for self-improvement. This is especially true of country people and laborers. They need to be provided with working conditions which will not block their human development but rather favor it.

Women are now employed in almost every area of life. It is appropriate that they should be able to assume their full proper role in accordance with their own nature. Everyone should acknowledge and favor the proper and necessary participation of women in cultural life.

Cultural Education

61. Today it is more difficult than ever for a synthesis to be formed of the various branches of knowledge and the arts. For while the mass and the diversity of cultural factors are increasing, there is a decline in the individual man's ability to grasp and unify these elements. Thus the ideal of the "universal man" is disappearing more and more. Nevertheless, it remains each man's duty to preserve a view of the whole human person, a view in which the values of intellect, will, conscience, and fraternity are pre-eminent. These values are all rooted in God the Creator and have been wonderfully restored and elevated in Christ.

The family is, as it were, the primary mother and nurse of this attitude. There, in an atmosphere of love, children can more easily learn the true structure of reality. There, too, tested forms of human culture impress themselves upon the mind of the developing adolescent in a kind of automatic way.

Opportunities for the same kind of education can also be found in modern society, thanks especially to the increased circulation of books and to the new means of cultural and social communication. All such opportunities can foster a universal culture.

The widespread reduction in working hours, for instance, brings increasing advantages to numerous people. May these leisure hours be properly used for relaxation of spirit and the strengthening of mental and bodily health. Such benefits are available through spontaneous study and activity and through travel, which refines human qualities and enriches men with mutual understanding. These benefits are obtainable too from physical exercise and sports events, which can help to preserve emotional balance, even at the community level, and to establish fraternal relations among men of all conditions, nations, and races.

Hence let Christians work together to animate the cultural expressions and group activities characteristic of our times with a human and a Christian spirit.

All these benefits, however, cannot educate men to a full self-development unless at the same time deep thought is given to what culture and science mean in terms of the human person.

Harmony between Culture and Christian Formation

62. Although the Church has contributed much to the development of culture, experience shows that, because of circumstances, it is sometimes difficult to harmonize culture with Christian teaching.

These difficulties do not necessarily harm the life of faith. Indeed they can stimulate the mind to a more accurate and penetrating grasp of the faith.

For recent studies and findings of science, history, and philosophy raise new questions which influence life and demand new theological investigations.

Furthermore, while adhering to the methods and requirements proper to theology, theologians are invited to seek continually for more suitable ways of communicating doctrine to the men of their times. For the deposit of faith or revealed truths are one thing; the manner in which they are formulated without violence to their meaning and significance is another.

In pastoral care, appropriate use must be made not only of theological principles, but also of the findings of the secular sciences, especially of psychology and sociology. Thus the faithful can be brought to live the faith in a more thorough and mature way.

Literature and the arts are also, in their own way, of great importance to the life of the Church. For they strive to probe the unique nature of man, his problems, and his experiences as he struggles to know and perfect both himself and the world. They are preoccupied with revealing man's place in history and in the world, with illustrating his miseries and joys, his needs and strengths, and with foreshadowing a better life for him. Thus they are able to elevate human life as it is expressed in manifold forms, depending on time and place.

Efforts must therefore be made so that those who practice these arts can feel that the Church gives recognition to them in their activities, and so that, enjoying an orderly freedom, they can establish smoother relations with the Christian community. Let the Church also acknowledge new forms of art which are adapted to our age and are in keeping with the characteristics of various nations and regions. Adjusted in their mode of expression and conformed to liturgical requirements, they may be introduced into the sanctuary when they raise the mind to God.

In this way the knowledge of God can be better revealed. Also, the preaching of the gospel can become clearer to man's mind and show its relevance to the conditions of human life.

May the faithful, therefore, live in very close union with the men of their time. Let them strive to understand perfectly their way of thinking and feeling, as expressed in their culture. Let them blend modern science and its theories and the understanding of the most recent discoveries with Christian morality and doctrine. Thus their religious practice and morality can keep pace with their scientific knowledge and with an ever-advancing technology. Thus too they will be able to test and interpret all things in a truly Christian spirit.

Through a sharing of resources and points of view, let those who teach in seminaries, colleges, and universities try to collaborate with men well versed in the other sciences. Theological inquiry should seek a profound understanding of revealed truth without neglecting close contact with its own times. As a result, it will be able to help those men skilled in various fields of knowledge to gain a better understanding of the faith.

This common effort will very greatly aid in the formation of priests. It will enable them to present to our contemporaries the doctrine of the Church concerning God, man, and the world in a manner better suited to them, with the result that they will receive it more willingly. Furthermore, it is to be hoped that many laymen will receive an appropriate formation in the sacred sciences, and that some will develop and deepen these studies by their own labors. In order that such persons may fulfill their proper function, let it be recognized that all the faithful, clerical and lay, possess a lawful freedom of inquiry and of thought, and the freedom to express their minds humbly and courageously about those matters in which they enjoy competence.

Evangelization in the Modern World

Excerpts Concerning Evangelization and Culture from the Apostolic Exhortation *Evangelii Nuntiandi* of Paul VI, December 8, 1975, in Follow-up to the 1974 Synod of Bishops

To the Episcopate, to the Clergy and to All the Faithful of the Entire World

Venerable Brothers and Dear Sons and Daughters: Health and Apostolic Blessing

Special Commitment to Evangelization

1. There is no doubt that the effort to proclaim the Gospel to the people of today, who are buoyed up by hope but at the same time often oppressed by fear and distress, is a service rendered to the Christian community and also to the whole of humanity.

For this reason the duty of confirming the brethren – a duty which with the office of being the Successor of Peter we have received from the Lord, and which is for us a "daily preoccupation," a program of life and action, and a fundamental commitment of our Pontificate – seems to us all the more noble and necessary when it is a matter of encouraging our brethren in their mission as evangelizers, in order that, in this time of uncertainty and confusion, they may accomplish this task with ever increasing love, zeal and joy.

On the Occasion of Three Events

2. This is precisely what we wish to do here, at the end of this Holy Year during which the Church, "striving to proclaim the Gospel to all people,"[3] has had the single aim of fulfilling her duty of being the messenger of the Good News of Jesus Christ – the Good News proclaimed through two fundamental commands: "Put on the new self" and "Be reconciled to God."

We wish to do so on this tenth anniversary of the closing of the Second Vatican Council, the objectives of which are definitively summed up in this single one: to make the Church of the twentieth century ever better fitted for proclaiming the Gospel to the people of the twentieth century.

We wish to do so one year after the Third General Assembly of the Synod of Bishops, which, as is well known, was devoted to evangelization; and we do so all the more willingly because it has been asked of us by the Synod Fathers themselves. In fact, at the end of that memorable Assembly, the Fathers decided to remit to the Pastor of the universal Church, with great trust and simplicity, the fruits of all their labors, stating that they awaited from him a fresh forward impulse, capable of creating within a Church still more firmly rooted in the undying power and strength of Pentecost a new period of evangelization.

Theme Frequently Emphasized in the Course of Our Pontificate

3. We have stressed the importance of this theme of evangelization on many occasions, well before the Synod took place. On 22 June 1973 we said to the Sacred College of Cardinals: "The conditions of the society in which we live oblige all of us therefore to revise methods, to seek by every means to study how we can bring the Christian message to modern man. For it is only in the Christian message that modern man can find the answer to his questions and the energy for his commitment of human solidarity." And we added that in order to give a valid answer to the demands of the Council which call for our attention, it is absolutely necessary for us to take into account a heritage of faith that the Church has the duty of preserving in its untouchable purity, and of presenting it to the people of our time, in a way that is as understandable and persuasive as possible.

In the Line of the 1974 Synod

4. This fidelity both to a message whose servants we are and to the people to whom we must transmit it living and intact is the central axis of evangelization. It poses three burning questions, which the 1974 Synod kept constantly in mind:

– In our day, what has happened to that hidden energy of the Good News, which is able to have a powerful effect on man's conscience?

– To what extent and in what way is that evangelical force capable of really transforming the people of this century?

– What methods should be followed in order that the power of the Gospel may have its effect?

Basically, these inquiries make explicit the fundamental question that the Church is asking herself today and which may be expressed in the following terms: after the Council and thanks to the Council, which was a time given her by God, at this turning-point of history, does the Church or does she not find herself better equipped to proclaim the Gospel and to put it into people's hearts with conviction, freedom of spirit and effectiveness?

Invitation to Meditation

5. We can all see the urgency of giving a loyal, humble and courageous answer to this question, and of acting accordingly.

In our "anxiety for all the Churches," we would like to help our Brethren and sons and daughters to reply to these inquiries. Our words come from the wealth of the Synod and are meant to be a meditation on evangelization. May they succeed in inviting the whole People of God assembled in the Church to make the same meditation; and may they give a fresh impulse to everyone, especially those "who are assiduous in preaching and teaching," so that each one of them may follow "a straight course in the message of the truth," and may work as a preacher of the Gospel and acquit himself perfectly of his ministry.

Such an exhortation seems to us to be of capital importance, for the presentation of the Gospel message is not an optional contribution for the Church. It is the duty incumbent on her by the command of the Lord Jesus, so that people can believe and be saved. This message is indeed necessary. It is unique. It cannot be replaced. It does not permit either indifference, syncretism or accommodation. It is a question of people's salvation. It is the beauty of the Revelation that it represents. It brings with it a wisdom that is not of this world. It is able to stir up by itself faith – faith that rests on the power of God.[11] It is truth. It merits having the apostle consecrate to it all his time and all his energies, and to sacrifice for it, if necessary, his own life.

★ ★ ★ ★ ★

Excerpt from Chapter II: What Is Evangelization?

Complexity of Evangelizing Action

17. In the Church's evangelizing activity there are of course certain elements and aspects to be specially insisted on. Some of them are so important that there will be a tendency simply to identify them with evangelization. Thus it has been possible to define evangelization in terms of proclaiming Christ to those who do not know him, of preaching, of catechesis, of conferring Baptism and the other Sacraments.

Any partial and fragmentary definition which attempts to render the reality of evangelization in all its richness, complexity and dynamism does so only at the risk of impoverishing it and even of distorting it. It is impossible to grasp the concept of evangelization unless one tries to keep in view all its essential elements.

These elements were strongly emphasized at the last Synod, and are still the subject of frequent study, as a result of the Synod's work. We rejoice in the fact that these elements basically follow the lines of those transmitted to us by the Second Vatican Council, especially in *Lumen Gentium, Gaudium et Spes* and *Ad Gentes.*

Renewal of Humanity

18. For the Church, evangelizing means bringing the Good News into all the strata of humanity, and through its influence transforming humanity from within and making it new: "Now I am making the whole of creation new." But there is no new humanity if there are not first of all new persons renewed by Baptism and by lives lived according to the Gospel. The purpose of evangelization is therefore precisely this interior change, and if it had to be expressed in one sentence the best way of stating it would be to say that the Church evangelizes when she seeks to convert, solely through the divine power of the Message she proclaims, both the personal and collective consciences of people, the activities in which they engage, and the lives and concrete milieux which are theirs.

And of the Strata of Humanity

19. Strata of humanity which are transformed: for the Church it is a question not only of preaching the Gospel in ever wider geographic areas or to ever greater numbers of people, but also of affecting and as it were upsetting, through the power of the Gospel, mankind's criteria of judgment, determining values, points of interest, lines of thought, sources of inspiration and models of life, which are in contrast with the Word of God and the plan of salvation.

Evangelization of Cultures

20. All this could be expressed in the following words: what matters is to evangelize man's culture and cultures (not in a purely decorative way as it were by applying a thin veneer, but in a vital way, in depth and right to their very roots), in the wide and rich sense which these terms have in *Gaudium et Spes*, always taking the person as one's starting-point and always coming back to the relationships of people among themselves and with God.

The Gospel, and therefore evangelization, are certainly not identical with culture, and they are independent in regard to all cultures. Nevertheless, the Kingdom which the Gospel proclaims is lived by men who are profoundly linked to a culture, and the building up of the Kingdom cannot avoid borrowing the elements of human culture or cultures. Though independent of cultures, the Gospel and evangelization are not necessarily incompatible with them; rather they are capable of permeating them all without becoming subject to any one of them.

The split between the Gospel and culture is without a doubt the drama of our time, just as it was of other times. Therefore every effort must be made to ensure a full evangelization of culture, or more correctly of cultures. They have to be regenerated by an encounter with the Gospel. But this encounter will not take place if the Gospel is not proclaimed.

Primary Importance of Witness of Life

21. Above all the Gospel must be proclaimed by witness. Take a Christian or a handful of Christians who, in the midst of their own community, show their capacity for understanding and acceptance, their sharing of life and destiny with other people, their solidarity with the efforts of all for whatever is noble and good. Let us suppose that, in addition, they radiate in an altogether simple and unaffected way their faith in values that go beyond current values, and their hope in something that is not seen and that one would not dare to imagine. Through this wordless witness these Christians stir up irresistible questions in the hearts of those who see how they live: Why are they like this? Why do they live in this way? What or who is it that inspires them? Why are they in our midst? Such a witness is already a silent proclamation of the Good News and a very powerful and effective one. Here we have an initial act of evangelization. The above questions will perhaps be the first that many non-Christians will ask, whether they are people to whom Christ has never been proclaimed, or baptized people who do not practice, or people who live as nominal Christians but according to principles that are in no way Christian, or people who are seeking, and not without suffering, something or someone whom they sense but cannot name. Other questions will arise, deeper and more demanding ones, questions evoked by this witness which involves presence, sharing, solidarity, and which is an essential element, and generally the first one, in evangelization.

All Christians are called to this witness, and in this way they can be real evangelizers. We are thinking especially of the responsibility incumbent on immigrants in the country that receives them.

Need of Explicit Proclamation

22. Nevertheless this always remains insufficient, because even the finest witness will prove ineffective in the long run if it is not explained, justified —what Peter called always having "your answer ready for people who ask you

the reason for the hope that you all have"–and made explicit by a clear and unequivocal proclamation of the Lord Jesus. The Good News proclaimed by the witness of life sooner or later has to be proclaimed by the word of life. There is no true evangelization if the name, the teaching, the life, the promises, the Kingdom and the mystery of Jesus of Nazareth, the Son of God are not proclaimed. The history of the Church, from the discourse of Peter on the morning of Pentecost onwards, has been intermingled and identified with the history of this proclamation. At every new phase of human history, the Church, constantly gripped by the desire to evangelize, has but one preoccupation: whom to send to proclaim the mystery of Jesus? In what way is this mystery to be proclaimed? How can one ensure that it will resound and reach all those who should hear it? This proclamation–*kerygma*, preaching or catechesis –occupies such an important place in evangelization that it has often become synonymous with it; and yet it is only one aspect of evangelization.

For a Vital and Community Acceptance

23. In fact the proclamation only reaches full development when it is listened to, accepted and assimilated, and when it arouses a genuine adherence in the one who has thus received it. An adherence to the truths which the Lord in his mercy has revealed; still more, an adherence to a program of life–a life henceforth transformed–which he proposes. In a word, adherence to the Kingdom, that is to say the "new world," to the new state of things, to the new manner of being, of living, of living in community, which the Gospel inaugurates. Such an adherence, which cannot remain abstract and unincarnated, reveals itself concretely by a visible entry into a community of believers. Thus those whose life has been transformed enter a community which is itself a sign of transformation, a sign of newness of life: it is the Church, the visible sacrament of salvation. But entry into the ecclesial community will in its turn be expressed through many other signs which prolong and unfold the sign of the Church. In the dynamism of evangelization, a person who accepts the Church as the Word which saves normally translates it into the following sacramental acts: adherence to the Church, and acceptance of the Sacraments, which manifest and support this adherence through the grace which they confer.

Involving a New Apostolate

24. Finally: the person who has been evangelized goes on to evangelize others. Here lies the test of truth, the touchstone of evangelization: it is unthinkable that a person should accept the Word and give himself to the Kingdom without becoming a person who bears witness to it and proclaims it in his turn.

To complete these considerations on the meaning of evangelization, a final observation must be made, one which we consider will help to clarify the reflections that follow.

Evangelization, as we have said, is a complex process made up of varied elements: the renewal of humanity, witness, explicit proclamation, inner adherence, entry into the community, acceptance of signs, apostolic initiative. These elements may appear to be contradictory, indeed mutually exclusive. In fact they are complementary and mutually enriching. Each one must always be seen in relationship with the others. The value of the last Synod was to have constantly invited us to relate these elements rather than to place them in opposition one to the other, in order to reach a full understanding of the Church's evangelizing activity.

It is this global vision which we now wish to outline, by examining the content of evangelization and the methods of evangelizing and by clarifying to whom the Gospel message is addressed and who today is responsible for it.

★ ★ ★ ★ ★

Excerpt from Chapter III: The Content of Evangelization

Message Touching Life as a Whole

29. But evangelization would not be complete if it did not take account of the unceasing interplay of the Gospel and of man's concrete life, both personal and social. This is why evangelization involves an explicit message, adapted to the different situations constantly being realized, about the rights and duties of every human being, about family life without which personal growth and development is hardly possible, about life in society, about international life, peace, justice and development—a message especially energetic today about liberation.

A Message of Liberation

30. It is well known in what terms numerous Bishops from all the continents spoke of this at the last Synod, especially the Bishops from the Third World, with a pastoral accent resonant with the voice of the millions of sons and daughters of the Church who make up those peoples. Peoples, as we know, engaged with all their energy in the effort and struggle to overcome everything which condemns them to remain on the margin of life: famine, chronic disease, illiteracy, poverty, injustices in international relations and especially in commercial exchanges, situations of economic and cultural neo-colonialism

sometimes as cruel as the old political colonialism. The Church, as the Bishops repeated, has the duty to proclaim the liberation of millions of human beings, many of whom are her own children—the duty of assisting the birth of this liberation, of giving witness to it, of ensuring that it is complete. This is not foreign to evangelization.

Necessarily Linked to Human Advancement

31. Between evangelization and human advancement—development and liberation—there are in fact profound links. These include links of an anthropological order, because the man who is to be evangelized is not an abstract being but is subject to social and economic questions. They also include links in the theological order, since one cannot dissociate the plan of creation from the plan of Redemption. The latter plan touches the very concrete situations of injustice to be combatted and of justice to be restored. They include links of the eminently evangelical order, which is that of charity: how in fact can one proclaim the new commandment without promoting in justice and in peace the true, authentic advancement of man? We ourself have taken care to point this out, by recalling that it is impossible to accept "that in evangelization one could or should ignore the importance of the problems so much discussed today, concerning justice, liberation, development and peace in the world. This would be to forget the lesson which comes to us from the Gospel concerning love of our neighbor who is suffering and in need."

The same voices which during the Synod touched on this burning theme with zeal, intelligence and courage have, to our great joy, furnished the enlightening principles for a proper understanding of the importance and profound meaning of liberation, such as it was proclaimed and achieved by Jesus of Nazareth and such as it is preached by the Church.

Without Reduction or Ambiguity

32. We must not ignore the fact that many, even generous Christians who are sensitive to the dramatic questions involved in the problem of liberation, in their wish to commit the Church to the liberation effort are frequently tempted to reduce her mission to the dimensions of a simply temporal project. They would reduce her aims to a man-centered goal; the salvation of which she is the messenger would be reduced to material well-being. Her activity, forgetful of all spiritual and religious preoccupation, would become initiatives of the political or social order. But if this were so, the Church would lose her fundamental meaning. Her message of liberation would no longer have any originality and would easily be open to monopolization and manipulation by ideological systems and political parties. She would have no more

authority to proclaim freedom as in the name of God. This is why we have wished to emphasize, in the same address at the opening of the Synod, "the need to restate clearly the specifically religious finality of evangelization. This latter would lose its reason for existence if it were to diverge from the religious axis that guides it: the Kingdom of God, before anything else, in its fully theological meaning. . . ."

Evangelical Liberation

33. With regard to the liberation which evangelization proclaims and strives to put into practice one should rather say this:

– it cannot be contained in the simple and restricted dimension of economics, politics, social or cultural life; it must envisage the whole man, in all his aspects, right up to and including his openness to the absolute, even the divine Absolute;

– it is therefore attached to a certain concept of man, to a view of man which it can never sacrifice to the needs of any strategy, practice or short-term efficiency.

Centered on the Kingdom of God

34. Hence, when preaching liberation and associating herself with those who are working and suffering for it, the Church is certainly not willing to restrict her mission only to the religious field and dissociate herself from man's temporal problems. Nevertheless she reaffirms the primacy of her spiritual vocation and refuses to replace the proclamation of the Kingdom by the proclamation of forms of human liberation; she even states that her contribution to liberation is incomplete if she neglects to proclaim salvation in Jesus Christ.

On an Evangelical Concept of Man

35. The Church links human liberation and salvation in Jesus Christ, but she never identifies them, because she knows through revelation, historical experience and the reflection of faith that not every notion of liberation is necessarily consistent and compatible with an evangelical vision of man, of things and of events; she knows too that in order that God's Kingdom should come it is not enough to establish liberation and to create well-being and development.

And what is more, the Church has the firm conviction that all temporal liberation, all political liberation – even if it endeavors to find its justification in such or such a page of the Old or New Testament, even if it claims for its ideological postulates and its norms of action theological data and conclusions, even if it pretends to be today's theology—carries within itself the germ of its own negation and fails to reach the ideal that it proposes for itself, whenever its profound motives are not those of justice in charity, whenever its zeal lacks a truly spiritual dimension and whenever its final goal is not salvation and happiness in God.

Involving a Necessary Conversion

36. The Church considers it to be undoubtedly important to build up structures which are more human, more just, more respectful of the rights of the person and less oppressive and less enslaving, but she is conscious that the best structures and the most idealized systems soon become inhuman if the inhuman inclinations of the human heart are not made wholesome, if those who live in these structures or who rule them do not undergo a conversion of heart and of outlook.

Excluding Violence

37. The Church cannot accept violence, especially the force of arms—which is uncontrollable once it is let loose—and indiscriminate death as the path to liberation, because she knows that violence always provokes violence and irresistibly engenders new forms of oppression and enslavement which are often harder to bear than those from which they claimed to bring freedom. We said this clearly during our journey in Colombia: "We exhort you not to place your trust in violence and revolution: that is contrary to the Christian spirit, and it can also delay instead of advancing that social uplifting to which you lawfully aspire." "We must say and reaffirm that violence is not in accord with the Gospel, that it is not Christian; and that sudden or violent changes of structures would be deceitful, ineffective of themselves, and certainly not in conformity with the dignity of the people."

Specific Contribution of the Church

38. Having said this, we rejoice that the Church is becoming ever more conscious of the proper manner and strictly evangelical means that she possesses in order to collaborate in the liberation of many. And what is she doing? She is trying more and more to encourage large numbers of Christians to devote themselves to the liberation of men. She is providing these Christian "liberators" with the inspiration of faith, the motivation of fraternal love, a social teaching which the true Christian cannot ignore and which he must make the foundation of his wisdom and of his experience in order to translate it concretely into forms of action, participation and commitment. All this must char-

acterize the spirit of a committed Christian, without confusion with tactical attitudes or with the service of a political system. The Church strives always to insert the Christian struggle for liberation into the universal plan of salvation which she herself proclaims.

What we have just recalled comes out more than once in the Synod debates. In fact we devoted to this theme a few clarifying words in our address to the Fathers at the end of the Assembly.

It is to be hoped that all these considerations will help to remove the ambiguity which the word "liberation" very often takes on in ideologies, political systems or groups. The liberation which evangelization proclaims and prepares is the one which Christ himself announced and gave to man by his sacrifice.

Religious Liberty

39. The necessity of ensuring fundamental human rights cannot be separated from this just liberation which is bound up with evangelization and which endeavors to secure structures safeguarding human freedoms. Among these fundamental human rights, religious liberty occupies a place of primary importance. We recently spoke of the relevance of this matter, emphasizing "how many Christians still today, because they are Christians, because they are Catholics, live oppressed by systematic persecution! The drama of fidelity to Christ and of the freedom of religion continues, even if it is disguised by categorical declarations in favor of the rights of the person and of life in society!"

★ ★ ★ ★ ★

Excerpt from Chapter V: The Beneficiaries of Evangelization

Proclamation to the Multitudes

57. Like Christ during the time of his preaching, like the Twelve on the morning of Pentecost, the Church too sees before her an immense multitude of people who need the Gospel and have a right to it, for God "wants everyone to be saved and reach full knowledge of the truth."

The Church is deeply aware of her duty to preach salvation to all. Knowing that the Gospel message is not reserved to a small group of the initiated, the privileged or the elect but is destined for everyone, she shares Christ's anguish at the sight of the wandering and exhausted crowds "like sheep without a shepherd" and she often repeats his words: "I feel sorry for all these people." But the Church is also conscious of the fact that, if the preaching of the

Gospel is to be effective, she must address her message to the heart of the multitudes, to communities of the faithful whose action can and must reach others.

Ecclesial "Small Communities"

58. The last Synod devoted considerable attention to these "small communities," or *communautés de base*, because they are often talked about in the Church today. What are they, and why should they be the special beneficiaries of evangelization and at the same time evangelizers themselves?

According to the various statements heard in the Synod, such communities flourish more or less throughout the Church. They differ greatly among themselves, both within the same region and even more so from one region to another.

In some regions they appear and develop, almost without exception, within the Church, having solidarity with her life, being nourished by her teaching and united with her pastors. In these cases, they spring from the need to live the Church's life more intensely, or from the desire and quest for a more human dimension such as larger ecclesial communities can only offer with difficulty, especially in the big modern cities which lend themselves both to life in the mass and to anonymity. Such communities can quite simply be in their own way an extension on the spiritual and religious level – worship, deepening of faith, fraternal charity, prayer, contact with pastors – of the small sociological community such as the village, etc. Or again their aim may be to bring together, for the purpose of listening to and meditating on the Word, for the Sacraments and the bond of the agape, groups of people who are linked by age, culture, civil state or social situation: married couples, young people, professional people, etc., people who already happen to be united in the struggle for justice, brotherly aid to the poor, human advancement. In still other cases they bring Christians together in places where the shortage of priests does not favor the normal life of a parish community. This is all presupposed within communities constituted by the Church, especially individual Churches and parishes.

In other regions, on the other hand, *communautés de base* come together in a spirit of bitter criticism of the Church, which they are quick to stigmatize as "institutional" and to which they set themselves up in opposition as charismatic communities, free from structures and inspired only by the Gospel. Thus their obvious characteristic is an attitude of fault-finding and of rejection with regard to the Church's outward manifestations: her hierarchy, her signs. They are radically opposed to the Church. By following these lines their main inspiration very quickly becomes ideological, and it rarely happens that they do not quickly fall victim to some political option or current of thought, and then to a system, even a party, with all the attendant risks of becoming its instrument.

The difference is already notable: the communities which by their spirit of opposition cut themselves off from the Church, and whose unity they wound, can well be called *communautés de base,* but in this case it is a strictly sociological name. They could not, without a misuse of terms, be called ecclesial *communautés de base,* even if, while being hostile to the hierarchy, they claim to remain within the unity of the Church. This name belongs to the other groups, those which come together within the Church in order to unite themselves to the Church and to cause the Church to grow.

These latter communities will be a place of evangelization, for the benefit of the bigger communities, especially the individual Churches. And, as we said at the end of the last Synod, they will be a hope for the universal Church to the extent:

–that they seek their nourishment in the Word of God and do not allow themselves to be ensnared by political polarization or fashionable ideologies, which are ready to exploit their immense human potential;

–that they avoid the ever present temptation of systematic protest and a hypercritical attitude, under the pretext of authenticity and a spirit of collaboration;

–that they remain firmly attached to the local Church in which they are inserted, and to the universal Church, thus avoiding the very real danger of becoming isolated within themselves, then of believing themselves to be the only authentic Church of Christ, and hence of condemning the other ecclesial communities;

–that they maintain a sincere communion with the pastors whom the Lord gives to his Church, and with the Magisterium which the Spirit of Christ has entrusted to these pastors;

–that they never look on themselves as the sole beneficiaries or sole agents of evangelization–or even the only depositaries of the Gospel–but, being aware that the Church is much more vast and diversified, accept the fact that this Church becomes incarnate in other ways than through themselves;

–that they constantly grow in missionary consciousness, fervor, commitment and zeal;

–that they show themselves to be universal in all things and never sectarian.

On these conditions, which are certainly demanding but also uplifting, the ecclesial *communautés de base* will correspond to their most fundamental vocation: as hearers of the Gospel which is proclaimed to them and privileged beneficiaries of evangelization, they will soon become proclaimers of the Gospel themselves.

Man's Entire Humanity Is Expressed in Culture

Address of John Paul II to UNESCO, The United Nations Educational, Scientific and Cultural Organization, Paris, June 2, 1980

Mr. President of the General Conference,

Mr. President of the Executive Council,

Mr. Director General,

Ladies and Gentlemen,

1. I wish in the first place to express my very cordial thanks for the invitation that Mr. Amadou Mahtar-M'Bow, Director General of the United Nations Educational, Scientific and Cultural Organization, extended to me several times, even at the first of the visits he has done me the honor of paying me. There are many reasons for which I am happy to be able to accept today this invitation, which I highly appreciated immediately.

For the kind words of welcome they have just addressed to me, I thank Mr. Napoleon Leblanc, President of the General Conference, Mr. Chams Eldine El-Wakil, President of the Executive Council, and Mr. Amadou Mahtar-M'Bow, Director General of the Organization. I also wish to greet all those who are gathered here for the 109th session of UNESCO's Executive Council. I cannot conceal my joy at seeing gathered on this occasion so many delegates from nations all over the world, so many eminent personalities, so many authorities, so many illustrious representatives of the world of culture and science.

Through my intervention, I will try to bring my modest stone to the edifice you are constructing with assiduity and perseverance, Ladies and Gentlemen, through your reflections and your resolutions in all the fields that are in UNESCO's sphere of competence.

2. Allow me to begin by referring to the *origins of your Organization.* The events that marked the foundation of UNESCO inspire me with joy and gratitude to Divine Providence: the signature of its constitution on 16 November 1945; the coming into force of this constitution and the establishment of the Organization on 4 November 1946; the agreement between UNESCO and

the United Nations Organization approved by the General Assembly of the U.N. in the same year. Your Organization is, in fact, the work of the nations which, after the end of the terrible Second World War, were impelled by what could be called a spontaneous desire for peace, union and reconciliation. These nations looked for the means and the forms of a collaboration capable of establishing this new understanding and of deepening it and ensuring it in a lasting way. So UNESCO came into being, like the United Nations Organization, because the peoples knew that at the basis of the great enterprises intended to serve peace and the progress of humanity over the whole globe, there was *the necessity of the union of nations*, mutual respect and international cooperation.

3. Prolonging the action, thought and message of my great predecessor Pope Paul VI, I had the honor of speaking before the United Nations General Assembly, in the month of October last, on the invitation of Mr. Kurt Waldheim, Secretary General of U.N. Shortly afterwards, on 12 November 1979, I was invited by Mr. Edouard Saouma, Director General of the United Nations Food and Agricultural Organization in Rome. On these occasions I had the honour of dealing with questions deeply linked with all the problems connected with man's peaceful future on earth. In fact, all these problems are closely linked. We are in the presence, so to speak, of a vast system of communicating vessels: the problems of culture, science and education do not arise, in the life of nations and in international relations, independently of the other problems of human existence, such as those of peace or hunger. The problems of culture are conditioned by the other dimensions of human existence, just as the latter, in their turn condition them.

4. All the same there is – and I stressed it in my address to the U.N., referring to the Universal Declaration of Human Rights – one fundamental dimension which is capable of shaking to their very foundations the systems that structure mankind as a whole and of freeing human existence, individual and collective, from the threats that weigh on it. This fundamental dimension is man, man in his integrality, man who lives at the same time in the sphere of material values and in that of spiritual values. Respect for the inalienable rights of the human person is at the basis of everything (cf. Address to the U.N., nos. 7 and 13).

Any threat to human rights, whether in the framework of man's spiritual goods or in that of his material goods, does violence to this fundamental dimension. That is why, in my address to FAO, I emphasized that no man, no country and no system in the world can remain indifferent to the "geography of hunger" and the gigantic threats that will ensue if the whole direction of economic policy, and in particular the hierarchy of investments, do not change in an essential and radical way. That is also why, referring to the origins of your Organization, I stress the necessity of mobilizing all forces which direct the spiritual dimension of human existence, and which bear witness to the primacy of the spiritual in man—and of what corresponds to the dignity of his intelligence, his will and his heart—in order not to succumb again to the monstrous alienation of collective evil, which is always ready to use material powers in the exterminating struggle of men against men, of nations against nations.

5. At the origin of UNESCO, as also at the basis of the Universal Declaration on Human Rights, there are, therefore, these first noble impulses of human conscience, intelligence and will. I appeal to this origin, to this beginning, to these premises and to these first principles. It is in their name that I come today to Paris, to the headquarters of your Organization, with an entreaty: that at the end of a stage of over thirty years of your activities, you will unite even more round these ideals and principles on which the beginning was based. It is in their name also that I shall now take the liberty of proposing to you some really fundamental considerations, for it is only by their light that there shines forth fully the meaning of this institution, which has as its name UNESCO, the United Nations Educational, Scientific and Cultural Organization.

6. *Genus humanum arte et ratione vivit* (Humanity lives by creativity and intellect; cf. St. Thomas, commenting on Aristotle, in Post. Analyt., n. 1). These words of one of the greatest geniuses of Christianity, who was at the same time a fruitful continuer of the thought of antiquity, take us beyond the circle and contemporary meaning of Western culture, whether it is Mediterranean or Atlantic. They have a meaning that applies to humanity as a whole, where the different traditions that constitute its spiritual heritage and the different periods of its culture, meet. The essential meaning of culture consists, according to these words of St. Thomas Aquinas, in the fact that it is a characteristic of human life as such. *Man lives a really human life thanks to culture.* Human life is culture in this sense too that, through it, man is distinguished and differentiated from everything that exists elsewhere in the visible world: man cannot do without culture.

Culture is a specific way of man's "existing" and "being." Man always lives according to a culture which is specifically his, and which, in its turn, creates among men a tie which is also specifically theirs, determining the interhuman and social character of human existence. In the unity of culture as the specific way of human existence, there is rooted at the same time the *plurality of cultures* in the midst of which man lives. In this plurality, man develops without losing, however, the essential contact with the unity of culture as the fundamental and essential dimension of his existence and his being.

7. Man who, in the visible world, is the only ontic *subject of culture,* is also its only *object and its term.* Culture is that through which man, as man, becomes more man, "is" more, has more access to "being." The fundamental

distinction between what man is and what he has, between being and having, has its foundation there too. Culture is always in an essential and necessary relationship to what man is, whereas its relationship to what he has, to his "having," is not only secondary, but entirely relative. All man's "having" is important for culture, is a factor creative of culture, only to the extent to which man, through his "having," can at the same time "be" more fully as a man, become more fully a man in all the dimensions of his existence, in everything that characterizes his humanity. The experience of various eras, without excluding the present one, proves that people think of culture and speak about it in the first place in relation to *the nature of man,* then only in a secondary and indirect way in relation *to the world of his products.* That in no way detracts from the fact that we judge the phenomenon of culture on the basis of what man produces, or that we draw from that, at the same time, conclusions about man. Such an approach – a typical way of the "a posteriori" process of knowledge – contains in itself the possibility of going back, in the opposite direction, to ontic-causal dependencies. Man, and only man, is the "protagonist" or "architect" of culture; man, and only man, expresses himself in it and finds his own balance in it.

8. All of us present here meet on the *ground of culture,* the fundamental reality which unites us and which is at the basis of the establishment and purposes of UNESCO. We thereby meet around man and, in a certain sense, in him, in man. This man, who expresses himself and objectivizes himself in and through culture, is unique, complete and indivisible. He is at once subject and architect of culture. Consequently, he cannot be envisaged solely as the resultant – to give only one example – of the production relations that prevail at a given period. Is this criterion of production relations not at all, then, a key to the understanding of man's historicity, to the understanding of his culture and of the multiple forms of his development? Certainly, this criterion is a key, and even a precious key, but it is not the fundamental, constitutive one. Human cultures reflect, there is no doubt, the various systems of production relations; however, it is not such and such a system that is at the origin of culture, but man, man who lives in the system, who accepts it or tries to change it. A culture without human subjectivity and without human causality is inconceivable; in the cultural field, man is always the first fact: *man is the prime and fundamental fact* of culture.

And he is so, always, in his totality: in his *spiritual* and *material* subjectivity as a *complete whole.* If the distinction between spiritual culture and material culture is correct with respect to the character and content of the products in which the culture is manifested, it is necessary to note at the same time that, on the one hand, the works of material culture always show a "spiritualization of matter," a submission of the material element to man's spiritual forces – that is, his intelligence and will – and that, on the other hand, the works of spiritual culture manifest, specifically, a "materialization" of the spirit, an incarnation of what is spiritual. In cultural works, this double characteristic seems to be equally of prime importance and equally permanent.

Here is, therefore, by way of theoretical conclusion, a sufficient basis to understand culture through the complete man, through the whole reality of his subjectivity. Here is also – in the field of action – a sufficient basis to seek always in culture the complete man, the whole man, in the whole truth of his spiritual and corporeal subjectivity; the basis which is sufficient in order not to superimpose on culture – a truly human system, a splendid synthesis of spirit and body – preconceived divisions and oppositions. In fact, whether it is a question of an absolutization of matter in the structure of the human subject, or, inversely, of an absolutization of the spirit in this same structure, neither expresses the truth about man or serves his culture.

9. I would like to stop here at another essential consideration, a reality of a quite different order. We can approach it by noting the fact that the Holy See is represented at UNESCO by its permanent Observer, whose presence is set in the perspective of the very nature of the Apostolic See. This presence is, even more widely, in harmony with the nature and mission of the Catholic Church and, indirectly, with that of the whole of Christianity. I take the opportunity which is offered to me today to express a deep personal conviction. The presence of the Apostolic See in your Organization – though motivated also by the specific sovereignty of the Holy See – has its justification above all in the *organic and constitutive link* which exists between *religion* in general and Christianity in particular, on the one hand, and *culture*, on the other hand. This relationship extends to the multiple realities which must be defined as concrete expressions of culture in the different periods of history and all over the world. It will certainly not be an exaggeration to state in particular that, through a multitude of facts, the whole of Europe – from the Atlantic to the Urals – bears witness, in the history of each nation as in that of the whole community, to the link between culture and Christianity.

Recalling this, it is not at all my intention to belittle the heritage of other continents, or the specific character and value of this same heritage which is derived from the other sources of religious, humanistic and ethical inspiration. What is more, I wish to pay the deepest and most sincere tribute to all the cultures of the human family as a whole, from the most ancient to the contemporary. It is in thinking of all cultures that I wish to say in a loud voice, here in Paris, at the headquarters of UNESCO, with respect and admiration: "Here is man!" I wish to proclaim my admiration before the creative riches of the human spirit, before its incessant efforts to know and strengthen *the identity of man*: this man who is always present in all the particular forms of culture.

10. Speaking, on the contrary, of the place of the Church and of the

Apostolic See in your Organization, I am thinking not only of all the works of culture in which, in the course of the last two millennia, the man who had accepted Christ and the Gospel expressed himself, or of the institutions of different kinds that came into being from the same inspiration in the fields of education, instruction, charity, social work and in so many others. I am thinking above all, Ladies and Gentlemen, of the fundamental *link* between the *Gospel,* that is, the *message of Christ and the Church,* and man in his *very humanity.* This link is in fact a creator of culture in its very foundation. To create culture, it is necessary to consider, to its last consequences and entirely, man as a particular and autonomous value, as the subject bearing the transcendency of the person. Man must be affirmed for himself, and not for any other motive or reason: solely for himself! What is more, man must be loved because he is man; love must be claimed for man by reason of the particular dignity he possesses. The whole of the affirmations concerning man belongs to the very substance of Christ's message and of the mission of the Church, in spite of all that critics may have declared about this matter, and all that the different movements opposed to religion in general and to Christianity in particular may have done.

In the course of history, we have already been more than once, and we still are, witnesses of a process of a very significant phenomenon. Where religious institutions have been suppressed, where ideas and works born of religious inspiration, particularly of Christian inspiration, have been deprived of their citizenship, men find again these same humanizing elements outside institutional channels. These they discover through the confrontation exercized, in truth and interior effort, between what constitutes their humanity and what is contained in the Christian message.

Ladies and Gentlemen, you will kindly forgive my making this statement. Proposing it, I did not want to offend anyone at all. I beg you to understand that, in the name of what I am, I could not abstain from giving this testimony. It also bears within it this truth – which cannot be passed over in silence – on culture, if we seek in it everything that is human, the elements in which man expresses himself or through which he wants to be the subject of his existence. And in so speaking, I wanted at the same time to manifest all the more my gratitude for the ties that unite UNESCO with the Apostolic See, these ties of which my presence today is intended as a particular expression.

11. A certain number of fundamental conclusions can be drawn from all that. In fact, the considerations I have just made show clearly that the *primary and essential task of culture* in general, and also of all culture, is *education.* Education consists in fact in enabling man to become more man, to "be" more and not just to "have" more and consequently, through everything he "has," everything he "possesses," to "be" man more fully. For this purpose man must be able to "be more," not only "with others," but also "for others." Education

is of fundamental inportance for the formation of inter-human and social relations. Here too, I touch upon a set of axioms on the basis of which the traditions of Christianity that have sprung from the Gospel meet the educative experience of so many well-disposed and deeply wise men, so numerous in all centuries of history. In our age, too, there is no lack of them, of these men who reveal themselves as great, simply through their humanity which they are able to share with others, in particular with the young. At the same time, the symptoms of crises of all kinds to which there succumb environments and societies which are among those best-off in other ways—crises which affect above all young generations—vie with each other in bearing witness that the work of man's education is not carried out only with the help of institutions, with the help of organized and material means, however excellent they may be. They also show that the most important thing is always man, man and his *moral authority* which comes from the truth of his principles and from the conformity of his actions with these principles.

12. As the world Organization most competent in all problems of culture, UNESCO cannot neglect this other question which is absolutely fundamental: What can be done in order that man's education may be carried out above all in *the family*?

What is the state of public morality which will ensure the family, and above all the parents, the moral authority necessary for this purpose? What type of instruction? What forms of legislation sustain this authority or, on the contrary, weaken it or destroy it? The causes of success and failure in the formation of man by his family always lie both within the fundamental creative environment of culture which the family is, and also at a higher level, that of the competence of the State and the organizations on which these causes depend. These problems cannot but cause reflection and solicitude in the forum where the qualified representatives of the State meet.

There is no doubt that the first and fundamental cultural fact is the spiritually mature man, that is, a fully educated man, a man capable of educating himself and educating others. Nor is there any doubt that the first and fundamental dimension of culture is healthy morality: *moral culture.*

13. Certainly, there are many particular questions in this field, but experience shows that everything is connected; and that these questions are set in systems that plainly depend upon one another. For example, in the process of education as a whole, and of scholastic education in particular, has there not been a unilateral shift towards *instruction in the narrow sense of the word*? If we consider the proportions assumed by this phenomenon, as well as the systematic increase of instruction which refers solely to what man possesses, is not man himself put more and more in the shade? That leads, then, to a real *alienation of education*: instead of working in favor of what man must "be," it works solely in favor of what man can take advantage of in the field of "hav-

ing," of "possession." The further stage of this alienation is to accustom man, by depriving him of his own subjectivity, to being the object of *multiple manipulations*: ideological or political manipulations which are carried out through public opinion; those that are operated through monopoly or control, through economic forces or political powers, and the media of social communication; finally, the manipulation which consists of teaching life as a specific manipulation of oneself.

These dangers in the field of education seem to threaten above all societies with a more developed technical civilization. These societies are confronted with man's specific crisis which consists of a growing *lack of confidence with regard to his own humanity,* to the meaning of the fact of being a man, and to the affirmation and joy derived from it, which are a source of creation. Modern civilization tries to impose on man a series of *apparent imperatives,* which its spokesmen justify by recourse to the principle of development and progress. Thus, for example, instead of respect for life, "the imperative" of getting rid of life and destroying it; instead of love which is the responsible communion of persons, "the imperative" of the maximum sexual enjoyment apart from any sense of responsibility; instead of the primacy of truth in actions, the "primacy" of behavior that is fashionable, of the subjective, and of immediate success.

In all that there is indirectly expressed a great *systematic renunciation* of the healthy ambition of being a man. Let us be under no illusions: the system constructed on the basis of these false imperatives, these fundamental renunciations, may determine the future of man and the future of culture.

14. If, in the name of the future of culture, it must be proclaimed that man has the right to "be" more, and if for the same reason it is necessary to demand a healthy *primacy of the family* in the overall work of educating man to real humanity, *the law of the Nation* must be set along the same line; it, too, must be placed *at the basis of culture and education.*

The Nation is, in fact, the great community of men who are united by various ties, but above all, precisely by culture. The Nation exists *"through" culture and "for" culture,* and it is therefore the great educator of men in order that they may "be more" in the community. It is this community which possesses a history that goes beyond the history of the individual and the family. It is also in this community, with respect to which every family educates, that the family begins its work of education with what is the most simple thing, language, thus enabling man who is at the very beginning to learn to speak in order to become a member of the community of his family and of his Nation.

In all that I am now proclaiming, which I will develop still further, my words express a particular experience, a particular testimony in its kind. I am the son of a Nation which has lived the greatest experiences of history, which its neighbors have condemned to death several times, but which has survived and remained itself. It has kept its identity, and it has kept, in spite of partitions and foreign occupations, its national sovereignty, not by relying on the resources of physical power, but solely by *relying on its culture.* This culture turned out in the circumstances to be more powerful than all other forces.

What I say here concerning the right of the Nation to the foundation of its culture and its future is not, therefore, the echo of any "nationalism," but it is always a question of a stable element of human experience and of the *humanistic perspective of man's development.* There exists a fundamental sovereignty of society which is manifested in the culture of the Nation. It is a question of the sovereignty through which, at the same time, man is supremely sovereign. When I express myself in this way, I am also thinking, with deep interior emotion, of the cultures of so many *ancient peoples* which did not give way when confronted with the civilizations of the invaders: and they still remain for man the source of his "being" as a man in the interior truth of his humanity. I am also thinking with admiration of the *cultures of new societies,* those that are awakening to life in the community of their own Nation – just as my Nation awakened to life ten centuries ago – and that are struggling to maintain their own identity and their own values against the influences and pressure of models proposed from outside.

15. Addressing you, Ladies and Gentlemen, you who have been meeting in this place for over thirty years now in the name of the primacy of the cultural realities of man, human communities, peoples and Nations, I say to you: With all the means at your disposal, watch over this fundamental sovereignty that every Nation possesses by virtue of its own culture. Cherish it like the apple of your eye for the future of the great human family. Protect it! Do not allow this fundamental sovereignty to become the prey of some political or economic interest. Do not allow it to become a victim of totalitarian and imperialistic systems or hegemonies, for which man counts only as an object of domination and not as the subject of his own human existence. For them, too, the Nation – their own Nation or others – counts only as an object of domination and a bait for various interests, and not as a subject: the subject of sovereignty coming from the true culture which belongs to it as its own. Are there not, on the map of Europe and the world, Nations which have a *marvelous historic sovereignty* derived from their culture, and which are, nevertheless, deprived of their full sovereignty at the same time? Is this not an important point for the future of human culture, important above all in our age, when it is so urgent to eliminate the vestiges of colonialism?

16. This sovereignty which exists and which draws its origin from the specific culture of the Nation and society, from the primacy of the family in the work of education, and finally from the personal dignity of every man, must remain the fundamental criterion of the manner of dealing with the problem, an important one for humanity today, namely, that of the *media of social*

communication (of the information which is bound up with them, and also of what is called "mass culture"). Since these media are "social" media of communication, they cannot be *means of domination* over others, on the part of agents of political power as well as of financial powers which impose their program and their model. They must become the means—and what an important means!—of *expression of this society* which uses them, and which also ensures their existence. They must take into account the real needs of this society. They must take into account the culture of the Nation and its history. They must respect the responsibility of *the family in the field of education.* They must take into consideration the good of man, his dignity. They cannot be subjected to the criterion of interest, of the sensational and of immediate success but, taking into account ethical requirements, they must serve the construction of a "more human" life.

17. *Genus humanum arte et ratione vivit.* (Humanity lives by creativity and intellect.) Fundamentally, it is affirmed that man is himself *through truth,* and *becomes more himself through increasingly perfect knowledge of truth.* I would like to pay tribute here, Ladies and Gentlemen, to all the merits of your Organization and at the same time to the commitment and to all the efforts of the States and Institutions which you represent, in regard to the *popularization of instruction* at all grades and all levels, as regards the elimination of illiteracy, which signifies the lack of all instruction, even the most elementary, a lack which is painful not only from the point of view of the elementary culture of individuals and environments, but also from the point of view of socio-economic progress. There are distressing indications of delay in this field, bound up with a distribution of goods that is often radically unequal and unjust; think of the situations in which there exist, alongside a plutocratic oligarchy limited in numbers, multitudes of starving citizens living in want. This delay can be eliminated, not by way of bloody struggles for power, but above all, by means of systematic campaigns for the spread and popularization of instruction. An effort in this direction is necessary if it is then desired to carry out the necessary changes in the socio-economic field. Man, who "is more," thanks also to what he "has," and to what he "possesses," must *know how to possess,* that is, *to order and administer* the means he possesses, for his own good and for the common good. For this purpose, instruction is indispensable.

18. The problem of instruction has always been closely linked with the *mission of the Church.* In the course of the centuries, she founded schools at all levels; she gave birth to the medieval Universities in Europe: in Paris and in Bologna, in Salamanca and in Heidelberg, in Krakow and in Louvain. In our age, too, she offers the same contribution wherever her activity in this field is requested and respected. Allow me to claim in this place for *Catholic families* the right which belongs to all families to educate their children in schools which correspond to their own view of the world, and in particular

the strict right of Christian parents not to see their children subjected, in schools, to programs inspired by atheism. That is, indeed, one of the fundamental rights of man and of the family.

19. The system of education is organically connected with the system of the different orientations given to the way of *practicing and popularizing science,* a purpose which is served by high-level educational establishments, Universities and also, in view of the present development of specialization and scientific methods, specialized institutes. These are institutions of which it would be difficult to speak without deep emotion. They are the work benches at which man's vocation to knowledge, as well as the constitutive link of humanity with truth as the aim of knowledge, become a daily reality, become, in a sense, the daily bread of so many teachers, venerated leaders of science, and around them, of young researchers dedicated to science and its applications, as also of the multitude of students who frequent these centers of science and knowledge.

We find ourselves here, as it were, at the highest rungs of the ladder which man has been climbing, since the beginning, towards knowledge of the reality of the world around him, and towards knowledge of the mysteries of his humanity. This historical process has reached in our age possibilities previously unknown; it has opened to human intelligence horizons hitherto unsuspected. It would be difficult to go into detail here for, on the way to knowledge, the orientations of specializations are as numerous as the development of science is rich.

20. Your Organization is a place of meeting, a meeting which embraces, in its widest sense, the whole field, so essential, of human culture. This audience is therefore the very place to greet all men of science, and to pay tribute particularly to those who are present here and who have obtained for their work the highest recognition and the most eminent world distinctions. Allow me, consequently, to express also certain wishes which, I do not doubt, will reach the thought and the hearts of the members of this august assembly.

Just as we are edified in scientific work—edified and made deeply happy—by this march of the *disinterested knowledge of truth* which the scholar serves with the greatest dedication and sometimes at the risk of his health and even his life, we must be equally concerned by everything that is in contradiction with the principles of disinterestedness and objectivity, everything that would make *science an instrument* to reach aims that have nothing to do with it. Yes, we must be concerned about everything that proposes and presupposes only these non-scientific aims, demanding of men of science that they should put themselves in their service without permitting them to judge and decide, in all independence of mind, *the human and ethical honesty* of these purposes, or threatening them with bearing the consequences when they refuse to contribute to them.

Do these non-scientific aims of which I am speaking, this problem that I am raising, need proofs or comments? You know what I am referring to; let it suffice to mention the fact that among those who were brought before the international courts, at the end of the last world war, there were also men of science. Ladies and Gentlemen, I beg you to forgive me these words, but I would not be faithful to the duties of my office if I did not utter them, not in order to return to the past, but to defend *the future of science and human culture*; even more, to defend the future of man and the world! I think that Socrates who, in his uncommon integrity, was able to sustain that knowledge is at the same time moral virtue, would have to climb down from his certainty if he could consider the experience of our time.

21. We realize it, Ladies and Gentlemen, *the future of man and of the world is threatened*, radically threatened, in spite of the intentions, certainly noble ones, of men of learning, men of science. It is threatened because the marvelous results of their researches and their discoveries, especially in the field of the sciences of nature, have been and continue to be exploited – to the detriment of the ethical imperative – for purposes that have nothing to do with the requirements of science, and even for purposes of *destruction and death*, and that to a degree never known hitherto, causing really unimaginable damage. Whereas science is called to be in the service of man's life, it is too often a fact that it is subjected to purposes that destroy the real dignity of man and of human life. That is the case when scientific research itself is directed towards these purposes or when its results are applied to purposes contrary to the good of mankind. That happens in the field of genetic manipulations and biological experimentations as well as in that of chemical, bacteriological or nuclear armaments.

Two considerations lead me to submit particularly to your reflection the nuclear threat which is weighing upon the world today and which, if it is not staved off, could lead to the destruction of the fruits of culture, the products of civilization elaborated throughout the centuries by successive generations of men who believed in the primacy of the spirit and who did not spare either their efforts or their fatigue. The first consideration is the following. Geopolitical reasons, economic problems of world dimension, terrible incomprehension, wounded national pride, the materialism of our age and the decadence of moral values have led our world to a situation of instability, to a frail balance which runs the risk of being destroyed any moment as a result of errors of judgment, information or interpretation.

Another consideration is added to this disquieting perspective. Can we be sure, nowadays, that the upsetting of the balance would not lead to war, and to a war that would not hesitate to have recourse to nuclear arms? Up to now it has been said that nuclear arms have constituted a force of dissuasion which has prevented a major war from breaking out, and it is probably true.

But we may wonder at the same time if it will always be so. Nuclear arms, of whatever order of magnitude or of whatever type they may be, are being perfected more and more every year, and they are being added to the arsenal of a growing number of countries. How can we be sure that the use of nuclear arms, even for purposes of national defense or in limited conflicts, will not lead to an *inevitable escalation,* leading to a destruction that mankind can never envisage or accept? But it is not you, men of science and culture, that I must ask not to close your eyes to what a nuclear war can represent for the whole of humanity (cf. Homily for the World Day of Peace, 1 January 1980).

22. Ladies and Gentlemen, the world will not be able to continue for long along this way. A conviction, which is at the same time a *moral imperative,* forces itself upon anyone who has become aware of the situation and the stake, and who is also inspired by the elementary sense of responsibilities that are incumbent on everyone: consciences must be mobilized! The efforts of *human consciences* must be increased in proportion to the tension between good and evil to which men at the end of the twentieth century are subjected. We must convince ourselves of the priority of ethics over technology, of the primacy of the person over things, of the superiority of spirit over matter (cf. *Redemptor Hominis,* no. 16). The cause of man will be served if science forms an alliance with conscience. The man of science will really help humanity if he keeps "the sense of man's transcendence over the world and of God's over man" (Address to the Pontifical Academy of Sciences, 10 November 1979, no. 4).

Thus, seizing the opportunity of my presence at the headquarters of UNESCO today, I, a son of humanity and Bishop of Rome, directly address you, men of science, you who are gathered here, you the highest authorities in all fields of modern science. And through you I address your colleagues and friends of all countries and all continents.

I address you in the name of this terrible threat which weighs over mankind, and at the same time, in the name of the future and the good of humanity all over the world. I beseech you: *let us make every effort* to establish and respect the primacy of ethics, in all fields of science. Let us do our utmost particularly to preserve the human family from the horrible perspective nuclear war!

I tackled this subject before the General Assembly of the United Nations Organization, in New York, on 2 October of last year. I am speaking about it today to you. I appeal to your intelligence and your heart, above passions, ideologies and frontiers. I appeal to all those who, through their political or economic power, would be and are often led to impose on scientists *the conditions of their work and its orientation.* Above all I appeal to every scientist individually and to the whole international scientific community.

All together you are an enormous power: the power of intelligences and consciences! Show yourselves to be more powerful than the most powerful in our modern world! Make up your mind to give proof of the most noble solidarity with mankind: the solidarity founded on the dignity of the human person. Construct peace, beginning with the foundation: *respect for all the rights of man,* those which are connected with his material and economic dimension as well as those which are connected with the spiritual and interior dimension of his existence in this world. May wisdom inspire you! May love guide you, this love which will suffocate the growing threat of hatred and destruction! Men of science, commit all your moral authority to save mankind from nuclear destruction.

23. Today I have been given the possibility of realizing one of the deepest desires of my heart. I have been given the possibility of penetrating, here, within the Areopagus which is that of the whole world. I have been given the possibility of saying to all, to you, members of the United Nations Educational, Scientific and Cultural Organization, to you who are working for the good and for the reconciliation of men and peoples through all fields of culture, science and information, to say to you and to cry to you from the inmost depths of my soul: Yes! The future of man depends on culture! Yes! The peace of the world depends on the *primacy of the Spirit*! Yes! The peaceful future of mankind depends on *love*!

Your personal contribution, Ladies and Gentlemen, is important, it is vital. It lies in the correct approach to the problems, to the solution of which you dedicate your service.

My final word is the following: Do not stop. Continue. Continue always.

Address of John Paul II to First Meeting of the Pontifical Council for Culture, Vatican City, January 18, 1983

Your Eminences,

Your Excellencies,

Ladies and Gentlemen,

1. It is with special joy that I welcome, for the first time, and officially, the Pontifical Council for Culture. First of all, I would like to thank the members of the international Council whom I recently appointed and who responded so quickly to the invitation to meet in Rome in order to discuss the orientation and the future activities of the Pontifical Council for Culture. Your presence on this Council is an honor and a source of hope for the Church. Your acknowledged reputations in widely diverse areas of culture, of the sciences, of the humanities, of the media, in universities, and in sacred disciplines, allows one to anticipate fruitful work from this new Council that I decided to create, taking my inspiration from the directives of the Second Vatican Council.

2. The Second Vatican Council has given a new dynamism in the domain of culture, especially in the Constitution *Gaudium et Spes.* Today it is indeed an arduous task to understand the extreme variety of cultures, of customs, of traditions, and of civilizations. At first sight, the challenge can seem to be beyond us, but is not this very challenge proportionate to our faith and to our *hope*? During the Second Vatican Council, the Church recognized that a dramatic gap had established itself between the Church and culture. The modern world is fascinated by its conquests, and its scientific and technological achievements. But, too often the modern world gives itself over to ideologies, to ethical criteria dictated by practicality, to behavior which is in contradiction to the Gospels, or which, at least, calmly discounts Christian values.

3. Therefore, it is in the name of the Christian faith that the Second Vatican Council committed the whole Church *to listen to modern man* in order to understand him and to invent a new kind of dialogue which would permit the originality of the Gospel message to be carried to the heart of contemporary mentalities. We must then rediscover the apostolic creativity and the prophetic power of the first disciples in order to face new cultures. Christ's word must appear in all of its freshness to the young generations whose atti-

tudes are sometimes so difficult to understand for the traditional-minded, but who are far from being closed to spiritual values.

4. Many times I have affirmed that the dialogue between the Church and the cultures of the world has assumed a vital importance for the future of the Church and of the world. If I may be allowed today to do so, I would like to return to this subject in order to emphasize two principal and complementary aspects which correspond to the two areas in which the Church is active: that of *the evangelization of cultures* and that of *the defense of man and of his cultural advancement.* Both of these tasks demand that new pathways of dialogue between the Church and the cultures of our period be elaborated.

This dialogue is absolutely indispensable for the Church, because otherwise evangelization will remain a dead letter. Saint Paul did not hesitate to say: "Woe to me if I do not preach the Gospel!" At the end of the twentieth century, as in the Apostle's time, the Church must be all things to all people, embracing today's cultures sympathetically. There are still classes and mentalities, countries, and entire areas to be evangelized, which presupposes a long and courageous *process of inculturation* so that the Gospel can penetrate the soul of living cultures, fulfilling their highest expectations and making them grow proportionately in Christian faith, hope, and charity. The Church, through its missionaries, has already accomplished incomparable work on all continents, but this missionary work is never completed, because sometimes cultures have only been affected superficially, and, in any case, as cultures continually change, they demand a renewed approach. Let us even add that this noble term of mission applies henceforth to old civilizations marked by Christianity, but which are now threatened with indifference, agnosticism, or even irreligion. In addition, new sectors of culture are appearing, with diverse objectives, methods, and languages. Intercultural dialogue is therefore a must for Christians in all countries.

5. In order to evangelize effectively, it is necessary to adopt resolutely an attitude of *exchange and of comprehension* in order to sympathize with the cultural identity of nationalities, of ethnic groups, and of varied sectors of modern society. Moreover, it is necessary to work for a greater closeness among cultures, so that the universal values of man will be accepted everywhere in a spirit of fraternity and solidarity. Consequently, evangelization presupposes the penetration of the specific identity of each culture and also favors exchanges among cultures, opening all of them to universal values and, I would even say, to the values of catholicity.

It was in thinking of this heavy responsibility that I wanted to create the Pontifical Council for Culture, in order to give the whole Church, both its leaders and the faithful, a strong incentive to become aware of the duty that is incumbent upon all to listen carefully to modern man, not in order to approve all of his behavior, but rather in order to discover first of all his latent hopes and aspirations. This is why I have invited bishops, those who work in the various services of the Holy See, international Catholic organizations, universities, and all men of faith and of culture to commit themselves with conviction to a dialogue among cultures, bringing to this dialogue the salvific word of the Gospel.

6. We must, in addition, remember that *Christians have much to receive* in this dynamic relationship between the Church and the contemporary world. The Ecumenical Council of Vatican II emphasized this point and it is appropriate to remember it. The Church has been greatly enriched by acquisitions from so many civilizations. The secular experience of so many nationalities, the progress of science, the hidden treasures of diverse cultures, through which the nature of man becomes more fully visible, and through which new paths toward the truth open up, all of that is an indisputable advantage for the Church as the Council recognized (cf. *Gaudium et Spes,* no. 44). And this enrichment continues. Indeed, think of the results of scientific research which have led to a better knowledge of the universe, to a deeper understanding of the mystery of man; think of the advantages that the new means of communication and contact among men have procured for society and for the Church; think of the capacity of producing innumerable economic and cultural goods, and especially of promoting the education of the masses, and of healing formerly incurable diseases. What admirable achievements! All of this is to man's credit. And all of this has greatly benefited the Church itself, in its life, its organization, its work, and its own labor. Thus, it is understandable that the People of God, in solidarity with the world in which they live, would recognize the discoveries and accomplishments of our contemporaries and participate in them as much as is possible so that man himself may grow and develop to the full extent of his potentiality. This presupposes a great capacity to accept and to admire, but also a clear *sense of discernment.* And, now, I would like to elaborate upon this last point.

7. In urging us to evangelize, our faith inspires us *to love man himself.* And, man, today, more than ever before, needs to be defended against the threats which weigh upon his development. The love that we draw from the spring of the Gospel, in the wake of the mystery of the Incarnation of the Word, brings us to proclaim that man merits honor and love for himself and must be respected in his dignity. Thus, brothers must learn again to speak to each other as brothers, to respect each other, to understand each other, so that man himself may survive and grow in dignity, liberty, and honor. To the extent that the modern world stifles dialogue among cultures, it heads towards *conflicts* which run the risk of being fatal for the future of human civilization. Beyond prejudices and cultural barriers of racial, linguistic, religious, and ideological separation, human beings must recognize themselves as brothers and sisters, and accept each other in their diversity.

8. The lack of understanding among men makes them run a fatal risk. But man is also threatened in his *biological being* by the irreparable deterioration of the environment, by the risk of genetic manipulations, the attacks against unborn life, and by torture which is currently still seriously widespread. Our love for man must give us the courage to denounce ideas which reduce the human being to a thing that one can manipulate, humiliate, or arbitrarily eliminate.

Man is also insidiously threatened in his *moral being,* because he is subject to hedonistic currents which exacerbate his instincts and fascinate him with illusions of consumption without discrimination. Public opinion is manipulated by the deceitful suggestions of powerful advertising, the one-dimensional values of which ought to make us critical and vigilant.

In addition, man is currently humiliated by *economic systems* that exploit entire collectivities. Furthermore, man is also the victim of certain *political or ideological regimes* that imprison the soul of the people. As Christians, we cannot keep silent and we must denounce this cultural oppression which prevents people and ethnic groups from being themselves in conformity with their profound vocation. It is through these cultural values that the individual or collective man lives a truly human life and one cannot tolerate that his reasons for living be destroyed. History will judge our period severely to the extent that it has stifled, corrupted, and brutally enslaved cultures in so many areas of the world.

9. It is in this sense that I was eager to proclaim to UNESCO, before the assembly of all nations, what I am permitting myself to repeat to you today: "It is essential *to affirm man for himself,* and not for any other motive or reason: uniquely for himself! Moreover, it is necessary to love man because he is man, it is necessary to demand love for man because of the particular dignity that he possesses. The whole of these affirmations concerning man belong to the very substance of Christ's message and of the mission of the Church, despite everything that critics have been able to declare on the matter, and everything that the diverse currents opposed to religion in general and to Christianity in particular may have done." (Address to UNESCO, June 2, 1980, no. 10.) This message is fundamental for making possible the work of the Church in the contemporary world. This is why I wrote in the conclusion of the encyclical *Redemptor hominis* that "man is and is always becoming the 'way' for the daily life of the Church" (no. 21). Yes, man is "the way of the Church," because without this respect for man and his dignity, how could one announce to him the words of life and of truth?

10. Thus, it is in remembering these two principles of orientation – evangelization of cultures and defense of man – that the Pontifical Council for Culture will pursue its own work. On one hand, it is required that *the evangelizer familiarize himself with the socio-cultural environments* in which he must

announce the word of God; more important, the Gospel is itself a leavening agent for culture to the extent that it reaches man in his manner of thinking, behaving, working, enjoying himself, that is, as it reaches him in his cultural specificity. On the other hand, our faith gives us confidence in man – in man created in the image of God and redeemed by Christ – in man whom we want to defend and to love for himself, conscious as we are that he is man only because of his culture, that is, because of his freedom to grow integrally and with all of his specific abilities. Your task is difficult but splendid. Together you must contribute to blazing new paths for the Church's dialogue with the contemporary world. How can one speak to the heart and to the intelligence of modern man in order to announce to him the salvific word? How can one make our contemporaries more sensitive to the intrinsic value of the human being, to the dignity of each individual, to the hidden wealth in each culture? Your role is great, because you must *help the Church to become a creator of culture* in its relationship with the modern world. We would be unfaithful to our mission to evangelize the present generations if we left Christians without an understanding of new cultures. We would also be unfaithful to the spirit of charity which must animate us if we didn't see in what respects man is today threatened in his humanity and if we did not proclaim, by our words and actions, the necessity of defending individual and collective man, of saving him from the oppressions and enslavements which humiliate him.

11. In your work you are invited to collaborate with all *men of good will.* You will discover that the spirit of good is mysteriously at work in so many of our contemporaries, even in some of those who do not claim affiliation with any religion, but who seek to accomplish honestly and with courage their human vocation. Think of so many fathers and mothers, so many teachers and students, of workers dedicated to their tasks, of so many men and women devoted to the cause of peace, the common good, international cooperation, and justice. Think also of all of the researchers who devote themselves with moral constancy and rigor to their useful work for society, of all the eager artists and creators of beauty. Do not hesitate to enter into dialogue with all of these persons of good will, many of whom perhaps secretly hope for the testimony and support of the Church in order better to defend and promote the true progress of man.

12. I warmly thank you for having come to work with us. In the name of the Church, the Pope is counting a great deal upon you, because as I said in the letter by which I created it, your Council "will bring regularly to the Holy See the echo of the great cultural aspirations throughout the world, delving into the expectations of contemporary civilizations and exploring new paths of cultural dialogue." Your Council will have above all else the *value of witnessing.* You must show Christians and the world the deep interest that the Church has in the progress of culture and in a fruitful dialogue among cul-

tures, as in their beneficial encounter with the Gospel. Your role cannot be defined once and for all and *a priori*: experience will teach you the most efficacious means of action and those best adapted to the circumstances. Keep in regular contact with the Executive Committee of the Council – whom I congratulate and encourage – participate in their actions and in their research, propose your initiatives to them, and inform them of your experiences. What is evidently requested of the Council for Culture is to implement its activity by means of dialogue, inspiration, testimony, and research. There is in those activities a particularly fruitful manner for the Church to be present in the world and to reveal to it the always new message of Christ the Redeemer.

With the approach of the Jubilee of the Redemption, I pray Christ to inspire you, to help you, so that your work will serve his plan, his Work of salvation. And, with all my heart, I thank you in advance for your cooperation, I bless you, in the name of the Father, the Son, and the Holy Spirit.

Address of John Paul II to Second Annual Meeting of the Pontifical Council for Culture, Vatican City, January 16, 1984

Dear Brothers in the Episcopate,

Dear Friends,

I extend a most hearty welcome to all of you, and I am happy to meet you during your annual reunion in Rome for a few special moments of reflection and orientation with the Pope. In you I greet with respect persons of culture throughout the world. You know the vital importance which I attach to the development of our contemporary cultures and their profitable encounter with the saving Word of Christ the Liberator, source of grace and of cultures also.

1. During your working session, you are analyzing the activities of the Pontifical Council for Culture, so as to plan its future action with a Christian outlook on cultures at the end of the twentieth century.

I hope that this Council, the most recent addition to the Roman Curia, will gradually exercise its own role, and I thank you for all that you have done since its foundation in May 1982. I thank especially Cardinal Carrone, President of the Committee of Presidency, Cardinal Sales, Archbishop Paul Poupard, President of the Executive Committee, Archbishop Antonio Javierre Ortas, Counsellor, Father Carrier, Secretary, and their collaborators who are all working hard at the primary tasks of exploration and planning, and the distinguished members of the International Council whose competent help is and will be very valuable.

Already the Holy See and the Church, through the ecclesiastical universities and academies, specialized commissions, libraries and archives, have always made a *contribution* of the first order to the world *in terms of education, teaching and research* in the sacred arts and sciences. Various sections of the Curia share in this work, and it is certainly desirable that their involvement grow in response to the needs of our contemporary world and especially that it be most unified and better known. Your Council has an original part to play in this activity and cooperation.

2. Your role is especially to form strong links with *the world of culture,* in the Church as well as outside of ecclesial institutions, with bishops, reli-

gious and lay people involved in this field or representing official or private cultural associations, academic people, researchers and artists, all those who are interested in the thorough study of the cultural problems of our day. In conjunction with the local Churches, you see to it that these qualified representatives make known to the Church the results of their experiences, research and productions for the benefit of culture, things which the Church cannot ignore in its pastoral dialogue and which are a source of human enrichment, and that they receive for this the esteem of Christians.

3. One naturally thinks of *international organizations* such as UNESCO and the Council of Europe whose specific activities are dedicated to the service of culture and education. Your Council can contribute, as it has already done, to strengthening suitable cooperation with these organizations which are already in contact with the Holy See.

You are also in a good position to participate, along with other representatives of the Holy See and of the Church, in important *congresses* which deal with cultural problems and human sciences. In such fields, the presence of the Church, to the extent that it is wanted, is particularly significant and a source of great growth for the world and for itself, and it is important that it direct all of its attention to this.

4. The usual work of the Council is also to *study* in depth major cultural questions where the faith is challenged and the Church especially involved. This is a valuable service to the Pope, the Holy See and to the Church. The collection "Cultures and Dialogue," whose first and interesting volume on the case of Galileo is already known, can also make a useful contribution, as well as various projects which you are planning for dialogue between cultures and the Gospel.

5. In carrying out your projects, it is good, as you have the care to do, that you should call on *the Episcopal Conferences* so as to learn from them about initiatives which put into practice, in their areas, the objectives of the Second Vatican Council and especially of the Constitution *Gaudium et Spes* on culture. A better understanding of how the local Churches come to grips with the evolution of mentalities and cultures in their countries will help to direct better their evangelizing action. Interesting pastoral experiments in this line have been tried since the Council, allowing local Churches to deal in the light of the Gospel with complex problems produced by the rise of new cultures, the challenge of inculturation, new trends of thought, the often violent clash of cultures, and the loyal search for dialogue between them and the Church.

Some episcopates have already created a distinct commission for culture. Some dioceses have named an individual, sometimes an auxiliary bishop, responsible for the new problems arising from modern pastoral applications in this line. As you know, this is the solution I chose myself for the Diocese of Rome.

It will be very good to make known the results which these initiatives have produced, thus giving rise to useful exchanges of information and healthy competition.

6. Quite rightly also, you seek to collaborate with *international Catholic organizations,* many of which are especially interested in cultural problems and have expressed the desire to cooperate with you. These coordinate the activity carried out by Catholics in the promotion of culture, education and intercultural dialogue. That is why I am happy that your Council pays such attention to this important sector, working with the Pontifical Council for the Laity, whose duty it is, in general, to follow the apostolate of international Catholic organizations.

7. On the other hand, many *religious men and women* do important work in this realm of culture. A number of religious institutes devoted to education and cultural progress, and to the understanding and evangelizing of cultures, have expressed their desire to participate actively in the work of the Pontifical Council for Culture, so as to seek together, in a spirit of fraternal cooperation, the best ways to promote the objectives of the Second Vatican Council in this vast field. In connection with the Sacred Congregation for Religious and for Secular Institutes, your Council will be able to help these religious men and women in the specific work of evangelization which is theirs for the cultural advancement of the human person.

8. Through these few words, one can easily appreciate the importance and urgency of the mission entrusted to the Pontifical Council for Culture, a mission which finds its place and specific aspect in that of the organisms of the Holy See and in that of the entire Church, responsible for bringing the Good News to men quite marked by cultural progress but also by its limitation. More than ever, in fact, man is seriously threatened by *anti-culture* which reveals itself, among other ways, in growing violence, murderous confrontations, exploitation of instincts and selfish interests. In working for the progress of culture, the Church is always trying to see to it that collective wisdom triumphs over divisive interests. We must allow our generations to build a *culture of peace.* May our contemporaries rediscover a liking and esteem for culture, true victory of reason, brotherly understanding and sacred respect for man who is capable of love, creativity, contemplation, solidarity, transcendence!

In this Jubilee Year of the Redemption, which has already given me the occasion to receive in pious pilgrimage many men and women of culture, I implore the blessings of the Lord on your difficult and fascinating task. May the message of reconciliation, liberation and love rising from the living spring of the Gospel purify and enlighten the cultures of our contemporaries in search of hope!

Address of John Paul II to the Third Annual Meeting of the Pontifical Council for Culture, Vatican City, January 15, 1985

Dear Brothers in the Episcopate,

Dear Friends,

1. My joy is great this morning in receiving you in Rome on the occasion of the third annual meeting of the International Council of the Pontifical Council for Culture.

I sincerely thank you for your active presence and for having agreed to devote your time and energies to this close collaboration with the Apostolic See. I greet with particular affection Cardinal Gabriel-Marie Garrone, president of your Committee of Presidency, and also Cardinal Eugenio de Araujo Sales. I likewise turn with gratitude toward the executive leadership of the Pontifical Council for Culture represented by its President, Archbishop Paul Poupard and its Secretary, Father Hervé Carrier, who, together with their zealous collaborators, both men and women, strive to accomplish a work that is outstanding both in quantity and in quality.

2. The Pontifical Council for Culture is invested, in my view, with a significance that is symbolic and full of hope. Indeed, I perceive you as qualified witnesses of Catholic culture throughout the world, charged to reflect likewise on the evolutions and the expectations of the different cultures in the regions, as in the sectors of activity which are your own. In virtue of the mission which I have entrusted to you, you are called to assist the Holy See, with competence, to understand better the profound and diverse aspirations of the cultures of today and to discern better how the universal Church can respond to these. For, throughout the world, the orientations, the mentalities, the ways of thinking and of conceiving the meaning of life are changing, exerting mutual influence on each other, confronting one another no doubt in a manner more striking than ever before. This is noted by all those who devote themselves with commitment to the advancement of man. It is good that your work of study, of consultation and of animation – undertaken in conjunction with the other departments of the Roman Curia, with the universities, the religious institutes, the International Catholic Organizations and several impor-

tant international agencies devoted to the promotion of cultures – gives you a clear awareness of the stakes presented by cultural activity in the broad sense of the term.

3. Beyond this respectful and disinterested openness to cultural realities in order to understand them better, the Christian cannot prescind from the question of evangelization. The Pontifical Council for Culture participates in the mission of the See of Peter for the evangelization of cultures and you share in the responsibility of the local Churches in the apostolic tasks required by the meeting of the Gospel with the cultures of our time. To this end, an immense work is demanded of all Christians and the challenge should mobilize their energies within each people and each human community.

To you who have accepted the assignment of supporting the Holy See in its universal mission to the cultures of our time, I entrust the particular task of studying and examining in depth what the *evangelization of the cultures* today means for the Church. Certainly, the concern for evangelizing cultures is not new for the Church, but it presents problems that have an aspect of novelty in a world characterized by pluralism, by the clashing of ideologies and by profound changes in mentality. You must help the Church to respond to these fundamental questions for the cultures of today: how is the message of the Church accessible to the new cultures, to contemporary forms of understanding and of sensitivity? How can the Church of Christ make itself understood by the modern spirit, so proud of its achievements and at the same time so uneasy for the future of the human family? *Who is Jesus Christ* for the men and women of today?

Yes, the entire Church should ask itself these questions, in the spirit of what my predecessor Paul VI said after the synod on evangelization: "What matters is to evangelize man's culture and cultures . . . in the wide and rich sense which these terms have in *Gaudium et Spes,* always taking the person as one's starting point and always coming back to the relationship of people among themselves and with God" (*Evangelii Nuntiandi,* no. 20). He then added: "The Kingdom which the Gospel proclaims is lived by men who are profoundly linked to a culture, and the building up of the Kingdom cannot avoid borrowing the elements of human culture or cultures" (ibid.).

It is then a complex but essential task: to help Christians to discern in the traits of their culture what can contribute to the appropriate expression of the Gospel message and to the building up of the Kingdom of God, and to disclose what is contrary to this. And in this way, the announcing of the Gospel to those of our contemporaries who do not as yet adhere to it will have a better chance of being realized through an authentic dialogue.

We cannot but evangelize: so many regions, so many cultural milieus remain still insensitive to the good news of Jesus Christ. I am thinking of the vast areas of the world still marginal to the Christian faith. But I am also thinking of the large cultural sectors in traditionally Christian countries which today seem indifferent – if not resistant – to the Gospel. I am speaking, of course, of appearances, for one must not prejudge the mystery of personal beliefs and the secret action of grace. The Church respects all cultures and imposes on no one her faith in Jesus Christ, but she invites all people of good will to promote a true civilization of love, founded on the evangelical values of brotherhood, justice and dignity for all.

4. All this demands a new approach of cultures, attitudes, behaviors, aimed at in-depth dialogue with cultural centers and at rendering fruitful their meeting with the message of Christ. This work demands also on the part of responsible Christians a faith illumined by continual reflection confronted with the sources of the Church's message, and a continual spiritual discernment pursued in prayer.

The Pontifical Council for Culture, for its part, is therefore called to investigate the important questions raised by the challenges of our time for the Church's mission of evangelization. By study, by meetings, reflection groups, consultations, exchanges of information and experiences, by the collaboration of the correspondents who have agreed, in great numbers, to labor with you in various parts of the world, I earnestly urge you to illumine these new dimensions in the light of theological reflection, of experience and of the contribution of the human sciences.

Be sure that I will gladly support the work and the initiatives which will enable you to make the various agencies of the Church sensitive to these problems. And, as a pledge of the support which I desire to bring to your task, so useful to the Church, I impart to you, and also to all your collaborators, and to your families my special Apostolic Blessing.

One Church, Many Cultures

Annual Christmas Address of John Paul II to the College of Cardinals, Vatican City, December 21, 1984

Your Eminencies, Venerated Brothers and Collaborators:

1. "*Dominus prope est*" (The Lord is near) (Phil. 4:5).

The now imminent recurrence of the holy feast of Christmas has once more brought us together for this beautiful custom of exchanging good wishes. The cardinal dean has given expression to our common sentiments. By means of appropriate and lofty words, he has brought us into that atmosphere filled with joyous hope which belongs to this festivity so dear to the hearts of all.

I thank him with fraternal affection, and, together with him, thank all of you for being here today. In your presence I am pleased to see confirmation of that will for communion in service to the church which renders daily labor unanimously noble and religiously meaningful.

"*Dominus prope est.*" With our souls brimming with gratitude we get ready to kneel down with the shepherds before the manger on that holy night: before that manger at which the "virgin-mother" announced by the prophet Isaiah (7:14) keeps watch with trembling affection. We know that in that frail human creature, still incapable of uttering a word, the eternal word of God, the uncreated wisdom which rules the universe, comes near to us. He is the light of God which "shines in the darkness," as the apostle John says. But John at once adds with bitter realism that the "darkness did not overcome it" (Jn. 1:5).

Light and darkness confront each other before the manger where the child lies: the light of truth and the darkness of error. It is a confrontation which does not permit neutrality: One must choose on which side to stand. This is a choice in which every human being has his future at stake. The child in the manger would one day become an adult and say: "If you live according to my teaching, you are truly my disciples; then you will know the truth, and the truth will set you free" (Jn. 8:31ff).

2. In becoming flesh so as to dwell among us (cf. Jn. 1:14), the word of God comes to bring us the priceless gift of knowledge of the truth: the truth about him, the truth about us and about our transcendental destiny. Man can-

not build himself nor his own freedom except on the foundation of this truth. It is therefore an extremely valuable gift: It must be guarded and defended. Loss of only a part of the whole truth, throbbing in the heart of that child "wrapped in swaddling clothes" and lying in the manger (Lk. 2:12), would mean man prejudicing full realization of himself, to a greater or lesser degree.

The church is aware of this. She knows that she was constituted the depository and guardian of such truth. So she feels invested with a special mission, making her duty-bound to a particular service to mankind: To every generation which arrives to populate the earth she has to reveal the marvelous design which God predisposed in his only begotten Son for the good of every son of man disposed to accept the marvelous initiative of his love in faith.

This is why the church, and, in the church, the Roman See of Peter particularly, keeps watch by the crib at Bethlehem. She is vigilant in order that those transcendent values which the Creator has offered to mankind—the truth and liberty in truth, which is as much as to say love,—shall not be obscured, even less, deformed. She keeps watch in order that, in spite of all contrary currents, such values may continually relive and affirm themselves ever more and more in the lives of individuals and families, the Christian community and the civil community—in a word, in the life of the whole human family.

3. The church has a consciousness of these values which is at once manifold and unitary. This was well brought out by the dogmatic constitution *Lumen Gentium,* in a well-known passage. The twentieth anniversary of promulgation of that dogmatic constitution fell just a month ago. In No. 13 of that fundamental council document a reminder is given of the church's attitude in regard to the "wealth of capacities and customs" pertaining to the various peoples. The church sees them as so many "gifts," which the various cultures bring her. She is therefore well content to accept them, yet feels herself duty-bound to purify them, consolidate them and elevate them.

In particular, by reason of that characteristic of universality which adorns and distinguishes her, the church knows that she must harmonize those "gifts" in a higher unity, in order that they may contribute to progressive affirmation of Christ's one single kingdom. So it is that "by virtue of this catholicity each individual part of the church contributes through its special gifts to the good of the other parts and of the whole church. Through this common sharing of gifts and through the common effort to attain fullness in unity, the whole and each of the parts are reinforced."

There is more: Continuing that line of thought, the council text propounds a fundamental thesis of Catholic ecclesiology. It states that "in the ecclesiastical communion the particular churches hold a rightful place. These churches retain their own traditions without in any way lessening the primacy of Peter. This chair presides over the whole assembly of charity and protects legitimate differences; at the same time it sees that such differences shall not hinder unity, but contribute toward it."

It would be difficult to express that with greater clarity and depth: The universal church is presented as a communion of churches, and indirectly as a communion of nations, languages, cultures. Each of these brings its own "gifts" to the whole, just as do single human generations and epochs, particular scientific and social gains, and the stages of civilization which are gradually attained.

4. There is much insistence today on the "special" Christian experiences which particular churches have in the sociocultural contexts in which each is called to live. Such specific experiences, it is emphasized, concern both the word of God, which ought to be read and comprehended in the light of facts emerging from one's own existential path, and they concern liturgical prayer. The latter should look to the culture in which it is rooted for the signs, gestures and words that serve for adoration, worship and celebration. They concern theological reflection, which ought to draw on the categories of thought typical of each culture. Finally, they concern the ecclesial community itself. It has its roots in the eucharist, but depends in its concrete development on historical-temporal conditionings that derive from being rooted in the environment of a certain country or a certain part of the world.

These perspectives are not without interest, because of lines of theological research which they seem to open up in regard to the inexhaustible mystery of the church, and, even more, the possibilities which they offer the faithful for perceiving the immense wealth of new life brought by Christ and making them more fully their own.

But they are views which, in order to be fruitful, presuppose respect for an unavoidable condition. The condition is that such experiences must not be lived in an isolated way or in an independent – not to say adverse – fashion as regards those who live in the church in other parts of the world. In order to constitute authentic experiences of church, they entail the necessity of being in tune with those which other Christians, in contact with different cultural contexts, feel called to live in order to be faithful to demands arising from the one single and identical mystery of Christ.

5. The affirmation touches upon a central point of Catholic ecclesiology and deserves to be repeated and stressed. Indulging "isolationist" orientations and favoring outright "centrifugal" tendencies is contary to the ecclesiology of the Second Vatican Council. In the already-cited No. 13, *Lumen Gentium* brings out the possibilities involved in healthy pluralism. But it also defines its frontiers with great clarity: True pluralism is never a factor for division, but an element contributing to construction of unity in the universal communion of the church.

An ontological relationship of reciprocal inclusion actually exists among the particular churches: Inasmuch as it is a realization of the one single church of Christ, every particular church is present in some way in all the particular churches "in which and from which the unique Catholic Church has its existence" (*Lumen Gentium,* 23). This ontological relationship ought to be expressed on the dynamic plane of concrete life if the Christian community does not wish to enter into contradiction with itself: The basic ecclesial choices made by the faithful of a community ought to be able to harmonize with those of the faithful of the other communities so as to give rise to that communion of minds and of hearts for which Christ prayed at the Last Supper: "As you, Father, are in me, and I in you . . . that they may be one in us. . . . That their unity may be complete" (Jn. 17:21–23).

6. A particular task of the Apostolic See consists exactly in serving this universal unity. Indeed, that is where its specific office lies, and, we may say, the charism of Peter and his successors. Was it not to him that Christ said, before the dark night of betrayal: "But I have prayed for you that your faith may never fail; you in turn must strengthen your brothers" (Lk. 22:32)? He is in fact the "rock" upon whom Christ willed to build his church (cf. Mt. 16:18). And it is precisely from the foundation that one expects the compact solidity of the entire edifice to arise. Therefore, after the resurrection, Jesus left Peter the following exigent mandate, in a dialogue charged with pathos: "Feed my lambs. . . . Feed my sheep" (Jn. 21:15ff). Certainly, the unique supreme pastor is the incarnate Word, Christ the Lord.

The pope therefore, with spontaneous impulsion, makes these words of St. Augustine his own: "We are pastors (shepherds) to you, but we are sheep with you under that shepherd. . . . We are teachers to you from this place, but under that one teacher in this school we are fellow disciples with you" (*Enarrationes in Psalmum,* 126:31). However, this does not do away with the fact that each has a specific task in the church and will have to render account of it to Christ himself one day.

Over the centuries the popes have keenly felt the responsibility of the service to Catholic unity which has been entrusted to them and have tried to provide for it in many ways, surrounding themselves with experienced collaborators in order to face up better to the manifold requirements of their office. Recently, in response to suggestions from the council assembly, the will to "internationalize" the Curia has been expressed, so that the presence there of officeholders coming from the various parts of the world could facilitate dialogue with the churches living on the various continents. This morning I have the joy of meeting with select representatives of the offices in which the Roman Curia is organized. I willingly take advantage of the occasion, dearest brothers in Christ, to express my appreciation to you and thank you for the skillful collaboration which you generously give me in my daily performance of the offices inherent in my ministry.

You live, as I do, that "solicitude for all the churches" which constitutes the "daily tension" mentioned by the apostle Paul (2 Cor. 11:28). It constitutes the daily tension of every pope. It pertains to the successors of Peter in fact to provide for those "gifts," to which the council text already alludes, to flow together toward the center of the church; it is for them again to ensure that those same "gifts," enhanced through reciprocal comparison, may be able to flow out again into the various members of the mystical body of Christ, bearing fresh impulses of life and fervor to them.

Ordinary means exist for meeting that apostolic commitment. Among these stand out *ad limina* visits: In the course of the present year I have had the joy of receiving the episcopal conferences of the Pacific Ocean, El Salvador, Taiwan, Togo, Lesotho, Peru, Greece, Sri Lanka, Venezuela, Argentina, Chile, Guinea, Ecuador, the Antilles, Bolivia, Paraguay.

And there are extraordinary means. Among these, the pope's visits and pilgrimages to particular churches on the various continents are showing themselves to be particularly effective. Still lively in my mind is the pleasing memory of the apostolic journey made at the beginning of May to Korea, Papua, New Guinea, the Solomon Islands and Thailand, for the sake of sharing the concerns and hopes of the young and promising churches of those lands.

Significant likewise was the journey which took me to Switzerland in the month of June. It enabled me to confirm the See of Rome's ties of communion with the noble churches of that nation.

Also unforgettable are the emotions lived during the journey in Canada, in contact both with persons who live their faith at the heart of a highly advanced society and with persons who have received the gospel message in the context of ancient aboriginal civilizations.

Finally, the journey which I made in the middle of October was important, though rapid. During it I touched upon Spain, and arrived at Santo Domingo, the land where evangelization shone for the first time on the new continent, five centuries ago. On that occasion I was similarly able to meet the people of Puerto Rico.

I joyfully also remember the pastoral visits made in Italy over the course of the year: to Bari, Bitonto, Viterbo, Fano, Alatri; then, at the beginning of October, to the churches of Calabria; then the pilgrimage made last November to the places sacred to the memory of St. Charles, on the fourth centenary of his death.

The Apostolic See maintains a thick network of contacts with all the particular churches, in continual concern not to allow the loss of any "gift" from on high" (cf. Jas. 1: 17), and at the same time to safeguard the invaluable treasure of the truth of God, together with everything of perennial validity which it has caused to sprout in the fertile soil of Christian generations in the course of the centuries. So, neither preconceived conclusions nor deplorable ignorance, but constant attention to "the Spirit's word to the churches" (Rv. 2:7), so that everything authentically proceeding from him may be to the advantage of the entire structure of the mystical body of Christ.

7. In this context there is need to emphasize as well the special responsibility which—*cum Petro et sub Petro*—the entire episcopate has in regard to "the deposit of faith," which Christ entrusted to the church, in order that it may be integrally safeguarded and faithfully taught to human generations of all ages. How can we not indeed recall the solemn words with which Jesus took farewell of his apostles at the moment of his return to the Father? They constitute a precise mandate: "Full authority has been given to me both in heaven and on earth. Go, therefore, and make disciples of all nations. . . . Teach them to carry out everything I have commanded you" (Mt. 28:18ff). Everything. No part of the "deposit" may be set aside, mishandled or neglected. In awareness of that, the apostle Paul addressed a categorical imperative to the disciple Timothy. *Depositum custodi.*—Guard what has been committed to you (1 Tm. 6:20). And he enjoined him: "I charge you to preach the word, to stay with this task whether convenient or inconvenient—correcting, reproving, appealing—constantly teaching and never losing patience" (2 Tm. 4:2).

Every historical epoch is actually exposed to the temptation "not to tolerate sound doctrine," but to "surround themselves with teachers who tickle their ears, they will stop listening to the truth and wander off to fables" (cf. ibid. 3ff).

Our epoch too is exposed to this temptation. A precise duty is therefore incumbent on today's pastors and guides of the people of God: that of defending the authenticity of the gospel teaching from everything infecting or deforming it. Certainly, we ought to know how to recognize and receive what "good" our generation can give expression to, so as "to purify it, consolidate it and elevate it." The council reminded us of this (cf. *Lumen Gentium,* 13). But we must also courageously reject what bears the mark of error and of sin; that which entails essential threats to the truth and morality of man; that which spreads itself in society with underhanded maneuvers and overbearing impositions, and attacks the dignity of the person and the inalienable rights of individuals and of nations.

The church has the right to keep watch in order to defend the integrity of the Catholic faith and doctrine, issuing warnings against what insidiously seeks to infect them. That is her precise task; she cannot abdicate it.

8. For its part also, the Holy See carries through this task of promotion and safeguard in regard to the *depositum fidei* with the aid especially of the Congregation for the Doctrine of the Faith. As is well known, after the Second Vatican Council, the procedure which that sacred dicastery follows in examining persons and writings subjected to its judgment was somewhat modified, with intent to offer every guarantee to the persons concerned: Safe-

guard of the truth is a sacrosanct and inseparable duty of the church's, and is not attained by in any way overriding the dignity and rights of persons.

Whoever will look at things with dispassionate objectivity cannot but recognize—also in the light of recent occurrences—that the dicastery in question is constantly inspired, in its interventions, by rigorous criteria of respect for the persons with which it enters into relationship. It may be wished and hoped that an equally respectful attitude may always be assumed by such persons in regard to the dicastery itself, when it befalls them to pronounce in private or in public on its workings. The same principle ought to apply to every other member of the people of God, since that dicastery has no other aim than that of safeguarding from all insidious dangers what is the greatest good which Christianity possesses, the authenticity and integrity of the faith.

It is certainly very important for a sincere and open dialogue to be introduced within the church among the various components of the people of God. But such dialogue must be understood as the way of searching after what is true and right, not as an occasion for indulging in words and attitudes which appear to be difficult to reconcile with an authentic spirit of dialogue. Everyone ought to bear in mind the duty which he or she has in regard to the truth, most of all that which God has revealed and of which the church is custodian.

9. Before concluding, I would also make reference to a point which is particularly felt today, "the preferential option for the poor." The church solemnly promised to make it in the Second Vatican Council, when it declared: "As Christ . . . so the church encompasses with love all those who are afflicted with human weakness. Indeed she recognizes in the poor and the suffering the likeness of her poor and suffering founder. She does all she can to relieve their need, and in them she strives to serve Christ" (*Lumen Gentium,* 8).

This "option" is emphasized with particular force by the episcopates of Latin America today; it has been repeatedly confirmed by me, after the example, in any case, of my unforgettable predecessor, Pope Paul VI. I willingly take this opportunity to repeat and stress that the commitment to the poor constitutes a dominant motive of my pastoral action and the constant solicitude accompanying my daily service to the people of God.

I have made and I do make that "option" my own; I identify with it. And I feel that it could not be otherwise, since this is the everlasting message of the Gospel. Thus did Christ, thus did the apostles of Christ, thus has the church done over the course of her 2,000-year history.

In view of the contemporary forms of exploitation of the poor, the church may not be silent. She also reminds the rich of their precise duties. Strong with God's word (cf. Is. 5:8; Jer. 5:25–28; Jas. 5:1, 3–4), she condemns the not few injustices which unfortunately are committed today also against the poor.

Yes, the church makes the preferential option for the poor her own. A preferential option, note well, not an exclusive or excluding option, for the message of salvation is meant for all. An option, moreover, which is essentially based on the word of God, not on criteria offered by human sciences or adverse ideologies, which often reduce the poor to abstract socio-political or economic categories. In any case, a firm and irrevocable option. As I said at Santo Domingo recently: "The pope, the church, and her hierarchy will to go on being present in the cause of the poor man, his dignity, his promotion, his rights as a person, his aspiration to unpostponable social justice" (*L'Osservatore Romano,* Oct. 13, 1984, p. 4).

10. Through the special mission entrusted to it, the Apostolic See participates, however, in the church's experiences in the various parts of the world and therefore knows that the forms of poverty to which contemporary man is subjected are manifold; it feels itself to be under a moral obligation toward those other forms of poverty too.

Beside, and in a certain sense in face of, the poverty against which the episcopal conferences of Medellín and Puebla raised their voices, stands that which derives from being deprived of those spiritual goods to which man has a right by his very nature. Is not that man also poor who is subjected to totalitarian regimes which deprive him of those fundamental liberties in which his dignity as an intelligent and responsible person is expressed? Is not that man poor who is wounded by others like himself in his interior relationship with the truth, in his conscience, in his most personal convictions, in his religious faith? That is what I have recalled in my preceding interventions, particularly in the encyclical *Redemptor Hominis* (17) and in the speech delivered to the General Assembly of the United Nations in 1979 (14–20), when I spoke of violations committed today in the sphere of man's spiritual goods. There is not only poverty which strikes the body; there is another more insidious poverty which strikes the conscience, violating the most intimate sanctuary of personal dignity.

Into this context of authentic option for the poor on the part of the church enters an event which has had great resonance this year: publication, that is, of the "Instruction on Certain Aspects of the Theology of Liberation." Contrary to a number of distorted interpretations which have been given of it, that document does not oppose the option for the poor, but rather constitutes an authoritative confirmation of it and effects a clarification and deepening of it at the same time.

By bringing out the intimate and constitutive bond which joins liberty to truth, the instruction defends the poor from illusory and dangerous ideological proposals for liberation. These begin from real, dramatic situations of misery and would make the poor and their suffering the pretext for fresh, sometimes graver, oppressions. Reduction of the gospel message to the sociopolitical dimension alone robs the poor of what constitutes a supreme right to them: that of receiving from the church the gift of the entire truth on man and on the presence of the living God in their history.

Reducing the human being to a political sphere alone does not in fact constitute only a threat to the dimension of "having," but it also constitutes a threat to the dimension of "being." As the instruction rightly affirms, only the integrity of the message of salvation can guarantee the integrity of man's liberation.

It is for this liberation that the church has fought and fights beside the poor, making herself the advocate of their downtrodden rights, raising up social works of every kind for their protection and defense, and announcing the word of God which calls all to reconciliation and penance. It is not by chance that the recent exhortation which I published in light of the conclusions reached by the sixth general assembly of the Synod of Bishops reproposes the basic gospel theme of conversion of heart, in conviction that the first liberation to obtain for man is from the moral evil which nests in his heart, for there also lies the cause of "social sin" and oppressive structures.

11. In this commitment to liberation of man from the various forms of poverty which mortify full realization of liberation, the church opens up dialogue with all, with an attitude of sincerity and trust. She declared this will of hers through the lips of Pope John XXIII, who was constantly intent on searching for "that which unites rather than that which divides" men. She repeated it with the voice of Paul VI, who dedicated his first encyclical, *Ecclesiam Suam*, to this theme. She finally confirmed that will with particularly authoritative witness in the Second Vatican Council. For the council, "the most eloquent demonstration of the church's solidarity, respect and love for the entire family of mankind cannot be given except by 'entering a dialogue with it,'" a dialogue based on the dignity of the human person and on the profound significance of his activity in the world (cf. *Gaudium et Spes,* 3 and 40).

He who, through the inscrutable divine design, sits today on the chair of Peter, confirms his will to continue along the path of respectful and sincere dialogue with the contemporary world and the authorities representing it, that it may have trust in the possibilities for good in human nature, and in the renewing power of the redemption of Christ acting in history. It is my profound conviction – and I uttered it in the message for World Peace Day 1983 – that "dialogue is a central and essential element of ethical thinking among people, whoever they may be" (6). For such dialogue to be able to bear its fruit, however, it is necessary that others' fields of competence not to be invaded and that the church keep her identity and liberty. "The role and competence of the church being what it is, she must in no way be confused with the political community, nor bound to any political system." Exactly for this reason "she remains the sign and safeguard of the transcendence of the human person."

12. Imbued with the light and warmth which comes from these truths, we set foot upon the threshold of Bethlehem. He who was born "in poverty" asks us to turn in thought and with the heart to the various forms of poverty which oppress contemporary man: He asks us to go to meet him.

"Jesus Christ . . . made himself poor for us, that we might become rich by his poverty" (cf. 2 Cor. 6:9).

Only by making room for Christ in our lives and in the lives of our communities can we solve the problem of the manifold poverties from which we suffer, can we really become "rich," that is, fully human.

So the real problem remains this: that of acknowledging rights of citizenship to Christ in the various "worlds" of which the modern world is composed. He alone possesses the secret for filling up every "poverty" of ours and arousing the joy of true richness in our hearts, that is, in the end, the riches of love.

May he flood your hearts with this joy, venerated brethren, and those of your fellow workers. May Christmas bring you and them, children of the church and all men and women on earth, a foretaste of the unutterable peace of that new world of which the birth of the son of God in time made a beginning, felicitously and irrevocably. May the holy Virgin, who sheltered the incarnate Word in her womb, dispose us to receive him with living faith and grateful love.

Statements on Church and Culture by John Paul II, 1978–82

Selected and Summarized by Paul Poupard

1. The first text, and this is very significant, is dated the very day of his enthronement in St. Peter's Square, October 22, 1978; it has become famous: "Have no fear, open wide the doors to Christ . . . the frontiers of states, the economic and political systems, the immense domains of culture, of civilization, of development. . . ." (Cf. Poupard, "Eglise et cultures," Paris, Ed. S.O.S., 1980, p. 9.)

2. November 30, 1978, in his message to the Diocese of Cracow for the ninth centennial of Saint Stanislaus, speaking of the foundation of the thousand-year-old identity of Poland: "Let us surround ourselves with a great love of the heritage of our Polish Christian culture, which bears the mark of Saint Stanislaus" (1979, 256; here and throughout, these numbers give the year and page of *Documentation Catholique,* Paris).

3. December 22, 1978, in his allocution to the College of Cardinals, John Paul II announced the opening of the secret archives of the Vatican up to the end of the pontificate of Leo XIII, adding this commentary: "to serve historical truth, and also to witness to the always active presence of the Church in the world of culture" (1979, 5).

4. January 25, 1979, passing through France on the way to Latin America, in a message to the president of the Republic: "I am happy to express to the French people my interest in their culture, my esteem for their concern for the rights of man and my confidence in their spiritual vitality" (179).

5. In his meeting with the Oaxaca Indians at Cuilapan, Mexico, January 29, 1979, John Paul underlined the importance of culture to transmit the faith: "for this there must be no distinction of races and of cultures" (1973).

6. January 30, 1979, in his homily in the sanctuary of Notre Dame of Zapopan: "popular piety is the true expression of the soul of the people when it is touched by grace and forged by the fortunate encounter of the work of evangelization and local culture" (183).

7. January 31, 1979, speaking to students of the Catholic universities in front of the Basilica of Our Lady of Guadalupe, John Paul asked "the promotion of an integral culture, that is looking toward the complete development of the human person with its values of intelligence, will, conscience, frater-

nity, all based on the creator and which have been marvelously elevated in Christ, a culture which intends the good of the community and all of society in a disinterested and authentic manner" (187).

8. February 15, 1979, in a message to the students of Latin America: "Culture forges the spiritual image of society, the particular foundation of its identity, that is, the heritage by which new generations are formed. . . . Access to all the goods of the culture is the goal which must be proposed to every society and to the entire human race. The condition and the criterion of authentic human progress is that minds and hearts partake of its goods. The victory of peace and justice in the life of nations and of each continent depends to a large degree on this" (522).

9. February 24, 1979, receiving the members of the Council of the International Federation of Catholic Universities and the rectors of Catholic universities of Europe, John Paul underlined the importance of the intellectual ministry and the necessity "to evangelize completely and durably the vast world of culture." He asked them to form people who "will realize a personal synthesis between faith and culture" (335).

10. March 30, 1979, at the European Society of Physics: "Your society also makes an appeal to the cultural unity of all the countries of Europe." In keeping with *Gaudium et Spes* (no. 59), the Pope stressed "the legitimate autonomy of culture, and especially of science" (418).

11. April 6, 1979, to a group of Hungarian pilgrims who had come to Rome for the fourth centennial of the foundation of the German-Hungarian College and to the fiftieth anniversary of the Ecclesiastical Institute of Hungary, he underlined the fundamental and prime importance of holy and cultured priests (507).

12. April 24, 1979, to the pilgrims of Brescia, he recalled how Paul VI had been particularly sensitive to the exigencies of modern culture (461).

13. April 26, 1979, to the Pontifical Biblical Commission he developed the theme of their meeting: The Cultural Insertion of Revelation. After having recalled all the cultures in which revelation has been expressed, John Paul underlined two consequences:

> a) The great value of cultures, already a presence in germ of the Divine Logos: Thus cultures are called, in a manner of speaking, by a certain analogy with the humanity of Christ, to participate in the dignity of the Divine Word himself.
>
> b) The purely instrumental character of cultures undergoes powerful mutations: "To define the existing relationships between the variations of culture and the constancy of revelation is rightly the task, arduous but exalted, of biblical studies as of the whole life of the Church" (456).

14. April 27, 1979, in his allocution to the Secretariat for Non-Christians, John Paul underlined the "importance of dialogue in the different cultural regions." (460).

15. In the Apostolic Constitution *Sapientia Christiana,* on the ecclesiastical universities and faculties, April 29, 1979: "It is necessary that all the culture of humanity be penetrated with the Gospel. Actually, the cultural milieu in which people live exercises a great influence on their manner of thinking, and consequently on their habits of acting. This is why the divorce of faith and culture is such a serious obstacle to evangelization. On the other hand, a culture which is impregnated with the Christian spirit is an instrument which favors the diffusion of the Gospel. Furthermore, the Gospel, which is destined to all peoples of all times and all places, is not bound exclusively to any particular culture, but it is capable of impregnating all cultures, by casting on them the light of divine revelation, by purifying and by restoring in Christ the customs of the people" (551).

16. May 25, 1979, to a Bulgarian delegation: "Culture and religious faith are not only not opposed to one another, but are related to one another as the fruit to the tree. One needs only to study the origin of the cultures of various people to see how culture has been and remains an authentic manifestation of some of the most profound needs of man, who tries to express in art and in customs that which seems to him true, good, beautiful, just and worthy of being loved. . . . It is a historical fact that the Christian Churches of the East and the West have fostered and propagated throughout the centures love of their own culture and respect for the culture of others" (573).

17. June 3, 1979, to young people at Gniezno: "Culture is the expression of man, it is the confirmation of humanity. Man creates it, and by it man creates himself. At the same time he creates culture in communion with others" (613).

18. June 5, 1979, to the Polish bishops at Jasna Gora, he reminded the Polish episcopate that it is the guardian of Polish culture, wholly impregnated with the light of Christianity: "The culture is the first and fundamental evidence of the identity of the nation" (622).

19. In the Apostolic Exhortation *Catechesi Tradendae,* October 16, 1979: All of section 53 concerns the evangelical message at the heart of cultures. It is necessary, therefore, to know them, to respect their values, and to insert into them the power of the Gospel which is "transformative and regenerative everywhere . . . by communicating to their legitimate values the fullness of Christ . . . which does not rise up spontaneously in any cultural soil" (914).

20. November 5, 1979, to the cardinals meeting for the first time in an Extraordinary Assembly, the Pope spoke of a central question which could not be avoided. He added these words, often repeated: "The dialogue of the Church with the cultures of our times is that vital domain in which the destiny of

the Church and the world is at stake, during this end of the twentieth century" (1007).

21. November 17, 1979, at the Angelicum University, Rome, on the occasion of the first centennial of the encyclical *Aeterni Patris* of Leo XIII, John Paul showed how "the adoption by the Church of the philosophy of Saint Thomas does not compromise the rightful plurality of cultures and the progress of human thought, which has a right to all that is true" (1070).

22. February 2, 1980, in a talk to the African community of Rome, the Pope underlined the spiritual and cultural values of the African continent and insisted on the evangelization of cultures, recalling *Catechesi Tradendae,* no. 53 (202).

23. February 9, 1980, to eight-thousand professors, students, and alumni of the Roman Colleges, he recalled the cultural goals of a Catholic school, which "is the place or the community of apprenticeship and of the culture." It acts "finally to direct all human culture toward the message of salvation" (*Gravissium Eductionis,* 8), (210).

24. April 1, 1980, to academics from forty-three countries: Before the menaces of fragmented culture, John Paul underlined the necessity for the interior unity of man as a necessity for coherence and plenitude: "Science and culture attain a full, coherent, and unitary sense if they are directed to the realization of the final goal of man, the glory of God" (417).

25. May 3, 1980, to the bishops of Zaire, at Kinshasa: "One of the aspects of evangelization is the inculturation of the Gospel, the Africanization of the Church. The Gospel, certainly, is not identified with cultures and transcends all of them. But the Kingdom which the Gospel announces is lived by men profoundly linked to a culture. The building up of the Kingdom cannot but be marked with elements of human cultures (cf. *Evangelii Nuntiandi,* no. 20). In fact, evangelization must help these to bring forth from their own living tradition original expressions of Christian life, celebration, and thought (cf. *Catechesi Tradendae,* no. 53).

"The Holy Spirit asks us to believe that the yeast of the Gospel, in its authenticity, has the power to nourish Christians in diverse cultures with all the riches of their inheritance, purified and transfigured" (504–505).

26. May 4, 1980, to the academics and intellectuals of Zaire, at Kinshasa: "Historically the Church founded the universities. And these have been the instruments of the formation and the diffusion of the culture of their own countries, contributing powerfully to forging the sense of national identity. . . . Authentic cultural pluralism is linked to the way that each people journeys toward the one truth" (515).

27. May 7, 1980, at Uhuru Park in Kenya: the responsibility to incarnate the Gospel in the African cultures (530).

28. May 7, 1980, to the bishops of Kenya: "The acculturation or incultura-

tion which you rightly seek will be truly a reflection of the incarnation of the Word when a culture, transformed and regenerated by the Gospel, produces original expressions of Christian life, celebration, and thought, out of its own living tradition. . . . Christ, in his members and body, is himself African (534).

29. May 11, 1980, to 200,000 young people gathered at Yamous-soukro on the Ivory Coast: "Keep your African roots. Safeguard the values of your culture" (547).

30. May 27, 1980, over French television: on the influence of culture . . . (551).

31. June 1, 1980, at the Institut Catholique of Paris: "Cast into the thinking world a Christian yeast" (583).

32. June 2, 1980, at UNESCO, Paris, major themes of the Pope's address:

- –Man lives a truly human life thanks to culture.
- –Culture is that by which man as man becomes more man.
- –We recognize each other in the area of culture, the fundamental reality which unites us.
- –Man is the primordial and fundamental ingredient of culture.
- –The organic and constitutive bond which exists between religion in general and Christianity in particular, on the one hand, and culture, on the other: . . . the fundamental bond of the Gospel, that is the message of Christ and the Church with man, in his very humanity. This bond is, in effect, the creator of culture in its very foundation.
- –The first and essential task of culture is education.
- –The nation exists by culture and for culture . . . the power which is the greatest of all other forces, evoked with emotion and admiration, as much by the people of antiquity as the cultures of the new societies: "Genus humanum arte et ratione vivit." [The human race lives by creativity and reason.] I want to say to you, to cry to you from the depth of my soul: Yes, the future of man depends on culture! (603–609).

33. June 12, 1980, receiving the prime minister of Greece: "Greek civilization expresses a sublime conception of man. . . . The implanting of Christianity in Greek and Hellenistic civilization could not but be fortunate and fruitful. The Greek language incarnated the word of God in the New Testament" (689).

34. June 28, 1980, before the Roman Curia, John Paul evoked his encounters with men of culture and science (674).

35. June 30, 1980, at Brasília: "The Culture of Brazil Born of the Cross": "Despite the obstacles and defeats it has met, the Catholic faith, not only in its abstract formulations but in its practical expressions, in the norms it in-

spires and the activities it sustains, is at the origin of the formation of Brazil and in particular of its culture" (734).

36. July 1, 1980, at Rio de Janeiro in a meeting with men of culture: The place where Church encounters culture is the world, and in it, man who is a being of the world. To create culture is to give to man, to all of man and to the community of men, the human and divine dimension. In this work of culture God makes covenant with man, He himself becomes a craftsman of culture for the development of man. The work of culture is a work of love (743–745).

37. July 7, 1980, at Salvador de Bahia: "Yes, the culture of each people is sacred and worthy of respect in its essential elements. . . . But it is important to remember that . . . Christ is the light which, integrated into the most diverse cultures, enlightens and raises them from within. . . . The Church wishes to enter into contact with all people and all cultures. She wishes to enrich herself with the true values of the most diverse cultures. The liturgy is one of these domains, but certainly it is not the only one, where this exchange between the Church and cultures is effected. . . . From this permanent and fecund exchange the indigenous culture as well as black culture and European culture must draw benefits, as indeed—why not say it?—the Church herself in your country" (786–787).

38. October 19, 1980, at the University of the Propagation of the Faith in Rome: "In a special way the problem of the encounter of the Christian message with different cultures is found here in a manner that is always alive and actual. The power of the Gospel must penetrate to the very heart of different cultures and different traditions" (1981, 9–10).

39. November 15, 1980, in the cathedral of Cologne at a meeting with scientists and students: A call to struggle for a new humanism in the crisis of the orientation of culture (1136–1140).

40. November 19, 1980, to twenty-five hundred artists and journalists at Munich, John Paul recalled the chasm which has been dug between the Church and art, literature, theater, films, and the substantially new relations established by the Second Vatican Council, particularly *Gaudium et Spes,* between the Church and modern culture. For the Church and art have man as their object, and are at the service of human truth. The Church needs art, image, space to celebrate its worship (1162–1165).

41. The evening of the same day, in his farewell to Germany: "Heirs of an eminent culture, become more and more the pioneers of that civilization of love which alone can make our world more worthy of man" (1171).

42. December 22, 1980, before the College of Cardinals: Men of culture are the guardians of the most authentic patrimony of humanity and artisans of the future of the nations. Civilization is in their hands (57, 1981).

43. January 12, 1981, before the diplomatic corps to the Apostolic See: Cul-

ture is the life of the mind. It is the key which gives access to the deepest and most jealously guarded secrets of the life of peoples. . . . Culture is the great educator of man, the source of his being as man in the interior truth of his humanity, the foundation of the lives of people, the root of their profound identity, the support of their survival and their independence, the highest expression of the life of each person, the splendid synthesis of mind and body (102–103).

44. February 17, 1981, to the bishops of the Philippines at Manila: Introduce the Gospel in all cultures (261).

45. February 21, 1981, on Radio Veritas, Manila, in his message to the Peoples of Asia: Homage to their cultures (281).

46. February 24, 1981, to the diplomatic corps at Tokyo: the dialogue of cultures (326).

47. February 24, 1981, in a meeting with scholars: relationship of culture-science-technology (327–330).

48. October 5, 1981, to the Council of the Laity: to renew culture, which is the expression of the integrated person (955–956).

49. January 15, 1982, to the bishops of Lombardy: for a pastoral ministry of popular culture as a collection of principles and values which constitute the ethos of a people, the power which unifies them in depth (187–190).

50. January 15, 1982, to the national congress of the Mouvement Ecclesial d'Engagement Culturel: "The synthesis between culture and faith is not only a necessity of culture but also of faith. A faith which does not become a culture is a faith which is not fully accepted, thought out completely, and faithfully lived."

51. February 15, 1982, to the bishops of Nigeria at Lagos: to acculturate the Gospel and to evangelize the culture. The road of culture is the road of man, and it is on this road that man encounters the One who reunites in Himself the values of all cultures and fully reveals the man of each culture to himself. The Gospel of Christ, the Word incarnate, inserts itself into the road of culture (249).

52. February 24, 1982, to a general audience: The passage to the stage of African Church requires, as one of the fundamental tasks, the evangelization of culture. The African culture is a magnificent substratum which awaits the incarnation of Christianity (301).

53. April 18, 1982, to the university professors at Bologna: the common passion for the truth of man. The Church needs the university in order that faith can be incarnated and become culture (483–485).

54. May 15, 1982, at Coimbra, Portugal: The Church is involved at the highest point of culture. Culture is man's, coming from man and for man. It encompasses the totality of the life of a people. The human incarnation of Jesus was also a cultural incarnation (547–550).

55. June 28, 1982, to the Vatican Curia: "Relationships with the world of culture, solicitude for which haunts me constantly and is an obligatory point of reference for my pontifical service . . . have found official expression for deepened and organic action in the recent institution of the Pontifical Council for Culture, to which I have confided specific tasks to advance the fundamental relationship between the Church and culture. The Second Vatican Council in the Pastoral Constitution *Gaudium et Spes,* 53–62, gave the command and the foundations. We must now truly engage in the encounter with cultures, the place of privileged dialogue in the search for a new humanism for our times. May the Lord bless these new tasks which open for the action of the Apostolic See!" (704–705).

56. September 12, 1982, to the University of Padua: authentic culture and freedom (1983, 21–23).

57. September 13, 1982, to Congress of Catholic Intellectuals: Orient contemporary society (920).

58. September 24, 1982, to the bishops of Mozambique: Incarnate, evangelize African culture. Cultural incarnation: may the Gospel become your own blood, your own soul. Integrate these two vital poles: faith and cultures (917).

59. October 15, 1982, to the Symposium of the Bishops of Europe: The crises of European culture are the crises of Christian culture (1152–1154).

60. October 21, 1982, for the Fourth Centennial of Matteo Ricci, a bridge between the Church and culture: inculturation of the Gospel message to incarnate it in the Chinese culture (1983, 18).

61. November 3, 1982, discourse to university students of Madrid: openness to the universal; service of integral man; reception of the transcendent (1099–1101).

62. November 13, 1982, to the bishops of Cameroun: After the announcement of the Gospel there is above all a second stage, which is the evangelization in depth of the culture, of African cultures (1983, 84–86).

63. November 18, 1982, to the French bishops of the Provence region: There exists an evident correlation between popular culture and the faith of the people. There is a massive absence of the religious dimension in the world of communication media. The love of the people to be defended and promoted must guide ministry (1133–1136).

64. November 20, 1982, the University of Palermo, Sicily: "I beg you, as men of culture, liberate Christ from all incrustations, exploitations, and unworthy appropriations" (1983, 75).

65. November 23, 1982, to the College of Cardinals: "The dimension of culture, by its particular specificity, conditions in different ways evangelization, catechesis, the Christian mission of the family. If the orientation of the Apostolic See must enter into the pastoral dimension, then a particular organization which discerns the cultural contexts and seeks contact with them

must not be lacking. . . . This organization is already working with ardor" (1983, 3).

66. November 26, 1982, to participants of the Symposium Familiaris Consortio: The truth which the Church announces must become life. This truth intends to inspire a familial culture. Ths process of inculturation is made up of two closely united moments: a critical judgment, but this is not sufficient. One must create a matrimonial and familial culture (1983, 92).

67. December 16, 1982, to the French bishops of the Midi region: It has rarely been so indispensable to reassign our projects and our resources, not only to maintain but to elevate the level of Christian culture in the Church (1983, 71–73).

"Culture" in the Discourses of John Paul II, 1983–84

Selected and Summarized by Hervé Carrier

References are to *L'Osservatore Romano* (*OR*) and to its English edition (*OR*e).

1. To the Pontifical Council for Culture, *OR* January 19, *OR*e No. 9, February 28, 1983. Two main orientations: the evangelization of cultures; the cultural defense and promotion of humankind.
2. To the Bavarian bishops, *OR* January 29, 1983. Cult and Culture are indissociable.
3. To the Catholic Schools of Latium (Italy), *OR* January 30, *OR*e No. 10, March 7, 1983. The link between the Gospel and humankind is a creator of culture.
4. To the Quezaltenango Indians (Guatemala), *OR* March 9, *OR*e No. 19, May 9, 1983. "Your native cultures are the wealth of your peoples."
5. To the Latin-American University world, *OR* March 9, *OR*e No. 17, April 25, 1983. For a better distribution of the advantages of culture.
6. Letter from Cardinal Casaroli to the Rector of the Catholic University, Milan, *OR* April 10, *OR*e No. 22, May 30, 1983. Culture: the ennoblement of humankind.
7. To the bishops of Zaire, *OR* April 13, April 21, and April 30; *OR*e No. 19, May 9; No. 22, May 30; No. 31, August 1, 1983. Conditions for the inculturation of faith.
8. To the Catholicos Kareine II Sarkissian, visiting Rome, *OR* April 17, *OR*e No. 19, May 9, 1983. The Armenian culture is born of faith.
9. To a group of scientists, *OR* May 9–10, *OR*e No. 22, May 30, 1983. The Galileo case, dialogue between the Church and science.
10. To the Opera of the Scala, Milan, to personalities connected with art and culture, *OR* May 22, *OR*e No. 25, June 25, 1983. The life of mind. There is needed an "ecology of the Spirit."
11. To the professors of Milan University, *OR* May 23–24; *OR*e No. 25, May 23, 1983. Culture and the future of the world.
12. For the beatification of the martyrs in China, *OR* May 16–17, *OR*e No. 21, May 23, 1983. Christianity is at ease in every culture.
13. To an international symposium on Vjaceslav Ivanov, *OR* May 29, *OR*e

No. 32, August 18, 1983. The Slav spirit, rooted in faith, belongs both to the Orient and the Occident.

14. To an international conference on "Paul VI and Modernity in the Church," *OR* June 5, *OR*e No. 32, August 8, 1983. Paul VI was an initiator of dialogue between the Church and the world.

15. The group "Nova Spes," composed of scientists, philosophers, and industrialists, *OR* June 11, *OR*e No. 32, August 8, 1983. Openness to all those who devote themselves to the progress of human values.

16. To the Jagellon University, Cracow, *OR* June 23, *OR*e No. 27, July 4, 1983. Its role in the creation and diffusion of culture in Poland.

17. Letter from Cardinal Casaroli to the 25th General Assembly of C.I.O., *OR* June 30–July 1, *OR*e No. 34–35, August 22–29, 1983. Cultural and religious forces add their voice to the concert of international relationships.

18. Message from Cardinal Casaroli to scientists meeting at Erice, Sicily, for a seminar on nuclear war, *OR* August 22–23, 1983. Diffuse the culture of peace throughout the world.

19. To the 33rd General Congregation of the Jesuits, *OR* September 3, *OR*e No. 37, September 12, 1983. Presence in the modern world and in all cultures.

20. To the General Chapter of the Dominicans, *OR* September 5–6, *OR*e No. 37, September 12, 1983. Submit modern man to the liberating power of God.

21. To the Director of UNESCO for 17th International Literacy day, *OR* September 8, *OR*e No. 40, October 3, 1983. To participate in the culture and life of society.

22. To the "European Vespers," Vienna, *OR* September 12–13; *OR*e No. 27, September 12, 1983. The European cultural community takes roots in the Christian message.

23. Meeting with the cultural world in Vienna, *OR* September 12–13; *OR*e No. 39, September 26, 1983. Nature and Art lead to the mystery of God.

24. At the Mass for the Italian Association of Saint Cecilia; *OR* September 26–27; *OR*e No. 42, October 17, 1983. May sacred music be true art.

25. To the friends of Louvain University, *OR* October 11; *OR*e No. 50, December 12, 1983. Culture at the service of Church and society.

26. To the Quebec Bishops, *OR* October 19; *OR*e No. 46, November 14, 1983. Faith should keep pace with culture and education.

27. To the bishops of the U.S.A., *OR* October 29; *OR*e No. 46, November 14, 1983. Catholic education is a privileged chapter in the history of the Church in the U.S.A.

28. To the Pontifical Academy of Sciences, *OR* November 12; *OR*e No. 47, November 21, 1983. Free knowledge from the violence of the rich and powerful.

29. To the Major Superiors of Europe, *OR* November 17, 1983; *OR*e No. 1–

2, January 9, 1984. Bear evangelical witness by penetrating the various cultures without becoming enslaved by them.

30. To the Delegates of F.U.C.I. and M.E.I.C., *OR* December 4, 1983; *OR*e No. 4, January 23, 1984. A link exists between faith and culture, between faith and history.

31. To European intellectuals, *OR* December 16, 1983. Christ is the Redeemer of humankind and of human culture.

32. To the Ambassador of Ecuador, *OR* December 19, 1983. Faith and culture in national progress.

33. To the Director and personnel of the Vatican Museums, *OR* December 20, 1983; *OR*e No. 3, January 16, 1984. A special and appreciated contribution to culture.

34. To Robert Hossein and his troupe, *OR* December 20, 1983. With respect to the spectacle: "A man called Jesus."

35. To the Pontifical Council for Culture, *OR* January 16–17, 1984. The Culture of peace must overcome anti-culture.

36. Homily for the first liturgical feast for Fra Angelico, *OR* February 18, 1984. Art can lead to Christian perfection.

37. To the Chinese Bishops of Formosa, *OR* February 29, 1984. To be present at the heart of values inspiring the culture of a nation.

38. To the jubilee of youth, *OR* April 16–17, 1984. Choose the culture of love against the culture of death.

39. To men and women of culture in Korea, *OR* May 6, 1984. Seek the evangelization of cultures and the promotion of the human being.

40. Homily at the Mass in the national stadium of Bangkok, *OR* May 11, 1984. In a culture marked by Buddhist wisdom live the wisdom of the Beatitudes.

41. Message for the Day of Social Comunications, *OR* May 28–29, 1984. Faith and culture should meet in the field of communications.

42. To Fribourg University, *OR* June 14, 1984. Truth, wisdom, freedom confronting the crisis of science and culture.

43. To Laval University, Canada, *OR* September 10–11, 1984. Promote a new culture, integrating tradition and modernity.

44. To the Indians of Canada, *OR* September 19, 1984. The Church respects your cultures and favors your progress.

45. Homily in Winnipeg, Canada, *OR* September 19, 1984. The identity and cooperation of diverse cultural groups toward a civilization of love.

46. To the Pontifical Academy of Sciences, *OR* October 3, 1984. Space belongs to the whole of humanity. Not to cultural imperialism.

47. To the Roman Curia, *OR* December 22, 1984. The universal Church and the community of local Churches: diversity of cultures and the unity of the Church.

Evangelization in Latin America's Present and Future

Excerpts from the Final Document of the Third General Conference of Latin American Episcopate, CELAM, Puebla, Mexico, January 27–February 13, 1979

PART ONE

PASTORAL OVERVIEW OF THE REALITY THAT IS LATIN AMERICA

The aim of this historical overview is:

– To *situate* our own evangelization in continuity with the evangelization carried out over the past five centuries. The pillars of that past evangelization still perdure, providing a radical Catholic substrate in Latin America. After Vatican II and the Second General Conference of the Latin American Episcopate in Medellín, this substrate was still further enlivened by the Church's increasingly clear and deepening awareness of its fundamental mission, namely, evangelization.

– To *examine* with a pastoral eye some of the aspects of the present sociocultural context in which the Church is carrying out its mission, and also the pastoral reality that confronts evangelization as it is operative today and as it moves into the future.

CHAPTER I

HISTORICAL OVERVIEW: MAJOR MILESTONES IN THE EVANGELIZATION OF LATIN AMERICA

The Church has been given the mission of bringing the Good News to human beings. To carry out this mission effectively, the Church in Latin America feels that it is necessary to know the Latin American people in their historical context and their varied circumstances. The Latin American people must continue to be evangelized as heirs to a past, protagonists of the present, fashioners of a future, and pilgrims journeying toward the definitive Kingdom.

Evangelization is the very mission of the Church. The history of the Church is fundamentally the history of the evangelization of a people that lives through an ongoing process of gestation, and that is born and integrated into the life of nations over the ages. In becoming incarnate, the Church makes a vital contribution to the birth of nationalities and deeply imprints a particular character on them. Evangelization lies at the origins of the New World that is Latin America. The Church makes its presence felt in the origins and in the present-day reality of the continent. And, within the framework of its own proper mission and its realization, the Church seeks to contribute its services to a better future for the peoples of Latin America, to their liberation and growth in all of life's dimensions. The Medellín Conference itself re-echoed the statement of Paul VI that the vocation of Latin America was to "fashion a new and genial synthesis of the ancient and the modern, the spiritual and the temporal, what others bequeathed to us and what is our own original creation" (Med-Intro.: 7).

In the sometimes painful confluence of the most varied cultures and races, Latin America forged a new mixture of ethnic groups as well as modes of thinking and living that allowed for the gestation of a new race that overcame the hard and fast separations that had existed previously.

The generation of peoples and cultures is always dramatic, enveloped in a mixture of light and shadow. As a human task, evangelization is subject to the vicissitudes of history; but it always tries to transfigure them with the fire of the Spirit on the pathway of Christ, the center and meaning of universal history and of each and every person. Spurred on by all the contradictions and lacerations of those founding epochs, and immersed in a gigantic process of domination and cultural growth that has not yet come to an end, the evangelization that went into the making of Latin America is one of the relevant chapters in the history of the Church. In the face of difficulties that were both enormous and unprecedented, the creative response was such that its vigor keeps alive the popular religiosity of the majority of our peoples.

Our radical Catholic substrate, with its flourishing, vital forms of religiosity, was established and animated by a vast legion of missionaries: bishops, religious, and lay people. First and foremost, there is the labor of our saints: Toribio de Mogrovejo, Rosa de Lima, Martín de Porres, Pedro Claver, Luis Beltrán, and others. . . . They teach us that the weakness and cowardice of the people who surrounded and sometimes persecuted them were overcome; that the Gospel in all its plenitude of grace and love was lived, and can be lived, in Latin America as a sign of spiritual grandeur and divine truth.

And then there were the intrepid champions of justice and proponents of the gospel message of peace: e.g., Antonio de Montesinos, Bartolomé de las Casas, Juan de Zumárraga, Vasco de Quiroga, Juan del Valle, Julián Garcés, José de Ancheita, Manuel Nóbrega, and all the others who defended the Indians against *conquistadores* and *encomenderos*—even unto death, as in the case of Bishop Antonio Valdivieso.* They prove, with all the force of actual fact, in what way the Church promotes the dignity and freedom of the Latin American person. And that is a reality thankfully acknowledged by John Paul II when he first stepped on the soil of the New World: ". . . those religious who came to announce Christ the Savior, to defend the dignity of the native inhabitants, to proclaim their inviolable rights, to foster their integral betterment, to teach brotherhood as human beings and as children of the same Lord and Father God" (HSD).

The evangelizing work of the Church in Latin America is the result of a unanimous missionary effort on the part of the whole people of God. We have the countless initiatives of charity, social assistance, and education; and we have the exemplary original syntheses of evangelization and human promotion by the missions of the Franciscans, Augustinians, Dominicans, Jesuits, Mercedarians, and others. We have the evangelical sacrifice and generosity of numerous Christians. Here women, by their abnegation and prayer, played an essential role. Inventiveness in teaching the faith was evident, along with a vast array of resources that brought together all the arts, ranging from music, song, and dance to architecture, painting, and the theater. This whole pastoral display of ability was associated with a time of great theological reflection and dynamic intellectual thinking that gave rise to universities, schools, dictionaries, grammars, catechisms in a variety of native languages, and extremely interesting historical accounts of the origins of our peoples. And then there was the extraordinary proliferation of lay organizations and confraternities, which came to serve as the vital heart and soul of the religious life of believers. They are the remote but fruitful source of the present-day community movements in the Latin American Church.

It is true that in its work of evangelization the Church had to bear the weight of its lapses, its acts of complicity with the earthly powers, its incomplete pastoral vision, and the destructive force of sin. But we must also recognize that evangelization, which makes Latin America a "continent of hope," has been far more powerful than the dark shadows that unfortunately accompanied it in the historical context through which it had to live. For us Christians today, this challenges us to measure up to our history at its best and to be capable of responding with creative fidelity to the challenges of our Latin American epoch.

After that era of evangelization in our lands, which was so decisive in

---

*Unfortunately, the problem of the African slaves did not attract sufficient evangelizing and liberation-oriented attention from the Church.

the formation of Latin America, there came a cycle of stabilization, weariness, and routinism. This was followed by the great crises in the nineteenth century and the early part of the twentieth century, which brought bitter experiences and persecutions to the Church. It was subjected to bouts of uncertainty and conflict that shook it to its very foundations. Overcoming this harsh test, the Church undertook a mighty effort and managed to rebuild and survive. Today, especially since Vatican II, the Church has been undergoing renewal and, with a vigorous evangelizing spirit, it has been paying heed to the needs and hopes of the peoples of Latin America. The energy that in past centuries brought its bishops together in Lima, Mexico City, São Salvador de Bahia, and Rome, has now manifested its vitality in the conferences of the Latin American Episcopate in Rio de Janeiro and Medellín. Those conferences activated the Church's energies and prepared it for the challenges of the future.

Since Medellín in particular, the Church, clearly aware of its mission and loyally open to dialogue, has been scrutinizing the signs of the times and is generously disposed to evangelize in order to contribute to the construction of a new society that is more fraternal and just; such a society is a crying need of our peoples. Thus the mutual forces of tradition and progress, which once seemed to be antagonistic in Latin America, are now joining each other and seeking a new, distinctive synthesis that will bring together the possibilities of the future and the energies derived from our common roots. And so, within this vast process of renewal that is inaugurating a new epoch in Latin America, and amid the challenges of recent times, we pastors are taking up the age-old episcopal tradition of Latin America and preparing ourselves to carry the Gospel's message of salvation hopefully and bravely to all human beings, but to the poorest and most forgotten by way of preference.

Throughout the course of a rich historical experience, filled with bright moments and dark shadows, the great mission of the Church has been its committed involvement in faith with the human being of Latin America: with that person's eternal salvation, spiritual victory, and full human development.

Taking inspiration from that great mission of yesteryear, we want to draw closer to the reality of today's Latin Americans with a pastoral eye and a Christian heart in order to understand and interpret it. Starting off from that reality, we want to proceed to analyze our pastoral mission.

CHAPTER II

PASTORAL OVERVIEW OF THE SOCIOCULTURAL CONTEXT

2.1. Introduction

As pastors, we journey with the people of Latin America through our history. There are many basic elements that are shared in common, but there are also shadings and differences peculiar to each nation. Starting off from the Gospel, which presents Jesus Christ doing good and loving all without distinction (Acts 10:38), and from our vision based on faith, we place ourselves in the reality of the Latin American as it finds expression in that human being's hopes, achievements, and frustrations. Our faith prompts us to discern the summonses of God in the signs of the times; to bear witness to, announce, and promote the evangelical values of communion and participation; and to denounce everything in our society that runs counter to the filiation originating in God the Father and the brotherhood rooted in Jesus Christ.

As pastors, we single out the successes and failures of recent years. In presenting this reality, we are not trying to dishearten people but rather to stimulate all those who can do something to improve it. The Church in Latin America has tried to help human beings to move on "from less human situations to more human ones" (PP: 20). It has made every effort to summon people to ongoing individual and social conversion. It asks all Christians to work together to change unjust structures and to communicate Christian values to the general culture in which they are living. It asks them to take cognizance of the successes achieved, to take heart from them, and thus to continue contributing to more and better successes.

We are happy to spell out some of the realities that fill us with hope:

–Latin Americans have an innate tendency to accept and shelter people; to share what they have with others; to display fraternal charity and generosity, particularly among the poor; and to share the distress of others in need. Latin Americans place high value on the special ties of friendship rooted in the family, the role of godparents, and the bonds thus created.

–Latin Americans have increasingly taken cognizance of their dignity as human beings and of the desire for political and social participation, despite the fact that in many areas these rights are crushed underfoot. There has been a proliferation of community organizations, such as cooperative movements, especially among the common people.

–There is growing interest in autochthonous values and in respecting the originality of indigenous cultures and their communities. There is also great love for the land.

–Ours is a young people; and where they have had opportunities to develop their abilities and organize, they have proved that they can win out and regain possession of their just rights and claims.

–The significant economic progress that has been experienced by our continent proves that it would be possible to root out extreme poverty and improve our people's quality of life. If that is possible, it becomes an obligation (PP: 76).

–We can see a growth in the middle class, though it has suffered decline in some areas.

–The forward strides in education are clear to be seen.

But in our many pastoral encounters with our people we also note what Pope John Paul II noted when he visited peasants, laborers, and students. It is the deeply felt plaint–fraught with anxieties, hopes, and aspirations–of those whose voice we wish to be: "The voice of those who cannot speak or who have been silenced" (AO).

So we place ourselves within the dynamic thrust of the Medellín Conference (Med-PC: 2), adopting its vision of reality that served as the inspiration for so many pastoral documents of ours in the past decade.

The real situation in our countries was lucidly reflected in the words of Paul VI: "We all know in what terms many bishops spoke during the recent Synod of Bishops. Bishops from every continent, particularly those from the Third World, spoke in pastoral accents that echoed the voices of millions of the Church's children who make up those peoples. We know only too well that all the energy and effort of those peoples are invested in the struggle to overcome the things that condemn them to live on the margin of life: hunger, chronic diseases, illiteracy, impoverishment, injustice in international relations and particularly in commercial interchanges, situations of economic and cultural neocolonialism that are sometimes as cruel as political neocolonialism, etc. The Church, said the bishops once again, has the duty to proclaim the liberation of millions of human beings, among whom are many of the Church's own children; the duty to help bring this liberation forth in the world, to bear witness to it and make sure that it is total. None of this is alien to evangelization" (EN: 30).

2.2. Sharing People's Anxieties

We are concerned about the anxieties of all those who make up the people, whatever their social condition may be. We are concerned about their loneliness, their family problems, and the lack of meaning in the lives of many of them. Today we wish in particular to share the anxieties that stem from their poverty.

Viewing it in the light of faith, we see the growing gap between rich and poor as a scandal and a contradiction to Christian existence (OAP: III, 2). The luxury of a few becomes an insult to the wretched poverty of the vast masses (PP: 3). This is contrary to the plan of the Creator and to the honor that is due him. In this anxiety and sorrow the Church sees a situation of social sinfulness, all the more serious because it exists in countries that call themselves Catholic and are capable of changing the situation: "They have a right to have the barriers of exploitation removed, . . . against which their best efforts at advancement are dashed" (AO).

So we brand the situation of inhuman poverty in which millions of Latin

Americans live as the most devastating and humiliating kind of scourge. And this situation finds expression in such things as a high rate of infant mortality, lack of adequate housing, health problems, starvation wages, unemployment and underemployment, malnutrition, job uncertainty, compulsory mass migrations, etc.

Analyzing this situation more deeply, we discover that this poverty is not a passing phase. Instead it is the product of economic, social, and political situations and structures, though there are also other causes for the state of misery. In many instances this state of poverty within our countries finds its origin and support in mechanisms which, because they are impregnated with materialism rather than any authentic humanism, create a situation on the international level where the rich get richer at the expense of the poor, who get ever poorer (OAP: III, 3). Hence this reality calls for personal conversion and profound structural changes that will meet the legitimate aspirations of the people for authentic social justice. Such changes either have not taken place, or else they have been too slow in coming in the concrete life of Latin America.

This situation of pervasive extreme poverty takes on very concrete faces in real life. In these faces we ought to recognize the suffering features of Christ the Lord, who questions and challenges us. They include:

–the faces of young children, struck down by poverty before they are born, their chance for self-development blocked by irreparable mental and physical deficiencies; and of the vagrant children in our cities who are so often exploited, products of poverty and the moral disorganization of the family;

–the faces of young people, who are disoriented because they cannot find their place in society, and who are frustrated, particularly in marginal rural and urban areas, by the lack of opportunity to obtain training and work;

–the faces of the indigenous peoples, and frequently of the Afro-Americans as well; living marginalized lives in inhuman situations, they can be considered the poorest of the poor;

–the faces of the peasants; as a social group, they live in exile almost everywhere on our continent, deprived of land, caught in a situation of internal and external dependence, and subjected to systems of commercialization that exploit them;

–the faces of laborers, who frequently are ill-paid and who have difficulty in organizing themselves and defending their rights;

–the faces of the underemployed and the unemployed, who are dismissed because of the harsh exigencies of economic crises, and often because of development-models that subject workers and their families to cold economic calculations;

–the faces of marginalized and overcrowded urban dwellers, whose lack of material goods is matched by the ostentatious display of wealth by other segments of society;

—the faces of old people, who are growing more numerous every day, and who are frequently marginalized in a progress-oriented society that totally disregards people not engaged in production.

We share other anxieties of our people that stem from a lack of respect for their dignity as human beings, made in the image and likeness of God, and for their inalienable rights as children of God.

Countries such as ours, where there is frequently no respect for such fundamental human rights as life, health, education, housing, and work, are in the position of permanently violating the dignity of the person.

To this are added other anxieties that stem from abuses of power, which are typical of regimes based on force. There are the anxieties based on systematic or selective repression; it is accompanied by accusations, violations of privacy, improper pressures, tortures, and exiles. There are the anxieties produced in many families by the disappearance of their loved ones, about whom they cannot get any news. There is the total insecurity bound up with arrest and detention without judicial consent. There are the anxieties felt in the face of a system of justice that has been suborned or cowed. As the Supreme Pontiffs point out, the Church, by virtue of "an authentically evangelical commitment" (OAP: III, 3), must raise its voice to denounce and condemn these situations, particularly when the responsible officials or rulers call themselves Christians.

Then there are the anxieties raised by guerilla violence, by terrorism, and by the kidnappings carried out by various brands of extremists. They, too, pose a threat to life together in society.

In many of our countries lack of respect for human dignity also finds expression in the lack of social participation on various levels. We want to allude, in particular, to labor unionization. In many places labor legislation is either applied arbitrarily or not taken into account at all. This is particularly true in countries where the government is based on the use of force. There they look askance at the organizing efforts of laborers, peasants, and the common people; and they adopt repressive measures to prevent such organizing. But this type of control over, or limitation on, activity is not app'plied to employer organizations, which can exercise their full power to protect their interests.

In some cases the over-politicization of labor unions at the top level distorts the aim of these organizations.

In recent years we have also seen deterioration in the political sphere. Much harm has been done to the participation of citizens in the conduct of their own affairs and destiny. We also frequently see a rise in what can be called institutionalized injustice (Med-P: 16). And by employing violent means, extremist political groups provoke new waves of repression against segments of the common people.

The free-market economy, in its most rigid expression, is still the prevailing system on our continent. Legitimated by liberal ideologies, it has increased the gap between the rich and the poor by giving priority to capital over labor, economics over the social realm. Small groups in our nations, who are often tied in with foreign interests, have taken advantage of the opportunities provided by these older forms of the free market to profit for themselves while the interests of the vast majority of the people suffer.

Marxist ideologies have also spread among workers, students, teachers, and others, promising greater social justice. In practice their strategies have sacrificed many Christian, and hence human, values; or else they have fallen prey to utopian forms of unrealism. Finding their inspiration in policies that use force as a basic tool, they have only intensified the spiral of violence.

In many instances the ideologies of National Security have helped to intensify the totalitarian or authoritarian character of governments based on the use of force, leading to the abuse of power and the violation of human rights. In some instances they presume to justify their positions with a subjective profession of Christian faith.

Our countries are going through cycles of economic crisis, despite the trend toward modernization and strong economic growth accompanied by varying degrees of hardship. These cycles intensify the sufferings of our people when a cold-hearted technocracy applies developmental models that extort a truly inhuman price from those who are poorest. And this is all the more unjust insofar as the price is not shared by all.

2.3. Cultural Aspects

Latin America is made up of different races and cultural groups characterized by varied historical processes; it is not a uniform, continuous reality. But there are elements that make up what might be called a common cultural patrimony of historical traditions and the Christian faith.

Unfortunately, the development of certain cultures is very precarious. In practice, values that are part of the rich, age-old tradition of our people are disregarded, marginalized, and even destroyed. But fortunately we also see the beginnings of a new valuation of our native cultures.

Due to dominant influences from abroad or the alienating imitation of imported values and lifestyles, the traditional cultures of our countries have been distorted and attacked. Our identity and our own specific values are threatened.

Hence we share our people's anxieties over the subversion of values that is at the root of many of the ills mentioned above:

–Individualistic materialism, the supreme value in the eyes of many of our contemporaries, works against communion and participation, posing obstacles to solidarity; and collectivist materialism subordinates the person to the State.

–Consumptionism, with its unbridled ambition to "have more," is suffocating modern human beings in an immanentism that closes them off to the evangelical values of generosity and austerity. It is paralyzing them when it comes to solidary communication and fraternal sharing.

–The deterioration of basic family values is disintegrating family communion, eliminating shared and responsible participation by all the family members and making them an easy prey to divorce or abandonment. In some cultural groups the woman finds herself in a position of inferiority.

–The deterioration of public and private integrity is evident. We also find frustration and hedonism leading people into such vices as gambling, drug addiction, alcoholism, and sexual licentiousness.

We must also consider education and social communication as transmitters of culture.

–Education has made great strides forward in recent years. School attendance has increased, though the drop-out rate is still high. Illiteracy has also diminished, though not enough in areas inhabited by indigenous peoples and peasants.

Despite these advances, however, there are also deformations that have depersonalized many people. This is due to manipulation by small power-groups who are trying to safeguard their own interests and inculcate their own ideologies.

–The aforementioned cultural traits are being strongly influenced by the media of social communication. Political, ideological, and economic power-groups succeed, through these media, in subtly penetrating both the environment and the lifestyle of our people. Information is manipulated by various authorities and groups. This is done particularly through advertising, which raises false expectations, creates fictitious needs, and often contradicts the basic values of our Latin American culture and the Gospel. The improper exercise of freedom in these media leads to an invasion of the privacy of persons, who generally are defenseless. Operating twenty-four hours a day, these media penetrate every area of human life: the home, work sites, places of recreation, and the streets. They also effect a cultural change that gives rise to a new idiom (EN:42).

2.4. The Underlying Roots of These Realities

We want to point out some of the underlying roots of these phenomena so that we can offer our help and cooperation in bringing about needed changes. Here we adopt a pastoral perspective that focuses more directly on the needs of the people.

a. We see the continuing operation of economic systems that do not regard the human being as the center of society, and that are not carrying out the profound changes needed to move toward a just society.

b. One of the serious consequences of the lack of integration among our nations is that we go before the world as small entities without any ability to push through negotiations in the concert of nations (MPLA: 8).

c. There is the fact of economic, technological, political, and cultural dependence; the presence of multinational conglomerates that often look after only their own interests at the expense of the welfare of the country that welcomes them in; and the drop in value of our raw materials as compared with the price of the finished products we buy.

d. The arms race, the great crime of our era, is both the result and the cause of tensions between our fellow countries. Because of it, enormous resources are allotted for arms purchases instead of being employed to solve vital problems (MPLA: 8).

e. There is a lack of structural reforms in agriculture that adequately deal with specific realities and decisively attack the grave social and economic problems of the peasantry. Such problems include access to land and to resources that would enable them to improve their productivity and their marketing.

f. We see a crisis in moral values: public and private corruption; greed for exorbitant profit; venality; lack of real effort; the absence of any social sense of practical justice and solidarity; and the flight of capital resources and brain power. All these things prevent or undermine communion with God and brotherhood.

g. Finally, speaking as pastors and without trying to determine the technical character of these underlying roots, we ourselves see that at bottom there lies a mystery of sinfulness. This is evident when the human person, called to have dominion over the world, impregnates the mechanisms of society with materialistic values (HSD: 3).

2.5. The Basic Setting: A Continent with Serious Demographic Problems

We note that almost all of our countries have experienced an accelerating rate of population growth. The vast majority of our population is composed of young people. Internal and external migrations bring with them a sense of uprooting. The cities are growing in a disorganized fashion; they are in danger of becoming uncontrollable megalopolises. It becomes harder every day to provide such basic services as housing, hospitals, schools, and so forth; and this increases social, cultural, and economic marginalization. The increase in those seeking work has outstripped the capacity of the present economic system to provide employment. And there are governments and international institutions that implement or support birth-control policies that are opposed to family morality.

* * * * *

Excerpt from Part Two: God's Saving Plan for Latin America, Chapter II: What Does Evangelizing Mean?

2. THE EVANGELIZATION OF CULTURE

2.1. Culture and Cultures

The new and important pastoral contribution of *Evangelii Nuntiandi* lies in Paul VI's summons to face up to the task of evangelizing culture and cultures (EN: 20).

The term "culture" means the specific way in which human beings belonging to a given people cultivate their relationship with nature, with each other, and with God in order to arrive at "an authentic and full humanity." It is the shared lifestyle that characterizes different peoples around the earth, and so we can speak about "a plurality of cultures" (GS: 53; EN: 20).

So conceived, culture embraces the whole life of a people. It is the whole web of values that inspire them and of disvalues that debilitate them; insofar as they are shared in common by all the members, they bring them together on the basis of a "collective consciousness" (EN: 18). Culture also embraces the forms in which these values or disvalues find configuration and expression – i.e., customs, language, societal institutions and structures – insofar as they are not impeded or suppressed by the intervention of other, dominant cultures.

In the context of this totality, evangelization seeks to get to the very core of a culture, the realm of its basic values, and to bring about a conversion that will serve as the basis and guarantee of a transformation in structures and the social milieu (EN: 18).

The essential core of a culture lies in the way in which a people affirms or rejects a religious tie with God, that is, in its religious values or disvalues. These values or disvalues have to do with the ultimate meaning of life. Their roots lie in the deeper zone where human beings formulate answers to the basic, ultimate questions that vex them. The answer may be a positively religious orientation on the one hand, or an atheistic orientation on the other hand. Thus religion or irreligion is a source of inspiration for all the other areas of a culture – family life, economics, politics, art, etc. They are either freed to seek out some transcendent meaning, or else they are locked up in their own immanent meaning.

Evangelization takes the whole human being into account, and so it seeks to reach the total human being through that being's religious dimension.

Culture is a creative activity of human beings. Thus it is in line with the vocation given to them by God to perfect all creation (Genesis), and hence their own spiritual and corporeal qualities and capabilities (GS: 53, 57).

Culture is continually shaped and reshaped by the ongoing life and historical experience of peoples; and it is transmitted by tradition from generation to generation. Thus human beings are born and raised in the bosom of a given society, conditioned and enriched by a given culture. They receive a culture, creatively modify it, and then continue to pass it on. Culture is a historical and social reality (GS: 53).

Cultures are continually subjected to new developments and to mutual encounter and interpenetration. In the course of their history they go through periods in which they are challenged by new values or disvalues, and by the need to effect new syntheses of their way of life. The Church feels particularly summoned to make its presence felt, to be there with the Gospel, when old ways of social life and value-organization are decaying or dying in order to make room for new syntheses (GS: 5). It is better to evangelize new cultural forms when they are being born than when they are already full-grown and established. This is the global challenge that confronts the Church today because we truly can "speak of a new age in human history" (GS: 54). Hence the Latin American Church seeks to give new impetus to the evangelization of our continent.

2.2. The Pastoral Option of the Latin American Church: To Evangelize Culture Today and for Tomorrow

The aim of evangelization. Christ sent his Church to announce the Gospel to all human beings, to all peoples (Matt. 28: 19; Mark 16: 15). Since every human being is born into a culture, the Church in its evangelizing activity seeks to touch, not only the individual, but also the culture of a people (EN: 18). Using the power of the Gospel, it tries "to reach and transform the criteria of judgment, the determining values, the points of interest, the lines of thought, the sources of inspiration, and the models of human life that are opposed to the Word of God and the plan of salvation. Perhaps we could put it this way: the work of evangelization is not to be a decorative veneer; it is to be done in a vital, in-depth manner so that it touches the very roots of human culture and cultures" (EN: 19–20).

Pastoral option. The evangelizing activity of our Latin American Church must have as its overall goal the ongoing evangelical renewal and transformation of our culture. In other words, the Gospel must penetrate the values and criteria that inspire our culture, convert the human beings who live by these values, and, insofar as it is necessary, change the structures in which they live and express themselves so that they may be more fully human.

If we are to do this, it is of the utmost importance that we pay heed to the religion of our peoples. Not only must we take it on as an object for evangelization. Insofar as it has already been evangelized, we must also accept it as an active, evangelizing force.

2.3. The Church, Faith, and Culture

Love for peoples and knowledge of their culture. To carry out and expand its evangelizing activity realistically, the Church must truly know the culture of Latin America. But even before that, it starts off with a profound attitude of love for peoples. Thus, basing its work not only on a scientific approach but also on the connatural effective understanding that comes with love, it will be able to learn and discern the specific modalities of our culture as well as its crises and historical challenges; and it will then be able to make common cause with our culture within the context of Latin America's history (OA: 1).

Here is one important criterion that must guide the Church in its effort to know our culture: it must note the overall direction in which the culture is heading rather than its side-pockets bound up with the past, its expressions that are operative today rather than those that are merely part of folklore.

The task of evangelizing our continent's culture must be organized against the backdrop of an established cultural tradition, now being challenged by the process of cultural change that has been affecting Latin America and the world in modern times and is now reaching its moment of crisis.

Faith's encounter with cultures. When the Church, the People of God, announces the Gospel and peoples accept it in faith, it becomes incarnate among them and assumes their cultures. This gives rise, not to an identification between the two, but to a close bond between them. On the one hand the faith transmitted by the Church is lived out on the basis of a presupposed culture. In other words, it is lived by believers who are deeply attached to a culture, and hence "the construction of the kingdom cannot help but take over elements from human culture and cultures" (EN: 20). On the other hand the principle of incarnation embodied in the old adage of St. Irenaeus remains valid in the pastoral realm: "what is not assumed is not redeemed."

The general principle of incarnation breaks down concretely into several specific criteria:

Cultures are not vacuums devoid of authentic values, and the evangelizing work of the Church is not a process of destruction; rather, it is a process of consolidating and fortifying those values, a contribution to the growth of the "seeds of the Word" present in cultures (GS:57).

The Church is even more interested in assuming the specifically Christian values that it encounters among peoples already evangelized, and that are lived out by those peoples in their own cultural forms.

In its evangelization, the Church begins with those seeds sown by Christ and with those values that are the fruit of its own evangelization.

All this implies that the Church – of course the local Church – makes every effort to adapt itself. It tries to translate the gospel message into the anthropological idiom and symbols of the culture in which it immerses itself (EN:53, 62–63; GS:58; DT:420–23).

When the Church proclaims the Good News, it denounces and corrects the presence of sinfulness in cultures; it purifies and exorcises their disvalues, thus establishing a critique of cultures. In the announcing of the Kingdom of God, the opposite side of the coin is the critical denunciation of various forms of idolatry, that is, of values that have been set up as idols or values that a culture has taken to be absolute when in fact they are not. The Church's mission is to bear witness to "the true God and one Lord."

So there is nothing insulting in the fact that evangelization invites peoples to abandon false conceptions of God, anti-natural patterns of conduct, and aberrant manipulations of some people by others.

The specific task of evangelization is to "proclaim Christ" (EN:53). This does not mean that cultures are to be invited to remain under the grip of an ecclesiastical regime. Instead they are to be invited to accept in faith the spiritual lordship of Christ, for they will not be able to attain their full measure outside of his truth and grace. Thus through evangelization the Church tries to make sure that cultures will be renovated, elevated, and perfected by the active presence of the risen Christ, the center of history, and of his Spirit (EN:18, 20, 23; GS:58, 61).

2.4. Evangelization of Culture in Latin America

We have indicated above the fundamental criteria governing the work of the Church in evangelizing cultures.

Our Church, for its part, carries out this work in the particular human area known as Latin America, whose historical and cultural process has already been described (see Part One).

So let us briefly review some of the principal items already established in Part One of this document so that we may be able to single out the challenges and problems posed to evangelization by the present moment of history.

Types of culture and stages in the cultural process. The origin of present-day Latin America lies in the encounter of the Spanish and Portuguese peoples with the pre-Columbian and African cultures. Racial and cultural intermingling has profoundly marked this process, and there is every indication that it will continue to do so now and in the future.

This fact should not prompt us to disregard the persistence of indigenous cultures or Afro-American cultures in a pure state, nor the existence of groups who are integrated into the nation in varying degrees.

Subsequently, during the last two centuries, new waves of immigrants have flowed into Latin America, and particularly into the southern cone of our continent. These immigrants brought their own characteristics with them, which basically were integrated with the underlying cultural stratum.

In the first epoch, from the sixteenth to the eighteenth centuries, were laid the bases of Latin American culture and its solid Catholic substrate. In that period evangelization was deep enough for the faith to become a constitutive part of Latin America's life and identity. It provided Latin America with a spiritual unity that still persists, despite later splintering into separate nations and divisions on the economic, social, and political planes.

So our culture is impregnated with the faith, even though it frequently has lacked the support of a suitable catechesis. This is evident in the distinctive religious attitudes of our people, which are imbued with a deep sense of transcendence and the nearness of God. It finds expression in a wisdom of the common people that has contemplative features and that gives a distinctive direction to the way our people live out their relationship with nature and their fellow human beings. It is embodied in their sense of work and festiveness, of solidarity, friendship, and kinship; and in their feel for their own dignity, which they do not see diminished by their own lives as simple, poor people.

Preserved more vividly as an articulation of life as a whole among the poor, this culture bears in particular the seal of the heart and its intuitions. Rather than finding expression in scientific categories and ways of thinking, it is more likely to find expression in artistic forms, in piety as a lived reality, and in solidary forms of social life.

From the eighteenth century on, this culture began to feel the impact of the dawning urban-industrial civilization, with its physico-mathematical brand of knowledge and its stress on efficiency. The impact was first felt by the *mestizo* culture, and then gradually by various enclaves of indigenous peoples and Afro-Americans.

The new urban-industrial civilization is accompanied by strong tendencies toward personalization and socialization. It produces a sharpened acceleration of history, demanding great efforts at assimilation and creativity from all peoples if they do not want to see their cultures left behind or even eliminated.

Urban-industrial culture, which has as a consequence the intense proletarianization of various social strata and even peoples, is controlled by the great powers in possession of science and technology. It is a historical process that tends to make the problem of dependence and poverty more and more acute.

The advent of urban-industrial civilization also entails problems on the ideological level, threatening the very roots of our culture. For in terms of real-life history and its workings, this civilization comes to us imbued with rationalism and inspired by two dominant ideologies: liberalism and Marxist collectivism. In both we find a tendency, not just to a legitimate and desirable secularization, but also to "secularism."

Within this basic historical process we see arising on our continent certain particular but important phenomena and problems: increased migration and displacement of the population from rural to urban areas; the rise of various religious phenomena, such as the invasion of sects, which should not be disregarded by evangelizers simply because they may seem to be marginal; the enormous influence of the media of social communication as vehicles of new cultural guidelines and models; the yearning of women to better their situation, in line with their dignity and distinctiveness, within the overall framework of society; and the emergence of a laborer's world that will be decisive in the new configuration of our culture.

Evangelizing activity: challenges and problems. The data given above also point to the challenges that must be faced by the Church. The problems are manifestations of the signs of the times, pointing toward the future where culture is now heading. The Church must be able to discern these signs if it is to consolidate the values and overthrow the idols that are feeding this historical process.

The coming world culture. This urban-industrial culture, which is inspired by the scientific-technological outlook, driven by the great powers, and characterized by the aforementioned ideologies, proposes to be a universal one. Various peoples, local cultures, and human groups are invited or even constrained to become an integral part of it.

In Latin America this tendency again brings to the fore the whole problem of integrating indigenous ethnic groups and realities into the political and cultural fabric of our nations. For our nations find themselves challenged to more toward greater development, to win new hands and lands for more efficient production, so that they can become a more integral and dynamic part of the accelerating thrust of world civilization.

This new universality has different levels. First, there is the level of scientific and technical elements, which are the instruments of development. Second, there is the level of certain values that are given new emphasis: e.g., labor and the increased possession of consumer goods. And then there is the whole matter of "lifestyle" as a whole, which entails a particular hierarchy of values and preferences.

Finding themselves at this critical juncture in history, some ethnic and social groups draw back into themselves, defending their own distinctive culture in and through a fruitless sort of isolationism. Other groups, on the other hand, allow themselves to be readily absorbed by lifestyles introduced by the new world culture.

In its work of evangelization, the Church itself moves ahead by a process of delicate and difficult discernment. By virtue of its own evangelical principles, the Church looks with satisfaction on the impulses of humanity leading toward integration and universal communion. By virtue of its specific mission it feels that it has been sent, not to destroy cultures, but to help them consolidate their being and identity. And it does this by summoning human beings of all races and peoples to unite in faith under Christ as one single People of the universal God.

The Church itself promotes and fosters things that go beyond this catholic union in the same faith, things that find embodiment in forms of communion between cultures and of just integration on the economic, social, and political levels.

But the Church, as one would expect, calls into question any "universality" that is synonymous with uniformity or levelling, that fails to respect different cultures by weakening them, absorbing them, or annihilating them. With even greater reason the Church refuses to accept universality when it is used as a tool to unify humanity by inculcating the unjust, offensive supremacy and domination of some peoples or social strata over other peoples and social strata.

The Church of Latin America has resolved to put fresh vigor into its work of evangelizing the culture of our peoples and the various ethnic groups. It wants to see the faith of the Gospel blossom or be restored to fresh life. And with this as the basis of communion, it wants to see it burgeon into forms of just integration on all levels—national, continental Latin American, and universal. This will enable our peoples to develop their own culture in such a way that they can assimilate the findings of science and technology in their own proper way.

The city. In the transition from an agrarian culture to an urban-industrial one, the city becomes the moving force behind the new world civilization. This fact calls for a new type of discernment on the part of the Church. In general, it should find its inspiration in the vision of the Bible. On the one hand the Bible has a positive view of the human tendency to create cities, where human beings can live together in a more corporate and humane way; on the other hand it is highly critical of the inhumanness and sinfulness that has its origin in urban life.

In the present situation, therefore, the Church does not favor as an ideal the creation of huge metropolises, which become inhuman beyond all repair.

Nor does it favor an excessively accelerated pace of industrialization that will cost today's generations their own happiness and require inhuman sacrifices.

The Church also recognizes that urban life and industrial change pose unprecedented problems. They undermine traditional patterns of behavior and institutions: the family, the neighborhood, and work life. And hence they also undermine the living situation of the religious human being, the faithful, and the Christian community (OA: 10).

These characteristics are aspects of what is called "the process of secularization," which is evidently bound up with the emergence of science and technology and the increase in urbanization.

There is no reason to assume that the elemental forms of religious awareness are exclusively bound up with agrarian culture. The transition to an urban-industrial civilization need not entail the abolition of religion. But it obviously poses a challenge because it entails new forms and structures of living that condition religious awareness and the Christian life.

So the Church is faced with a challenge. It must revitalize its work of evangelization so that it will be able to help the faithful live as Christians amid the new conditioning factors created by the urban-industrial society. And it must realize that these new factors do have an influence on the practice of holiness, on prayer and contemplation, on interhuman relationships (that have now become more functional and anonymous), on people's work life, production, and consumption.

Secularism. The Church accepts the process of secularization insofar as it means the legitimate autonomy of the secular realm. Taking it in this sense (GS: 36; EN: 55), it regards it as just and desirable. But the fact is that the shift to an urban-industrial society, viewed in terms of the real-life process of western history rather than in the abstract, has been inspired by the ideology that we call "secularism."

Secularism essentially separates human beings from God and sets up an opposition between them. It views the construction of history as purely and exclusively the responsibility of human beings, and it views them in merely immanent terms. The world "is explained solely on its own terms, without any necessary reference to God. God, then, is superfluous, if not a downright obstacle. So in order to recognize the power of human beings, this brand of secularism ends up bypassing God, or even denying God altogether. The result seems to be new forms of atheism—an anthropocentric atheism that is practical and militant rather than abstract and metaphysical. And bound up with this atheistic secularism we find a consumer civilization, a hedonism exalted as the supreme value, a will to power and domination, and discrimination of all sorts. These are some of the other inhuman tendencies of this 'humanism'" (EN: 55).

Committed to its task to evangelize people and to arouse faith in God, the provident Father, and in Jesus Christ, who is actively present in history, the Church finds itself in a radical confrontation with this secularistic movement. It sees it as a threat to the faith and the very culture of our Latin American peoples. Hence one of the fundamental commitments in the new drive toward evangelization must be to revivify and reorganize the proclamation of the content of evangelization, basing our efforts on the very faith of our peoples. Our aim is that they themselves will be able to incorporate the values of the new urban-industrial civilization into a new vital synthesis, which will continue to be grounded on faith in God rather than on the atheism that is the logical consequence of the movement toward secularism.

Conversion and structures. We have alluded to the inconsistency that exists between the culture of our people, whose values are imbued with the Christian faith, and the impoverished condition in which they are often forced to live by injustice.

Undoubtedly situations of injustice and acute poverty are an indictment in themselves, indicating that the faith was not strong enough to affect the criteria and the decisions of those responsible for ideological leadership and the organization of our people's socio-economic life together. Our peoples, rooted in the Christian faith, have been subjected to structures that have proved to be wellsprings of injustice. These structures are linked with the expansion of liberal capitalism, though in some areas they have been transformed under the inspiration of Marxist collectivism; but they arise out of the ideologies of the dominant cultures, and they are inconsistent with the faith that is part of our people's culture.

The Church thus calls for a new conversion on the level of cultural values, so that the structures of societal life may then be imbued with the spirit of the Gospel. And while it calls for a revitalization of evangelical values, it simultaneously urges a rapid and thoroughgoing transformation of structures. For by their very nature these structures are supposed to exert a restraining influence on the evil that arises in the human heart and manifests itself socially; and they are also meant to serve as conditioning pedagogical factors for an interior conversion on the plane of values (Med-P: 16).

Other problems. Within this general situation and its overall challenges are inscribed certain specific problems of major importance that the Church must heed in its new effort at evangelization. They include the following:

– Starting off from a sound knowledge of the cultural conditions of our peoples and a solid penetration into their lifestyle, the Church must organize an adequate catechesis. And there must be enough native pastoral workers of varied sorts to satisfy the right of our peoples not to stay immersed in ignorance about the faith or at the most rudimentary levels of knowledge.

– There must be a critical yet constructive examination of the educational system established in Latin America.

–Using past experience and imagination, the Church must draw up criteria and approaches for a pastoral effort directed at city life, where the new cultural styles are arising. At the same time the Church must also work to evangelize and promote indigenous groups and Afro-Americans.

–The Church must establish a new evangelizing presence among workers as well as intellectual and artistic elites.

–Humanistically and evangelically the Church must contribute to the betterment of women, in line with their specific identity and femininity.

3. EVANGELIZATION AND THE PEOPLE'S RELIGIOSITY

3.1. Basic Statements about this Notion

By the religion of the people, popular religiosity, or popular piety (EN: 48), we mean the whole complex of underlying beliefs rooted in God, the basic attitudes that flow from these beliefs, and the expressions that manifest them. It is the form of cultural life that religion takes on among a given people. In its most characteristic cultural form, the religion of the Latin American people is an expression of the Catholic faith. It is a people's Catholicism.

Despite the defects and the sins that are always present, the faith of the Church has set its seal on the soul of Latin America (HZ:2). It has left its mark on Latin America's essential historical identity, becoming the continent's cultural matrix out of which new peoples have arisen.

It is the Gospel, fleshed out in our peoples, that has brought them together to form the original cultural and historical entity known as Latin America. And this identity is glowingly reflected on the *mestizo* countenance of Mary of Guadalupe, who appeared at the start of the evangelization process.

This people's religion is lived out in a preferential way by the "poor and simple" (EN:48). But it takes in all social sectors; and sometimes it is one of the few bonds that really brings together the people living in our nations, which are so divided politically. But of course we must acknowledge that there is much diversity amid this unity, a diversity of social, ethnic, and even generation groups.

At its core the religiosity of the people is a storehouse of values that offers the answers of Christian wisdom to the great questions of life. The Catholic wisdom of the common people is capable of fashioning a vital synthesis. It creatively combines the divine and the human, Christ and Mary, spirit and body, communion and institution, person and community, faith and homeland, intelligence and emotion. This wisdom is a Christian humanism that radically affirms the dignity of every person as a child of God, establishes a basic fraternity, teaches people how to encounter nature and understand work, and provides reasons for joy and humor even in the midst of a very hard life. For the common people this wisdom is also a principle of discernment and an evangelical instinct through which they spontaneously sense when the Gospel is served in the Church and when it is emptied of its content and stifled by other interests (OAP: III, 6).

Because this cultural reality takes in a very broad range of social strata, the common people's religion is capable of bringing together multitudes. Thus it is in the realm of popular piety that the Church fulfills its imperative of universality, Knowing that the message "is not reserved for a small group of initiates or a chosen, privileged few, but is meant for all" (EN: 57), the Church accomplishes its task of convening the masses in its sanctuaries and religious feasts. There the gospel message has a chance, not always pastorally utilized, of reaching "the heart of the masses" (EN: 57).

The people's religious life is not just an object of evangelization. Insofar as it is a concrete embodiment of the Word of God, it itself is an active way in which the people continually evangelize themselves.

In Latin America this Catholic piety of the common people has not adequately impregnated certain autochthonous cultural groups and ones of African origin. Indeed in some cases they have not even been evangelized at all. Yet these groups do possess a rich store of values and "seeds of the Word" as they await the living Word.

Though the popular religiosity has set its seal on Latin American culture, it has not been sufficiently expressed in the organization of our societies and states. It has left standing what John Paul II has once again called "sinful structures" (HZ: 3). The gap between rich and poor, the menacing situation faced by the weakest, the injustices, and the humiliating disregard and subjection endured by them radically contradict the values of personal dignity and solidary brotherhood. Yet the people of Latin America carry these values in their hearts as imperatives received from the Gospel. That is why the religiosity of the Latin American people often is turned into a cry for true liberation. It is an exigency that is still unmet. Motivated by their religiosity, however, the people create or utilize space for the practice of brotherhood in the more intimate areas of their lives together: e.g., the neighborhood, the village, their labor unions, and their recreational activities. Rather than giving way to despair, they confidently and shrewdly wait for the right opportunities to move forward toward the liberation they so ardently desire.

Due to lack of attention on the part of pastoral agents and to other complicated factors, the religion of the people shows signs of erosion and distortion. Aberrant substitutes and regressive forms of syncretism have already surfaced. In some areas we can discern serious and strange threats to the religion of the people, framed in terms that lay excessive stress on apocalyptic fantasies.

3.2. A Description of the People's Religiosity

We can point to the following items as positive elements of the people's piety: the trinitarian presence evident in devotions and iconography; a sense of God the Father's providence; Christ celebrated in the mystery of his Incarnation (the Nativity, the child Jesus), in his crucifixion, in the Eucharist, and in the devotion to the Sacred Heart. Love for Mary is shown in many ways. She and "her mysteries are part of the very identity of these peoples and characterize their popular piety" (HZ: 2). She is venerated as the Immaculate Mother of God and of human beings, and as the Queen of our individual countries as well as of the whole continent. Other positive features are: veneration of the saints as protectors; remembrance of the dead; an awareness of personal dignity and of solidary brotherhood; awareness of sin and the need to expiate it; the ability to express the faith in a total idiom that goes beyond all sorts of rationalism (chant, images, gesture, color, and dance); faith situated in time (feasts) and in various places (sanctuaries and shrines); a feel for pilgrimage as a symbol of human and Christian existence; filial respect for their pastors as representatives of God; an ability to celebrate the faith in expressive and communitarian forms; the deep integration of the sacraments and sacramentals into their personal and social life; a warm affection for the person of the Holy Father; a capacity for suffering and heroism in withstanding trials and professing their faith; a sense of the value of prayer; and acceptance of other people.

For some time now the religion of the people has been suffering from a divorce between elites and the common people. This indicates that there has been a lack of education, catechesis, and dynamic activity, due to a lack of proper pastoral concern on the part of the Church.

The negative aspects that we can point to are varied in origin. Some are of an ancestral type: superstition, magic, fatalism, idolatrous worship of power, fetishism, and ritualism. Some are due to distortions of catechesis: static archaism, misinformation and ignorance, syncretistic reinterpretation, and reduction of the faith to a mere contract with God. Some negative aspects are threats to the faith today: secularism as broadcasted by the media of social communication; consumptionism; sects; oriental and agnostic religions; ideological, economic, social, and political types of manipulation; various secularized forms of political messianism; and uprooting and urban proletarianization as the result of cultural change. We can state that many of these phenomena are real obstacles to evangelization.

3.3. Evangelizing the People's Religiosity: The Process, Attitudes, and Criteria

Like the Church as a whole, the religion of the people must be constantly evangelized over again. In Latin America, where the Gospel has been preached and the general population baptized for almost five hundred years, the work of evangelization must appeal to the "Christian memory of our peoples." Evangelization will be a work of pastoral pedagogy in which the Catholicism of the common people is assumed, purified, completed, and made dynamic by the Gospel. In practice this means renewing a pedagogical dialogue based on the last links that the evangelizers of yesteryear had forged in the heart of our people. To do this, we must know the symbols, the silent nonverbal language of the people. Only then can we engage in a vital dialogue with them, communicating the Good News through a renewed process of informational catechesis.

Guided by the light of the Holy Spirit and imbued with "pastoral charity," the agents of evangelization will know how to elaborate a "pedagogy of evangelization" (EN: 48). Such a pedagogy demands that they love the people and be close to them; that they be prudent, firm, constant, and audacious. Only then can they educate this precious faith, which is sometimes in a very weakened state.

Concrete forms and pastoral processes must be evaluated on the basis of the criteria that characterize the Gospel as lived in the Church. Everything should help to make the baptized more truly children of God in the Son, more truly brothers and sisters in the Church, and more responsible missionaries in spreading the Kingdom. That is the direction which the maturing of the people's religion should take.

3.4. Tasks and Challenges

We face an urgent situation. The shift from an agrarian to an urbanized, industrial society is subjecting the people's religion to a decisive crisis. As this millennium draws to a close in Latin America, the great challenges posed by the people's piety entail the following pastoral tasks:

a. We must offer adequate catechesis and evangelization to the vast majority of the people who have been baptized but whose popular Catholicism is in a weakened state.

b. We must mobilize apostolic movements, parishes, base-level ecclesial communities, and church militants in general so that they may be a "leaven in the dough" in a more generous way. We must re-examine the spiritual practices, attitudes, and tactics of church elites vis-à-vis the common people's religiosity. As the Medellín Conference pointed out: "Given this type of religious sense among the masses, the Church is faced with the dilemma of either continuing to be a universal Church or, if it fails to attract and vitally incorporate such groups, of becoming a sect" (Med-PM: 3). We must develop in our militants a mystique of service designed to evangelize the religion of their people. That task is even more to the point today, and it is up to elites to accept the spirit of their people, purify it, scrutinize it, and flesh it out in a prominent way. To this end elites must participate in the assemblies and public manifestations of the people so that they may offer their contribution.

c. We must proceed to put more planned effort into transforming our sanctuaries so that they might be "privileged locales" of evangelization (HZ: 5). This would entail purifying them of all forms of manipulation and commercialism. A special effort in this direction is demanded of our national sanctuaries, which stand as symbols of the interaction between the faith and the history of our peoples.

d. We must pay pastoral attention to the popular piety of the peasants and the indigenous peoples, so that they might enjoy growth and renewal in line with their own proper identity and development and in accordance with the emphases spelled out by Vatican II. This will ensure better preparation for more generalized cultural change.

e. We must see to it that the liturgy and the common people's piety crossfertilize each other, giving lucid and prudent direction to the impulses of prayer and charismatic vitality that are evident today in our countries. In addition, the religion of the people, with its symbolic and expressive richness, can provide the liturgy with creative dynamism. When examined with proper discernment, this dynamism can help to incarnate the universal prayer of the Church in our culture in a greater and better way.

f. We must try to provide the religiosity of the common people with the necessary reformulations and shifts of emphasis that are required in an urban-industrial civilization. The process is already evident in the big cities of the continent, where the Catholicism of the people is spontaneously finding new forms of expression and enriching itself with new values that have matured within its own depths. In this respect we must see to it that the faith develops a growing personalization and a liberative solidarity. The faith must nurture a spirituality that is capable of ensuring the contemplative dimension, i.e., gratitude to God and a poetic, sapiential encounter with creation. The faith must be a wellspring of joy for the common people and a reason for festivity even in the midst of suffering. In this way we can fashion cultural forms that will rescue urban industrialization from oppressive tedium and cold, suffocating economicism.

g. We must support the religious expressions of the common people *en masse* for the evangelizing force that they possess.

h. We must assume the religious unrest and excitement that is arising as a form of historical anxiety over the coming end of the millennium. This unrest and excitement must be framed in terms of the lordship of Christ and the providence of the Father, so that the children of God may enjoy the peace they need while they struggle and labor in time.

If the Church does not reinterpret the religion of the Latin American people, the resultant vacuum will be occupied by sects, secularized political forms of messianism, consumptionism and its consequences of nausea and indifference, or pagan pansexualism. Once again the Church is faced with stark alternatives: what it does not assume in Christ is not redeemed, and it becomes a new idol replete with all the old malicious cunning.

4. EVANGELIZATION, LIBERATION, AND HUMAN PROMOTION

In this section we shall discuss evangelization in terms of its connection with human promotion, liberation, and the social doctrine of the Church.

4.1. A Word of Encouragement

We fully recognize the efforts undertaken by many Latin American Christians to explore the particularly conflict-ridden situations of our peoples in terms of the faith and to shed the light of God's Word on them. We encourage all Christians to continue to provide this evangelizing service and to consider the criteria for reflection and investigation; and we urge them to put special care into preserving and promoting ecclesial communion on both the local and the universal levels.

We are also aware of the fact that since the Medellín Conference pastoral agents have made significant advances and encountered quite a few difficulties. Rather than discouraging us, this should inspire us to seek out new paths and better forms of accomplishment.

4.2. The Social Teaching of the Church

The contribution of the Church to liberation and human promotion has gradually been taking shape in a series of doctrinal guidelines and criteria for action that we now are accustomed to call "the social teaching of the Church." These teachings have their source in Sacred Scripture, in the teaching of the Fathers and major theologians of the Church, and in the magisterium (particularly that of the most recent popes). As is evident from their origin, they contain permanently valid elements that are grounded in an anthropology that derives from the message of Christ and in the perennial values of Christian ethics. But they also contain changing elements that correspond to the particular conditions of each country and each epoch.*

Following Paul VI (OA: 4), we can formulate the matter this way: attentive to the signs of the time, which are interpreted in the light of the Gospel and the Church's magisterium, the whole Christian community is called upon

---

*See the explanatory note at the start of *Gaudium et Spes,* which explains why that conciliar Constitution is called "pastoral."

to assume responsibility for concrete options and their effective implementation in order to respond to the summons presented by changing circumstances. Thus these social teachings possess a dynamic character. In their elaboration and application lay people are not to be passive executors but rather active collaborators with their pastors, contributing their experience as Christians, and their professional, scientific competence (GS: 42).

Clearly, then, it is the whole Christian community, in communion with its legitimate pastors and guided by them, that is the responsible subject of evangelization, liberation, and human promotion.

The primary object of this social teaching is the personal dignity of the human being, who is the image of God, and the protection of all inalienable human rights (PP: 14–21). As the need has arisen, the Church has proceeded to spell out its teaching with regard to other areas of life: social life, economics, politics, and cultural life. But the aim of this doctrine of the Church, which offers its own specific vision of the human being and humanity (PP: 13), is always the promotion and integral liberation of human beings in terms of both their earthly and their transcendent dimensions. It is a contribution to the construction of the ultimate and definitive Kingdom, although it does not equate earthly progress with Christ's Kingdom (GS: 39).

If our social teachings are to be credible and to be accepted by all, they must effectively respond to the serious challenges and problems arising out of the reality of Latin America. Human beings who are diminished by all sorts of deficiencies and wants are calling for urgent efforts of promotion on our part, and this makes our works of social assistance necessary. Nor can we propose our teaching without being challenged by it in turn insofar as our personal and institutional behavior is concerned. It requires us to display consistency, creativity, boldness, and total commitment. Our social conduct is an integral part of our following of Christ. Our reflection on the Church's projection into the world as a sacrament of communion and salvation is a part of our theological reflection. For "evangelization would not be complete if it did not take into account the reciprocal appeal that arises in the course of time between the Gospel on the one hand and the concrete personal and social life of human beings on the other" (EN: 29).

Human promotion entails activities that help to arouse human awareness in every dimension and to make human beings themselves the active protagonists of their own human and Christian development. It educates people in living together, it gives impetus to organization, it fosters Christian sharing of goods, and it is an effective aid to communion and participation.

If the Christian community is to bear consistent witness in its efforts for liberation and human betterment, each country and local Church will organize its social pastoral effort around ongoing and adequate organisms. These organisms will sustain and stimulate commitment to the community, ensuring the needed coordination of activities through a continuing dialogue with all the members of the Church. Caritas and other organisms, which have been doing effective work for many years, can offer valuable help to this end.

If they are to be faithful and complete, theology, preaching, and catechesis must keep in mind the whole human being and all human beings. In timely and adequate terms they must offer people today "an especially vigorous message concerning liberation" (EN: 29), framing it in terms of the "overall plan of salvation" (EN: 38). So it seems that we must offer some clarifying remarks about the concept of liberation itself at this present moment in the life of our continent.

4.3. Discerning the Nature of Liberation in Christ

At the Medellín Conference we saw the elucidation of a dynamic process of integral liberation. Its positive echoes were taken up by *Evangelii Nuntiandi* and by John Paul II in his message to this conference. This proclamation imposes an urgent task on the Church, and it belongs to the very core of an evangelization that seeks the authentic realization of the human being.

But there are different conceptions and applications of liberation. Though they share common traits, they contain points of view that can hardly be brought together satisfactorily. The best thing to do, therefore, is to offer criteria that derive from the magisterium and that provide us with the necessary discernment regarding the original conception of Christian liberation.

There are two complementary and inseparable elements. The first is liberation from all the forms of bondage, from personal and social sin, and from everything that tears apart the human individual and society; all this finds its source to be in egotism, in the mystery of iniquity. The second element is liberation for progressive growth in being through communion with God and other human beings; this reaches its culmination in the perfect communion of heaven, where God is all in all and weeping forever ceases.

This liberation is gradually being realized in history, in our personal history and that of our peoples. It takes in all the different dimensions of life: the social, the political, the economic, the cultural, and all their interrelationships. Through all these dimensions must flow the transforming treasure of the Gospel. It has its own specific and distinctive contribution to make, which must be safeguarded. Otherwise we would be faced with the situation described by Paul VI in *Evangelii Nuntiandi*: "The Church would lose its innermost significance. Its message of liberation would have no originality of its own. It would be prone to takeover or manipulation by ideological systems and political parties" (EN: 32).

It should be made clear that this liberation is erected on the three great pillars that John Paul II offered us as defining guidelines: i.e., the truth about Jesus Christ, the truth about the Church, and the truth about human beings.

Thus we mutilate liberation in an unpardonable way if we do not achieve liberation from sin and all its seductions and idolatry, and if we do not help to make concrete the liberation that Christ won on the cross. We do the very same thing if we forget the crux of liberative evangelization, which is to transform human beings into active subjects of their own individual and communitarian development. And we also do the very same thing if we overlook dependence and the forms of bondage that violate basic rights that come from God, the Creator and Father, rather than being bestowed by governments or institutions, however powerful they may be.

The sort of liberation we are talking about knows how to use evangelical means, which have their own distinctive efficacy. It does not resort to violence of any sort, or to the dialectics of class struggle. Instead it relies on the vigorous energy and activity of Christians, who are moved by the Spirit to respond to the cries of countless millions of their brothers and sisters.

We pastors in Latin America have the most serious reasons for pressing for liberative evangelization. It is not just that we feel obliged to remind people of individual and social sinfulness. The further reason lies in the fact that since the Medellín Conference the situation has grown worse and more acute for the vast majority of our population.

We are pleased to note many examples of efforts to live out liberative evangelization in all its fullness. One of the chief tasks involved in continuing to encourage Christian liberation is the creative search for approaches free of ambiguity and reductionism (EN: 32) and fully faithful to the Word of God. Given to us in the Church, that Word stirs us to offer joyful proclamation to the poor as one of the messianic signs of Christ's Kingdom.

John Paul II has made this point well: "There are many signs that help us to distinguish when the liberation in question is Christian and when, on the other hand, it is based on ideologies that make it inconsistent with an evangelical view of humanity, of things, and of events (EN: 35). These signs derive from the content that the evangelizers proclaim or from the concrete attitudes that they adopt. At the level of content one must consider how faithful they are to the Word of God, to the Church's living tradition, and to its magisterium. As for attitudes, one must consider what sense of communion they feel, with the bishops first of all, and then with the other sectors of God's People. Here one must also consider what contribution they make to the real building up of the community; how they channel their love into caring for the poor, the sick, the dispossessed, the neglected, and the oppressed; and how, discovering in these people the image of the poor and suffering Jesus, they strive to alleviate their needs and to serve Christ in them (LG: 8). Let us make no mistake about it: as if by some evangelical instinct, the humble and simple faithful spontaneously sense when the Gospel is being served in the Church and when it is being eviscerated and asphyxiated by other interests" (OAP: III, 6).

Those who hold to the vision of humanity offered by Christianity also take on the commitment not to measure the sacrifice it costs to ensure that all will enjoy the status of authentic children of God and brothers and sisters in Jesus Christ. Thus liberative evangelization finds its full realization in the communion of all in Christ, as the Father of all people wills.

4.4. Liberative Evangelization for a Human Societal Life Worthy of the Children of God

Other than God, nothing is divine or worthy of worship. Human beings fall into slavery when they divinize or absolutize wealth, power, the State, sex, pleasure, or anything created by God–including their own being or human reason. God himself is the source of radical liberation from all forms of idolatry, because the adoration of what is not adorable and the absolutization of the relative leads to violation of the innermost reality of human persons: i.e., their relationship with God and their personal fulfillment. Here is the liberative word par excellence: "You shall do homage to the Lord your God; him alone shall you adore" (Matt. 4:10; cf. Deut. 5:6ff). The collapse of idols restores to human beings their essential realm of freedom. God, who is supremely free, wants to enter into dialogue with free beings who are capable of making their own choices and exercising their responsibilities on both the individual and communitarian levels. So we have a human history that, even though it possesses its own consistency and autonomy, is called upon to be consecrated to God by humanity. Authentic liberation frees us from oppression so that we may be able to say yes to a higher good.

Humanity and earthly goods. By virtue of their origin and nature, by the will of the Creator, worldly goods and riches are meant to serve the utility and progress of each and every human being and people. Thus each and every one enjoys a primary, fundamental, and absolutely inviolable right to share in the use of these goods, insofar as that is necessary for the worthy fulfillment of the human person. All other rights, including the right of property and free trade, are subordinate to that right. As John Paul II teaches: "There is a social mortgage on all private property" (OAP:III,4). To be compatible with primordial human rights, the right of ownership must be primarily a right of use and administration; and though this does not rule out ownership and control, it does not make these absolute or unlimited. Ownership should be a source of freedom for all, but never a source of domination or special privilege. We have a grave and pressing duty to restore this right to its original and primary aim (PP:23).

Liberation from the idol of wealth. Earthly goods become an idol and a serious obstacle to the Kingdom of God (Matt. 19:23–26) when human beings devote all their attention to possessing them or even coveting them. Then earthly goods turn into an absolute, and "you cannot give yourself to God and money" (Luke 16:13).

Turned into an absolute, wealth is an obstacle to authentic freedom. The cruel contrast between luxurious wealth and extreme poverty, which is so visible throughout our continent and which is further aggravated by the corruption that often invades public and professional life, shows the great extent to which our nations are dominated by the idol of wealth.

These forms of idolatry are concretized in two opposed forms that have a common root. One is liberal capitalism. The other, a reaction against liberal capitalism, is Marxist collectivism. Both are forms of what can be called "institutionalized injustice."

Finally, as already noted, we must take cognizance of the devastating effects of an uncontrolled process of industrialization and a process of urbanization that is taking on alarming proportions. The depletion of our natural resources and the pollution of the environment will become a critical problem. Once again we affirm that the consumptionist tendencies of the more developed nations must undergo a thorough revision. They must take into account the elementary needs of the poor peoples who constitute the majority of the world's population.

The new humanism proclaimed by the Church, which rejects all forms of idolatry, "will enable our contemporaries to enjoy the higher values of love and friendship, of prayer and contemplation, and thus find themselves. This is what will guarantee humanity's authentic development—its transition from less than human conditions to truly human ones" (PP:20). In this way economic planning will be put in the service of human beings rather than human beings being put in the service of economics (PP:34). The latter is what happens in the two forms of idolatry mentioned above (liberal capitalism and Marxist collectivism). The former is the only way to make sure that what human beings "have" does not suffocate what they "are" (GS:35).

Human beings and power. The various forms of power in society are a basic part of the order of creation. Hence in themselves they are essentially good, insofar as they render service to the human community.

Authority, which is necessary in every society, comes from God (Rom. 13:1; John 19:11). It is the faculty of giving commands in accordance with right reason. Hence its obligatory force derives from the moral order (PT:47), and it should develop out of that ground in order to oblige people in conscience: "Authority is before all else a moral force" (Pt:48; GS:74).

Sin corrupts humanity's use of power, leading people to abuse the rights of others, sometimes in more or less absolute ways. The most notorious example of this is the exercise of political power. For this is an area that involves decisions governing the overall organization of the community's temporal welfare, and it readily lends itself to abuses. Indeed, it may lead not only to abuses by those in power but also to the absolutizing of power itself (GS: 73) with the backing of public force. Political power is divinized when in practice it is regarded as absolute. Hence the totalitarian use of power is a form of idolatry; and as such, the Church completely rejects it (GS: 75). We grieve to note the presence of many authoritarian and even oppressive regimes on our continent. They constitute one of the most serious obstacles to the full development of the rights of persons, groups, and even nations.

Unfortunately, in many instances this reaches the point where the political and economic authorities of our nations are themselves made subject to even more powerful centers that are operative on an international scale. This goes far beyond the normal range of mutual relationships. And the situation is further aggravated by the fact that these centers of power are ubiquitous, covertly organized, and easily capable of evading the control of governments and even international organisms.

There is an urgent need to liberate our peoples from the idol of absolutized power so that they may live together in a society based on justice and freedom. As a youthful people with a wealth of culture and tradition, Latin Americans must carry out the mission assigned to them by history. But if they are to do this, they need a political order that will respect human dignity and ensure harmony and peace to the community, both in its internal relations and its relations with other communities. Among all the aspirations of our peoples, we would like to stress the following:

–Equality for all citizens. All have the right and the duty to participate in the destiny of their society and to enjoy equality of opportunity, bearing their fair share of the burdens and obeying legitimately established laws.

–The exercise of their freedoms. These should be protected by basic institutions that will stand surety for the common good and respect the fundamental rights of persons and associations.

–Legitimate self-determination for our peoples. This will permit them to organize their lives in accordance with their own genius and history (GS: 74) and to cooperate in a new international order.

–The urgent necessity of re-establishing justice. We are not talking only about theoretical justice recognized merely in the abstract. We are talking also about a justice that is effectively implemented in practice by institutions that are truly operative and adequate to the task.*

---

*Hedonism, too, has been set up as an absolute on our continent. Liberation from the idol of pleasure-seeking and consumptionism is an imperative demand of Christian social teaching. We shall consider this issue more fully in Part Three, Chapter I, when we deal with educating people for love and family life (see nos. 582–89 below).

5. EVANGELIZATION, IDEOLOGIES, AND POLITICS

5.1. Introduction

Recent years have seen a growing deterioration in the sociopolitical life of our countries.

They are experiencing the heavy burden of economic and institutional crises, and clear symptoms of corruption and violence.

The violence is generated and fostered by two factors: (1) what can be called institutionalized injustice in various social, political, and economic systems; and (2) ideologies that use violence as a means to win power.

The latter in turn causes the proliferation of governments based on force, which often derive their inspiration from the ideology of National Security.

As a mother and teacher whose expertise is humanity, the Church must examine the conditions, systems, ideologies, and political life of our continent – shedding light on them from the standpoint of the Gospel and its own social teaching. And this must be done even though it knows that people will try to use its message as their own tool.

So the Church projects the light of its message on politics and ideologies, as one more form of service to its peoples and as a sure line of orientation for all those who must assume social responsibilities in one form or another.

5.2. Evangelization and Politics

The political dimension is a constitutive dimension of human beings and a relevant area of human societal life. It has an all-embracing aspect because its aim is the common welfare of society. But that does not mean that it exhausts the gamut of social relationships.

Far from despising political activity, the Christian faith values it and holds it in high esteem.

Speaking in general, and without distinguishing between the roles that may be proper to its various members, the Church feels it has a duty and a right to be present in this area of reality. For Christianity is supposed to evangelize the whole of human life, including the political dimension. So the Church criticizes those who would restrict the scope of faith to personal or family life; who would exclude the professional, economic, social, and political orders as if sin, love, prayer, and pardon had no relevance in them.

The fact is that the need for the Church's presence in the political arena flows from the very core of the Christian faith. That is to say, it flows from the lordship of Christ over the whole of life. Christ sets the seal on the definitive brotherhood of humanity, wherein every human being is of equal worth: "All are one in Christ Jesus" (Gal. 3:28).

From the integral message of Christ there flows an original anthropology and theology that takes in "the concrete personal and social life of the human being" (EN: 29). It is a liberating message because it saves us from the bondage of sin, which is the root and source of all oppression, injustice, and discrimination.

These are some of the reasons why the Church is present in the political arena to enlighten consciences and to proclaim a message that is capable of transforming society.

The Church recognizes the proper autonomy of the temporal order (GS: 36). This holds true for governments, parties, labor unions, and other groups in the social and political arena. The purpose that the Lord assigned to his Church is a religious one; so when it does intervene in the sociopolitical arena, it is not prompted by any aim of a political, economic, or social nature. "But out of this religious mission itself come a function, a light, and an energy which can serve to structure and consolidate the human community according to the divine law" (GS: 42).

Insofar as the political arena is concerned, the Church is particularly interested in distinguishing between the specific functions of the laity, religious, and those who minister to the unity of the Church–i.e., the bishop and his priests.

5.3. Notions of Politics and Political Involvement

We must distinguish between two notions of politics and political involvement. First, in the broad sense politics seeks the common good on both the national and international plane. Its task is to spell out the fundamental values of every community–internal concord and external security–reconciling equality with freedom, public authority with the legitimate autonomy and participation of individual persons and groups, and national sovereignty with international coexistence and solidarity. It also defines the ethics and means of social relationships. In this broad sense politics is of interest to the Church, and hence to its pastors, who are ministers of unity. It is a way of paying worship to the one and only God by simultaneously desacralizing and consecrating the world to him (LG: 34).

So the Church helps to foster the values that should inspire politics. In every nation it interprets the aspirations of the people, especially the yearnings of those that society tends to marginalize. And it does this with its testimony, its teaching, and its varied forms of pastoral activity.

Second, the concrete performance of this fundamental political task is normally carried out by groups of citizens. They resolve to pursue and exercise political power in order to solve economic, political, and social problems in accordance with their own criteria or ideology. Here, then, we can talk about "party politics." Now even though the ideologies elaborated by such groups may be inspired by Christian doctrine, they can come to differing conclusions. No matter how deeply inspired in church teaching, no political party can claim the right to represent all the faithful because its concrete program can never have absolute value for all (cf. Pius XI, *Catholic Action and Politics,* 1937).

Party politics is properly the realm of lay people (GS:43). Their lay status entitles them to establish and organize political parties, using an ideology and strategy that is suited to achieving their legitimate aims.

In the social teaching of the Church lay people find the proper criteria deriving from the Christian view of the human being. For its part the hierarchy will demonstrate its solidarity by contributing to their adequate formation and their spiritual life, and also by nurturing their creativity so that they can explore options that are increasingly in line with the common good and the needs of the weakest.

Pastors, on the other hand, must be concerned with unity. So they will divest themselves of every partisan political ideology that might condition their criteria and attitudes. They then will be able to evangelize the political sphere as Christ did, relying on the Gospel without any infusion of partisanship or ideologization. Christ's Gospel would not have had such an impact on history if he had not proclaimed it as a religious message: "The Gospels show clearly that for Jesus anything that would alter his mission as the Servant of Yahweh was a temptation (Matt. 4:8; Luke 4:5). He does not accept the position of those who mixed the things of God with merely political attitudes (Matt. 22:21; Mark 12:17; John 18:36)" (OAP:I,4).

Priests, also ministers of unity, and deacons must submit to the same sort of personal renunciation. If they are active in party politics, they will run the risk of absolutizing and radicalizing such activity; for their vocation is to be "men dedicated to the Absolute." As the Medellín Conference pointed out: "In the economic and social order . . . and especially in the political order, where a variety of concrete choices is offered, the priest, as priest, should not directly concern himself with decisions or leadership nor with the structuring of solutions" (Med-PR:19). And the 1971 Synod of Bishops stated: "Leadership or active militancy on behalf of any political party is to be excluded by every priest unless, in concrete and exceptional circumstances, this is truly required by the good of the community and receives the consent of the bishop after consultation with the priests' council and, if circumstances call for it, with the episcopal conference" ("The Ministerial Priesthood," Part Two, no. 2). Certainly the present thrust of the Church is not in that direction.

By virtue of the way in which they follow Christ, and in line with the distinctive function that is theirs within the Church's mission because of their specific charism, religious also cooperate in the evangelization of the political order. Living in a society that is far from fraternal, that is taken up with consumptionism, and that has as its ultimate goal the development of its material forces of production, religious will have to give testimony of real austerity in their lifestyle, of interhuman communion, and of an intense relationship with God. They, too, will have to resist the temptation to get involved in party politics, so that they do not create confusion between the values of the Gospel and some specific ideology.

Close reflection upon the recent words of the Holy Father addressed to bishops, priests, and religious will provide valuable guidance for their service in this area: "Souls that are living in habitual contact with God and that are operating in the warm light of his love know how to defend themselves easily against the temptations of partisanship and antithesis that threaten to create painful divisions. They know how to interpret their options for the poorest and for all the victims of human egotism in the proper light of the Gospel, without succumbing to forms of sociopolitical radicalism. In the long run such radicalism is untimely, counterproductive, and generative of new abuses. Such souls know how to draw near to the people and immerse themselves in their midst without calling into question their own religious identity or obscuring the 'specific originality' of their own vocation, which flows from following the poor, chaste, and obedient Christ. A measure of real adoration has more value and spiritual fruitfulness than the most intense activity, even apostolic activity. This is the most urgent kind of 'protest' that religious should exercise against a society where efficiency has been turned into an idol on whose altar even human dignity itself is sometimes sacrificed" (RMS).

Lay leaders of pastoral action should not use their authority in support of parties or ideologies.

5.4. Reflections on Political Violence

Faced with the deplorable reality of violence in Latin America, we wish to express our view clearly. Condemnation is always the proper judgment on physical and psychological torture, kidnapping, the persecution of political dissidents or suspect persons, and the exclusion of people from public life because of their ideas. If these crimes are committed by the authorities entrusted with the task of safeguarding the common good, then they defile those who practice them, notwithstanding any reasons offered.

The Church is just as decisive in rejecting terrorist and guerrilla violence, which becomes cruel and uncontrollable when it is unleashed. Criminal acts can in no way be justified as the way to liberation. Violence inexorably engenders new forms of oppression and bondage, which usually prove to be more serious than the ones people are allegedly being liberated from. But most importantly violence is an attack on life, which depends on the Creator alone.

And we must also stress that when an ideology appeals to violence, it thereby admits its own weakness and inadequacy.

Our responsibility as Christians is to use all possible means to promote the implementation of nonviolent tactics in the effort to re-establish justice in economic and sociopolitical relations. This is in accordance with the teaching of Vatican II, which applies to both national and international life: "We cannot fail to praise those who renounce the use of violence in the vindication of their rights and who resort to methods of defense which are otherwise available to weaker parties too, provided that this can be done without injury to the rights and duties of others or of the community" (GS: 78).

"We are obliged to state and reaffirm that violence is neither Christian nor evangelical, and that brusque, violent structural changes will be false, ineffective in themselves, and certainly inconsistent with the dignity of the people" (Paul VI, Address in Bogotá, 23 August 1968). The fact is that "the Church realizes that even the best structures and the most idealized systems quickly become inhuman if human inclinations are not improved, if there is no conversion of heart and mind on the part of those who are living in those structures or controlling them" (EN: 36).

5.5. Evangelization and Ideologies

Here we shall consider the exercise of discernment with regard to the ideologies existing in Latin America and the systems inspired by them.

Of the many different definitions of ideology that might be offered, we apply the term here to any conception that offers a view of the various aspects of life from the standpoint of a specific group in society. The ideology manifests the aspirations of this group, summons its members to a certain kind of solidarity and combative struggle, and grounds the legitimacy of these aspirations on specific values. Every ideology is partial because no one group can claim to identify its aspirations with those of society as a whole. Thus an ideology will be legitimate if the interests it upholds are legitimate and if it respects the basic rights of other groups in the nation. Viewed in this positive sense, ideologies seem to be necessary for social activity, insofar as they are mediating factors leading to action.

But in themselves ideologies have a tendency to absolutize the interests they uphold, the vision they propose, and the strategy they promote. In such a case they really become "lay religions." People take refuge in ideology as an ultimate explanation of everything: "In this way they fashion a new idol, as it were, whose absolute and coercive character is maintained, sometimes unwittingly" (OA: 28). In that sense it is not surprising that ideologies try to use persons and institutions as their tools in order to achieve their aims more effectively. Herein lies the ambiguous and negative side of ideologies.

But ideologies should not be analyzed solely in terms of their conceptual content. In addition, they are dynamic, living phenomena of a sweeping and contagious nature. They are currents of yearning tending toward absolutization, and they are powerful in winning people over and whipping up redemptive fervor. This confers a special "mystique" on them, and it also enables them to make their way into different milieus in a way that is often irresistible. Their slogans, typical expressions, and criteria can easily make their way into the minds of people who are far from adhering voluntarily to their doctrinal principles. Thus many people live and struggle in practice within the atmosphere of specific ideologies, without ever having taken cognizance of that fact. This aspect calls for constant vigilance and re-examination. And it applies both to ideologies that legitimate the existing situation and to those that seek to change it.

To exercise the necessary discernment and critical judgment with regard to ideologies, Christians must rely on "a rich and complex heritage, which *Evangelii Nuntiandi* calls the social doctrine, or social teaching, of the Church" (OAP: III,7).

This social doctrine or teaching of the Church is an expression of its "distinctive contribution: a global perspective on the human being and on humanity" (PP: 13). The Church accepts the challenge and contribution of ideologies in their positive aspects, and in turn challenges, criticizes, and relativizes them.

Neither the Gospel nor the Church's social teaching deriving from it are ideologies. On the contrary, they represent a powerful source for challenging the limitations and ambiguities of all ideologies. The ever fresh originality of the gospel message must be continually clarified and defended against all efforts to turn it into an ideology.

The unrestricted exaltation of the State and its many abuses must not, however, cause us to forget the necessity of the functions performed by the modern State. We are talking about a State that respects basic rights and freedoms; a State that is grounded on a broad base of popular participation involving many intermediary groups; a State that promotes autonomous development of an equitable and rapid sort, so that the life of the nation can withstand undue pressure and interference on both the domestic and international fronts; a State that is capable of adopting a position of active cooperation with the forces for integration into both the continental and the international community; and finally, a State that avoids the abuse of monolithic power concentrated in the hands of a few.

In Latin America we are obliged to analyze a variety of ideologies:

a. First, there is capitalist liberalism, the idolatrous worship of wealth in individualistic terms. We acknowledge that it has given much encouragement to the creative capabilities of human freedom, and that it has been a stimulus to progress. But on the other side of the coin it views "profit as the chief spur to economic progress, free competition as the supreme law of economics, and private ownership of the means of production as an absolute right, having no limits nor concomitant social obligations" (PP:26). The illegitimate privileges stemming from the absolute right of ownership give rise to scandalous contrasts, and to a situation of dependence and oppression on both the national and international levels. Now it is true that in some countries its original historical form of expression has been attenuated by necessary forms of social legislation and specific instances of government intervention. But in other countries capitalist liberalism persists in its original form, or has even retrogressed to more primitive forms with even less social sensitivity.

b. Second, there is Marxist collectivism. With its materialist presuppositions, it too leads to the idolatrous worship of wealth—but in collectivist terms. It arose as a positive criticism of commodity fetishism and of the disregard for the human value of labor. But it did not manage to get to the root of that form of idolatry, which lies in the rejection of the only God worthy of adoration: the God of love and justice.

The driving force behind its dialectics is class struggle. Its objective is a classless society, which is to be achieved through a dictatorship of the proletariat; but in the last analysis this really sets up a dictatorship of the party. All the concrete historical experiments of Marxism have been carried out within the framework of totalitarian regimes that are closed to any possibility of criticism and correction. Some believe it is possible to separate various aspects of Marxism—its doctrine and its method of analysis in particular. But we would remind people of the teaching of the papal magisterium on this point: "It would be foolish and dangerous on that account to forget that they are closely linked to each other; to embrace certain elements of Marxist analysis without taking due account of their relation with its ideology; and to become involved in the class struggle and the Marxist interpretation of it without paying attention to the kind of violent and totalitarian society to which this activity leads" (OA:34).

We must also note the risk of ideologization run by theological reflection when it is based on a praxis that has recourse to Marxist analysis. The consequences are the total politicization of Christian existence, the disintegration of the language of faith into that of the social sciences, and the draining away of the transcendental dimension of Christian salvation.

Both of the aforementioned ideologies—capitalist liberalism and Marxism—find their inspiration in brands of humanism that are closed to any transcendent perspective. One does because of its practical atheism; the other does because of its systematic profession of a militant atheism.

c. In recent years the so-called Doctrine of National Security has taken a firm hold on our continent. In reality it is more an ideology than a doctrine.

It is bound up with a specific politico-economic model with elitist and verticalist features, which suppresses the broad-based participation of the people in political decisions. In some countries of Latin America this doctrine justifies itself as the defender of the Christian civilization of the West. It elaborates a repressive system, which is in line with its concept of "permanent war." And in some cases it expresses a clear intention to exercise active geopolitical leadership.

We fully realize that fraternal coexistence requires a security system to inculcate respect for a social order that will permit all to carry out their mission with regard to the common good. This means that security measures must be under the control of an independent authority that can pass judgment on violations of the law and guarantee corrective measures.

The Doctrine of National Security, understood as an absolute ideology, would not be compatible with the Christian vision of the human being as responsible for carrying out a temporal project, and to its vision of the State as the administrator of the common good. It puts the people under the tutelage of military and political elites, who exercise authority and power; and it leads to increased inequality in sharing the benefits of development.

We again insist on the view of the Medellín Conference: "The system of liberal capitalism and the temptation of the Marxist system would appear to exhaust the possibilities of transforming the economic structures of our continent. Both systems militate against the dignity of the human person. One takes for granted the primacy of capital, its power, and its discriminatory utilization in the function of profit-making. The other, although it ideologically supports a kind of humanism, is more concerned with collective humanity, and in practice becomes a totalitarian concentration of state power. We must denounce the fact that Latin America finds itself caught between these two options and remains dependent on one or the other of the centers of power that control its economy" (Med-JU: 10).

In the face of this situation, the Church chooses "to maintain its freedom with regard to the opposing systems, in order to opt solely for the human being. Whatever the miseries or sufferings that afflict human beings, it is not through violence, power-plays, or political systems but through the truth about human beings that they will find their way to a better future" (OAP: III, 3). Grounded on this humanism, Christians will find encouragement to get beyond the hard and fast either-or and to help build a new civilization that is just, fraternal, and open to the transcendent. It will also bear witness that eschatological hopes give vitality and meaning to human hopes.

For this bold and creative activity Christians will fortify their identity in the original values of Christian anthropology. The Church "does not need to have recourse to ideological systems in order to love, defend, and collaborate in the liberation of the human being. At the center of the message of which the Church is the trustee and herald, it finds inspiration for acting in favor of brotherhood, justice, and peace; and against all forms of domination, slavery, discrimination, violence, attacks on religious liberty, and aggression against human beings and whatever attacks life" (OAP: III, 2).

Finding inspiration in these tenets of an authentic Christian anthropology, Christians must commit themselves to the elaboration of historical projects that meet the needs of a given moment and a given culture.

Christians must devote special attention and discernment to their involvement in historical movements that have arisen from various ideologies but are distinct from them. The teaching of *Pacem in Terris* (PT: 55 and 152), which is reiterated in *Octogesima Adveniens,* tells us that false philosophical theories cannot be equated with the historical movements that originated in them, insofar as these historical movements can be subject to further influences as they evolve. The involvement of Christians in these movements imposes certain obligations to persevere in fidelity, and these obligations will facilitate their evangelizing role. They include:

a. Ecclesial discernment, in communion with their pastors, as described in *Octogesima Adveniens* (OA: 4).

b. The shoring up of their identity by nourishing it with the truths of faith, their elaboration in the social teaching or doctrine of the Church, and an enriching life of prayer and participation in the sacraments.

c. Critical awareness of the difficulties, limitations, possibilities, and values of these convergences.

5.6. The Dangers of the Church and Its Ministers' Activity Being Used as a Tool

In propounding an absolutized view of the human being to which everything, including human thought, is subordinated, ideologies and parties try to use the Church or deprive it of its legitimate independence. This manipulation of the Church, always a risk in political life, may derive from Christians themselves, and even from priests and religious, when they proclaim a Gospel devoid of economic, social, cultural, and political implications. In practice this mutilation comes down to a kind of complicity with the established order, however unwitting.

Other groups are tempted in the opposite direction. They are tempted to consider a given political policy to be of primary urgency, a precondition for the Church's fulfillment of its mission. They are tempted to equate the Christian message with some ideology and subordinate the former to the latter, calling for a "re-reading" of the Gospel on the basis of a political option (OAP: 1,4). But the fact is that we must try to read the political scene from the standpoint of the Gospel, not vice-versa.

Traditional integrism looks for the Kingdom to come principally through a stepping back in history and reconstructing a Christian culture of a medieval cast. This would be a new Christendom, in which there was an intimate alliance between civil authority and ecclesiastical authority.

The radical thrust of groups at the other extreme falls into the same trap. It looks for the Kingdom to come from a strategic alliance between the Church and Marxism, and it rules out all other alternatives. For these people it is not simply a matter of being Marxists, but of being Marxists in the name of the faith (see nos. 543–46 above).

5.7. Conclusion

The mission of the Church is immense and more necessary than ever before, when we consider the situation at hand: conflicts that threaten the human race and the Latin American continent; violations of justice and freedom; institutionalized injustice embodied in governments adhering to opposing ideologies; and terrorist violence. Fulfillment of its mission will require activity from the Church as a whole: pastors, consecrated ministers, religious, and lay people. All must carry out their own specific tasks. Joined with Christ in prayer and abnegation, they will commit themselves to work for a better society without employing hatred and violence; and they will see that decision through to the end, whatever the consequences. For the attainment of a society that is more just, more free, and more at peace is an ardent longing of the peoples of Latin America and an indispensable fruit of any liberative evangelization.

* * * * *

Excerpt from Part Three: Evangelization in the Latin American Church, Chapter I: Centers of Communion and Participation

2. BASE-LEVEL ECCLESIAL COMMUNITIES (CEBs), THE PARISH, AND THE LOCAL CHURCH

Besides the Christian family, the first center of evangelization, human beings live their fraternal vocations in the bosom of the local Church, in communities that render the Lord's salvific design present and operative, to be lived out in communion and participation.

Thus within the local Church we must consider the parishes, the CEBs, and other ecclesial groups.

The Church is the People of God, which expresses its life of communion and evangelizing service on various levels and under various historical forms.

2.1. The Situation

In general we can say that in our Latin American Church today we find a great longing for deeper and more stable relationships in the faith, sustained and animated by the Word of God. We see an intensification in common prayer and in the effort of the people to participate more consciously and fruitfully in the liturgy.

We note an increase in the co-responsibility of the faith, both in organization and in pastoral action.

There is more wide-ranging awareness and exercise of the rights and duties appropriate to lay people as members of the community.

We notice a great yearning for justice and a sincere sense of solidarity, in a social milieu characterized by growing secularism and other phenomena typical of a society in transformation.

Bit by bit the Church has been dissociating itself from those who hold economic or political power, freeing itself from various forms of dependence, and divesting itself of privileges.

The Church in Latin America wishes to go on giving witness of unselfish and self-denying service in the face of a world dominated by greed for profit, lust for power, and exploitation.

In the direction of greater participation, there has been an increase of ordained ministries (such as the permanent diaconate), non-ordained ministries, and other services such as celebrators of the Word and community animators. We also note better collaboration between priests, religious, and lay people.

More clearly evident in our communities, as a fruit of the Holy Spirit, is a new style of relationship between bishops and priests, and between them and their people. It is characterized by greater simplicity, understanding, and friendship in the Lord.

All this is a process, in which we still find broad sectors posing resistance of various sorts. This calls for understanding and encouragement, as well as great docility to the Holy Spirit. What we need now is still more clerical openness to the activity of the laity and the overcoming of pastoral individualism and self-sufficiency. On the other hand, the impact of the secularized milieu has sometimes produced centrifugal tendencies in the community and the loss of an authentic ecclesial sense.

We have not always found effective ways to overcome the meager education of our people in the faith. Thus they remain defenseless before the onslaughts of shaky theological doctrines, sectarian proselytism, and pseudo-spiritual movements.

In particular we have found that small communities, especially the CEBs, create more personal inter-relations, acceptance of God's Word, re-examination of one's life, and reflection on reality in the light of the Gospel. They accentuate committed involvement in the family, one's work, the neighborhood, and the local community. We are happy to single out the multiplication of small communities as an important ecclesial event that is peculiarly ours, and as the "hope of the Church" (EN: 58). This ecclesial expression is more evident on the periphery of large cities and in the countryside. They are a favorable atmosphere for the rise of new lay-sponsored services. They have done much to spread family catechesis and adult education in the faith, in forms more suitable for the common people.

But not enough attention has been paid to the training of leaders in faith-education and Christian directors of intermediate organisms in the neighborhoods, the world of work, and the rural farm areas. Perhaps that is why not a few members of certain communities, and even entire communities, have been drawn to purely lay institutions or have been turned into ideological radicals, and are now in the process of losing any authentic feel for the Church.

The parish has been going through various forms of renewal that correspond to the changes in recent years. There is a change in outlook among pastors, more involvement of the laity in pastoral councils and other services, ongoing catechetical updating, and a growing presence of the priest among the people, especially through a network of groups and communities.

In the area of evangelization the parish embodies a twofold relationship of communication and pastoral communion. On the diocesan level parishes are integrated into regions, vicarages, and deaneries. And within the parish itself pastoral work is diversified in accordance with different areas, and there is greater opening to the creation of smaller communities.

But we still find attitudes that pose an obstacle to the dynamic thrust of renewal. Primacy is given to administrative work over pastoral care. There is routinism and a lack of preparation for the sacraments. Authoritarianism is evident among some priests. And sometimes the parish closes in on itself, disregarding the overall apostolic demands of a serious nature.

On the level of the local Church we note a considerable effort to arrange the territory so that greater attention can be paid to the People of God. This is being done by the creation of new dioceses. There is also concern to provide the Churches with organisms that will foster co-responsibility through channels suited for dialogue: e.g., priest councils, pastoral councils, and diocesan committees. These are to inspire a more organic pastoral effort suited to the specific reality of a given diocese.

Among religious communities and lay movements we also see a greater awareness of the necessity of being involved in the mission of the local Church and evincing an ecclesial spirit.

On the national level there is a noticeable effort to exercise greater collegiality in episcopal conferences, which are continuously being better organized and fitted with subsidiary organisms. Deserving of special mention is the growth and effectiveness of the service that CELAM offers to ecclesial communion throughout Latin America.

On the worldwide level we note the fraternal interchange promoted by the sending of apostolic personnel and economic aid. These relationships have been established with the episcopates of Europe and North America, with the help of CAL; their continuation and intensification offer ampler opportunities for interecclesial participation, which is a noteworthy sign of universal communion.

2.2. Doctrinal Reflection

The Christian lives in community under the activity of the Holy Spirit. The Spirit is the invisible principle of unity and communion, and also of the unity and variety to be found in states of life, ministries, and charisms.

In their families, which constitute domestic Churches, the baptized are summoned to their first experience of communion in faith, love, and service to others.

In small communities, particularly those that are better organized, people grow in their experience of new interpersonal relationships in the faith, in deeper exploration of God's Word, in fuller participation in the Eucharist, in communion with the pastors of the local Church, and in greater commitment to justice within the social milieu that surrounds them.

One question that might be raised is: When can a small community be considered an authentic base-level ecclesial community (CEB) in Latin America?

As a community, the CEB brings together families, adults and young people, in an intimate interpersonal relationship grounded in the faith. As an ecclesial reality, it is a community of faith, hope, and charity. It celebrates the Word of God and takes its nourishment from the Eucharist, the culmination of all the sacraments. It fleshes out the Word of God in life through solidarity and commitment to the new commandment of the Lord; and through the service of approved coordinators, it makes present and operative the mission of the Church and its visible communion with the legitimate pastors. It is a base-level community because it is composed of relatively few members as a permanent body, like a cell of the larger community. "When they deserve their ecclesial designation, they can take charge of their own spiritual and human existence in a spirit of fraternal solidarity" (EN: 58).

United in a CEB and nurturing their adherence to Christ, Christians strive for a more evangelical way of life amid the people, work together to challenge the egotistical and consumeristic roots of society, and make explicit their vocation to communion with God and their fellow humans. Thus they offer a valid and worthwhile point of departure for building up a new society, "the civilization of love."

The CEBs embody the Church's preferential love for the common people. In them their religiosity is expressed, valued, and purified; and they are given a concrete opportunity to share in the task of the Church and to work committedly for the transformation of the world.

The *parish* carries out a function that is, in a way, an integral ecclesial function because it accompanies persons and families throughout their lives, fostering their education and growth in the faith. It is a center of coordination and guidance for communities, groups, and movements. In it the horizons of communion and participation are opened up even more. The celebration of the Eucharist and the other sacraments makes the global reality of the Church present in a clearer way. Its tie with the diocesan community is ensured by its union with the bishop, who entrusts his representative (usually the parish priest) with the pastoral care of the community. For the Christian the parish becomes the place of encounter and fraternal sharing of persons and goods; it overcomes the limitations inherent in small communities. In fact, the parish takes on a series of services that are not within the reach of smaller communities. This is particularly true with respect to the missionary dimension and to the furthering of the dignity of the human person. In this way it reaches out to migrants, who are more or less stable, to the marginalized, to the alienated, to nonbelievers, and in general to the neediest.

In *the local Church,* which is shaped in the image of the universal Church, we find the one, holy, catholic, and apostolic Church of Christ truly existing and operating (LG: 23; CD: 11). The local Church is a portion of the People of God, defined by a broader sociocultural context in which it is incarnated. Its primacy in the complex of ecclesial communities is due to the fact that it is presided over by a bishop. The bishop is endowed, in a full, sacramental way, with the threefold ministry of Christ, the head of the mystical body: prophet, priest, and pastor. In each local Church the bishop is the principle and foundation of its unity.

Because they are the successors of the apostles, bishops—through their communion with the episcopal college and, in particular, with the Roman pontiff—render present the apostolicity of the whole Church. They guarantee fidelity to the Gospel. They make real the communion with the universal Church. And they foster the collaboration of their presbytery and the growth of the People of God entrusted to their care.

It will be up to the bishop to discern the charisms and promote the ministries that are needed if his diocese is to grow toward maturity as an evangelized and evangelizing community. That means his diocese must be a light and leaven in society as well as a sacrament of unity and integral liberation. It must be capable of interchange with other local Churches and animated by a missionary spirit that will allow its inner evangelical richness to radiate outside.

2.3. Pastoral Lines of Approach

As pastors, we are determined to promote, guide, and accompany CEBs in the spirit of the Medellín Conference (Med-JPP: 10) and the guidelines set forth by *Evangelii Nuntiandi* (no. 58). We will also foster the discovery and gradual training of animators for these communities. In particular, we must explore how these small communities, which are flourishing mainly in rural areas and urban peripheries, can be adapted to the pastoral care of the big cities on our continent.

We must continue the efforts at parish renewal: getting beyond the merely administrative aspects; seeking greater lay participation, particularly in pastoral councils; giving priority to organized forms of the apostolate; and training lay people to assume their responsibilities as Christians in the community and the social milieu.

We must stress a more determined option for an overall, coordinated pastoral effort, with the collaboration of religious communities in particular. We must promote groups, communities, and movements, inspiring them to an ongoing effort at communion. We must turn the parish into a center for promoting services that smaller communities cannot surely provide.

We must encourage experiments to develop the pastoral activity of all the parish agents, and we must support the vocational pastoral effort of ordained ministers, lay services, and the religious life.

Worthy of special recognition and a word of encouragement are priests and other pastoral agents, to whom the diocesan community owes support, encouragement, and solidarity. This holds true also for their fitting sustenance and social security, within the spirit of poverty.

Among priests we want to single out the figure of the parish priest. He is a pastor in the likeness of Christ. He is a promoter of communion with God, his fellow humans to whose service he dedicates himself, and his fellow priests joined around their common bishop. He is the leader and guide of the communities, alert to discern the signs of the time along with his people.

In the realm of the local Church efforts should be made to ensure the ongoing training and updating of pastoral agents. Spirituality and training courses should be provided by retreat centers and days of recollection. It is urgent that diocesan curias become more effective centers of pastoral promotion on three levels: that of catechetics, liturgy, and services promoting justice and charity. The pastoral value of administrative service should also be recognized. A special effort should be made to coordinate and integrate pastoral diocesan councils and other diocesan organisms. For even though they present problems, they are indispensable tools in planning, implementing, and keeping up with the pastoral activity in diocesan life.

The local Church must stress its missionary character and its aspect of ecclesial communion, sharing values and experiences as well as fostering the interchange of personnel and resources.

Through its pastors, episcopal collegiality, and union with the Vicar of Christ, the diocesan community ought to intensify its intimate communion with the center of church unity. It should also shore up its loyal acceptance of the service that is offered through the magisterium, nurturing its fidelity to the Gospel and its concrete life of charity. This would include collaboration on the continental level through CELAM and its programs.

We pledge to make every effort to ensure that this collegiality – of which this conference in Puebla and the two previous conferences are privileged instances – will be an even stronger sign of credibility for our proclamation of the Gospel and our service to it; that it will thereby foster fraternal communion in all of Latin America.

* * * * *

Excerpt from Chapter III: Agents of Communion and Participation

1. LITURGY, PRIVATE PRAYER, POPULAR PIETY

Private prayer and popular piety, present in the soul of our people, constitute evangelization values. The liturgy is the privileged moment of communion and participation for an evangelization that leads to integral, authentic Christian liberation.

1.1. The Situation

a. Liturgy. Liturgical renewal in Latin America is providing generally positive results. This is because we are rediscovering the real place of the liturgy in the Church's evangelizing mission, because the new liturgical books are encouraging greater comprehension and participation among the faithful, and because pre-sacramental catechesis is spreading.

All this has been inspired by the documents of the Holy See and episcopal conferences, as well as by meetings on various levels in Latin America – regional, national, etc.

This renewal has been facilitated by a common language, a rich cultural heritage, and popular piety.

We sense the need to adapt the liturgy to various cultures and to the situation of our people – young, poor, and simple (SC: 37–40).

The lack of ministers, the scattered population, and the geographical situation of our continent have prompted us to take greater cognizance of the usefulness of celebrations of the Word, and of the importance of utilizing the media of social communication (radio and television) to reach all.

But our observation is that we have not yet given pastoral work devoted to the liturgy the priority it deserves within our overall pastoral effort. Much harm is still being done by the opposition evident in some sectors between evangelization on the one hand and sacramentalization on the other. The liturgical training of the clergy is not being deepened as it should be, and we note a marked absence of liturgical catechesis designed for the faithful.

Participation in the liturgy does not have an adequate impact on the social commitment of Christians. Sometimes the liturgy is used as a tool in ways that disfigure its evangelizing value.

The failure to observe liturgical norms and their pastoral spirit has also been harmful, leading to abuses that cause disorientation and division among the faithful.

b. Private prayer. The popular religiosity of Latin Americans contains a rich heritage of prayer. Rooted in the native cultures, it was later evangelized by the forms of Christian piety introduced by missionaries and immigrants.

The age-old custom of coming together to pray at festivals and on special occasions is one that we regard as a rich treasure. More recently this prayer-life has been enriched by the biblical movement, new forms of contemplative prayer, and the prayer-group movement.

Many Christian communities that have no ordained minister accompany and celebrate events and feasts by coming together for prayer and song. These meetings simultaneously evangelize the community and imbue it with an evangelizing dynamism.

In large areas family prayer has been the only form of worship in existence. In fact, it has preserved the unity and faith of the family and the common people.

The invasion of the home by radio and TV has jeopardized the pious practices carried out in the bosom of the family.

Even though prayer often arises from merely personal needs and finds expression in traditional formulas that have not really been assimilated, people must not overlook the fact that the vocation of Christians should lead them to a moral, social, and evangelizing commitment.

c. Popular piety. A popular piety, a piety of the common people, is evident among all the Catholic people of Latin America. It is evident on every level and it takes quite a variety of forms. We bishops must not overlook this piety. It must be scrutinized with theological and pastoral criteria so that its evangelizing potential may be discovered.

Latin America is insufficiently evangelized. The vast majority of the people express their faith predominantly in forms of popular piety.

The forms of popular piety are quite diverse, and they are both communal and personal in character. Among them we find the cultic worship of the suffering, crucified Christ; devotion to the Sacred Heart; various devotions to the Most Blessed Virgin Mary; devotion to the saints and the dead; processions; novenas; feasts of patron saints; pilgrimages to sanctuaries; sacramentals; promises; and so forth.

Popular piety presents such positive aspects as a sense of the sacred and the transcendent; openness to the Word of God; marked Marian devotion; an aptitude for prayer; a sense of friendship, charity, and family unity; an ability to suffer and to atone; Christian resignation in irremediable situations; and detachment from the material world.

But popular piety also presents negative aspects: lack of a sense of belonging to the Church; a divorce between faith and real life; a disinclination to receive the sacraments; an exaggerated estimation of devotion to the saints, to the detriment of knowing Jesus Christ and his mystery; a distorted idea of God; a utilitarian view of certain forms of piety; an inclination, in some places, toward religious syncretism; the infiltration of spiritism and, in some areas, of Oriental religious practices.

Too often forms of popular piety have been suppressed without valid reasons, or without replacing them with something better.

* * * * *

PART FOUR

A MISSIONARY CHURCH SERVING EVANGELIZATION IN LATIN AMERICA

The Spirit of the Lord prompts the People of God in history to discern the signs of the times and to discover, in the deepest yearnings and problems of human beings, God's plan regarding the human vocation in the building up of society, making it more humane, just, and fraternal.

Thus in Latin America we see poverty as the palpable seal stamped on the vast majority. At the same time, however, the poor are open, not only to the Beatitudes and to the Father's predilection, but also to the possibility of being the true protagonists of their own development.

For Jesus, the evangelization of the poor was one of the messianic signs. For us, too, it will be a sign of evangelical authenticity.

Furthermore, the young people of Latin America wish to construct a better world and, sometimes without even knowing it, they are seeking the evangelical values of truth, justice, and love. Evangelization of them will not only fulfill their generous yearnings for personal fulfillment but also guarantee the preservation of a vigorous faith on our continent.

Thus poor people and young people constitute the treasure and the hope of the Church in Latin America, and so evangelization of them is a priority task.

The Church also calls upon all its children, working within the framework of their own specific responsibilities, to be a leaven in the world and to share in building a new society on both the national and international levels. On our continent in particular, since it is Christian for the most part, people should be a source of growth, light, and transforming power.

CHAPTER I

A PREFERENTIAL OPTION FOR THE POOR

1.1. From Medellín to Puebla

With renewed hope in the vivifying power of the Spirit, we are going to take up once again the position of the Second General Conference of the Latin American episcopate in Medellín, which adopted a clear and prophetic option expressing preference for, and solidarity with, the poor. We do this despite the distortions and interpretations of some, who vitiate the spirit of Medellín, and despite the disregard and even hostility of others (OAP: Intro.). We affirm the need for conversion on the part of the whole Church to a preferential option for the poor, an option aimed at their integral liberation.

The vast majority of our fellow humans continue to live in a situation of poverty and even wretchedness that has grown more acute.* We wish to take note of all that the Church in Latin America has done, or has failed to do, for the poor since the Medellín Conference. This will serve as a starting point for seeking out effective channels to implement our option in our evangelizing work in Latin America's present and future.

We see that national episcopates and many segments of lay people, reli-

---

*We referred to this in nos. 15ff. of this document. Here we would simply recall that the vast majority of our people lack the most elementary material goods. This is in contrast to the accumulation of wealth in the hands of a small minority, frequently the price being poverty for the majority. The poor do not lack simply material goods. They also miss, on the level of human dignity, full participation in sociopolitical life. Those found in this category are principally our indigenous peoples, peasants, manual laborers, marginalized urban dwellers and, in particular, the women of these social groups. The women are doubly oppressed and marginalized.

gious men and women, and priests have made their commitment to the poor a deeper and more realistic one. This witness, nascent but real, led the Latin American Church to denounce the grave injustices stemming from mechanisms of oppression.

The poor, too, have been encouraged by the Church. They have begun to organize themselves to live their faith in an integral way, and hence to reclaim their rights.

The Church's prophetic denunciations and its concrete commitments to the poor have in not a few instances brought down persecution and oppression of various kinds upon it. The poor themselves have been the first victims of this oppression.

All this has produced tensions and conflicts both inside and outside the Church. The Church has frequently been the butt of accusations, either of being on the side of those with political or socioeconomic power, or of propounding a dangerous and erroneous Marxist ideology.

Not all of us in the Latin American Church have committed ourselves sufficiently to the poor. We are not always concerned about them, or in solidarity with them. Service to them really calls for constant conversion and purification among all Christians. That must be done if we are to achieve fuller identification each day with the poor Christ and our own poor.

1.2. Doctrinal Reflection

Jesus evangelizes the poor. As the pope has told us, the evangelical commitment of the Church, like that of Christ, should be a commitment to those most in need (Luke 4:18–21; OAP:III,3). Hence the Church must look to Christ when it wants to find out what its evangelizing activity should be like. The Son of God demonstrated the grandeur of this commitment when he became a human being. For he identified himself with human beings by becoming one of them. He established solidarity with them and took up the situation in which they find themselves—in his birth and in his life, and particularly in his passion and death where poverty found its maximum expression (Phil. 2: 5–8; LG:8; EN:30; Med-JU:1,3).

For this reason alone, the poor merit preferential attention, whatever may be the moral or personal situation in which they find themselves. Made in the image and likeness of God (Gen. 1:26–28) to be his children, this image is dimmed and even defiled. That is why God takes on their defense and loves them (Matt. 5:45; James 2:5). That is why the poor are the first ones to whom Jesus' mission is directed (Luke 4:18–21), and why the evangelization of the poor is the supreme sign and proof of his mission (Luke 7:21–23).

This central feature of evangelization was stressed by Pope John Paul II:

"I have earnestly desired this meeting because I feel solidarity with you, and because you, being poor, have a right to my special concern and attention. I will tell you the reason: the pope loves you because you are God's favorites. In founding his family, the Church, God had in mind poor and needy humanity. To redeem it, he sent his Son specifically, who was born poor and lived among the poor to make us rich with his poverty (2 Cor. 8:9)" (Address in the Barrio of Santa Cecilia, 30 January 1979).

In her Magnificat (Luke 1:46–55), Mary proclaims that God's salvation has to do with justice for the poor. From her, too, "stems authentic commitment to other human beings, our brothers and sisters, especially to the poorest and neediest, and to the necessary transformation of society" (HZ:4).

Service to our poor brothers and sisters. When we draw near to the poor in order to accompany them and serve them, we are doing what Christ taught us to do when he became our brother, poor like us. Hence service to the poor is the privileged, though not the exclusive, gauge of our following of Christ. The best service to our fellows is evangelization, which disposes them to fulfill themselves as children of God, liberates them from injustices, and fosters their integral advancement.

It is of the utmost importance that this service to our fellow human beings take the course marked out for us by Vatican II: "The demands of justice should first be satisfied, lest the giving of what is due in justice be represented as the offering of a charitable gift. Not only the effects but also the causes of various ills must be removed. Help should be given in such a way that the recipients may gradually be freed from dependence on others and become self-sufficient" (AA:8).

Commitment to the poor and oppressed and the rise of grassroots communities have helped the Church to discover the evangelizing potential of the poor. For the poor challenge the Church constantly, summoning it to conversion; and many of the poor incarnate in their lives the evangelical values of solidarity, service, simplicity, and openness to accepting the gift of God.

Christian poverty. For the Christian, the term "poverty" does not designate simply a privation and marginalization from which we ought to free ourselves. It also designates a model of living that was already in evidence in the Old Testament, in the type known as "the poor of Yahweh" (Zeph. 2:3; 3:12–20; Isa. 49:13; 66:2; Ps. 74:19; 149:4), and that was lived and proclaimed by Jesus as blessedness (Matt. 5:3; Luke 6:20). St. Paul spelled out this teaching, telling us that the attitude of the Christian should be that of a person who uses the goods of this world (whose makeup is transitory) without absolutizing them, since they are only means to reach the Kingdom (1 Cor. 7:29–

31). This model of the poor life is one that the Gospel requires of all those who believe in Christ; so we can call it "evangelical poverty" (Matt. 6:19–34). Religious live this poverty, required of all Christians, in a radical way when they commit themselves by vows to live the evangelical counsels (see nos. 733–35 above).

Evangelical poverty combines the attitude of trusting confidence in God with a plain, sober, and austere life that dispels the temptation to greed and haughty pride (1 Tim. 6:3–10).

Evangelical poverty is also carried out in practice through the giving and sharing of material and spiritual goods. It is not forced on others but done out of love, so that the abundance of some might remedy the needs of others (2 Cor. 8:1–15).

The Church rejoices to see many of its children, particularly the more modest members of the middle class, living this Christian poverty in concrete terms.

In today's world this poverty presents a challenge to materialism, and it opens the way for alternative solutions to a consumer society.

1.3. Pastoral Guidelines

Objective. The objective of our preferential option for the poor is to proclaim Christ the Savior. This will enlighten them about their dignity, help them in their efforts to liberate themselves from all their wants, and lead them to communion with the Father and their fellow human beings through a life lived in evangelical poverty. "Jesus Christ came to share our human condition through his sufferings, difficulties, and death. Before transforming day-to-day life, he knew how to speak to the heart of the poor, liberate them from sin, open their eyes to a light on the horizon, and fill them with joy and hope. Jesus Christ does the same thing today. He is present in your Churches, your families, and your hearts" (AWM:8).

This option, demanded by the scandalous reality of economic imbalances in Latin America, should lead us to establish a dignified, fraternal way of life together as human beings and to construct a just and free society.

The required change in unjust social, political, and economic structures will not be authentic and complete if it is not accompanied by a change in our personal and collective outlook regarding the idea of a dignified, happy human life. This in turn, disposes us to undergo conversion (Med-JV:1, 3; EN:30).

The gospel demand for poverty, understood as solidarity with the poor and as a rejection of the situation in which most people on this continent live, frees the poor person from being individualistic in life, and from being attracted and seduced by the false ideals of a consumer society. In like manner the witness of a poor Church can evangelize the rich whose hearts are attached to wealth, thus converting and freeing them from this bondage and their own egotism.

Means. To live out and proclaim the requirement of Christian poverty, the Church must re-examine its structures and the life of its members, particularly that of its pastoral agents, with the goal of effective conversion in mind.

Such conversion entails the demand for an austere lifestyle and a total confidence in the Lord, because in its evangelizing activity the Church will rely more on the being and power of God and his grace than on "having more" and secular authority. In this way it will present an image of being authentically poor, open to God and fellow human beings, ever at their disposal, and providing a place where the poor have a real chance for participation and where their worth is recognized.

Concrete actions. Committed to the poor, we condemn as anti-evangelical the extreme poverty that affects an extremely large segment of the population on our continent.

We will make every effort to understand and denounce the mechanisms that generate this poverty.

Acknowledging the solidarity of other Churches, we will combine our efforts with those of people of good will in order to uproot poverty and create a more just and fraternal world.

We support the aspirations of laborers and peasants, who wish to be treated as free, responsible human beings. They are called to share in the decisions that affect their lives and their future, and we encourage all to improve themselves (AO; AWM).

We defend their fundamental right "to freely create organizations to defend and promote their interests, and to make a responsible contribution to the common good" (AWM: 3).

The indigenous cultures have undeniable values. They are the peoples' treasure. We commit ourselves to looking on them with sympathy and respect and to promoting them. For we realize "how important culture is as a vehicle for transmitting the faith, so that human beings might progress in their knowledge of God. In this matter there can be no differences of race or culture" (AO: 2).

With its preferential but not exclusive love for the poor, the Church present in Medellín was a summons to hope for more Christian and humane goals, as the Holy Father pointed out (AWM). This Third Episcopal Conference in Puebla wishes to keep this summons alive and to open up new horizons of hope.

PUEBLA DOCUMENT ABBREVIATIONS

HSD	Homily in the Cathedral of Santo Domingo, 25 January 1979, John Paul II.
MPLA	Message to People of Latin America, Puebla Conference.
PP	*Populorum Progressio,* encyclical of Paul VI. Eng. trans., *The Pope Speaks,* 1967, 12: 144–72.
GS	*Gaudium et Spes,* Vatican II. Pastoral Constitution on the Church in the Modern World.
AO	Address to the Indians of Oaxaca and Chiapas, 29 January 1979, Oaxaca, John Paul II.
HZ	Homily in Zapopan, 30 January 1979, John Paul II.
MED-PC	Medellín document on Poverty of the Church.
DT	*Documento de trabajo,* working document of Puebla Conference.
EN	*Evangelii Nuntiandi,* exhortation of Paul V.
MED-P	Medellín document on Peace.
OAP	Opening Address at Puebla, John Paul II.
MED-PM	Medellín document on Pastoral Care of the Masses.
LG	*Lumen Gentium,* Vatican II. Dogmatic Constitution on the Church.
PT	*Pacem in Terris,* encyclical of John XXIII.
MED-PR	Medellín document on Priests.
RMS	Address to Religious Major Superiors, 24 November 1978, John Paul II.
CD	*Christus Dominus,* Vatican II. Decree on the Bishops' Pastoral Office in the Church.
MED-JPP	Medellín document on Joint Pastoral Planning.
SC	*Sacrosanctum Concilium,* Vatican II. Constitution on the Sacred Liturgy.
AA	*Apostolicam Actuositatem,* Vatican II. Decree on the Apostolate of the Laity.
MED-JU	Medellín document on Justice.
MED-JV	Medellín document on Youth
AWM	Address to Workers in Monterrey, 31 January 1979, John Paul II.

The Hispanic Presence: Challenge and Commitment

Excerpts from the Pastoral Letter of the Bishops of the United States on Hispanic Ministry, January 10, 1984

I. A CALL TO HISPANIC MINISTRY

1. At this moment of grace we recognize the Hispanic community among us as a blessing from God. We call upon all persons of good faith to share our vision of the special gifts which Hispanics bring to the body of Christ, his pilgrim church on earth (1 Cor. 12:12–13).

Invoking the guidance of the Blessed Virgin Mary, we desire especially to share our reflections on the Hispanic presence in the United States with the Catholic laity, religious, deacons and priests of our country. We ask Catholics, as members of the body of Christ, to give our words serious attention in performing the tasks assigned to them. This Hispanic presence challenges us all to be more "catholic," more open to the diversity of religious expression.

2. Although many pastoral challenges face the church as a result of this presence, we are pleased to hear Hispanic Catholics voicing their desire for more opportunities to share their historical, cultural and religious gifts with the church they see as their home and heritage. Let us hear their voices; let us make all feel equally at home in the church ("The Bishops Speak with the Virgin," pastoral letter of the Hispanic bishops of the United States, I, b and III, c); let us be a church which is in truth universal, a church with open arms, welcoming different gifts and expressions of our "one Lord, one faith, one baptism, one God and Father of all" (Eph. 4:5–6).

3. Hispanics exemplify and cherish values central to the service of church and society. Among these are:

- Profound respect for the dignity of each person, reflecting the example of Christ in the Gospels;
- Deep and reverential love for family life, where the entire extended family discovers its roots, its identity and its strength;
- A marvelous sense of community that celebrates life through "fiesta";

– Loving appreciation for God's gift of life and an understanding of time which allows one to savor that gift;
– Authentic and consistent devotion to Mary, the mother of God.

4. We are all called to appreciate our own histories and to reflect upon the ethnic, racial and cultural origins which make us a nation of immigrants. Historically the church in the United States has been an "immigrant church" whose outstanding record of care for countless European immigrants remains unmatched. Today that same tradition must inspire in the church's approach to recent Hispanic immigrants and migrants a similar authority, compassion and decisiveness.

Although the number of Hispanics is increasing in our country, it would be misleading to place too much emphasis on numerical growth only. Focusing primarily on the numbers could very easily lead us to see Hispanics simply as a large pastoral problem, while overlooking the even more important fact that they present a unique pastoral opportunity.

The pastoral needs of Hispanic Catholics are indeed great; although their faith is deep and strong, it is being challenged and eroded by steady social pressures to assimilate. Yet the history, culture and spirituality animating their lively faith deserve to be known, shared and reinforced by us all. Their past and present contributions to the faith life of the church deserve appreciation and recognition.

Let us work closely together in creating pastoral visions and strategies which, drawing upon a memorable past, are made new by the creative hands of the present.

5. The church has a vast body of teaching on culture and its intimate link with faith. "In his self-revelation to his people culminating in the fullness of manifestation in his incarnate Son, God spoke according to the culture proper to each age. Similarly the church has existed through the centuries in varying circumstances and has utilized the resources of different cultures in its preaching to spread and explain the message of Christ, to examine and understand it more deeply, and to express it more perfectly in the liturgy and in various aspects of the life of the faithful" (*Gaudium et Spes,* 58).

As with many nationalities with a strong Catholic tradition, religion and culture, faith and life are inseparable for Hispanics. Hispanic Catholicism is an outstanding example of how the Gospel can permeate a culture to its very roots (*Evangelii Nuntiandi,* 20). But it also reminds us that no culture is without defects and sins. Hispanic culture, like any other, must be challenged by the Gospel.

Respect for culture is rooted in the dignity of people made in God's image. The church shows its esteem for this dignity by working to ensure that pluralism, not assimilation and uniformity, is the guiding principle in the life of communities in both the ecclesial and secular societies. All of us in the church should broaden the embrace with which we greet our Hispanic brothers and sisters and deepen our commitment to them.

Hispanic Reality

6. No other European culture has been in this country longer than the Hispanic. Spaniards and their descendants were already in the Southeast and Southwest by the late sixteenth century. In other regions of our country a steady influx of Hispanic immigrants has increased their visibility in more recent times. Plainly, the Hispanic population will loom larger in the future of both the wider society and the church in the United States.

Only 30 years ago the U.S. census estimated there were six million Hispanics in the country. The 1980 census counted almost 15 million—a figure which does not include the population on the island of Puerto Rico, many undocumented workers, recent Cuban refugees, those who have fled spiraling violence in Central and South America, nor countless other Hispanics missed in the census. A number of experts estimate a total U.S. Hispanic population of at least 20 million.

The United States today ranks fifth among the world's Spanish-speaking countries: only Mexico, Spain, Argentina and Colombia have more Hispanics.

Hispanic Catholics are extremely diverse. They come from nineteen different Latin American republics, Puerto Rico and Spain. The largest group, comprising 60 percent, is Mexican-American. They are followed by Puerto Ricans, 17 percent, and Cubans, 8 percent. The Dominican Republic, Peru, Ecuador, Chile and increasingly Central America, especially El Salvador—as well as other Latin American countries—are amply represented.

Hispanics vary in their racial origins, color, history, achievements, expressions of faith and degree of disadvantage. But they share many elements of culture, including a deeply rooted Catholicism, values such as commitment to the extended family and a common language, Spanish, spoken with different accents.

They are found in every state of the union and nearly every diocese. Although many, especially in the Southwest, live in rural areas, over 85 percent are found in large urban centers like New York, Chicago, Miami, Los Angeles, San Antonio and San Francisco. In places like Hartford, Washington, D.C., and Atlanta, a growing number of advertisements in Spanish and English, as well as large Hispanic barrios, are increasing evidence of their presence.

It is significant that Hispanics are the youngest population in our country. Their median age, 23.2, is lower than that of any other group; 54 percent are age 25 or less.

Socio-Economic Conditions

7. In general, most Hispanics in our country live near or below the poverty level. While limited improvements in their social and economic status have occurred in the last generation, the Hispanic community as a whole has yet to share equitably in this country's wealth–wealth they have helped produce. Despite rising expectations, Hispanic political participation in the political process is limited by economic and social underdevelopment. Thus Hispanics are severely underrepresented at decision-making levels in church and society.

The annual median income for non-Hispanic families is $5,000 higher than the median for Hispanic families; 22.1 percent of Hispanics live below the poverty level, compared with 15 percent of the general population.

Historically, unemployment has been higher among Hispanics than other nationalities. The Puerto Ricans are the hardest hit, with unemployment rates generally a third higher than other Hispanics. In times of crisis, such as in the economic downturn of the early 1980s, Hispanics are among the last hired and the first fired.

Well over half the employed Hispanics work at non-professional, non-managerial jobs, chiefly in agricultural labor and urban service occupations. In both occupational areas the courageous struggle of workers to obtain adequate means of negotiation for just compensation has yet to succeed.

Lack of education is an important factor keeping Hispanics poor. While more Hispanics now finish high school and college than did ten years ago, only 40 percent graduate from high school, compared with 66 percent of the general population. Hispanics are underrepresented even within the Catholic school system, where they account for only 9 percent of the student population.

Educational opportunities are often below standard in areas of high Hispanic concentration. Early frustration in school leads many young Hispanics to drop out without the skills they need, while many of those who stay find themselves in an educational system which is not always supportive. Often Hispanic students are caught in a cultural cross fire–living their Hispanic culture at home, while feeling pressured at school and at work to assimilate and forsake their heritage.

Impersonal data tells us that Hispanics are numerous, rapidly increasing, of varied national origins, found everywhere in the United States, socio-economically disadvantaged and in need of greater access to education and the decision-making processes. But there is a human reality behind the dry, sometimes discouraging, data. We see in the faces of Hispanics a profound serenity, a steadfast hope and a vibrant joy; in many we recognize an evangelical sense of the blessing and prophetic nature of poverty.

* * * * *

III. URGENT PASTORAL IMPLICATIONS

10. We urge all U.S. Catholics to explore creative possibilities for responding innovatively, flexibly and immediately to the Hispanic presence. Hispanics and non-Hispanics should work together, teach and learn from one another and together evangelize in the fullest and broadest sense. Non-Hispanic clergy – especially religious, priests and bishops who have been at the forefront of the Hispanic apostolates – are needed more than ever today to serve with the Hispanic people.

The Church's Mission and the Hispanic Presence

11. From an ecclesial perspective, evangelization, which is the church's central mission and purpose, consists not just in isolated calls to individual conversion, but in an invitation to join the people of God (EN, 15). This is reflected in the Hispanic experience of evangelization, which includes an important communitarian element expressed in an integral or "holistic" vision of faith and pastoral activity carried out in community (*II Encuentro Nacional Hispano de Pastoral,* I, 4c).

This experience is summed up in the concept of the *pastoral de conjunto,* a pastoral focus and approach to action arising from shared reflection among the agents of evangelization (Final Document of the Third General Conference of Latin American Bishops, Puebla, 650, 122 and 1307). Implicit in a *pastoral de conjunto* is the recognition that both the sense of the faithful and hierarchical teaching are essential elements in the articulation of the faith. This pastoral approach also recognizes that the church's essential mission is best exercised in a spirit of concord and in group apostolate (*Apostolicam Actuositatem,* 18).

An effective Hispanic apostolate includes the application of this experience, which can benefit the church in all its efforts to fulfill its mission. Essential to this is an integral vision, forged in community, which encompasses the totality of human challenges and opportunities as religious concerns.

Creative Possibilities

12. We therefore invite all our priests, deacons, and religious and lay leaders to consider the following creative opportunities.

A. Liturgy. Universal in form, our church "respects and fosters the spiritual adornments and gifts of the various races and peoples" in its liturgical life (*Sacrosanctum Concilium,* 37). As applied to the Hispanic presence, this requires making provision for Spanish and bilingual worship according to the traditions and customs of the people being served. We are thus challenged to greater study of Hispanic prayer forms. It is encouraging in this regard that Hispanic Catholic artists and musicians are already contributing to the liturgy in our country.

The presence of Hispanic liturgists on parish and diocesan commissions is essential. Every effort should be made to bring this about.

As their homes have been true "domestic churches" for many Hispanic Catholics, so the home has traditionally been for them the center of faith and worship. The celebration of traditional feasts and special occasions in the home should therefore be valued and encouraged.

The choice of liturgical art, gestures and music, combined with a spirit of hospitality, can refashion our churches and altars into spiritual homes and create in our communities an inviting environment of family *fiesta.*

B. Renewal of preaching. The recasting and proclamation of the word in powerful, new, liberating images are unavoidable challenges for Hispanic ministry. As the apostle Paul asked, "How can they believe unless they have heard of him? And how can they hear unless there is someone to preach?" (Rom. 10:14).

Those who preach should always bear in mind that the ability to hear is linked to the hearer's language, culture and real-life situation. In proclaiming the gospel message they should strive to make these characteristics and realities their own, so that their words will transmit the Gospel's truly liberating content.

Thirsting for God's word, Hispanics want clear and simple preaching on its message and its application to their lives. They respond to effective preaching, and they often express a keen desire for better, more powerful preaching which expresses the gospel message in terms they can understand.

We strongly recommend that priests engaged in ministry with Hispanics, such as parish priests and chaplains, enroll in Spanish courses so that they can readily speak with and listen to Hispanics. Similarly, we urge Hispanic permanent deacons to develop their preaching skills. We ask that these men be called on more often to exercise the ministry of the word. The continuing education of permanent deacons and periodic evaluation of their ministry are necessary in this regard.

C. Catechesis. Like initial evangelization, catechesis must start where the hearer of the Gospel is (EN, 44). In the case of Hispanics this suggests not merely the use of Spanish, but also an active dialogue with their culture and their needs (National Catechetical Directory, 229). Since religious education is a lifelong process for the individual (NCD, 32), parishes should provide an atmosphere for catechesis which in every respect encourages the ongoing formation of adults as well as children. Such efforts will match the effectiveness of grade-level programs for children among the English-speaking and explore new methods in adult catechesis.

It is essential too that dioceses sponsor catechist-formation courses in Spanish for Hispanics. They should be assured of having appropriate, effective materials and programs in Spanish (NCD 194, 195). Catechists should take advantage of every "teachable moment" to present the church's doctrine to Hispanic Catholics. Hispanic family celebrations like baptisms, *quinceanos,* weddings, anniversaries, *fiestas patrias, novenarios, velorios* and funerals often provide excellent teachable moments which are also "moments of grace" enabling the catechist to build upon the people's traditions and use them as living examples of gospel truths (Puebla, 59 and *Catechesi Tradendae,* 53).

Throughout our country there is a deep yearning and hunger—"not a famine for bread or a thirst for water, but for hearing the word of the Lord" (Amos 8:11). We urge continuing efforts to begin Bible study groups in Hispanic communities and to call forth Hispanic leaders to guide and direct such programs.

D. Vocation and formation of lay ministers. Adequate training must have a high priority in Hispanic ministry. In planning such training the goals of enhancing pluralism and catholicity will suggest the means. Formation should aim to incorporate the knowledge and practical experience necessary to minister effectively, while also fostering a serious commitment of service.

Although Hispanics lack sufficient clergy trained to minister with them, there are among them many lay people who are well disposed to respond to the call to be apostles (AA, 3). From this we conclude that fostering vocations and training for lay ministries will help provide the much-needed laborers in the vineyard.

One model in this direction is the *escuela de ministerios* which helps train lay leaders, calls youths to greater participation in the church and is likely to serve as a place of election for priestly and religious vocations.

* * * * *

K. Migrants. As noted, Hispanics are highly mobile and are found in both urban and rural settings. As a result, they tend to escape the attention and care of the urban church. This underlines the need for adaptations in pastoral care, particularly in the case of migrant workers.

There are three major migrant streams in the United States. In the East farmworkers migrate from Mexico, South America and Florida north to New York and New England, working on sugar cane, cotton, tobacco, apple and grape crops. In the Central Plains migrants go north from Texas to the Great Lakes to harvest fruits, vegetables and grains. There is also a substantial number of Puerto Rican seasonal laborers, most of them young and single, who work mainly in the Northeast. In the West migrants move northward through California, Nevada and Idaho up to the Northwest; some even go as far as Alaska in search of seasonal jobs. Migration usually begins in the spring and ends in the late fall when the migrants return to their southern home bases.

Abuses of farmworkers are notorious, yet they continue to go unrelieved. Conditions are worsening in many regions. Men and women are demoralized to the point where the riches of Hispanic culture, strong family ties and the profound faith life are sometimes lost. We denounce the treatment of migrants as commodities–cheap labor–rather than persons. We urge others to do the same. Economic conditions often require children to be part of the labor force. Along with the other problems associated with mobility, their education suffers. In the same vein, we find deplorable the abuse of the rights of undocumented workers. All this makes it imperative for the church to support the right of migrant farmworkers to organize for the purpose of collective bargaining.

Experience in the Hispanic apostolate suggests the need for mobile missionary teams and various forms of itinerant ministries. Dioceses and parishes in the path of migrant streams also have a responsibility to support this work and coordinate the efforts of sending and receiving dioceses.

Undoubtedly, too, Hispanic migrants themselves, whose agricultural understanding of life so closely resembles that of Jesus the Galilean, have much to contribute to meeting the challenge.

L. Social justice and social action. The integral evangelization described earlier as the central focus of the pastoral strategy we envisage will be incomplete without an active component of social doctrine and action. As we said in our pastoral letter on war and peace, "at the center of all Catholic social teaching are the transcendence of God and the dignity of the human person. The human person is the clearest reflection of God's presence in the world" ("The Challenge of Peace," I). This thought must be applied specifically to the reality of the Hispanic presence and the ministry which responds to it.

In the past twenty years Catholic teaching has become increasingly specific about the meaning of social justice. From Pope John XXIII's encyclical *Pacem in Terris* to Pope John Paul II's *Laborem Exercens,* we have seen social teaching define as human rights such things as good governance, nutrition, health, housing, employment and education. In the United States we have applied these teachings to the problems of our time and nation.

Now we call attention to those social concerns which most directly affect the Hispanic community, among them voting rights, discrimination, immigration rights, the status of farmworkers, bilingualism and pluralism. These are social justice issues of paramount importance to ministry with Hispanics and to the entire church.

As it engages in social teaching, the church embraces the quest for justice as an eminently religious task. Persons engaged in this endeavor must be involved with, informed by and increasingly led by those who know from experience the paradoxical blessings of poverty, prejudice and unfairness (Mt. 5:3). Accordingly, we urge Hispanics to increase their role in social action and non-Hispanics increasingly to seek out Hispanics in a true partnership.

M. Prejudice and racism. Within our memory, Hispanics in this country have experienced cruel prejudice. So extensive has it been in some areas that they have been denied basic human and civil rights. Even today Hispanics, blacks, the recent Southeast Asian refugees and native Americans continue to suffer from such dehumanizing treatment—treatment which makes us aware that the sin of racism lingers in our society. Despite great strides in eliminating racial prejudice, both in our country and in our church, there remains an urgent need for continued purification and reconciliation. It is particularly disheartening to know that some Catholics hold strong prejudices against Hispanics and others and deny them the respect and love due their God-given human dignity.

This is evident even in some parish communities where one finds a reluctance among some non-Hispanics to serve with Hispanics or to socialize with them at parochial events. We appeal to those with this un-Christian attitude to examine their behavior in the light of Jesus' commandment of love and to accept their Hispanic brothers and sisters as full partners in the work and life of their parishes. Our words in our pastoral letter on racism deserve repeating:

"Racism is not merely one sin among many, it is a radical evil dividing the human family and denying the new creation of a redeemed world. To struggle against it demands an equally radical transformation in our own minds and hearts as well as the structure of our society" ("Brothers and Sisters to Us," p. 10).

We urge those who employ Hispanics to provide them with safe working conditions and to pay them salaries which enable them to provide adequately for their families. The inhuman condition of pervasive poverty forced on many Hispanics is at the root of many social problems in their lives. Decent working conditions and adequate salaries are required by justice and basic fairness.

N. Ties with Latin America. Hispanics in our midst are an as-yet untapped resource as a cultural bridge between North and South in the Americas. The wellspring of Hispanic culture and faith is historically and geographically located in Latin America. For this reason, a dynamic response to the Hispanic presence in the United States will necessarily entail an ever greater understanding of and linkage with Latin American society and church.

Latin America, the home of 350 million Catholics, continues to experience grave socio-economic injustice and, in many nations, a severe deprivation of the most basic human rights. These conditions are oppressive and dehumanizing; they foster violence, poverty, hatred and deep divisions in the social fabric; they are fundamentally at variance with gospel values. And yet our fellow Catholics in Latin America, especially the poor, are often vibrant witnesses to the liberating quality of the Gospel, as they strive to build a "civilization of love" (Puebla, 9).

We shall continue to support and assist the church in Latin America. We also look forward to a continuing exchange of missionaries, since the cooperation we envision is not onesided. For our part, we shall continue to send those most prepared to evangelize in Latin America, including our Hispanic personnel as they grow in numbers. With careful regard to circumstances in the areas from which they come, we welcome Latin American and other priests and religious who come to serve Hispanics in the United States. We recommend that upon arrival they receive special language and cultural preparation for pastoral activity. The church in the United States has much to learn from the Latin American pastoral experience; it is fortunate to have in the Hispanic presence a precious human link to that experience.

O. Popular Catholicism. Hispanic spirituality is an example of how deeply Christianity can permeate the roots of a culture. In the course of almost 500 years in the Americas, Hispanic people have learned to express their faith in prayer forms and traditions that were begun and encouraged by missionaries and passed from one generation to the next.

Paul VI recognized the value inherent in popular Catholicism. While warning against the possible excesses of popular religiosity, he nonetheless enumerated values that often accompany these prayer forms. If well-oriented, he pointed out, popular piety manifests a thirst for God, makes people generous and imbues them with a spirit of sacrifice. It can lead to an acute awareness of God's attributes, such as his fatherhood, his providence, and his loving and constant presence (EN, 48).

Hispanic spirituality places strong emphasis on the humanity of Jesus, especially when he appears weak and suffering, as in the crib and in his passion and death. This spirituality relates well to all that is symbolic in Catholicism; ritual, statues and images, holy places and gestures. It is also a strongly devotional spirituality. The Blessed Virgin Mary, especially under the titles of Our Lady of Guadalupe (Mexico), Our Lady of Providence (Puerto Rico) and Our Lady of Charity (Cuba), occupies a privileged place in Hispanic popular piety.

A closer dialogue is needed between popular and official practice, lest the former lose the guidance of the Gospel and the latter lose the active participation of the unsophisticated and the poorest among the faithful (Final Document of the Second General Conference of Latin American Bishops, Medellín, 3). An ecclesial life vibrant with a profound sense of the transcendent, such as is found in Hispanic popular Catholicism, can also be a remarkable witness to the more secularized members of our society.

P. Comunidades eclesiales de base. Hispanics in the Americas have made few contributions to the church more significant than the *comunidades eclesiales de base* (basic ecclesial communities). The small community has appeared on the scene as a ray of hope in dealing with dehumanizing situations that can destroy people and weaken faith. A revitalized sense of fellowship fills the church in Latin America, Africa, Europe and Asia with pastoral joy and hope. The Synod of Bishops in 1974 witnessed an outpouring of such hope from Latin American pastors, who saw in *comunidades eclesiales de base* a source of renewal in the church. Since these communities are of proven benefit to the church (EN, 58), we highly encourage their development.

The *comunidad eclesial de base* is neither a discussion or study group nor a parish. It is "the first and fundamental ecclesiastical nucleus, which on its own level must make itself responsible for the richness and expansion of the faith, as well as of the worship of which it is an expression" (Joint Pastoral Planning, Medellín, 10). It should be an expression of a church that liberates from personal and structural sin; it should be a small community with personal relationships; it should form part of a process of integral evangelization; and it should be in communion with other levels of the church. The role of the parish in particular is to facilitate, coordinate and multiply the *comunidades eclesiales de base* within its boundaries and territories. The parish should be a community of communities. The ideal *comunidad eclesial de base* is a living community of Christians whose active involvement in every aspect of life is nourished by profound commitment to the Gospel.

* * * * * *

Excerpt from IV: Statement of Commitment

Convocation for the III Encuentro

18. We ask our Hispanic peoples to raise their prophetic voices to us once again, as they did in 1972 and 1977, in a *III Encuentro Nacional Hispano de Pastoral,* so that together we can face our responsibilities well. We call for

the launching of an *encuentro* process, from *comunidades eclesiales de base* and parishes, to dioceses and regions, and to the national level, culminating in a gathering of representatives in Washington, D.C., in August 1985.

Toward a Pastoral Plan

19. Beyond the *encuentro* process, in which we shall take part, we recognize that integral pastoral planning must avoid merely superficial adaptations of existing ministries. We look forward to reviewing the conclusions of the *III Encuentro* as a basis for drafting a national pastoral plan for Hispanic ministry to be considered in our general meeting at the earliest possible date after the *encuentro.*

Conclusion

20. As we continue our pilgrimage together with our Hispanic brothers and sisters, we frame our commitment in the same spirit as our brother bishops of Latin America gathered at Puebla ("Message to the Peoples of Latin America," Puebla, 9):

–We call upon the entire Catholic Church in the United States, laity, religious, deacons and priests, to join us in our pledge to respond to the presence of our Hispanic brothers and sisters;

–We honor and rejoice in the work that has taken place before us, and we pledge our best efforts to do even better henceforth;

–We envisage a new era of ministry with Hispanics, enriched by the gifts of creativity placed providentially before us and by the Spirit of Pentecost, who calls us to unity, to renewal and to meeting the prophetic challenge posed by the Hispanic presence;

–We commit ourselves to engage in a thorough, conscientious and continuing pastoral effort to enhance the catholicity of the church and the dignity of all its members;

–We look hopefully to the greater blessings Hispanics can bring to our local churches.

May this commitment receive the blessing, the encouragement and the inspiration of our Lord. May his blessed mother, patroness of the Americas, accompany us in our journey. Amen.

What We Have Seen and Heard

Excerpts from the Pastoral Letter of the Ten Black Catholic Bishops of the United States, on Evangelization, September 9, 1984

INTRODUCTION

Within the history of every Christian community there comes the time when it reaches adulthood. This maturity brings with it the duty, the privilege and the joy to share with others the rich experience of the "word of life." Always conscious of the need to hear the word and ever ready to listen to its proclamation, the mature Christian community feels the irresistible urge to speak that word:

"This is what we proclaim to you: what was from the beginning, what we have heard, what we have seen with our eyes, what we have looked upon and our hands have touched—we speak the word of life. (This life became visible; we have seen and bear witness to it, and we proclaim to you the eternal life that was present to the Father and became visible to us.) What we have seen and heard we proclaim in turn to you so that you may share life with us. This fellowship of ours is with the Father and with his Son, Jesus Christ. Indeed, our purpose in writing you this is that our joy may be complete" (1 Jn. 1:1–4).

We, the ten black bishops of the United States, chosen from among you to serve the people of God, are a significant sign among many other signs that the black Catholic community in the American church has now come of age. We write to you as brothers that "you may share life with us." We write also to all those who by their faith make up the people of God in the United States that "our joy may be complete." And what is this joy? It is that joy that the Ethiopian eunuch, the treasurer of the African queen, expressed in the Book of Acts when he was baptized by the deacon, Philip: He "went on his way rejoicing" (Acts 8:39). We rejoice because, like this African court official, we, the descendants of Africans brought to these shores, are now called to share our faith and to demonstrate our witness to our risen Lord.

We write to you, black brothers and sisters, because each one of us is called to a special task. The Holy Spirit now calls us all to the work of evangelization. As he did for Peter, the Lord Jesus has prayed for us that our faith might not fail (Lk. 22:32), and with Paul we all are compelled to confess: "Yet preaching the Gospel is not the subject of a boast; I am under compulsion and have no choice. I am ruined if I do not preach it!" (1 Cor. 9:16).

Evangelization is both a call and a response. It is the call of Jesus reverberating down the centuries: "Go into the whole world and proclaim the good news to all creation" (Mk. 16:15). The response is, "Conduct yourselves, then, in a way worthy of the Gospel of Christ" (Phil. 1:27). Evangelization means not only preaching but witnessing; not only conversion but renewal; not only entry into the community but the building up of the community; not only hearing the word but sharing it. Evangelization, said Pope Paul VI, "is a question not only of preaching the Gospel in ever wider geographic areas or to ever greater numbers of people, but also of affecting and as it were upsetting, through the power of the Gospel, mankind's criteria of judgment, determining values, points of interest, lines of thought, sources of inspiration and models of life, which are in contrast with the word of God and the plan of salvation."

Pope Paul VI issued that call to the peoples of Africa when he said to them at Kampala in Uganda, "You are now missionaries to yourselves." And Pope Paul also laid out for all sons and daughters of Africa the nature of the response, "You must now give your gifts of blackness to the whole church."

We believe that these solemn words of our Holy Father Paul VI were addressed not only to Africans today but also to us, the children of the Africans of yesterday. We believe that the Holy Father has laid a challenge before us to share the gift of our blackness with the church in the United States. This is a challenge to be evangelizers, and so we want to write about this gift, which is also a challenge. First, we shall write about the gifts we share, gifts rooted in our African heritage. Then we will write about the obstacles to evangelization that we must still seek to overcome.

Grateful Remembrance for Our Own Evangelization

Before we go on, however, we must at the beginning remember those who brought us to new birth within the faith. When we as black Catholics speak of missionaries, we shall never forget the devoted service that many white priests, vowed religious and laypersons gave to us as a people and still give to us daily. We shall remember and never forget that this ministry was often given at great personal sacrifice and hardship. The same holds true today.

We remember especially that those of us who have grown up in the faith owe this faith to the black men and women who have gone before us strong in the faith and steadfast in their personal conviction. If we have reached adulthood in the fullness of the age of Christ, it is most of all thanks to our fathers and mothers and all our ancestors who kept alive an unflagging commitment to Christ and to his church throughout bitter days of slavery and the troubled times of racial segregation. Their faith was passed on to us despite the peculiar structures of racism and bondage that marred the Catholic Church in America in an earlier time.

I. THE GIFTS WE SHARE

Black Culture and Values: Informed by Faith

There is a richness in our black experience that we must share with the entire people of God. These are gifts that are part of an African past. For we have heard with black ears and we have seen with black eyes and we have understood with an African heart. We thank God for the gifts of our Catholic faith, and we give thanks for the gifts of our blackness. In all humility we turn to the whole church that it might share our gifts so that "our joy may be complete."

To be Catholic is to be universal. To be universal is not to be uniform. It does mean, however, that the gifts of individuals and of particular groups become the common heritage shared by all. Just as we lay claim to the gift of blackness, so we share these gifts within the black community at large and within the church. This will be our part in the building up of the whole church. This will also be our way of enriching ourselves. "For it is in giving that we receive." Finally, it is our way to witness to our brothers and sisters within the black community that the Catholic Church is both one and also home to us all.

Scripture

African-American spirituality is based on the sacred scriptures. In the dark days of slavery, reading was forbidden, but for our ancestors the Bible was never a closed book. The stories were told and retold in sermons, spirituals and shouts. Proverbs and turns of phrase borrowed freely from the Bible. The Bible was not for our ancestors a mere record of the wonderful works of God in a bygone age; it was a present record of what was soon to come. God will lead his people from the bondage of Egypt. God will preserve his children in the midst of the fiery furnace. God's power will make the dry bones scattered on the plain snap together, and he will breathe life into them. Above all, the birth and death, the suffering and the sorrow, the burial and the resurrection tell how the story will end for all who are faithful, no matter what the present tragedy is.

For black people the story is our story; the Bible promise is our hope.

Thus when the word of scripture is proclaimed in the black community, it is not a new message but a new challenge. Scripture is part of our roots; the Bible has sunk deep into our tradition; and the good news of the Gospel has been enmeshed in our past of oppression and pain. Still the message was heard, and we learned to celebrate in the midst of sorrow, to hope in the depths of despair and to fight for freedom in the face of all obstacles. The time has now come to take this precious heritage and to go and "tell it on the mountain."

Our Gift of Freedom

The good news of the Gospel is the message of liberation. "You will know the truth," said Jesus, "and the truth will set you free" (Jn. 8:32). Recently our Holy Father, Pope John Paul II, spoke at length on the relation between truth and freedom:

"Jesus himself links 'liberation' with knowledge of the truth: 'You will know the truth, and the truth will make you free' (Jn. 8:32). In this affirmation is the deep meaning of freedom that Christ gives man as a consequence coming from knowledge of the truth. It is a question of a spiritual process of maturing, by means of which man becomes a representative and spokesman of 'righteousness and holiness' (Eph. 4:24) at the different levels of personal, individual and social life. But this truth is not mere truth of a scientific or historical nature; it is Christ himself—the word incarnate of the Father—who can say of himself, 'I am the way, the truth, the life' (Jn. 14:6). For this reason, Jesus, although aware of what was in store for him, repeatedly and forcefully, with firmness and with decision, opposed 'non-truth' in his earthly life.

"This service of truth, participation in the prophetic service of Christ, is a task of the church, which tries to carry it out in the different historical contexts. It is necessary to call clearly by name injustice, the exploitation of man by man, the exploitation of man by the state or by the mechanisms of systems and regimes. It is necessary to call by name all social injustice, all discrimination, all violence inflicted on man with regard to his body, his spirit, his conscience, his dignity as a person, his life."

Black people know what freedom is because we remember the dehumanizing force of slavery, racist prejudice and oppression. No one can understand so well the meaning of the proclamation that Christ has set us free than those who have experienced the denial of freedom. For us, therefore, freedom is a cherished gift. For its preservation, no sacrifice is too great.

Hence, freedom brings responsibility. It must never be abused, equated with license or taken for granted. Freedom is God's gift, and we are accountable to him for our loss of it. And we are accountable for the gift of freedom in the lives of others. We oppose all oppression and all injustice, for unless all are free, none are free. Moreover, oppression by some means freedom's destruction for both the oppressor and the oppressed, and liberation liberates the oppressor and the oppressed.

Our African-American ancestors knew the liberating hand of God. Even before emancipation they knew the inner spiritual freedom that comes from Jesus. Even under slavery they found ways to celebrate that spiritual freedom which God alone can give. They left us the lesson that without spiritual freedom we cannot fight for the broader freedom which is the right of all who are brothers and sisters in Christ. This is the gift we have to share with the whole church. This is the responsibility that freedom brings; to teach to others its value and work to see that its benefits are denied to none.

The Gift of Reconciliation

The gospel message is a message that liberates us from hate and calls us to forgiveness and reconciliation. As a people we must be deeply committed to reconciliation. This is a value coming from our African heritage and deepened by our belief in the gospel teaching. When in recent years we rejected "token integration" for "self-determination," it was not to choose confrontation in place of cooperation, but to insist on collaboration with mutual respect for the dignity and unique gifts of all. Reconciliation can never mean unilateral elevation and another's subordination, unilateral giving and another's constant receiving, unilateral flexibility and another's resistance. True reconciliation arises only where there is mutually perceived equality. This is what is meant by justice.

Without justice, any meaningful reconciliation is impossible. Justice safeguards the rights and delineates the responsibility of all. A people must safeguard their own cultural identity and their own cultural values. Likewise they must respect the cultural values of others. For this reason sincere reconciliation builds on mutual recognition and mutual respect. On this foundation can be erected an authentic Christian love.

"But now in Christ Jesus you who once were far off have been brought near through the blood of Christ. It is he who is our peace, and who made the two of us one by breaking down the barrier of hostility that kept us apart" (Eph. 2:13–14).

We seek justice, then, because we seek reconciliation, and we seek reconciliation because by the blood of Christ we are made one. The desire for reconciliation is for us a most precious gift, for reconciliation is the fruit of liberation. Our contribution to the building up of the church in America and in the world is to be an agent of change for both.

Finally, as we speak of reconciliation, let us note that as members of a truly universal church our efforts must never be limited to the black community in this country alone. Our minds and hearts turn toward the church of the poor in the Third World, especially those "who hunger and thirst for justice" in Africa, Asia, and Latin America. We turn also to the members of the "church of silence" and to the various minority groups in the East and in the West.

We shall remind ourselves and our compatriots that we are called to be "instruments of peace." This peace is the fruit of justice. We must be a part of those movements for justice that seek to reduce bombs and increase bread, to replace bullets with the printing of books. We must work with all who strive to make available the fruits of creation to all God's children everywhere. It was in chains that our parents were brought to these shores and in violence were we maintained in bondage. Let us who are the children of pain be now a bridge of reconciliation. Let us who are the offspring of violence become the channels of compassion. Let us, the sons and daughters of bondage, be the bringers of peace.

Our Spirituality and Its Gifts

Black Americans are a people rich with spiritual gifts. Some aspects of this spirituality have already been mentioned. It is fitting, however, to present briefly the major characteristics of what can be termed "black spirituality." As members of a church universal both in time and place, we have no difficulty with this term. All peoples and all cultures have been molded by the Holy Spirit, and the Holy Spirit has distributed his gifts in the language, culture and traditions of each.

Black spirituality has four major characteristics: It is contemplative. It is holistic. It is joyful. It is communitarian.

The Contemplative Dimension

Black spirituality is contemplative. By this we mean that prayer is spontaneous and pervasive in the black tradition. Every place is a place for prayer because God's presence is heard and felt in every place. Black spirituality senses the awe of God's transcendence and the vital intimacy of his closeness. God's power breaks into the "sin-sick world" of everyday. The sense of God's presence and power taught our ancestors that no one can run from him and no one need hide from him.

Black spirituality has taught us what it means to "let go" and "to lean on God." In an age of competition and control we have learned to surrender to God's love and to let him work his power through us. In an age of technology and human engineering our spiritual heritage has never let us forget that God takes us each by the hand and leads us in ways we might not understand. It is this sense of God's power in us that calls us to work for evangelization in the modern world.

Holistic

Black spirituality, in contrast with much of Western tradition, is holistic. Like the biblical tradition, there is no dualism. Divisions between intellect and emotion, spirit and body, action and contemplation, individual and community, sacred and secular are foreign to us. In keeping with our African heritage, we are not ashamed of our emotions. For us, the religious experience is an experience of the whole human being—both the feelings and the intellect, the heart as well as the head. Moreover, we find foreign any notion that the body is evil. We find our own holistic spiritual approach to be in accord with the scriptures and the logic of the incarnation.

In sharing this approach we contribute greatly to evangelization in our day. St. Paul wrote Timothy, "Everything God created is good; nothing is to be rejected when it is received with thanksgiving" (1 Tm. 4:4). The material world need not lead us away from God, but can and should bring us closer to him.

We dare to suggest that black spirituality in its holistic approach also presents a solution to one of the problems of our time: the progressive dehumanization brought about by a technocratic society. Not only is it possible to counteract the dehumanizing forces in our world and our work, but we can restore the human. We can put back the human factor by rediscovering that "the world is charged with the grandeur of God" and that "the whole world is in his hands." We affirm that the advances in technology, when understood with God's presence in all things, will be a powerful force for the coming of the kingdom and the human progress of all people.

The Gift of Joy

Joy is a hallmark of black spirituality. Joy is first of all celebration. Celebration is movement and song, rhythm and feeling, color and sensation, exultation and thanksgiving. We celebrate the presence and the proclamation of the word.

This joy is a sign of our faith and especially our hope. It is never an escape from reality, however harsh it may be. Indeed this joy is often present even in the midst of deep anguish and bitter tears.

"You will weep and mourn while the world rejoices; you will grieve for a time, but your grief will be turned into joy" (Jn. 16:20).

This joy is a result of our conviction that "in the time of trouble, he will lead me." This joy comes from the teaching and wisdom of mothers and fathers in the faith that, looking at Jesus, we must burst forth into song so that all might hear, "He's sweet I know. . . ."

This gift of joy is something we must share. If the message of evangelization is the "good news" about Jesus, we must react with joy. If we do indeed feel a profound joy, we shall know that we have heard and that we have understood; and we are thus enabled to share our good news.

One who is joyful is impelled to love and cannot hate. A joyful person seeks to reconcile and will not cause division. A joyful person is troubled by the sight of another's sadness. A joyful person seeks to console, strives to encourage and brings to all true peace.

Such is the gift so clearly needed in our time. Such is the gift that Jesus passed on to us on the evening he died. "All this I tell you that my joy be yours and your joy may be complete" (Jn. 15:11).

Community

In African culture the "I" takes its meaning in the "we." In other words, individual identity is to be found within the context of the community. Even today black Christianity is eminently a social reality. The sense of community is a major component of black spirituality.

This communal dimension of our spirituality is a gift we also need to share. In the world in which we live, a high value is placed on competition. Hence, so many of us become "losers" so that others might prevail as "winners." And again so many place personal profit and personal advancement before the good of the community and the benefit of the whole.

The communal dimension of black spirituality permeates our experience of liturgy and worship. Worship must be shared. Worship is always a celebration of community. No one stands in prayer alone. One prays and acts within and for the community. Each one supports, encourages and enriches the other and is in turn enriched, encouraged and supported.

Community, however, means social concern and social justice. Black spirituality never excludes concern for human suffering and other people's concerns. "As often as you did it for one of my least brothers, you did it for me" (Mt. 25:40) are the words of Christ that cut through any supposed tension between secular concerns and the sacred or between prayerful pursuits and the profane. Ours is a spiritual heritage that always embraces the total human person.

* * * * *

Excerpt from Part II: The Call of God to His People

Black Initiative

We call upon our black Catholic sisters and brothers to shoulder the responsibility laid upon us by our baptism into the body of Christ. This responsibility is to proclaim our faith and to take an active part in building up the church. The Second Vatican Council in its Decree on the Missionary Activity of the Church stated:

"The church has not been truly established and is not yet fully alive, nor is it a perfect sign of Christ among men, unless there exists a laity worthy of the name working along with the hierarchy. . . .

"Their main duty . . . is the witness which they are bound to bear to Christ by their life and works in the home, in their social group and in their own professional circle. . . . They must give expression to this newness of life in the social and cultural framework of their own homeland, according to their own national traditions. They must heal it and preserve it. . . . Let them also spread the faith of Christ among those with whom they live. . . . This obligation is all the more urgent, because very many men can hear of the Gospel and recognize Christ only by means of the laity who are their neighbors."

The black community in the United States for a long time has been a component of the missionary enterprise of the American church. In this sense these words from the Decree on Missionary Activity are perfectly valid for the American black community. We are conscious of the debt of gratitude we owe to those who have served among us as home missionaries.

Yet we are also aware that we, like other African-Americans, are also descendants of slaves and freedmen. Like them we are victims of oppression and racism, and like them we are fighters for the same freedom and dignity. We likewise speak with the same accents and sing the same songs, and we are heirs of the same cultural achievements. Thus we have a privileged position to gain access to the hearts and minds of the African-American community. Hence, we have the solemn responsibility to take the lead in the church's work within the black community.

On the other hand, we are in a position to counter the assumption which many have advanced that to become a Catholic is to abandon one's racial heritage and one's people! The Catholic Church is not a "white church" nor a "Euro-American church." It is essentially universal and hence Catholic. The black presence within the American Catholic Church is a precious witness to the universal character of Catholicism.

The church, however, must preserve its multicultural identity. As Paul VI wrote, "Evangelization loses much of its force and effectiveness if it does not take into consideration the actual people to whom it is addressed, if it does not use their language, their signs and symbols, if it does not answer the questions they ask and if it does not have an impact on their concrete life."

In our response to the invitation to evangelize, we as black Catholics have before us several opportunities to assure the universal aspect of the American church. We can do so by permitting the Catholic Church in this country to reflect the richness of African-American history and its heritage. This is our gift to the church in the United States, this is our contribution to the building up of the universal church.

Authorization and Encouragement

Since African-American members of the American church are to assume the responsibility to which the church and our racial heritage call us, black leaders in the church—clergy, religious and lay—need encouragement and the authorization to use their competencies and to develop their expertise. Unhappily we must acknowledge that the major hindrance to the full development of black leadership within the church is still the fact of racism. The American Catholic bishops wrote in the pastoral letter on racism:

"The church . . . must be constantly attentive to the Lord's voice as he calls on his people daily not to harden their hearts (Ps. 94:8). We urge that on all levels the Catholic Church in the United States examine its conscience regarding attitudes and behavior toward blacks, Hispanics, native Americans and Asians. We urge consideration of the evil of racism as it exists in the local church and reflection upon the means of combating it. We urge scrupulous attention at every level to ensure that minority representation goes beyond mere tokenism and involves authentic sharing in the responsibility and decision making."

These words have not had the full impact on the American church that was originally hoped. Blacks and other minorities still remain absent from many aspects of Catholic life and are only meagerly represented on the decision-making level. Inner-city schools continue to disappear, and black vocational recruitment lacks sufficient support. In spite of the fact that Catholic schools are a principal instrument of evangelization, active evangelization is not always a high priority.

This racism, at once subtle and masked, still festers within our church as within our society. It is this racism that in our minds remains the major impediment to evangelization within our community. Some little progress has been made, but success is not yet attained. This stain of racism on the American church continues to be a source of pain and disappointment to all, both black and white, who love it and desire it to be the bride of Christ "without stain or wrinkle" (Eph. 5:27). This stain of racism, which is so alien to the

Spirit of Christ, is a scandal to many, but for us it must be the opportunity to work for the church's renewal as part of our task of evangelization. To "profess the truth in love" (Eph. 4:15) to our brothers and sisters within the faith remains for black Catholics the first step in proclaiming the gospel message. We, like St. John the Baptist, proclaim a baptism of repentance for the forgiveness of sins, and we call on the American church to produce the fruit of repentance and not presume to tell themselves we have Abraham for our father, for we all belong to the family of God (cf. Lk. 3:1–9).

Our demand for recognition, our demand for leadership roles in the task of evangelization, is not a call for separatism but a pledge of our commitment to the church and to share in her witnessing to the love of Christ. For the Christ we proclaim is he who prayed on the night before he died "that all may be one as you, Father, are in me, and I in you; I pray that they may be (one) in us, that the world may believe that you sent me" (Jn. 17:21).

⋆ ⋆ ⋆ ⋆ ⋆

Excerpt from Opportunities for Evangelization

Liturgy

The celebration of the sacred mysteries is that moment when the church is most fully actualized and most clearly revealed. No treatment of evangelization would be complete without a discussion of the role of liturgy in this regard.

In the African-American tradition the communal experience of worship has always had a central position. In our heritage the moment of celebration has always been a time for praise and thanksgiving, and the affirmation of ourselves as God's children. It is a moment of profound expression, not a flight from reality (as some have suggested), but an experience of God's power and love.

From the standpoint of evangelization in the black community, the liturgy of the Catholic Church has always demonstrated a way of drawing many to the faith and also of nourishing and deepening the faith of those who already believe. We believe that the liturgy of the Catholic Church can be an even more intense expression of the spiritual vitality of those who are of African origin, just as it has been for other ethnic and cultural groups:

"The church has no wish to impose a rigid uniformity in matters which do not involve the faith or the good of the whole community. Rather she respects and fosters the spiritual adornments and gifts of the various races and peoples."

Through the liturgy, black people will come to realize that the Catholic Church is a homeland for black believers just as she is for people of other cultural and ethnic traditions. In recent years remarkable progress has been made in our country by many talented black experts to adapt the liturgy to the needs and the genius of the African-American community. In order that this work can be carried on more fully within the Catholic tradition and at the same time be enriched by our own cultural heritage, we wish to recall the essential qualities that should be found in a liturgical celebration within the black Catholic community. It should be authentically black. It should be truly Catholic. And it should be well prepared and well executed.

Authentically Black

The liturgy is simultaneously a ritualization of the divine reality which transcends all human limitations and also an expression of what is most intimate and personal in the participants. What is expressed is the mystery of Christ, which transcends all cultures. The way, however, in which this mystery is expressed is mediated by the culture and traditions of the participants. All people should be able to recognize themselves when Christ is presented, and all should be able to experience their own fulfillment when these mysteries are celebrated. Hence, we can legitimately speak of an African-American cultural idiom or style in music, in preaching, in bodily expression, in artistic furnishings and vestments, and even in tempo. It is for this reason that we encourage those in pastoral ministry to introduce the African-American idiom into the expression of the Roman liturgy.

It is not our purpose at this time to detail all the characteristics this African-American cultural idiom may have nor to suggest the limits of cultural authenticity. It is important that from our own community there arise competent liturgical scholars and artists who will mutually contribute to a black Catholic liturgical critique.

We do wish to remind our fellow black Catholics, however, that the African-American cultural heritage is vast and rich. The cultural idiom of American black people has never been uniform, but has varied according to region and ethos. African, Haitian, Latin and West Indian cultural expressions also continue to this day to nurture the black American cultural expression. For this reason, an authentic black Catholic liturgy need never be confined to a narrowly based concept of what is truly black. There is a splendid opportunity for the vast richness of African-American culture to be expressed in our liturgy. It is this opportunity, thanks to the norms established in the revised Roman liturgy, which enables our work of evangelization to be filled with such promise for the future.

Truly Catholic

The liturgy not only expresses the worship of a given Catholic community, it also expresses the unity of the Catholic Church. Black Catholic liturgy should express not only our African-American cultural heritage, but also our Catholic faith and unity. In this way, unlike some other Christian communities in the black community, our worship is not confined to preaching the word alone, but also includes the sacrament as celebration.

For this reason neither the preaching nor the music nor any other ritual action has exclusive domain at liturgical celebration. If one or the other prevails, the evangelical dimension as well as the prayerful experience of the liturgy suffers.

"Evangelization thus exercises its full capacity when it achieves the most intimate relationship, or better still, a permanent and unbroken intercommunication, between the word and the sacraments. In a certain sense it is a mistake to make a contrast between evangelization and sacramentalization. . . . The role of evangelization is precisely to educate people in the faith in such a way as to lead each individual Christian to live the sacraments as true sacraments of faith—and not to receive them passively or reluctantly."

Both the liturgical preaching and the music should invite the worshiping community to a more profound participation in the total sacramental experience. Neither preaching nor music should overwhelm the liturgical worship and prevent it from exhibiting a balanced unified action.

Proper Preparation and Excellence in Execution

We wish to commend those who have tirelessly presented workshops and conferences on black liturgical expression. We urge the continued training of liturgists and musicians from the black Catholic community. We likewise wish to commend those who have generously given their talents as musicians and artists for the enhancement of our liturgical worship. We wish to encourage black artists, composers, musicians, and vocalists to continue to dedicate their skills in God's service. Finally, we urge men and women steeped in the African-American tradition and culture to collaborate with our liturgical scholars in the development of liturgical worship in our community. It is especially in this regard that we can use our rich gifts of blackness for the whole church.

In the liturgy, preparation begins with prayerful reflection and is completed and perfected by an execution that culminates in total prayer. We urge that this prayerful preparation and prayerful performance and execution be the result of a collaborative effort of many gifted people each Sunday in our parishes.

The Social Apostolate

The proclamation of the good news by Jesus began with the proclamation of justice and compassion in the context of social reform:

"When the book of the prophet Isaiah was handed him, he unrolled the scroll and found the passage where it was written: The spirit of the Lord is upon me; therefore he has anointed me. He has sent me to bring glad tidings to the poor, to proclaim liberty to captives, recovery of sight to the blind and release to prisoners, to announce a year of favor from the Lord" (Lk. 4:17–19).

For us the causes of justice and social concern are an essential part of evangelization. Our own history has taught us that preaching to the poor and to those who suffer injustice without concern for their plight and the systemic cause of their plight is to trivialize the Gospel and mock the cross. To preach to the powerful without denouncing oppression is to promise Easter without Calvary, forgiveness without conversion and healing without cleansing the wound.

Our concern for social justice, moreover, goes beyond denouncing injustice in the world around us. It brings us to the examination of our own hearts and intentions. It reminds us that it was the despised and rejected Samaritan who had the compassion to bind up the wounds of the other and to provide a lesson for the chosen (cf. Lk. 10:29–37). As black people in a powerful nation we must have concern for those who hunger and thirst for justice everywhere in the present world. We must not forget that in a world of suffering even compassion may still be selective. Let us not ignore those whom others tend to forget. It should be our concern to remind others of the plight of Haitian refugees, the hunger of drought-ridden Africans, the forgotten blacks in a war-torn Namibia and the many other forgotten minorities and ill-starred majorities in the world of the downtrodden and deprived. Political expedience and diplomatic advantages should not be bought with the human rights of others.

As a people we must have the courage to speak out and even contribute our efforts and money on behalf of any people or any segment of the human family that the powerful may seek to neglect or forget as a matter of policy. Be assured that we too must render an account for what the Lord has given us (cf. Ps. 116:12). When we share our talents and our possessions with the forgotten ones of this world, we share Christ. This is not the prelude to evangelization, it is the essence of evangelization itself.

Editor's Overview toward the Future

Joseph Gremillion

This book does more than record a particular conference hosted by Father Hesburgh at the University of Notre Dame, December 1983. It also signals a freshet of ecclesial-theological-pastoral reflection and discussion, writing and witness on the triune subjects of nature-culture-grace, of society-culture-Church into the coming generation. Culture will become a core concern of ecclesial consciousness, scholarship, and ministry for the 1990s and beyond—within the Church in general, not only among theologians.

Several foundational theologians began exploring these fruitful relations decades ago, to beget the *nouvelle theologie* of historicity which nourished Vatican II. While *Lumen Gentium* and *Gaudium et Spes* formally recognized and announced the germinal role of culture in human and ecclesial life, these new seeds needed two more decades of gestation and growth. Today, these young culture-kinder of Vatican II are not merely permitted to struggle for survival. They are nourished and propagated by the Pope himself.

1. John Paul II is deliberately moving forward the culture-consciousness of the Church from the solid takeoff platform of *Gaudium et Spes,* which led ten years later to Paul VI's "Evangelization in the World Today," engendered by the 1974 Synod of Bishops. The present Pope began applying the culture content of these two basic documents to the Church's global mission in his first encyclicals, and more particularly during his pastoral journeys to all the globe's cultural and ecclesial regions. On the first of these journeys in 1979, four months after assuming the Chair of Peter, the new Pope participated in the Puebla Conference of the Latin American Bishops, where regional Church and culture became dominant themes.

A year later John Paul II set forth his convictions and cultural agenda before the secular world with his own basic statement before UNESCO in 1980. This address, entitled "Man's Entire Humanity Is Expressed in Culture," introduced concepts on faith and culture, Church and society, of creative depth which now begin to stretch and challenge the minds of Churchpersons in both Americas. Before this secular worldwide body on education, science, and culture, John Paul set forth his own cultural creed as post-Vatican II Pope. A few quotes profile the Pope's own program of evangelization through humanization of culture, and the Gospel role for forming humanity:

Man lives a really human life thanks to culture.

Man who, in the visible world, is the only ontic *subject of culture,* is also its only *object and its term.* Culture is that through which man, as man, becomes more man, "is" more, has more access to "being."

This man, who expresses himself and objectivizes himself in and through culture, is unique, complete and indivisible. He is at once subject and architect of culture. Consequently, he cannot be envisaged solely as the resultant – to give only one example – of the production relations that prevail at a given period.

On the one hand, the works of material culture always show a "spiritualization of matter," a submission of the material element to man's spiritual forces – that is, his intelligence and will – and, on the other hand, the works of spiritual culture manifest, specifically, a "materialization" of the spirit, an incarnation of what is spiritual.

The presence of the Apostolic See in your Organization [UNESCO] . . . has its justification above all in the *organic and constitutive link* which exists between *religion* in general and Christianity in particular, on the one hand, and *culture,* on the other hand.

The Nation is, in fact, the great community of men who are united by various ties, but above all, precisely by culture. The Nation exists *"through" culture and "for" culture,* and it is therefore the great educator of men in order that they may "be more" in the community. It is this community which possesses a history that goes beyond the history of the individual and the family.

We realize it, Ladies and Gentlemen, *the future of men and of the world is threatened,* radically threatened, in spite of the intentions, certainly noble ones, of men of learning, men of science. . . . That happens in the field of genetic manipulations and biological experimentations as well as in that of chemical, bacteriological or nuclear armaments.

How can we be sure that the use of nuclear arms, even for purposes of national defense or in limited conflicts, will not lead to an *inevitable escalation,* leading to a destruction that mankind can never envisage or accept?

We must convince ourselves of the priority of ethics over technology, of the primacy of the person over things, of the superiority of spirit over matter. The cause of man will be served if science forms an alliance with conscience . . . [to keep] "the sense of men's transcendence over the world and of God's over man."

This papal address to UNESCO is so substantive and universal that it approaches an encyclical in its authority and future impact. It now becomes, in my judgment, the "constitution" of the Pontifical Council for Culture, established by John Paul in 1983. This new Vatican body *Pro Cultura* will animate and collaborate in the cultural concerns of Vatican departments, bishops conferences, religious communities, Catholic organizations, universities, and research centers, and with other appropriate religious and secular entities.

2. Having edited this book reporting our Notre Dame Conference on evangelization and culture within the regional Churches of Latin and North America, I risk a few brief thoughts about possible consequences of this papal-sponsored focus on culture, Church, and evangelization into the coming decade or two.

The duality of nature and grace, creation and revelation, natural and supernatural, secular society and Church, natural law and life of grace, this-world and the reign of God, has provided the basic bipolar formula and "raw material" for theologizing within the Christian community for fifteen hundred years. In 1965, Vatican Council II formally recognized *culture* as a third foundational element in the millennial experience of human-divine relations, and especially for societal-ecclesial concerns "in today's world." In the twenty years since, the Catholic Church has begun, deliberately and consciously as God's People, to probe the meaning of our fresh triad of nature-culture-grace – in spiritual life and liturgy, theology and doctrine, ministry and magisterium, personal options and social ethics.

Pope John Paul II is promoting this awakening of the Church to the reality and role of culture. He carries forward, especially, the cultural focus of evangelization, in line with the 1974 Synod and Paul VI in "Evangelization in the Modern World." The present Pope, however, now adds distinctive convictions about "humanization" by offering fresh insight into the depth of culture's role for *making man human.* Before the most secular of all world assemblies, UNESCO, Pope Wojtyla has affirmed: "Culture is that through which man, as man, becomes more man, 'is' more, has more access to 'being.'" John Paul explained further that, "Man lives a really human life thanks to culture. Human life is culture. . . . Culture is a specific way of man's 'existing' and 'being.'" It is by culture that "man is distinguished and differentiated from everything that exists elsewhere in the visible world; man cannot do without culture."

Culture therefore is constituent of the humanum. It is not merely an adjunct, tacked on to the nature of "man." By biological, genetic reproduction the *nature* of "man" is transmitted to another being. *Culture* however is *not* transmitted in this reproductive process; rather the capacity and potential for receiving and creating and sharing culture are inherited genetically by the human progeny. Actualization of that culture-capacity begins with the newborn, particularly until now in the family community. (Disputed views among scholars about this process are skipped over in this summary.)

In fact, the Pope goes on to affirm, "Human life is culture." Culture constitutes, forms, and shapes all humans; obviously, therefore, evangelization of humans must address their cultures—and always has, consciously or not, through twenty centuries. Now Vatican II marks the rise of a new quality and depth of ecclesial insight into the role of culture: for evangelization as well as humanization, unto their symbiosis. In consequence the implications possible for interactions among natural law and cultural law and the Gospel law of love become indeed portentous.

3. This fresh insight concerning culture comes forth within the Catholic Church as she probes anew her own self-awareness. Cause and effect operate here. Culture often becomes a mirror from which the reflecting Church acquires better self-sight and deeper self-understanding.

The papal magisterium began emphasizing *ecclesial consciousness* two decades before Vatican II through Pius XII's encyclical on the Mystical Body, which stressed the Church's inner life and being, ensouled by the Holy Spirit. The first purpose assigned the Council by John XXIII was to examine more deeply the nature of the Church. This was carried forward by the universal conciliar magisterium, *ad intra* and *ad extra,* by the two Constitutions "The Church" and "The Church in the Modern World." These most authoritative and magisterial *Acta Apostolica,* generated in the Spirit by the whole College of Bishops, 1962–65, document the degree in which this ecclesial self-reflection was nourished by the *ad extra* cultures of humankind, to beget new levels of striving for churchly self-awareness as "Sacramentum Mundi."

Vatican II's other documents—on the liturgy, revelation, mission, and ecumenism, about the laity, media, religious freedom, other faiths and philosophies—all have enhanced ecclesial consciousness. Each evokes reflective listening and participation in the communitarian mode, within the Church and with humankind as a whole in its multiple cultural contexts and societal systems.

This conciliar self-reflection and teaching on the "who-and-whatness" of the Church-and-the-world received vital sustenance and guidance during the 1960s from the papal magisterium, through the four great encyclicals of the Council's two Popes: *Mater et Magistra* and *Pacem in Terris* of John; *Ecclesiam Suam* and *Populorum Progressio* of Paul. The leitmotif of all four papal documents is Church and humankind awakening reciprocally to new levels of awareness and responsibility, under the twin impulse of the Spirit and the human creativity of culture.

4. The worldwide College of Bishops, having received after a lapse of centuries renewed constitutional status, began delving into Church-and-world awareness at local, national, regional, and global levels. The twenty-five hundred Catholic bishops acquired collegial voice and visible presence in the world via a periodic representative assembly. Paul VI first convoked the synod in 1967 to provoke reflection and exchange on the macro-structures of the Church (at the level of national and regional bishops conferences) and their relation to the Chair of Peter, the papacy.

The two hundred bishops, including presidents of all episcopal conferences, national and regional, who formed with Pope Paul the 1971 Synod, entered directly into Church-culture issues and ecclesial self-image with their Declaration on "Justice in the World." In 1974, the young synodal magisterium explored deeply the relations of evangelization and culture; this led to the seminal document of Paul VI on this subject, "Evangelization in the Modern World." (Key portions of this papal-synodal teaching are given in this volume.)

The collegial-episcopal magisterium began to address Church-culture-society issues also as regional bodies. CELAM, the Council of Latin American Bishops, led the way with their historic Medellín Conference in 1968, inaugurated by Paul VI in the first of his pastoral visits to the regional Churches of the Third World. African and Asian episcopal conferences of continental scale, and subregional bodies thereof, organized themselves according to their cultural and geopolitical contexts. Scores of documents addressing Church and world, evangelization-culture, and humanization have come forth from the episcopal magisteria of these regional Churches and pastors, always with the attentive overseeing of the Apostolic Chair.

After Vatican II, the new national conferences of bishops also began exercising their collegial teaching mission through hundreds of pastoral letters and prophetic statements on Church-world issues. Preparing these required collegial reflection, which generates ecclesial consciousness, at regional and national levels. Diocesan bishops now do the same, singly or as groups – by state, for example, or province. Religious communities also examine themselves and their apostolates since Vatican II in terms of the peoples and cultures among whom they minister. They produce fresh visions of their mission, such as "Faith at the Service of Justice" by the Jesuits.

5. It is John Paul II, however, who above all others stresses culture and ecclesial consciousness, evangelization and humanization, as major themes of his own papal magisterium. This began with his first encyclical, *Redemptor Hominis*, in 1979, only one year after assuming the Petrine Chair. He speaks of ecclesial self-awareness a dozen times, relating this repeatedly to culture, humanization, and mission:

> The Church's consciousness . . . fathoming more and more deeply both her divine mystery and her human mission, and even her human weakness . . . this consciousness is and must remain the first source of the Church's love. . . . The Church's consciousness must go with universal openness [which] is what gives her apostolic, or in other words her missionary, dynamism.
>
> The Church of today must be aware in an always new manner of man's situation. This means that she must be aware of his possibilities [and] of the threats to man and of all that seems to oppose the endeavor "to make human life ever more human."
>
> The ecumenical council gave a fundamental impulse to forming the Church's self-awareness by . . . presenting us a view of the terrestrial globe as a map of various religions . . . Superimposed on [this map is] the phenomenon of atheism in its various forms, beginning with the atheism that is programmed, organized, and structured as a political system.
>
> Seeking to see man as it were, with the eyes of Christ himself, the Church becomes more and more aware that she is the guardian of a great treasure . . . the treasure of humanity. . . .
>
> The Second Vatican Council [showed] how this "ontological" community of disciples and confessors must increasingly become, even from a "human" point of view, a community aware of its own life and activity.

These quotes from John Paul's encyclical *Redemptor Hominis* show the progression of the papal magisterium on the subject of ecclesial consciousness and the humanum during the forty years since *Mystici Corporis* of Pius XII.

6. Since the Council, the theological magisterium continues to serve ecclesial self-reflection among all the magisterial levels noted above. The conciliar, papal, synodal, collegial, and episcopal magisteria all receive stimulus and nurture from the theological schools, following the tradition and roles of Athanasius, Augustine, and the great Gregories, of Aquinas, Bonaventure, and Bellarmine, of Theresa of Avila, and Catherine of Siena. It is notable that these theological giants, 325 to 1575, were all native to the Mediterranean Basin, from the Bosphorus to Gibraltar. Compare this Greco-Roman cultural ecclesial geography with the "view of the terrestrial globe as a map of various religions" which Pope John Paul perceives today, on which is superimposed "the phenomenon of atheism . . . organized and structured as a political system."

Hermeneutics, interpretation-for-understanding, is a prevailing thrust of post-conciliar ecclesiology all over the globe. Interpretation requires introspection, which deepens ecclesial self-understanding in plural forms amidst the several cultural contexts of the diverse historico-religious, geopolitical regions of the globe.

In most regions this ecclesial-cultural introspection proceeds among theologian and pastors together—pastors who chair dioceses as well as clergy who head parishes, plus their pastoral teams which include religious women and men and increasingly lay leaders as well. In a pluriform Church, pastoral care and theologizing also become pluriform and participatory, among the whole People of God—who in turn become more conscious of becoming the Christian Communion both in their own cultural locality and globally. This universality of Catholic consciousness begins to animate personal prayer, meditation, and public liturgy, which are nourished by this ecclesial awareness—the seed of eschaton and Omega.

This Notre Dame Conference on the Latin and North America Churches did not cover all the subjects raised in this Overview. They were stirred up in this one participant as I pondered its meaning, as editor of this work. I have recorded them because they hint at the possible implications of and expectations for the Pope's new Council *Pro Cultura,* at all levels of the Church and especially in the several regions where conferences similar to our own will be held.

I would hope that reports comparable to this book will be written, so that these cultural-ecclesial components, region by region, might nourish and embrace and understand each other, to form more fully the whole Universal Church, increasingly conscious of Christ's call to evangelize and humanize all his human family, gifted by the Creator with our own creativity of culture.

Participants

Conference on the Church and Culture since Vatican II, University of Notre Dame, November 1983

COMMITTEE FOR ORGANIZATION AND PROGRAM

Archbishop Marcos McGrath, C.S.C.
Archbishop Paul Poupard
Rev. Hervé Carrier, S.J.
Rev. Theodore Hesburgh, C.S.C.
Rev. Richard McBrien

PARTICIPANTS FROM OUTSIDE NOTRE DAME

Braganza, Sr. Mary, R.S.C.J.
New Delhi, India
Carrier, Rev. Hervé, S.J.
Vatican City
Crowley, Bishop Joseph R.
South Bend, Indiana
Cuen, Dr. Fernando
Mexico City, Mexico
Dearden, Cardinal John
Detroit, Michigan
DeRoo, Bishop Remi
Victoria, B.C., Canada
Dougherty, Dean Jude P.
Washington, D.C.
Haas, Dr. John M.
Columbus, Ohio
Hehir, Rev. J. Bryan
Washington, D.C.
Higgins, Msgr. George G.
Washington, D.C.
Lambert, Rev. Bernard, O.P.
Quebec, Canada
Lobkowicz, Dr. Nikolaus
Munich, Germany
McGrath, Archbishop Marcos
Panama City, Panama
McManus, Bishop William E.
Fort Wayne, Indiana
McNamee, Sr. Catherine
St. Paul, Minnesota
Murphy, Msgr. Terrence J.
St. Paul, Minnesota
Outler, Dr. Albert C.
Dallas, Texas
Poupard, Archbishop Paul
Vatican City
Preus, Dr. David W.
Minneapolis, Minnesota
Prince, Rev. Bernard A.
Ottawa, Canada
Ryan, Rev. William J., S.J.
Toronto, Canada
Sauder, Dr. Carl B.
Ponce, Puerto Rico

Scannone, Rev. Juan C., S.J.
San Miguel, Argentina
Schmitz, Prof. Kenneth L.
Toronto, Canada
Tannenbaum, Rabbi Mark H.
New York, New York
Vachon, Archbishop Louis-Albert
Quebec, Canada
Warner, Rev. Richard, C.S.C.
South Bend, Indiana

PARTICIPANTS FROM NOTRE DAME

Bartell, Rev. Ernest, C.S.C.
Blantz, Rev. Thomas, C.S.C.
Burrell, Rev. David, C.S.C.
Burtchaell, Rev. James, C.S.C.
Christman, Dr. Elizabeth
Crosson, Dr. Frederick J.
Daly, Dr. Ann Carson
Daly, Dr. Maura
Dolan, Dr. Jay P.
Fitzsimons, Dr. M. A.
Francis, Dr. Michael J.
Gernes, Dr. Sonia G.
Gilligan, Hon. John J.
Gleason, Dr. Philip
Goulet, Dr. Denis
Gremillion, Msgr. Joseph
Gutting, Dr. Gary
Hauerwas, Dr. Stanley
Hesburgh, Rev. Theodore M., C.S.C.
Kertesz, Dr. Stephen
Loux, Dr. Michael J.
McBrien, Rev. Richard
O'Donnell, Dr. Guillermo
O'Meara, Rev. Thomas, O.P.
Pike, Dr. Fredrick B.
Plantinga, Dr. Alvin
Weigert, Dr. Andrew J.
Wilber, Dr. Charles K.
Yoder, Dr. John H.

Contributors

HERVÉ CARRIER, S.J., has been Secretary of the Vatican's Pontifical Council for Culture since its formation in 1982. He was formerly President of the International Federation of Catholic Universities and Rector of the Gregorian University, Rome. He is the author of many books, including *Higher Education Facing New Cultures* (Gregorian Press, 1982).

BISHOP REMI DEROO is Ordinary of Victoria, British Columbia and President of the Social Affairs Commission of the Canadian Conference of Catholic Bishops. He is a co-author of "Ethical Reflections on the Economic Crisis," issued by the Social Affairs Commission in January 1983.

DENIS A. GOULET is O'Neill Professor of Education for Justice in the Economics Department at the University of Notre Dame. Besides prior teaching and research posts in Brazil, Algeria, and Paris, he has served on development planning teams of several governments. Among his publications are *Ethics of Development* (Sao Paulo, 1966), *A New Moral Order, Development Ethics and Liberation Theology* (Orbis, 1974), *Mexico: Development Strategies for the Future* (University of Notre Dame Press, 1983), and *Theory and Practice of Participation* (forthcoming from the Catholic University of Sao Paulo).

MSGR. JOSEPH GREMILLION, now Director of the Institute for Pastoral and Social Ministry at the University of Notre Dame, served from 1967–74 as the first Secretary of the Vatican's Commission for Justice and Peace established by Pope Paul VI. His previous positions include Director of Social Development for Catholic Relief Services and Director of Social and Ecumenical Ministry for the Diocese of Shreveport. Among his seven books are *The Gospel of Peace and Justice* (Orbis, 1976) and *Food-Energy and the Major Faiths* (Orbis, 1978).

J. BRYAN HEHIR is Secretary for Social Development and World Peace, United States Catholic Conference, and a Professor of International Affairs at Georgetown University. He was formerly Director of International Justice and Peace, U.S.C.C.

Bernard Lambert, O.P., was a *peritus* during Vatican II, closely associated in elaboration of *Gaudium et Spes,* and theological advisor to Cardinal Maurice Roy as president of the Pontifical Commission on Justice and Peace. He is the author of several books, including *Nouvelle Image de l'église* and *Les Beatitudes et la culture aujourd'hui.*

Archbishop Marcos McGrath, C.S.C., former Bishop of Veraguas, Panama, is now Archbishop of Panama. He served as Vice President of CELAM and was very active in Vatican II, especially in the drafting of *Lumen Gentium* and *Gaudium et Spes.*

Albert C. Outler, Professor Emeritus in Perkins School of Theology, Southern Methodist University, was observer-delegate of the Methodist Church at all four sessions of Vatican II. He has long been active in the World Council of Churches and is a pioneer of the ecumenical movement. His books include *Psychotherapy and the Christian Message* (Harper, 1954); *St. Augustine* (Westminster, 1955); *Evangelism in the Wesleyan Spirit* (Tidings, 1972).

Archbishop Paul Poupard (named Cardinal in 1985) is President of the Vatican Secretariat for Non-Christians and of the Pontifical Council for Culture. A laureate of Académie Française, he is the author of twelve books, including *Eglise et culture, jalons pour une pastorale de l'intelligence* (Paris: S.O.S.) and editor of two quarterlies, *Athéisme et dialogue* and *Cultures et dialogue.*

Juan Carlos Scannone, S.J., a native of Argentina, is a Professor of Theology at the Universidad del Salvador. Former editor of the journal of philosophy and theology *Stromata,* he writes extensively on the theology of evangelization and of liberation, with particular attention to cultural issues and popular religion.

Index